THE BIPOLAR EXPRESS

THE BIPOLAR EXPRESS

Manic Depression and the Movies

David Coleman

ROWMAN & LITTLEFIELD
Lanham • Boulder • New York • Toronto • Plymouth, UK

Published by Rowman & Littlefield
4501 Forbes Boulevard, Suite 200, Lanham, Maryland 20706
www.rowman.com

10 Thornbury Road, Plymouth PL6 7PP, United Kingdom

British Library Cataloguing in Publication Information Available

Library of Congress Cataloging-in-Publication Data

Coleman, David, 1964–
The bipolar express : manic depression and the movies / David Coleman.
p. cm.
Includes bibliographical references and index.
ISBN 978-0-8108-9193-7 (hardback : alk. paper) — ISBN 978-0-8108-9194-4 (ebook) 1. Manic-depressive illness in motion pictures. I. Title.
PN1995.9.M275C65 2014
791.43'6561—dc23
2014010265

∞™ The paper used in this publication meets the minimum requirements of American National Standard for Information Sciences Permanence of Paper for Printed Library Materials, ANSI/NISO Z39.48-1992.

Printed in the United States of America

CONTENTS

ACKNOWLEDGMENTS

As author, I am deeply in debt to and owe gratitude to many. For their tireless research and worthy tomes of exhaustive biographical detail, historical film writers such as Patrick McGilligan, Donald Spoto, Peter Biskind, and others far too numerous to list deserve enormous thanks. You will nonetheless find their names and works of scholarship appearing profusely in the endnotes, and I urge the reader to seek the original texts and consult them for their merits independently of this book. Their work is not oriented specifically toward this book's thesis, but they chronicle their subjects with endless biographical detail that offers invaluable insights. Likewise, the works of bipolar medical research psychiatry by such writers as Kay Redfield Jamison and Anthony Storr are resources without which this book could not exist save in the most rudimentary form. To the numerous Internet organizations and libraries that provided access and materials, I also wish to sincerely express my thanks. For his endless patience and encouragement, my editor, Stephen Ryan, also gets a well-deserved round of applause.

The author also wishes to acknowledge the many millions of bipolar and unipolar depressive sufferers who have endured countless heartaches and private hells and who are not profiled in any significant way in this effort. Not every bipolar has filmic therapy to combat their illness. Not every depressive can achieve creative victory over a chronic episode. But many have found their own forms of creative therapy, despite lacking the resources and opportunities of their well-funded brethren in Hollywood and other film-production centers, and in so doing, have prevailed and endured. I also wish to thank their support groups and loved ones. Every bipolar who is in remission knows that without these angels there would be no wind beneath our wings or gentle words to bring us back to earth when necessary.

No writer is stand-alone in his or her efforts on any personal level in terms of professional work. The author acknowledges his profound gratitude to those who have taken the time to support this effort, if not the author himself, with both scholarly and personal contributions. The subject matter, my own vagaries of temperament, and the various complicated turns one encounters in life all threatened at times to derail this prolonged effort. Rather than list a series of names, I would like their owners to privately bask in their deserved personal spotlights as they read this, as I am confident you will recognize yourselves when you do so. The program may not list your name, but the performance could not have happened without your generosity and loyalty. There are, however, some that I would be remiss if I did not name. My lovely family rides the wild roller coaster of my disorder by my side with a grace and forgiveness I strive to better understand but freely admit is presently beyond my ability to comprehend. Their love and patience gives me hope that I will one day see their light from the inside, not merely bask in the one they protectively cast upon me. So for Ryan, Lindsay, and Andy, my eternal gratitude for, first, making life so richly possible, and second, helping to bring this book to fruition. And to my wife, Laura, who has been my source of unending faith and redemption through decades of personal travails owing to my illness, I dedicate this volume. In some small way, I hope it helps repay my overdrafted karmic balance with the same healing power with which you always restore my equilibrium.

INTRODUCTION

Some of the greatest film directors and actors in cinema history were and are bipolar or unipolar depressives. A brief litany of their names alone conjures renown and prestige in their respective art forms. By no means complete, a small sampling of filmmaking talent with severe mood disorders might include: James Dean, Nicholas Ray, Charlie Chaplin, Peter Sellers, Francis Ford Coppola, Vivien Leigh, Martin Scorsese, Klaus Kinski, Jim Carrey, Peter Bogdanovich, Ned Beatty, Carrie Fisher, Rainer Werner Fassbinder, Marilyn Monroe, Alfred Hitchcock, Robin Williams, Vincente Minnelli, Margot Kidder, Harrison Ford, Tim Burton, Robert Downey Jr., Busby Berkeley, Woody Allen, Catherine Zeta-Jones, Sam Peckinpah, Russell Brand, Gene Tierney, Richard Dreyfuss, Mel Gibson, Greta Garbo, Frederico Fellini, Lars Von Trier, Linda Hamilton, Orson Welles, Mariette Hartley, Spaulding Gray, Frances Farmer, Judy Garland, Bob Fosse, and Burgess Meredith. This list is only suggestive, not complete, and in no particular order of relevance save that the listed were or are all mood-disordered creators.

Such a list does not fully capture the impact these visionary performers and directors have had on movies and audiences in their respective eras. To gain a better perspective, let's stage an imaginary film festival of the greatest moments in cinema history. The only criteria for selection to our pretend screening series is that the works were *not* created by mood-disordered individuals in the capacity of writer, director, actor, or other key creative talent. As virtual programmer, our task is simple: if mood-disordered artists were involved, we simply do not show their works. Despite the relative ease implied, it's actually quite a daunting task to sort through, but let's try for argument's sake. For what is revealed by absence is every bit as powerful for our argument as what is present by comparison. At least, that is, in great works of film produced by manic depressives.

In our festival of notable absences via an alternative history where these artists never existed, bipolar actress Vivien Leigh will never cry "fiddle-dee-dee!" nor tell of her dependency on the kindness of strangers. No one else can be recast in her role, either, as all works by depressive playwright Tennessee Williams are also excluded. There goes Brando's signature cry of "Stella!" with Williams's dismissal, one of the actor's finest screen moments. Orson Welles will in this pretend scenario choose to hide his depressions from the world. Rather than create some of the best films ever made in Hollywood, Welles stays in Wisconsin and rules the local market as a much-in-demand birthday party magician. Emotionally unstable, Marilyn Monroe will never be assaulted by a train's steam engine, nor have her skirt blown aloft by a subway's venting blast. Zero any memories of Peter Sellers as Dr. Strangelove, Inspector Clouseau, and Chauncey Gardner for inclusion in our "neurotypicals only" fest. James Dean rides the ups and downs of his cyclothymia, but not his beloved motorcycle into screen immortality. Greta Garbo will never express her desire to be left alone in her depressive fugue, and John Barrymore will never bellow as Ahab, stalking his own manic obsession to its tragic conclusion. Nor will any other screen version of *Moby Dick* suffice in its place, as Herman Melville was bipolar as the source author.

The incredibly revealing list of talents afflicted with mood disorder who nevertheless achieved unparalleled success in Hollywood and beyond grows by their conspicuous removal. Slumbering angel of death Michael Corleone as envisioned by manic-depressive Francis Coppola is not qualified for our series, and neither is manic self-aggrandizer Col. Kilgore swearing the beach is safe to surf. Woody Allen may be doing fine as a stand-up comic in our parallel dimension of psychiatric exclusion, but the missing films we cherish are no laughing matter. There will be no more of Annie Hall's "lah-dee-dahs!" to echo Vivien Leigh's "fiddle-dee-dee!" as bookends, alas, and no Hannah or any of her charming sisters. Lovers of more masculine films will equally be disappointed when they scan the line-up. Martin Scorsese's rich oeuvre of downbeat taxi drivers and raging bulls is gone. When word spreads in the social media communities that no Little Tramp will be shown, owing to Chaplin's bipolarity, ticket sales plummet. Who can blame them? Our festival's task of finding great films and great performances that are not tinged with madness falters. Peter Bogdanovich tweets that he will be withdrawing all of his works in a symbolic stand of protest for his fellow mood sufferers. So hopes for a cast reunion at the festival for *The Last Picture Show* or *Paper Moon* are definitely now on hold. If one further widens the criteria to allow for the many careers launched by association with some of these key figures and their artistic triumphs, and then excludes these protege filmakers' works, as well? Our Festival of Exemptions quickly degenerates into a meaningless exercise in film programming. We are left to ponder if cinema is actually cinema as we have known it as we search for replacements. Given this book's position that filmmaking itself was created as an actual technical process by a likely manic depressive, one can argue that the premise of a non-bipolar movie festival is a contradiction in terms, as films, and film attendance, might not have otherwise been invented. Since the literal creation of filmmaking, mood-disordered directors and actors have not only played an integral part in film's popular transcendence, but in remarkably and disproportionately higher numbers than one might otherwise expect given bipolarity's low percentage of affliction in general population studies. But why is this the case? Hopefully this book will help shed light on this question.

By filtering cinema through the sieve of bipolarity, which the filmmakers were laboring under while making their films, one begins to gain perspective as to how cohesive many of their otherwise disparate movies are by comparison and grouping. It is not that only bipolars make great cinema, nor that mood disorder alone accounts for their respective talents. Nor is it true that works of artistic genius are always created by only mood-disordered artists. Rather, it is that the pressures of these disorders are so profound for the profiled artists, and, as we shall see, had and have such a life-altering impact, that to continue to ignore them as a major contributory influence is akin to deleting the German war machine from an accurate history of World War II. Nor is there any shame or disrespect being assigned herein for these courageous individuals and their unfortunate illnesses. In an older reality, the admission alone that one struggled with any form of mental illness was so taboo as to be career ending. Today, and often in large part because of the advocacy of many of those profiled, the so-called label of mental illness has been vastly reduced, though by no means erased. So any belief that the author has anything other than enormous respect, and indeed gratitude, for them and their positive affirmations in the face of much negative societal indifference or hypocrisy is not only a complete misreading of my intent, but also misses a deeper point. Writing about so many of my personal and professional heroes has not only been a lifetime honor, but also has illuminated how much we all owe them for the untold hours of pleasure they've bestowed upon us. The legacy of human compassion and cathartic immortality they bequeathed is beyond any book or even series of volumes to fully appreciate. It is especially sobering to comprehend, as I have throughout the writing, that so much of what we have been given came at great personal agony for the producing bipolar artists involved.

Their collective plight as people who have had to endure the high cost associated with being open about their medical condition is not one of distanced empathy for me. I have fought my own battles with bipolar disorder for over thirty years. During some of this, I was a professional screenwriter fortunate to work in the Hollywood studio system. As such, I was privileged to meet and briefly know some of my filmmaking idols. I never grew tired of this thrill, but over the years, a singular note of creeping realization would frequently arise in my brain's quieter moments. Why were so many of the talented, often wonderfully warm directors and actors with whom I was working so incredibly moody? I add with honesty that I did not always ask this question with admiration, particularly after creative meetings with such persons in which their brilliance and keen manic insights sometimes left my own talent and self-worth duly questioned as a result. But my hurt feelings aside, in our collaborations I was never less than astonished at the reservoir such mood-disordered visionaries would draw upon from their seemingly inexhaustible supply of manic-fueled energies. Nor was I ever more mystified than when these same vibrant artists would show up unexpectedly in the slumps, achingly depressed, their talents temporarily shelved, at the very next meeting—if they didn't cancel it without warning. If it had only been an occasional pattern, and if I had not been bipolar and recognized many of these markers as reflective of my own, then this book would not exist. But it was the recurrent nature of these repeated scenes in my career as a writer-for-hire to the studios that was the genesis of my questioning. The coincidences were beyond improbable, they were apocalyptic. The more I researched and wrote this book, the more I became convinced of the unrecognized enormity of bipolarity as expression in the cinematic arts. It is the author's sincerest hope that this recognition will be at long last forthcoming. To include their mental illness as a substantial influence on their artistic visions does nothing to belittle, only elevates, the true measure of their greatness. These brave human beings are not only my fellow sufferers, but also my daily and sometimes sleepless nightly inspiration. The movies they have lovingly crafted, using moviemaking as therapy for their disorder, have benefited me in every sense as an avid viewer. Their offspring films have become my adoptive children, and like all proud parents, I am passionate about them all.

I

A BRIEF OVERVIEW OF MANIC DEPRESSION AND HOW IT AFFECTS CREATIVITY

Though the term *mood disorder* is necessarily ambiguous, for our purposes in this book it specifically refers to bipolar, or manic-depressive, disorders and—to the extent that they share some similarities—unipolar depressive disorder. These two terms, short-formed to simply *bipolarity* and *depression*, encompass an enormous variety of clinical markers but share a significant series of symptoms among a large percentage of the diagnosed sufferers. Despite their respective differences, if for no other reason than both patient types spend much of their time in depressive states, they are virtually indistinguishable. In historical and geographical fact, the differences between bipolar and unipolar depression are less robust in the scientific literature. A simpler continuity exists between upper manic and lower depressive states in some European countries, where the disorder is considered as one, rather than diagnosable as two separate but closely aligned affective illnesses, as is the case in the United States.[1] Because they are distinct disorders, to the extent unipolar films are considered in this book it is because they more accurately reflect on the main emphasis, which is bipolar works of cinema.

This book also uses the term *mental illness* to include mood disordered patients, but it is important to note that the term *mental illness* also includes those suffering from schizophrenia and other significant neurological disorders besides bipolarity when generally used. So while mood-disordered individuals are often included in the larger context of being mentally ill, they concurrently have an acutely distinctive diagnosis as being either manic depressives or unipolar depressives, which also sets them apart from the larger whole. Indeed, the very success or failure of treatments depends on a correct early diagnosis by a qualified practitioner. Without a correct diagnosis, ineffective strategies, or even harmful side effects, are encountered in the first course of prescriptive care. To stress the relative groundbreaking times in which current research is being conducted and codified, it is worth remembering that the terms *bipolar* and *unipolar* as medical descriptors did not enter the lexicon until the 1960s and took until the 1980s in the United States to become commonplace in mental health care facilities. The field is truly in its infancy, or at least early childhood, in terms of common clinical terms, as well as reliable genetic data, high-tech imaging, and related scientific advances, not to mention universally effective therapies and treatments. As this book also demonstrates, the biased societal views to which those with bipolar disorder have been subjected are well documented in the historical medium of motion pictures. This is because movies, from their earliest inception in the late 1800s into the modern era, capture a popular snapshot of societal fascination with, and too often discrimination against, the mentally ill.

A manic-depressive person may experience periods of intense depression, or melancholia, in which normal interests and concerns offer no sense of value or return for the investment on the depressed person's behalf. A rare exception for many bipolars and depressives, however, and as this book illustrates, is therapeutic artistic self-expression, which not only can remain intact as a faculty, but can uncannily also be enhanced by mood swings. The depressed person feels less energy, and many will sleep excessively to negate their stupor. This avoidance behavior is common amongst bipolars. A sense of self-perpetuating helplessness quickly sets in. The patient retreats further from reality, therefore guaranteeing by inaction that reality's responsibilities will inevitably come crashing down on the depressed person's shoulders.[2] This is why it is called madness, in the most frank sense. It makes no sense to the perplexed outside observer why any sane, healthy individual would retreat from life's pleasures, no matter the disappointments, for too long. Nor does it make sense to endure the understandable wrath of one's peers and employers for failing at one's professional responsibilities despite repeated warnings and attempts at offering assistance. From the neurotypical's point of view, the depressed person is simply "acting crazy."

But the focus here is not on the mentally healthy but on those lacking the very ability during severe bouts of their affliction to keep even the most rudimentary precepts of common sense in balanced perspective. Indeed, it is a hallmark of bipolar disorder that self-defeating and self-destructive strategies and choices are underlying, contributing reasons why the illness is so difficult to effectively help. How to treat persons who are often not even aware they are their own worst advocates and, therefore, worst enemies, is the great problem in dealing with mood disorders. Whether it is simply taking care to groom themselves; to literally get out of the bed and move around in order to speed recovery; to eat a balanced, healthy diet; or any number of similar seemingly obvious and yet completely unmanageable everyday activities (from the depressed patient's point of view), the depressed person often must be coaxed and encouraged until the most pernicious side effects of the medical condition (such as mental fogginess, emotional disorientation, and in severe cases even catatonia, wherein the individual is frozen with a form of living rigor mortis for long stretches of time),[3] finally, often slowly, abate. Abatement is a relative term, with many suffering agonizing relapses.

As if such feelings of worthlessness were not bad enough, depressed people often feel an unending sense of intense guilt. They blame themselves for being unwilling to deal with their problem. They blame themselves for being unable to just "get my act together" in the face (and often in denial) of a clinical mental disorder. They blame themselves for feeling dependent upon others who assist them. They blame themselves for those who abandon them. They blame society for not understanding them. They blame themselves for blaming themselves. In a clinical depression, there is no limit to the amount of injurious self-blame the patient can inflict upon his or her already vulnerable psyche or upon those of others near him.[4] It is not without reason that suicide is a high-percentage conclusion to far too many sufferers of mood disorders involving recurrent depression.[5] While many neurotypical people will admit to suffering from occasional depression, thankfully far fewer will ever know the personal ravages of a sustained, months-, even years-long, depression. To face each new dawn, for weeks or months on end, after another sleepless night of unrelenting self-recrimination and massive self-doubt, is one of the tortures reserved for the damned on Earth, if such reservations are actually granted to be existent. As Edgar Allan Poe, himself likely bipolar,[6] wrote in the poem "For Annie" (1849) of his frequent spells and unending recoveries from his melancholia, "The sickness . . . the nausea . . . the pitiless pain . . . have ceased, with the fever that maddened my brain." In the same poem, he describes his illness by its characteristic "moaning and groaning, the sighing and sobbing."[7]

Other hallmark symptoms of clinical depression include a profound loss of energy, reduced or no sex drive, an inability to concentrate, a lack of appetite, psychomotor agitation or retardation, and obsessive thoughts of suicide.[8] Extreme irritability and anger are characteristics of a depressive in the full throes of an episode.[9] The afflicted is often attempting with all his or her personal energies and willpower to accomplish even the simplest task at hand, only to fail repeatedly despite their best efforts. The understandable frustration and feelings of helplessness can turn into anger and rage in an unstable person under duress of a clinical episode. The cyclic nature of bipolar disorder, in which the sufferer is genetically destined to experience severe bouts of clinical depression and/or mania in subsequent times of life,[10] adds an existential edge of perpetual angst to the afflicted's feelings and thoughts. There exists a definite feeling of suffering from a form of Sisyphus syndrome when one is bipolar; the shared camaraderie of realizing no matter how many times a patient rolls the rock to the top of the summit of self-control, a downward plummet back into the depths of depression is just one eventual slip of the foot away.

As there are many shades of gray, so there exist variants in the manic-depressive spectrum. Some patients experience one or two severe, months-long depressions, and then largely recover, only rarely experiencing similar symptoms later in life. Many more, however, are clinically predicted to have ongoing depression in recurrently severe attacks.[11] The only real question becomes to what degree their personal, unknown, and currently unknowable cycle of depression will afflict them when—not if—it returns. In cases where the return of the depressive symptoms is more frequent and/or longer lasting, the prognosis is less favorable than for the depressive who suffers less recurrences and/or shorter durations of episodes.[12] In worst-case scenarios, depressed patients commit suicide rather than continue seeking therapies or hope. It is worth noting by way of dubious distinction that, statistically speaking, bipolar suicides tend to wait until they're hypomanic (and therefore more likely to possess the energy to act on impulsive thoughts and plans without reservation) to attempt suicide, whereas unipolar depressives tend to act when they're most despondent.[13] Whatever the mood leading to suicide or its attempt, the devastation is the same for their grieving loved ones.

Mania, in stark contrast to depression, is a sense of euphoric certainty that often manifests itself in the patient exhibiting signs of self-grandiosity. This sense of superiority is based less in ego (although egomania is certainly one of the more prevalent forms of mania on evident display in the film business) and more in the rapid pace of thoughts most bipolars experience while "riding high" on mania. During such states manics will spend without discretion, work with little or no sleep, and articulate their ideas and passions with conviction and clarity that can be astonishing (at least to the overwhelmed listener). The rush of ideas, emotions, and insights is also overwhelming in the patient experiencing an episode. Tangential connections between arcane subject matter with seemingly little in the way of connective tissue can be instantly synthesized and articulated by a person under such a psychological state of disorder. Some researchers have referred to this ability of manics to rapidly shift from one thought to the next and reveal underlying meanings as a form of gestalt thinking, and that manics therefore may be "extraordinarily capable of accessing large numbers of gestalts."[14] Strangely, such expressive insights, derived from unstable states of psychological being, sometimes prove to have staying power over the non-afflicted, who do not experience mood swings, provided the visionary bipolar is not deranged beyond understanding in the artistic output. Schizophrenics having an episode often speak in a language that is coded with hidden meanings, which researchers can sometimes clinically establish as having an interior veracity and consistency of delusion,[15] however inaccessible to the average person. Bipolar artists equally can present intense expressions of feeling that strike the neurologically typical person as having profound meaning and keen artistic integrity, despite the neurotypical person's lack of his or her own filtering disorder. It is as if the disordered artist is somehow striking a personal chord of angst, joy, and/or despair, and the audience is responding from an individually supplied, but crowd-unified, perspective of feeling. The rapturous states of self-wonderment that many manics experience, especially while channeling their hyper energies into their cinematic works, often result in exuberantly expressive films, as we shall read throughout the coming chapters. Under the controlled delusion of his disorder, the manic filmmaker is able to stoke his imagination to heights and depths beyond even his own, more typically "normal" state of consciousness. Likewise, the manic actor is able to give in to his already unstable emotions with breathtaking speed and believability, often leaving other cast members momentarily unable to pick up their dropped beat. These qualities add an electricity to such creative endeavors as filmmaking, which are often dependent upon spontaneity and playfulness, qualities manics have in abundance (at least until they come crashing down).

So it can be said, with much evident truth, that manic and hypomanic states produce profoundly lasting works of art, at least when practiced by skillful artists with latent talents. Though it confers many life-challenging negatives, it is difficult to argue that mania does not also bestow at least some offsetting positives for both creator and society alike. This is a very unusual symbiosis in the fields of medical ailments, as most disorders and diseases offer little in the way of compensation for the pain and misery they inflict. It raises uncomfortable questions about trade-offs in terms of what benefits society reaps from the artistic harvest of a creative class of manic visionaries producing therapeutic works of cinema, for example, versus the inevitable decline possible in the field in question if such manic states are dimmed by medications and/or eliminated in some future scenario. Like the visions of a prehistoric shaman, works of art created under states of visionary mania offer glimpses into intense states of being otherwise inaccessible to the neurotypical viewer. Hence, such bipolar films remain strange and yet, as well, strangely familiar. And they should be, created as they are by artists both balanced and then unbalanced in the fluctuation of their profound mood disorders. It may be that the alternating mood swings experienced by the bipolar creator, subject as they are to accompanying changes in neurological functions (such as increased ability to envision solutions for difficult problems while manic, and then a decreased ability to censor gloomy or pessimistic thoughts while depressive),[16] constitute the underlying commonality of expression that gives bipolar-directed films such depths of power. By studying and feeling the artistic challenges from a variety of emotionally charged viewpoints, the bipolar director and actor are, in essence, expressing highly complicated, sometimes even conflicting tonalities. Through the balancing aspect of their disorder, the bipolar filmmaker integrates these complex emotional visions into coherent, cathartic works of art.

The artistic dreams and nightmares that we most cherish, and that are so often supplied by such visionary madmen, are peculiarly singular in nature in many cases. Because these bipolar expressionist works can have extreme states of emotion and vision, they move audiences in unexpected, unpredictable ways. They tend to be anything but typical, and often are lastingly memorable. We need only recall our latest disappointing visit to a local cinema or DVD rental kiosk and hear again our lament at the time of exit or return of the movie: "If only I could have cared something about the characters or the story!" The truly amusing aspect of this collective observation is that it obscures the actual psychological mechanics at play. The reason the viewer complains in retrospect is not that he or she could not care, but that a satisfying emotional crisis and resolution was lost for lack of caring. What is missed is not the caring, per se, but the release, the conclusion, the catharsis from the state of caring, in retrospect. In so many ways, cinema as therapy works as well as a metaphor for its creators as it does for its emotionally dependent viewers. It produces frustration and disappointment in the film-going patients who experience "bad therapy" when they go out for a needed night of emotional cleansing at the movies and find themselves unmoved by their latest hour and a half of overkill, loud explosions, and 3D imagery.

It is as if the manic, hypomanic, or depressed person is acting out on deeply ingrained impulses and thoughts without properly vetting them against a sober, judging sense of self-restraint. Like the effects of alcohol in reducing social inhibition, the manic-depressive's mood swings and erratic mental connections can cause him or her to make decisions and take actions he or she would not, in their so-called right mind, ever even consider, and therefore, they very often later regret them. And paradoxically, as this book will repeatedly demonstrate, this lack of restraint—when combined with an intense artistic nature and cinematic talent—is the very component that so often produces visionary cinema as its outcome.

THE NECESSITY OF ART CREATION AS EFFECTIVE BIPOLAR THERAPY

The diagnosis of bipolarity carries significant clinical risks in terms of the well-being of the patient. Within five years of receiving the diagnosis as being manic depressive, a significant percentage of patients will attempt suicide.[17] Despite valiant efforts, many are unable to overcome the difficult challenges of maintaining a strict medical and physical well-being regimen, saving face via constant social reintegration after the latest episode, and surviving the ravages of the disorder itself. For bipolar disorder manifests itself against all better judgment, willpower, and ability to negate when it is in full bloom. Bipolars are in this narrow sense proverbial victims of their own temporal wiring, unable to control their emotive centers during episodes any better than a person could remain calm while drowning. Drowning is a good analogy. The afflicted person's brain is submerged under an array of misfiring brain chemicals during an episode, and drowning horrifyingly captures the intensity of desperation and panic such mania and depression can induce in a patient. All reasons the brain might otherwise have supplied to avoid making such instant decisions as spending all of one's money on a shopping spree, or telling one's employer how ineffective their entire decision-making process is at a company meeting, vanishes under the insidious floodwaters of self-assured confidence and an unending bravado. But no matter the temporary brilliance or insanity (or, not infrequently, both) the disorder confers in the moment, the brain mightily swims but finally exhausts. All voices of reason sink beneath the choppy waves of a downward spiral, extinguishing the flame of creativity with it.

The negative aspects of a mood disorder often overshadow the creative aspects that the disorders sometimes convey or heighten in the afflicted artist. The personal biographies of manic-depressive filmmakers and actors can read like the diary of the Devil himself, full of angst, drama, and dissolution in all areas and aspects of life. And yet, conversely, their produced works often linger in their ability to emotionally connect to audiences. Beyond their actual lives' daily struggles as bipolar disordered, these artists' psychic pain is somehow captured, magnified, and retransmitted silently to the viewer in the magic that is truly the movies. This transcendent ability to go beyond their shared pain and inspire emotional reaction in others is a key component as to why bipolar filmic visions are so often successful. It also offers a glimpse into the how of the filmmakers themselves, who are channeling the vagaries and disappointments of their disorder into their creative outlets as a form of therapy and control. Their sufferings are devastating owing to their chronic mental conditions. For bipolar artists, this means a need to have an artistic outlet into which such unceasing pain can be effectively, if temporarily, alleviated by artistic expiration. Bipolar individuals who are able to utilize these artistic therapies tend to exhaust themselves and, therefore, their pent-up manic-depressive energies, with the very act of creativity itself.[18] By so doing, they achieve a form of spent normalcy, their worst clinical aspects absorbed into their art, rather than harmfully directed at themselves or others.

It is the demanding and all-encompassing production process, not the outcome only, that so often drives the bipolar filmmaker. Most of the bipolar filmmakers profiled herein are and were active from beginning to end on their productions. Quite often, fabled stories revolve around these very same filmmakers in which studios, producers, and/or loved ones had to intervene to remove the filmmaker from a project. If it is hard for a professional who is paid to do his or her job well and thoroughly to let go at the end of the long shooting day, so much more difficult for the bipolar filmmaker who is left with manic energies to burn at sunset and a potentially longer night ahead should there be no work at hand to accomplish. As one bipolar director with whom I once worked answered when I asked him how he knew when the film's editing was complete, "When they lock you out of the editing room, mate."

This driving need to work beyond normal endurance is a hallmark of the creative mood-disordered artist, though of course, it is sometimes shared by obsessive neurotypical directors who may not have any mental illness whatsoever. This noted, the likelihood of becoming the proverbial fanatic film type massively trends more toward bipolar filmmakers and performers than the average, albeit equally dedicated, talent. The former seemingly cannot divorce themselves from their creative sides even long enough to heal the wounds and rifts their artistic obsessions have naturally created between family, friends, and professional colleagues. There is a kind of "identity masking" present in bipolar filmmakers when they direct their creative energies into a sustained, prolonged filmic endeavor. The creative mask offers a continuous sense of artistic therapy with daily challenges that seem beneficial when their personal stresses and anxieties are lessened by these activities. The grander role of creative visionary is preferred rather than an individual- istic personal identity, entirely because the larger role is more stable by definition. It requires continuity in order to be effective, whereas the unstable personal bipolar identity threatens the production's natural flow toward completion. In this sense, the larger creative goal offers the bipolar filmmaker or actor a chance to remain professionally and artisti- cally committed to a performance-based stability regime that may be personally lacking owing to mania or depression. The lengthy, absorb- ing nature of the film production process in and of itself becomes a sort of shorter-term stay in the creative asylum, if you will, and many bipolar directors and actors are loath to leave this form of therapy simply be- cause production has ended.

Not without coincidence, as well as a hint of sardonic commentary, many filmmakers have likened directing a film to running a home for the mentally ill. Many of Hollywood's talented neurotypical practition- ers would probably qualify as emotionally and mentally temporarily unstable, in broad psychiatric terms, on any given day on the set owing to the latent pressures, even as the truly bipolar ones often offer mirac- ulous displays of controlled genius-level acting and directorial insight amid the chaos on set. Because many mood-swing creators endure the maelstrom of insanity with sometimes daily and nightly regularity, the buzz and tension involved in any large film production is de rigueur in terms of becoming just more background noise for the hardened bipo- lar. Thus, the pluses and the minuses of bipolarity and artistic influence are intertwined like hissing twin cobras, each poised to strike at the opposite's throat in defiance. This despite the fact that they're feeding one another, and both co-dependent on the opposite's strengths and gifts, springing forth as they do from the same, shared body. It is no mean feat to endure the making of even the most simply shot feature film, from beginning of conceptualization and writing to the pressures of promotion and completion for releasing, all the while hustling for the next project as is required in Hollywood for even the top talents. Add- ing the mixture of managing a psychiatric illness like bipolarity atop such an achievement and still creating not merely releasable, but vision- ary cinematic art, makes the manic depressive filmmaker appear mys- teriously superhuman at times. How is it that those who are so thoroughly afflicted with such a life-challenging disorder manage to not only cope and survive despite the odds in reality, but also excel and thrive in the filmic arts, despite their obstacles? Through examination of each afflicted individual struggle and their subsequent cinematic triumphs, one begins to appreciate the enormous tenacity and passion such persons have invested in the medium of movies, and how by doing so, they have literally helped create, shape, and define it in the long run. A deeper mystery lurks as connective thread, too. For by using film as therapy for their own tortured psyches, these bipolar filmmakers also help bring about changes in the real-world perceptions of the very illness they are attempting to therapeutically expunge. From the descent into artistic madness comes the Promethean fires of visionary redemption, for the bipolar film creator and the viewing audience.

2

THE EARLY CINEMA AND MENTAL ILLNESS

THE SPECULATIVE EARLY ORIGINS OF CINEMA AS BIPOLAR BY-PRODUCT

It's interesting to speculate that early American cinema invention itself was partially a by-product of bipolar disorder. Although a case can and will be shortly made to this effect, it is admitted beforehand that the indisputable physical evidence is as absent as was synchronized sound from early silent cinema. Which is to say: there actually *were* early attempts to synchronize sound with silent cinema, and the inventors of cinema did precisely this with a phonograph slaved to a film projector at cinema's dawn.[1] In other words: there is arguable proof a mood-disordered individual conceived and helped create filmmaking as a technical art form. For the fact is that the credited coinventor and, in many historical aspects, creator of cinema was once admitted to an asylum for what was euphemistically known in his era as a "nervous breakdown" on at least one occasion during his employment with Thomas Edison.[2]

William Kennedy-Laurie Dickson was creator of Edison's Kineto-graph and Kinetoscope processes, which effectively created the 35 mm film spool as production methodology. Dickson's 35 mm format remained the standard for most of cinema's history prior to digital takeover. It is true that Edison was passionate about the potential of movie-making as mass communication. He saw it as a natural by-product of the many patents he held in electrical lighting. It is also true that during the time of Dickson's many innovations while in Edison's employ, Edison was more obsessed with his $5 million investment in magnetically separating ore and was distracted with that potentially lucrative extraction process. That left the young Dickson to create much of cinema himself while his employer was away on other business. Edison failed at the magnetic ore enterprise, while Dickson, with considerably less investment, succeeded at the creation of a motion picture camera and projection device.[3] Edison and Dickson's combined aim had been to revolutionize the former peep show and zoetrope formats of fixed, static images. Dickson solved the dilemma by using looped film of continuously photographed imagery that unspooled in longer amounts of time, allowing for both moving images that changed and altered as well as primitive narrative possibilities. In no uncertain terms, Edison and Dickson tasked themselves with inventing everything that would become cinema and define its very essence, however crudely, from its inception. And it was Dickson, not Edison, who would solve the technical challenges, as well as establish the basic tenets of cinema as a production form and in content.

Dickson was an immigrant of Scottish and French ancestry who arrived penniless and friendless in America. He was a child from impoverished means owing to his father's early demise, a classic early stressor for adult-onset mood disorder.[4] Dickson sent a letter to Edison in New Jersey at the tender age of eighteen, introducing himself to the world-famous inventor and requesting an internship in Edison's Menlo Park idea factory and workshop.[5] Although Edison refused Dickson's request, Dickson must have impressed him when he later showed up at Edison's doorstep at the age of twenty-two, as Edison hired the famished young man. This was fortunate news for not only Dickson, but also his dependent, widowed mother and two impoverished sisters who had immigrated to the United States with him. Already a fanatical amateur photographer, as apprentice, Dickson must have felt as if he'd been handed the keys to the magical kingdom by Merlin, assigned as he was by Edison to work on Edison's moving-picture conception. As David Robinson recounts in his definitive book *From Peep Show to Palace: The Birth of American Film*, "Edison provided the facilities, perhaps the impetus, and sometimes the vision; but there is now little doubt that all the experimental and practical work on the Kinetoscope were Dickson's."[6]

Dickson was innovative beyond merely the technical creation of movies. He also pioneered and had built the first-ever movie studio in 1889. A small, two-sectioned structure with plenty of plate glass windows to allow sunlight throughout the shooting day, it was an early forerunner of the later Black Maria 360-degree revolving studio (itself a Dickson invention) subsequently constructed when motion picture production became a mainstay output of Edison's ongoing commercial enterprises.[7] There is reliable evidence Dickson once startled Edison upon Edison's return from a business trip in 1889 with a preview of sound movie production even before Dickson perfected the Kinetoscope itself. According to the employees of Edison who knew of the incident, and later research by early cinema historians such as Gordon Hendricks, Edison was greeted by Dickson's presentation of a phonograph synchronized in some crude, unknown fashion to a series of flipped, or possibly even projected, slide images that gave the viewer the illusion he was seeing a photographed person talk.[8] This effort has been lost, but later Dickson would produce the surviving "Dickson Experimental Sound Film" (1894), which shows Dickson playing violin beside a prototype for the Kinetophone as two men dance around him. Though the initial sound recording is missing for this earliest-known synchronized audio effort, film editor Walter Murch did a restoration of the seventeen-second film in 2002 in which the original-era-suggested music track was added with uncannily accurate results.[9] Dickson was the first cinema creator to realize the vast commercial potential of using celebrities and famous actors of the stage to appear in his earliest short film productions, which he helmed in every major creative aspect: writing, photographing, directing, editing, titling, sometimes starring, and even copyrighting them in his own name on Edison's behalf as routine procedure.[10] All of which means, by even the most stringent accounts, W. K. L. Dickson (as he was known in the fashion of his time) was an enormous, if not the most enormous, contributor to the birth of filmmaking, both as technical progenitor and aesthetic innovator of the form. As if in long overdue recognition, the United States post office printed a commemorative stamp of Dickson in 1996 acknowledging him as the inventor of the motion picture camera (and, more noteworthy, omitting Edison entirely), even if his name is all but forgotten despite many accomplishments.[11]

But was he bipolar? The only medical evidence is that the public debut of the Kinetoscope at the Chicago World's Fair of 1893 was canceled, despite anticipatory crowds and enormous hype, due in large part to Dickson's nervous breakdown. The furor had been created by Edison in the world press, promising that the Kinetoscope, the revolutionary motion picture process, would be unveiled for the first time at the fair. The actual notes later published in apology for the failure of the device to be demonstrated as promised only mentioned the device was not perfected.[12] For understandable business reasons no mention was made that the cause for the Kinetoscope's non-showing at its promised debut was that its chief creator was hospitalized in a sanitarium. But whether or not Dickson's mental breakdown was bipolar, there is no doubt that the delay of motion pictures as a public event was caused, at the very least, by mental illness severe enough to warrant hospitalization at the behest of Dickson. It is a historical fact that a sanitarium stay by its inventor slowed the introduction of the technology to the viewing public. And so the confluence between film and mental mood disorders is present from its inception, however coincidental or significant, as a seminal influence merely by this fact alone.

There are some other intriguing biographical clues regarding Dickson's bipolarity. One is his brilliance at such a young age, though genius is by no means associated exclusively with manic depression. He had a penchant for seeing solutions where even the visionary of visionaries himself, Thomas Edison, remained stuck in profound, though highly impractical, verbal conceits. As Margaret Julia Hames, a media studies professor at New York University surmised, "he ignored company policy, embarrassed his employer, and risked sanction. Dickson revealed that he possessed daring, risk-taking personality traits."[13] The latter are hallmarks of possible clinical mania. He also displayed a temperament that was obsessional in nature. There is not only the evidence of his devotion to photography from a young age, but the rather self-aggrandizing confidence to actually arrive, unannounced, with his tattered hat in hand, at Edison's place of business seeking employment. This after being rejected in the same request via writing by the great man himself—and in numerous subsequent letters by Edison's own private secretary! While some may view this as only chutzpah run amok, it is also a clinically accurate portrait of delusional self-aggrandizement during the manic phase. The idea that a poor immigrant lacking any introductions (save a series of prior rejection letters dismissing his requests for a meeting) would suddenly arrive in person without expectation is at the least a worthwhile piece of speculative evidence, in and of itself, of some form of potential personality disorder, if not mental imbalance.

Dickson had numerous business disputes with Edison that led not only to acrimonious results (a not infrequent outcome of collaborations with bipolars for obvious reasons). Dickson unethically (and perhaps even illegally) took the ideas he'd created with Edison and sold them, with slight modification, to Edison's business rivals.[14] Nor was Dickson's reputation on very firm ground prior to this incident. Edison's personal secretary, Alfred Ord Tate, sent an internal memorandum characterizing Dickson's attempt to share copyright with his employer as "the essence of gall."[15] But was it gall, or clinical delusions of grandeur? In fact, the final straw that led to Dickson's permanent estrangement from his former boss was when Edison ordered Dickson to properly re-copyright the earliest motion pictures back into Edison's holding company name. In the many lawsuits that would follow, it became apparent to many in the business community that Dickson was, at the very least, a man of unusual temperament and audacity. This reputation was born out if for no other reason than Dickson was willing to endure the litigation Edison was notorious for unleashing on all perceived competitors and/or enemies. (Edison seemed to often blend them into one and the same in his mind.) Dickson seemingly didn't care, cocksure he could withstand the onslaught by selling to Edison's rivals the heart and soul of the moviemaking process itself and therefore reap the profits to defend himself against Edison's lawyers. Dickson bet correctly, reinventing the wheel and devising a new process to compete with Edison's so that Dickson owned all the patents and copyrights to the new moviemaking format himself in conjunction with new partners. As Hames stated in her analysis after researching Dickson's archive of personal papers, such behavior "reveals another aspect to Dickson's personality: a tendency toward risk-taking to the point of self-harm."[16]

Dickson's devotion to his filmmaking creation was intense and beyond mere profit in orientation, yet another potential marker of being on the mood-disorder spectrum.[17] Consider Dickson's need to embark on the first-ever documentary film of war and actually risk his life in the process. Dickson dispatched himself from London to South Africa in 1899 and spent nearly three-fourths of a year filming the Boer War in battlefield locales under live fire. The undertaking is not to be discounted in terms of the technical difficulty of obtaining cinematic imagery, let alone surviving an armed conflict. Not content to release the first movie ever made in a war, Dickson also cowrote (along with his poet sister Antonia) a book about his exploits called *The Biograph in Battle* in 1900. This made him one of the first filmmakers to ever publish a proverbial "making of" account of their filmic exploits. He also cowrote two previous books (again with Antonia) while still in the employ of Edison, one of which—*History of the Kinetograph, Kinetoscope, and Kineto-Phonograph* (1895)—chronicled his single-handed contributions to filmmaking, largely omitting Edison, his then-current boss, by conscious design.[18]

Next consider that Dickson once spent four consecutive months in Rome fruitlessly trying to convince Pope Leo XIII to be recorded in the motion picture format. The operator would be none other than Dickson himself, his Biograph camera in hand. Day after day, Dickson patiently, and then impatiently, awaited an audience with the pope. Dickson desperately wanted to be the first person in history to show a pope in any movie format. But day after day, Dickson's polite but obsessive requests for a brief audience were denied through the pope's intermediaries. Dickson finally wore down the elderly Catholic prelate, who graciously allowed Dickson to briefly film him as he walked through the Vatican garden one day—gracious in that Dickson's behavior was borderline celebrity stalking in nature. Not only that, but Dickson convinced the pope to then bless his camera so that the footage would survive the trip to the lab—surely the first motion picture to receive a Catholic seal of approval in film history.[19] Significantly, this was five years before the pope would allow himself to be recorded for the first time in history on audio for a radio broadcast. In this regard, and given the constant daily rebuff, one wonders: what convinced Dickson that his efforts would eventually pay off if not maniacal self-belief? The heady drive to be the first and the best, as Dickson exhibited, is a definite hallmark of the clinical self-grandiosity one associates with egomania[20] (though by no means exclusively, as many ego-driven, neurotypical individuals demonstrate it, too).

The fact that Dickson lost his father at a young age should not be overlooked in his or any other mood-disordered person's biography. Research has borne out that the loss of a parent during childhood is a significant predictor of possible recurring bouts of clinical depression later in life, though whether it is a trigger or merely exacerbates the underlying bipolar disorder is unknown.[21] There are also the one- and two-word descriptors that seemingly leap out of the few texts regarding this era in relation to Dickson's characteristic moods that are emblematic of so many later bipolar filmmakers: "gifted" and "inventive enthusiasm" and even the classic euphemism "nervous breakdown." The latter is frequently encountered in biographies of stars and directors prior to the rise of modern terms and knowledge of manic depression and other mood-related disorders. Whether it is his personal ambition, his visionary aspects, his willingness to break the rules even as he was inventing them himself, his nervous breakdown, his defiance against powerful figures, his genius foresight to invent cinema not only once, but twice; these all are very good indicators of *possible* bipolarity. But they are admittedly far from clinical proof, and so the thesis must forever remain untested, in all likelihood, given the scant materials left in existence by Dickson himself addressing the specificity of his own mental well-being (even if what does exist demonstrates an evident bias toward self-inflation). Many records of his activities for Edison that may have favored Dickson's claim to be the creator of cinema were later destroyed by either Edison or his employees, perhaps to protect Edison's own claim as the originator.[22] In summation, in many of the markers self-evident in even Dickson's own far-from-modest accounts of his contributions to cinema, one will find archetypal bipolar tendencies. These repeating patterns of conduct, thought, and behavior as demonstrated by Dickson will be seen in clinically diagnosed bipolar creators in coming chapters. Elements of his life story—early childhood stressors, asylum stay, manic self-aggrandizement, risk taking beyond reason, rule breaking, compulsive behaviors, and obsessive genius—run parallel to those of many who will follow, in effectively prototypical expressions of bipolarity.

Dickson's contributions should be renowned, not obscure, regardless. He not only survived being sued by Edison, but profited handsomely in the process by building an entirely new moving picture process to rival Edison's fading Kinetoscope. Coincidentally, or perhaps not, Edison's movie output began to lose its marketing luster shortly after Dickson's departure, as Edison and others less visionary took the production reins from Dickson. Rather than be bogged down by Edison's patents, Dickson invented the Mutoscope, secretly passing the plans for its construction to his friend Herman Casler, also a former Edison employee.[23] Dickson would later cocreate and head the famous American Mutoscope Company out of New York, rivaling Edison for early commercial dominance. Dickson's innovations would continue while Edison's shrank. Dickson had William Zeiss, later founder of the optic dynasty, construct to personal specification the first set of prime lenses, specifically ordering lenses for both distance and close-up photography, as well as a magnifying lens for viewing 35 mm-sized film images.[24] He hired a young Billy Bitzer as an early Mutoscope camera operator, years before Bitzer would revolutionize silent filmmaking in the early Hollywood era for D. W. Griffith and the like with his cinematographic techniques. In every sense, Dickson was a visionary and successful early film tycoon, as well as progenitor of the cinematic form itself. And in at least some likelihood, based upon his unusually hypomanic nature, many present biographic markers, and history of an asylum stay, Dickson was bipolar.

THE ESCAPED LUNATIC AND OTHER EARLY BIPOLAR FILM DEPICTIONS

The first known movie to deal with inmates at a mental hospital was French pioneering filmmaker Georges Méliès' *Off to Bloomingdale Asylum* (1901). Released in his native France as *L'omnibus des toqués ou Blancs et Noirs*, or also *Les Echappes de Charenton*, the one-minute effort shows nothing but a single, static camera setup. It is clearly studio bound, the background charmingly though unrealistically painted as the fantasy horse-drawn carriage with Charenton (an asylum in Paris) written on the side. The strange horse stops and spills four blackface minstrel tourists in matching tweed suits. As they tumble to the ground, they spontaneously transform into whiteface clowns clad head-to-toe in white. They fight as they frantically dance, kicking one another until each reverts back into a blackface tourist. This action repeats, back and forth. Never do the dancers, black or white, vary their hyper dancing. A worried guard notices their manic actions and dashes away. Meanwhile, the blackface vaudevillians devour one another in a magical process until only one is left, his belly swollen to gigantic proportions. As he delightedly puffs on a huge cigar to finish his impromptu meal, the guard returns and shoves an unlit explosive up the poor glutton's derriere. Before the blackface man can react, the guard lights the fuse. The would-be patient is shot skyward like a bottle rocket and explodes into nothingness as black clouds of smoke waft through the streets, his only remains.

To say it has nothing to do with mental illness beyond the obvious asylum reference is self-apparent. What is interesting is to speculate why Méliès chose to take a film that merely shows the antics of some vaudevillian clowns and suggest, without any other alteration, that it depicts mentally ill patients. How was such a fantastic leap, every bit as illogical as the film itself, even possible? The answer may lie in the perception, created by the filmmaker himself, that the actors and facial expressions he portrayed in his early films were seen by the viewing public as depictions of excited states of mental imbalance. Jean Mauclair, reflecting in 1929 in a Parisian newspaper on the era's obsession with imagery from Méliès, which so often depicted hysterical patients whose heads were often made giant in proportion to their bodies and exploded violently, recalled them as "sentimentalo-epileptic dramas,"[25] referring to their peculiarly hyperactive manner. This was not without intent by its maker. Méliès maintained that his cinematic sleight-of-hand and compulsively transmuting screen figures could "drive the most fearless spectator crazy."[26] So it can be argued that one of cinema's founders of narrative language intended to induce temporary states of mental affliction in even the most balanced of spectators— surely a bizarre aesthetic by design, but nonetheless understandable given the befuddlement and mysticism a stage magician like Méliès would have been accustomed to providing his paying public. Also contributing to a perception among the public that the films he released were depicting the mentally afflicted were the frantic, spastic characters enacted with gusto by Méliès in multiple roles. The filmmaker related once how an American buyer who purchased the films from him was stupefied by the fact that Méliès was so normal off-screen after witnessing his latest projected antics. "He had probably imagined that I was, offstage, demented, a madman, completely crazy,"[27] Méliès recorded. While Méliès was anything but crazy, according to recorded history, the buyer's all-too-typical perceptual bias was rooted in the films themselves, as well as lingering taboos against the mentally ill in society.

But why the title change by the American distributor of the film to *Off to Bloomingdale Asylum* (when it wasn't alternately released, most likely in the South, as *The Darktown Comedians' Trip to Paris*)? The answer is all too readily apparent. Bloomingdale Insane Asylum was the only psychiatric treatment facility in all of New York State at one point in its initially illustrious beginning. Located in Manhattan, where Columbia University now resides, it was accessed by traveling Bloomingdale Avenue, later renamed Broadway.[28] Started with the best of humane intentions in 1821, it had fallen into terrible mismanagement by the time Julius Chambers, a young reporter for the *New York Tribune*, exposed its many institutional abuses in a series of scathing, well-publicized articles.[29] Chambers had committed himself as a patient with the help of his editors in order to gain access and information, which may be a partial source of inspiration for Samuel Fuller's later film *Shock Corridor* (1963), bearing as it does a similar plot line, albeit set in a modern asylum. Because of the exposé, the administration was changed and many inmates were set free, judged legally sane despite their being held at Bloomingdale's beyond their supposed recovery.

It is telling that the Edison Company, which acquired all U.S. rights from Méliès' own Star-Film, probably believed that the viewing public would accept by way of inference that the strange, unexplained madness on display was only because the frantically dancing clowns were de facto insane, as had Méliès when he made it. Watching the film today, the lingering impression, not far-fetched given the inherent racism at the time, is also created that the blackface stereotypes were seen as perhaps having a delusion of grandeur in that they pretend they're capable of becoming Caucasian, even if as "only" white clowns. Whatever the rationale, the Edison Company surely believed the notoriety of the Bloomingdale exposé would make sense to a public endlessly fascinated by the notorious case. To reiterate this probability of bias, consider the fact that the English company that acquired the rights changed the title to *Off to Bedlam Asylum* (after the notorious English asylum) instead of using the American variant Bloomingdale or the original Charenton. Having witnessed the success of the American and French releases with their respective asylum references, it only made economic sense, however insensitive from today's perspective. But *Off to Bloomingdale Asylum* is not really about an asylum or mental illness, being merely retitled into such distinction, thus its importance beyond being first is nominal. That is not to impugn Méliès or his clever, original production, which was quite novel and exciting for its era. However, it would take another work to actually feature mental illness as the subject matter, and, oddly enough, the first American film producer to see the value in a film about an asylum was none other than W. K. L. Dickson.

Whether or not Dickson's psychiatric condition influenced his productivity and emotional spectrum, one of his biggest hits in 1904 as creative head of production at American Mutoscope & Biograph was to approve and coproduce *The Escaped Lunatic* (1904). The plot alone, as detailed in the Biograph film sales sheet that nascent theater owners received when deciding to purchase or rent their fare, reads like an indictment of the entire sanitarium concept. To wit: "A lunatic confined in a barred cell, labors under the delusion that he is the Emperor Napoleon. In the first scene we see him in an altercation with his keepers over the quality of food furnished him. The keepers set upon him and beat him unmercifully and leave him unconscious. He comes to and determines to escape."[30] It is unknown whether or not Dickson's own stay in a sanitarium was by self-admission or forced intervention, nor whether or not his stay was agreeable or effective. So while it may be speculatively said that a possible negative reaction to his stay may have colored this trade sheet's copy as well as the film's themes of inmate rebellion, no such information has been unearthed to prove it. Still, it remains an intriguing hypothesis. And certainly, as detailed above, Dickson was a complete hands-on entrepreneur in every phase of his productions, so it again would not be beyond the facts to believe that he wrote, or at least approved, the all-important promotional materials for his films. Unlike today's gargantuan corporate enterprises, filmmaking was then a small-team affair.

It's worth further recapitulating the flowery language of American Mutoscope's sales sheets describing the plot after the inmate effects his escape, which reads very much like Dickson's own earlier books about himself:

> Then follows a series of thrilling and ludicrous chases through the mostly picturesque scenery. The lunatic is cornered on a bridge over a waterfall, but manages to overcome the keeper and hurls him into the rapids below. In another scene he crosses a torrent on a slender wire cable swinging loose above it. Time after time the lunatic succeeds in circumventing his keepers. Finally, however, he tires of the

chase and is seen running back to the asylum. He leaps the 30 feet
back to the window and when the keepers, all blown and covered
with mud, rush into the cell, Napoleon I, is calmly reading a newspaper.[31]

Credit for direction rightfully goes to Wallace McCutcheon, but as
suggested, Dickson in all probability had at least some creative contribution into the making of the tale, which again implies the dualistic
history of mental illness and motion picture production from its beginning. In terms of narrative technique alone, *The Escaped Lunatic* is
noted for being one of the first American films to be structured around
a chase sequence.[32] This formula, novel in 1904, would become the
biggest cliché in all of silent cinema—one need only think of the Key-
stone Cops, which followed in this film's frantic footsteps—but not
because Dickson and company failed to innovate. Contrarily, the formula was genius in its utter simplicity and circular-narrative construction, which is why every Hollywood silent film producer quickly aped it.
The formula is still used in today's cinema, with films still relying on the
same structural introductions made by *The Escaped Lunatic*, including
the use of an unbalanced character as lead instigator of the story's
nonstop rush of events. In its day, the impact was surely felt by jealous
rival Thomas Edison, who rushed a rip-off directed by none other than
Edwin S. Porter called *Maniac Chase* into production in 1904. It was
largely the same effort, shot by shot!

The Escaped Lunatic also created the concept of a fleeing mental
asylum patient as inherently, albeit comically, dangerous. Because the
disordered protagonist is depicted as having superhuman strength
when the asylum attendants chase him, the impression is established in
cinema that mental patients are not merely to be pitied, but also to
some extent feared, unless they are under constant confinement. Not
that *The Escaped Lunatic* injects anything other than comedy into most
of its run time. But when the so-called lunatic hurls one of the attendants head-first into a raging waterfall to his possible death, it's hard to
argue that the maniac is presented as forgiving or generous in nature.
And yet *The Escaped Lunatic* also offers the first genuine pathos in
regard to the afflicted. For prior to the inmate's escape, it is shown that
his living conditions are deplorable beyond acceptance. Further, he is
set upon by his handlers with savage fury for the smallest defiance.
There is never a sense that he is any real threat to them. Rather, a man

seems unnecessarily, violently beaten into submission—to sad effect, whatever his prior transgressions. *The Escaped Lunatic* makes no great point about the handling of the mentally ill beyond demonstrating the inhumane treatment the inmate receives at the battering hands of the guards. But this point is germane to all that will follow in films dealing with bipolar disorder. For it sets in motion the dueling nature of the way mentally ill people will be depicted in cinema, then and now: mostly to be feared, and occasionally pitied, when not the subject of laughter.

Other early films deserve recognition. In 1902, William Haggar, an early British filmmaker, produced his first short film effort entitled *The Maniac's Guillotine*. Little is known of the film today, as it is presumed lost. Surviving texts describe it in no detail save as a scene lifted from a stage play.[33] Still, whether or not the film involved mental illness in any capacity as content, its title alone was seminal. The word *maniac* is used for the first time, and while no one can be certain, it is probable that the relationship between a maniac and a weapon as deadly as a guillotine did not turn out positive by the end credits. Supporting this hypothesis is the fact that most of Haggar's movies were historically known not only for their self-evident artistic qualities, but also for their use of on-screen violence. This actually placed him at odds sometimes with local censors who were offended.[34] While this would of course be incredibly tame by today's blood-soaked standards, or lack thereof, in terms of screen mayhem, it also means in all likelihood that for viewing audiences the association between mania and violence was linked from cinematic inception by the film's title alone.

There were two contrasting visions of mania offered in 1906 cinema. The basic formula of escaped lunatic equaling mortal danger was continued without deviation in *The Madman's Fate*, produced in Great Britain. Director J. H. Martin merely added a new coda. In his version of the story, the dangerous escapee assaults a man's wife. As the intruder tries to stab her with a knife, her husband intervenes, accidentally killing the unbalanced attacker in the process. After the wife tearfully recounts her story to the horrified judge and jury, her husband is acquitted of all charges. The right to self-protection is invoked in *The Madman's Fate* as reason for showing the maniac's death as justifiable. Somewhat contradictorily, no motive is ever presented for the maniac's actions save a clinical illness. The implication is that mentally ill escapees are, by very definition of their sudden freedom, murderers should the opportunity arise, and for no apparent reason. Hardly a balanced portrait of the unbalanced, but revealing of the era's latent societal attitudes. However, mania of a nonviolent sort is illustrated in *The Puzzle Maniac*, also from Great Britain. This Gaumont production directed by Alf Collins shows a man who becomes so obsessed with finishing a puzzle that when he cannot figure out the final piece he winds up being carted off to an asylum. Not clinically accurate in its depiction of mania, *The Puzzle Maniac* was intended to provoke laughter, not horror, at the idea that one's mental stability could be so fragile as to shatter over even the most staid of personal hobbies. As a one-joke short film, it doesn't add much to the history of manic depression in cinema, but it does indicate the extraordinary lengths to which some bipolar patients will go to see their obsessions concluded, whatever the personal cost, when they're involved in creative endeavors, even one as mundane as assembling a picture puzzle.

If nothing else, American filmmaking from its birth was wrought with remakes, often from rival producers who simply copied their competitors' titles with little or no deviation from the prevailing, commercially demonstrated formula. Under such conditions, it was logical for studios to replicate their own successful movies, as their competition certainly would in time. And so American Mutoscope and Biograph self-capitalized upon their earlier, trendsetting *The Escaped Lunatic* with *Dr. Dippy's Sanitarium* (1906). The British Film Institute's plot encapsulation is precise: "The new attendant is attacked and pursued by the lunatics."[35] The four mental patients who constitute the diverse assembly include a bearded man who prefers to crawl like an animal rather than walk erect, another man who wears a ridiculous paper hat and is obsessed with throwing knives at people, a top-hatted patient who attacks anyone within reach with his bare hands, and a nymphomaniac who bats her eyes at the new attendant with evident, invitational lust. The inmates react with jealousy when they perceive her interest in the new man, and a melee between three asylum guards and the inmates breaks out. During the fight, the new man flees but is chased down by the now escaped, enraged inmates. They shove him into a huge wooden barrel and roll him with maniacal glee into a lake. After rescuing him, they tie him up and throw knives at him for enjoyment. Just then, the asylum's guards arrive and rescue the new man, distracting the inmates with a pie. As they gluttonously feed, the patients are easily rounded up for confinement.

Apart from the novel introduction of Dr. Dippy—the first known psychiatrist in the movies and hardly a flattering portrait including his ridiculous surname—the rest of the production merely echoes the already growing perception of mood-disordered patients as literally dangerous, as when the new man enters a door where the inmates are housed that boldly exclaims in capital letters, "DANGEROUS KEEP OUT!" Yet again the delusional behaviors of clinical sufferers of an incurable, agonizing medical condition are played for laughs, albeit with equal shadings of implicit terror at being in the company of anyone afflicted with mania or depression. Maniacs are sexually deviant and all too willing to attempt homicide for amusement, the film demonstrates. They are easily distracted with food and trinkets, like children or pets, the conclusion reveals. At no point do the patients appear to have any true humanity left as individuals. Rather, they have been reduced, or self-reduced by their disorder, into monomania types, sadly lacking even the depth of stereotypes. Those with mental disorders are to be laughed at, feared, or both. The echoes will continue along these lines for many years in film history, without much critical insight or variation. The extent to which these films were merely reflecting popular perceptions of the mentally ill versus actually influencing the public's opinion in such matters would be impossible to accurately distill, then or now. Suffice to say, the consistency of the portraits of madness in these earliest efforts suggest an underlying societal prejudice that is being reinforced by the filmmakers in the films, rather than the filmmakers originating any such biases in reality. It begs credulity to imagine that the pioneer filmmakers were actually creating the very form itself and simultaneously inventing the maniac murderer meme. The more mundane probability is that the directors and actors were distilling into crude photoplays the attitudes and suppositions about bipolarity they already knew from popular imagination. Crafting these earliest movies was technically challenging enough without the added need to invent new stereotypes. The first filmmakers knew that stereotypes were a desirable necessity of the form, in that they allowed audiences to quickly delineate who to like, and dislike, in the compressed, economical stories of their era. If not chosen for resonance, they were for convenience.

The now familiar motif of mania equaling danger is continued in *The Madman's Bride* (1907), directed by Lewin Fitzhamon. Instead of an escaped lunatic, the mentally ill killer is no less than a lord, who marries and then kills his honeymoon bride on their first night together. He is caught after a struggle and brought to justice. While the class differences do add a slight twist to the usual perception that mental illness is a lower-class disorder,[36] the bottom line is that mental illness equals homicidal mania, at least as the patterning occurs in primitive cinema. One dubious distinction is achieved by the effort: mania is forever linked with murder in screen history. In no uncertain terms, *The Madman's Bride* is the forerunner of every modern horror film that features a psychopathic maniac as killer, of which the examples are literally too numerous to list within the boundaries of this book. It is a very unfortunate image of mental degradation, a caricature that holds as much historical pain for sufferers of mood disorders as do racist and sexist stereotypes for other offended segments of the population. If it has been such a largely unacknowledged source of mean-spirited reductionism, then it is that much more self-evident that society has yet to fully understand the harm this hateful image has wrought.

Not to be outdone by their own success with *The Madman's Bride*, British film production company Hepworth renewed the whole cycle with their unofficial remake of *The Escaped Lunatic*, which they called *The Harmless Lunatic's Escape* (1908). The lone novelty was that the escapee takes the asylum director's car and crashes it headfirst into the sanitarium's wall. Otherwise, the only noteworthy addition to the previous trendsetting film was that the filmmakers sought to soften the harsh implication of the title by adding the adjective "harmless" to the established formula. Again, the implication is that as long as the insanity on display harms no one but the individual himself (who nevertheless may be in the throes of a painful, disorienting medical episode), it is okay to laugh, whereas if they are the "other kind" of lunatic, they are to be feared and guarded against. A truly humane portrait had yet to appear in any cinema worldwide at this point, but a progenitor of a new, less dismissive screen portrait was about to tackle the issue, and, in doing so, introduce a more modern perspective.

D. W. GRIFFITH AND THE SPECTER OF EDGAR ALLAN POE

Author, publisher, poet, and lecturer Edgar Allan Poe was without much doubt a manic depressive.[37] There can be no conclusive argument made, as Poe never recorded an admission as such with attendant psychiatric nomenclature (which would have been quite an accomplishment, given that the field's knowledge of bipolarity had yet to be generally even recognized or subsequently codified with such terms). But if one is to account for Poe's rapid-cycling nature by any other descriptor than the very ones most often present in Poe's own work—"melancholy" or "insane" or other mood disorde-related terms—then one is attempting to shake salt on the tail of a raven as the preferred capture methodology. All of Poe's work, his alcoholic life, and even his death during a disorienting, depressive fugue state,[38] indicate bipolar disorder as a probable, psychiatric postmortem assessment.

Not that Poe made any attempt to hide his overwhelming mania or depression. He was known for his fits of nearly catatonic stupor as well as for furiously penning long-winded and often ill-tempered manic critiques to his fellow published writers.[39] "His action was alternately vivacious and sullen,"[40] Poe wrote in the fictional guise of the titular protagonist in "The Fall of the House of Usher," but by his contemporaries' accounts, he may as well have been describing himself. He lived, and loved, a life of emotional extremes that only reading his life's work can truly evoke with any sense of authenticity. It is as if Poe captured his wounded psyche in all its lurid details and permutations on the pages as he scribbled his quill. "Thy soul shall find itself alone / 'Mid dark thoughts of the grey tombstone,"[41] he penned in the poem "Spirits of the Dead." He also scribed this chillingly revelatory stanza: "I dwelt alone / In a world of moan, / And my soul was a stagnant tide."[42] Though his tales of so-called madness witness many different locales and character names, they all read and feel as if they occurred but to the same lonely, bereft soul in terms of origination and sensibility. Indeed, Poe's very Gothic nature is not owed merely to his mastery of melancholic language only—though that is never to be discounted as the obvious supreme quality of his artistic abilities—but also to his sensibility, in the Victorian meaning of the word. Which is to say, the manner of life is equal to the expression of life, and surely, vice versa.

Trapped in such a world of super-codified societies and restrictive attitudes toward acceptable behavior, a manic depressive like Poe, unable
to fully participate with any continuity owing to his infirmary, would
have surely found himself a stranded, moody derelict in a world around
him seemingly gone mad. And this is precisely how he lived and wrote
about his own life. As poet Charles Baudelaire commented upon learn-
ing of Poe's death, "[It was] almost a suicide, a suicide prepared for a
long time."[43] As previously noted, recurrent thoughts of suicide are
latent potential markers of bipolarity and depression.

As one of the most famous authors of his time and indeed beyond,
Poe created the very idea of a superstar author, selling out various
lecture halls to adoring crowds as he read aloud from "The Raven" and
other best-selling poems and tales he'd published.[44] Likewise, the dark
nature of his personal life and his obsessive, ruinous relationships were
the stuff of legend and gossip. They added what would later become a
Byronesque quality to Poe's imaginatively sinister body of work, which
is ironic in that the teenaged Poe adored Lord Byron's poetry the most
of all.[45] Decadent but marvelously self-aware of their own pitiable state,
Poe's characters such as Roderick Usher and his largely unknown, unnamed narrators cast a spellbinding pall upon the public that has never
abated. "Very dreadfully nervous I had been and am! but why will you
say that I am mad?"[46] he used as the opening line of conceit for "The
Tell-Tale Heart." This uneasy tension in his work lies at the black heart
of his effectiveness as author, as Poe is forever positioning his narrators
as unworthy due to self-admitted states of often tragic insanity—as was
his own a tragic life in large part but with unexpected greatness occasionally dropped in for narrative surprise. Poe could hardly have
sketched his own life as gloomy fiction better than the depressing reality rendered without effort or assistance by life on his behalf. In truth,
his fiction is a thinly disguised redressing of his life's worst moments,
written as much for some form of personal exorcism as for any subsequent readers. How else does one account for the weird, unsettling
alignment between the actual, mostly sad life of the writer and the
obvious parallels in his work? Or his ruminative, hellish reviewing of
slightly fictionalized variations of such horrifying events as slowly losing
so many loved ones to terminal illnesses as Poe did, and as do his heroes
in so many permutations throughout his stories? And when his loved
ones weren't chronically ill, he would himself fall prey to his unstable

mood swings. "For ten days, I was totally deranged,"[47] Poe wrote of one of his many "lost weekend" manic-depressive episodes, with no indication this was atypical or perhaps even the worst of what he had suffered.

D. W. Griffith was an avid fan of Edgar Allan Poe's work. Early in his directorial career, he made a 1909 biographical short film about his literary hero when American Mutoscope and Biograph offered the chance. His short film *Edgar Allen Poe* (note the misspelled name, which adorns even the original Biograph film's title card) opens in a small, cramped bedroom with Poe's dying wife desperately in need of food and uplift. She lies on her bed, nearly comatose, eyes glassy as Poe paces the tiny set, unable to find inspiration. Poe notices a sinister raven has appeared inside his abode, perched atop a wardrobe dresser. He is seized with insight and dashes out his most famous poem. Next we see the starving young author peddling his poem to disinterested publishers. He seems without hope of even having his work read until one kindly publisher takes a shine to his plight and bothers to read Poe's poem. Amazed, the publisher agrees to publish Poe's work. Poe is overjoyed, especially when the publisher reaches into his pocket and stuffs a wad of bills into the author's hands, insisting he take it on the spot. The delighted Poe shakes his publisher's hand in lieu of signing any contract and leaves counting cash in hand (perhaps the first, and only, time in history such an arrangement between author and publisher has been so conducted). However, while he is away, his wife awakens to find herself alone and dies longing for Poe. Poe arrives home with a newly purchased bag of groceries, but drops them, grief-stricken, when he realizes his soul mate is dead. He rages in anguish at heaven, hell, and earth, and the iris closes in on his despair, fading to screen black.

To say Griffith has embellished known historical realities of Poe's life story and the loss of his wife is no small exaggeration. For example, she didn't die until two years after his successful publication of "The Raven."[48] And yet, by shortening the narrative of events, Griffith makes the tragedy all the more poignant. Robbed of even his wife's realization of his personal accomplishment, the desperately depressive poet is left with the emptiest of victories in having secured publication. As direct as it is bleakly human, *Edgar Allen Poe* is no masterpiece, but it nevertheless successfully captures the manic-depressive nature of the poet and author. At first, Poe is seen as an angry depressive, storming around his claustrophobic quarters and railing against the gods for his poverty and obscurity. Without much warning, Poe is manic, furiously writing with utter conviction. The poet judges the penned results to be magnificent, as the wildly exaggerated motions of the actor playing Poe demonstrate. Poe is self-aggrandizement personified as he reads his creation aloud to his dying wife. But in the next scene, he is once again down and out as he knocks on doors of publishing houses seeking to sell the same poem he was earlier convinced was masterful. Doubt is one thing, but Poe is clearly without personal resolve, resigned nearly to his fate and almost out the door when the publisher who agrees to print "The Raven" actually halts Poe's exit at the last possible second. And yet again, Poe's mood turns from darkly down to exalted as he delightedly takes the money offered by his new publisher. While all silent film acting is pitched beyond the naturalism that has since overtaken modern cinema, *Edgar Allen Poe* actually has a range of acting styles and emotive moments that portend the more realistic performances Griffith would later be credited with bringing to the movies in his more mature works.

As per the norm by this point, Edison and company rushed their own Edgar Allan Poe film into production, anticipating as they did that what was good enough for archrival American Mutoscope and Biograph was even better for the Edison Company. *Lunatics in Power* (1909) was anything but the serious melodramatic turn Griffith had more correctly captured. Instead of focusing on Poe, Edison's version takes the setting from Poe's story "The System of Dr. Tarr and Professor Fether" and plays it strictly for laughs. A reviewer from the *New York Dramatic Mirror* enjoyed the film's hysterical acting mannerisms. "At last we know what the Edison comedians are good for. They are precisely adapted to play the parts of inmates in a lunatic asylum," wrote the anonymous reviewer. "The crazy style of action . . . is quite appropriate in this one."[49] The reviewer evidently, if unconsciously, perceives the commonly held notion in society that the "appropriate" way to view mental illness is with a "crazy style of action." Given that headlines of the era and beyond portrayed the horrid realities for some psychiatric inmates, this seems at best ignorant. One sees the evident, unexamined bias in such statements as the reviewer's in appalling contrast to the well-publicized reality of the abuses at Bloomingdale Asylum in America, or those in England's Bethlem Royal Hospital (the latter in which citizens could pay to torture inmates for amusement on select, festive nights).[50] The sentiment that those who are housed in mental institutions are best rendered as spastic in nature seems callous, but such was the perception of the mentally ill in the era. Like much stereotyping in early cinema and the attendant actual prejudices in society, the mentally ill were perceived as dancing fools or dangerous psychopaths in cinema's primitive era, when they were shown to be human at all.

Not every reviewer was so insensitive as to miss the grotesque aspect of the film. An anonymous reviewer in a 1908 edition of *Moving Picture World* previewed the film and had a nascent realization that the subject matter could be perceived as objectionable by some. The reviewer wrote: "The advisability of using any affliction as serious as lunacy as a basis for sport is questionable, though aside from that the film is lively and not unattractive."[51] It's noteworthy the reviewer's objection is not actually with depictions, but with the loss of potential box office returns should any audience members find the subject matter distasteful. There were other progressive forces in society also at work seeking to address these early, harmful images of mental illness in plays, fiction, editorials, and filmed entertainment. The U.S. National Committee for Mental Hygiene of 1909 was established to promote a more accurate, less biased portrait of mental illness to the public, and this included movies.[52] It is possible that the turn in imagery from lunatics armed with guns and knives to a few more humanizing film examples of bipolarity that occurs subsequent to the committee's formation is proof that their early advocacy had some rehabilitating effect. However, since there is no measurable way to ascertain this possibility, it may have also been that early filmmakers were simply looking to flip the standard maniac-with-a-knife image, already growing stale, in order to get further mileage from it.

Lunatics in Power is the first Poe filmic adaptation, but many more would follow, some of which would be further Poe adaptations by Griffith himself. Modern variants continue to this day, including the *The Raven* (2012), arriving almost a century after the earliest screen version. Interestingly, the latter film, starring John Cusack as the writer, actually is more akin to Griffith's version in that it includes the author as protagonist in his own narrative creation instead of as disembodied, unidentified narrator, as in Poe's fictional version. And improbable as it reads, Sylvester Stallone, in one of his oddest screen passions, has been attempting to direct a Poe biography for over three decades, but to no success as of this writing, despite numerous announcements in the Hol-

lywood trades briefly associating various actors and production companies with upcoming, though never materialized, production start dates.
"It's a story for every young man or woman who sees themselves as a bit
outside the box, or has been ostracized during their life as an oddball or
too eccentric,"[53] Stallone explained as to why he has spent over thirty
years trying to produce an endlessly rewritten script. As we shall read, a
passion for Poe is a recurrent obsession in many mood-disordered filmmakers (though Stallone has not admitted to any mental illness himself), experiencing as they do an intense bond with the morbid states
the writer so expressively rendered. But as we see by Stallone's example, Poe's hold on the imagination extends across all neurological types
for almost two centuries, with little sign of abatement, perhaps his
greatest display of enduring genius.

Nor was Griffith done with mental illness as filmic subject matter.
He set *House of Darkness* (1913) in an asylum. The subtitle card that
follows the film's moniker states, "How the Mind of an Unfortunate
Was Brought to Reason by Music," which adequately sums up the film's
plot. The opening shot fades into an enclosed yard with many patients
sitting about, most of them gazing wanly at nothing, and then the shot
fades to black. The title card tells the viewer they have just witnessed
"Disordered Minds in the Asylum" in case there is any doubt. Griffith
then titles a card explaining how "Such Poor Unfortunates as These"
have come to arrive in the co-ed asylum by showing the case history of a
mother who could not bear the loss of her child and became mentally
unstable. At one point in the narrative, a character credited as The
Lunatic, aka The Unfortunate Patient (Charles Hill Mailes), is shown
struggling during a manic fit of anger with two orderlies, each of whom
must subdue the overwrought hysteric with considerable force. However, as soon as the patient hears a young nurse playing the piano inside
an asylum's room, he transforms, calming and thanking the orderlies for
their concern. Now docile, the patient is easily led to the communal
garden by the amazed caretakers, but they tragically make no mention
to anyone on the staff of the positive effect music had on his well-being.

No sooner have they turned their backs, however, than the patient is
upon one of the orderlies, assaulting him with his fists. The patient flees
and the orderlies give chase, albeit in a less comical manner than has
cinematically proceeded the already cliché "lunatic on the loose" formula. Two plainclothes guards are jumped by the escapee and one of

their guns is taken in the violent attack. Now armed, the madman wields the pistol with a gleam in his eyes, enjoying the power as the beaten guards run away, terrified. The maniac, facing the camera, mouths one huge word of satisfaction—"Yes!"—as he studies his new weapon. He winds up in the house of the newlywed doctor who runs the asylum. There he holds the doctor's wife hostage, aiming the gun at the back of her head, demanding she play the piano. When she nervously plays a melody, the patient immediately transforms, his maniacal spell broken, and becomes docile. He gives her the gun and is taken back into custody by the annoyed orderlies, apologizing as he's led away.

What is remarkable about Griffith's movie is not that it invokes the killer maniac formula that has so stereotypically been the norm to this point in cinema. Rather, Griffith directs the performance by Mailes with such empathy that Mailes comes across not as the usual madman beyond reason, but as an actual sufferer of a mental illness who does not remain in any one episode of clinical insanity for long. While no diagnosis is offered to the viewer of the man's condition beyond the ubiquitous catch phrase of "lunacy," his mercurial mood shifts from agitated to calm and then back into agitation, along with the complete lucidity he achieves between bouts of disorder, does suggest a form of rapid-cycling manic depression. The nuanced performance by Mailes is a screen first, as well. Rather than play either the manic side or the depressive side with grotesque exaggeration, the actor instead plays each role with an inner dignity. Griffith exploits each extreme by not directing his escapee to overplay with wild exaggerations, but instead, to hold back and suggest the boiling cauldron beneath the surface, which is always ready to explode. Mailes plays this well, at first a physical dynamo who is unstoppable by even armed guards, and then, adroitly, becoming an entranced, mild-mannered introvert when his attack subsides. When projected at its proper silent film speed so that the actions of the actors do not appear hyperactive, the pathos Mailes captures in his expressive performance is unexpectedly novel. One particularly effective image has him hiding behind the spokes of a chair, peering at the warden's wife, the spokes echoing the prison bars of his asylum confinement, even though he is technically free.

The fact that Griffith uses music as the calming agent, rather than a pharmaceutical one, is almost pointless given that no known drugs in

use were of any recorded significant benefit to the manic-depressive
patient of this time. In other words, while melodramatic and suspect as
a medical cure, and surely unrealistic since most manic-depressive episodes do not end without lingering negative consequences to the sufferer's psyche, the patient's love of music humanizes the plight of the
mentally ill rather than only exploiting it as a subject to be feared. While
it is true Griffith insists on having it both ways, he at least deserves
credit for treating the subject matter with historically groundbreaking
perspective. Whether intentional or accidental, *House of Darkness* im-
plicitly endorses a central tenet herein; that is, there exists an undeni-
able synchronicity between creativity and madness, and likewise, a sustained therapeutic benefit in creativity for the mentally ill.[54] While never earth shattering in terms of believability, Griffith creates great suspense with the volatile mood swings his escaped patient experiences,
surely putting the viewers of 1913 on the edge of their seats with such a
mercurial portrait of mental instability. Whereas every other character
on-screen is purely one-dimensional, Mailes achieves an early form of
pathos that Griffith would later become known for in his feature works.

It may seem tempting to condemn the early cinema pioneers for
their insensitivity in exploiting the mentally ill with the use of the word
"lunatic" in so many of their biggest commercial hits, as well as their
largely negative imagery of bipolarity. However, the blame game, if one
is to give each player his or her own honest due, has many other participants arranged around the shared table. The popular press would use
the term "lunatic" or "maniac" sensationally, wantonly applying it to
each new tabloid homicide. But as a recent landmark study concludes,
acts of violence are actually overwhelmingly committed more by neurotypicals under the influence of drugs or alcohol than by mentally ill
persons.[55] Newspaper editorial cartoons were rife with lunatic characters and name calling. Political figures were lunatics, as were all other
elected officials any editorial board at a magazine happened to disagree
with over policy matters. In short, the term was as abused over time as
it was abusive, and so came to actually be seen as a form of self-parody,
and not used in a more generalized, hurtful sense implying actual mental illness. But the interconnected nature of filmmaking and mental
illness is such that until the term lost its significance, it was a hurtful
designation not unlike the ones many African Americans and homosexual Americans faced until their own respective moments of true equal-

ity. It was designed and used to always reduce, and never elevate, anyone to whom it was applied. In a word, it was willfully ignorant of reality. In screen imagery, it was all jolly fun antics of the homicidal maniacs who were ready, willing, and able to murder at a moment's flickering notice. When the mentally ill looked upon the filmed imagery of themselves in this era, they must have felt like a black person watching their own racist portrayals in such fare as *The Birth of a Nation* (1915) half a century after the Civil War. The chasm between delusion and reality lay not merely with the mentally ill during episodes of affliction. There also existed a chasm between screen portrayals of manic depression and clinical reality that was just as delusionally presented to a seemingly gullible public. These primitive films were not only the foundation for a cinema to come, but also for echoing and distorting misconceptions about bipolar disorder as a real world illness widely afflicting the populace watching them.

3

THE GOLDEN AGE OF SILENT FILMS AND MANIC DEPRESSION

CHAPLIN'S MOTHER AND THE DEPRESSIVE PARENT AS BIPOLAR ARCHETYPE

The earliest silent movies and their sometimes crude legacy gave way under new practitioners. Substantial contributions were made by D. W. Griffith's epic use of intercutting to tell stories over multiple locales and times in *The Birth of a Nation* and *Intolerance.* In the comedy arena, the empathetic adventures of Charlie Chaplin's Little Tramp became an internationally beloved sensation. A down-and-out vagabond always on the verge of starvation between the next round of found food or drink, Chaplin created in his persona the Everyman, but brought to his thread-bare knees by poverty, lack of opportunity, or worse. "In 1915, he burst onto a war-torn world bringing it the gift of comedy, laughter and relief while it was tearing itself apart through World War I," wrote Martin Sieff in a review of the book *Chaplin: A Life* for the *Washington Times.* "It is doubtful any individual has ever given more entertainment, pleasure and relief to so many human beings when they needed it the most."[1] His usually luckless but resourceful Tramp was the original survivor type, and along with Mary Pickford as America's Sweetheart and Douglas Fairbanks as Adventurous Rogue personified, was one of the most popular figures in the movies of the era.

While an objective conclusion of Chaplin's impact can never be fully measured—for how does one judge adoration beyond the counting of box office receipts?—the subjective influences certainly can be considered, especially as to the themes and subject matter that he chose as filmmaker. Chaplin's biography highlights the impact of mental illness on not just the primary source parent, but also the affected offspring. This continuity in a family's history is a common marker in any clinical diagnosis of manic depression, and any prevalence of mood disorders in the family genealogy is an indicator of its possible existence for the patient.[2] None other than Dr. Sigmund Freud himself made this causal relationship literal in Chaplin's case. Freud wrote in a letter posthumously revealed in regard to Charlie Chaplin, who had just visited the good doctor in his Vienna office: "[Chaplin] is undoubtedly a great artist; certainly he always portrays one and the same figure; only the weakly poor, helpless, clumsy youngster for whom, however, things turn out well in the end. Now do you think for this role he has to forget about his own ego? On the contrary, he always plays only himself as he was in his dismal youth. He cannot get away from those impressions and humiliations of that past period of his life."[3]

Charlie Chaplin's mother spent time in and out of sanitariums battling mental illness throughout much of Chaplin's cruelly impoverished upbringing. Hannah Chaplin was a stage performer of some ability with vocals and as a ballerina, though her career was cut short by what Chaplin himself deemed "tragic promiscuity . . . an insatiable desire that was pathological."[4] This assessment appears in a thinly veiled portrait of her in his unfinished *Footlights*, a novel that apparently was Chaplin's attempt to review his life's history without being held accountable for its seamier realities. His mother's insatiable sexual appetite may have been a clinical mania, which is another common marker of potential bipolar disorder.[5] Hypersexuality and risk-taking behaviors combined to make Hannah's biographical truths understandably worthy of masking by her son, as there are unexplained incidents so wildly out of her character that to explain them as reasonable begs the question of sanity itself. Especially when the diagnosis of manic depression so aligns with the reality Chaplin alludes to, and is confirmed by historical records of his mother's often erratic behaviors and mood swings.

At one point when Chaplin was young, Hannah abandoned him and his bewildered father (who Chaplin doubted was his biological father due to his mother's constant affairs), running off during a gold rush with speculator Sydney Hawkes to prospect for riches he assured her were awaiting in South Africa.[6] They would hear nothing more from her, despite Chaplin's closeness to her, until her shabby, unannounced return six months later, when she would come back to England sans Hawkes but pregnant with Sydney Jr. Chaplin's unbelievably accepting father actually adopted Charlie's half-brother as his own and forgave Hannah. This was perhaps done out of recognition that his wife was mentally unstable and prone to impulsive, delusional decisions. But his kindness was not rewarded, as she had another opportunity and/or clinical episode six years later, this time abandoning her family (including Sydney) to run off with Leo Dryden without warning. As previously when her evident mania had seized her and then expired, she returned home exhausted and again pregnant. Dryden inherited their child, either by force or agreement. While the record is unclear, the implication is not: if the child was agreed to be given to the man rather than the woman in this time, it indicated some probable detriment in the mother's case. If the child was forcibly taken, it bespeaks of Dryden's apparent need to remove the infant from its biological mother, possibly because he feared to leave the child with Hannah. In any case, Chaplin's namesake father abandoned his family at this point and forced Charlie to make his way in life with only his mentally ill mother and half-brother Sydney at his side.

Making matters worse than his mother's grinding poverty and lack of support were the endless lovers, at least from her confused son's perspective.[7] Hannah marginally supported the two boys as a poorly paid ballet girl at the famed Empire Theater in Leicester Square. Perhaps a kinder explanation for her ceaseless carnal activities was that she was preoccupied with finding a suitable partner for marriage and replacement father figure. Grimmer speculation is that she may have prostituted herself in order to make ends meet for herself and her malnourished children.[8] While no arrest record or autobiography exists to make Hannah's prostitution definitive, the fact that she contracted syphilis, which would later, perhaps comorbidly, accelerate her declining mental health, is historical. After admission to the poorhouse known as Lambeth during an acute episode, she was diagnosed as suffering from delusions and tertiary syphilis, according to the Lambeth Hospital Register of Lunatics (HI/L/B17/Vol. 16, p. 364).[9] She was then admitted to Cane Hill Lunatic Asylum for treatment and recovery. Her stay at Cane Hill for three months resulted in her being released in a state of declared remission. Alas, she would be readmitted twice more in the coming years, each time with worsening mental illness. This effectively ended her already impoverished career as an entertainer, and made survival a daily hardship for Chaplin and his half-brother, left with only one another for long stretches of time.

As Stephen M. Weissman, author of *Chaplin: A Life*, surmises in an article entitled "Charlie Chaplin's Film Heroines," the influence on the Little Tramp character is evident when one considers the archetype of Rescued Woman of Trouble that Chaplin invokes throughout his career. Whether it is Georgia, the dance hall whore in *The Gold Rush*, or as Weissman states, "the high class courtesan in *A Woman of Paris*, the unwed mother in *The Kid*, the suicidally depressed ballet dancer in *Limelight*, and the two other dance hall girls in *A Dog's Life* and *A Countess from Hong Kong* . . . [each] represents an ambiguous amalgam of a more and less innocent way of viewing a young woman whose problematic sexuality echoes significant issues in Chaplin's own mother's life: before he lost her to a mental illness when he was still a child."[10] The magic of the Little Tramp was that he seemed abandoned, a genuine orphan to the world's cruelties, and yet somehow, always managed to rise to the occasion and better himself. This was particularly true when in behest of a loved one, usually a woman, who was in desperate need of emotional support despite her own best efforts. This is the archetype of the character's very screen essence, and as the linkage between Chaplin's biography and filmic output indicates, it was not coincidental. Like the horrific scene that concludes Samuel Fuller's *I Shot Jesse James* (1949), in which Robert Ford is forever doomed to reenact his own cowardly assassination of his friend on stage for hissing audiences who relish their chance to jeer Ford's despicable act, so Chaplin was so devastated by his mother's illness that he felt a compulsive need to recreate their plight in his screen work.[11] And, notably, Chaplin made the new versions end with hope, for his fictionalized recreations of his challenging childhood usually resulted in the Tramp redeeming the troubled avatar of his mother. With each of her incarcerations in an asylum, Chaplin was removed from his mother, more distant by degrees, until he lost her entirely to insanity. Left alone and without adult supervision for long stretches of his depressive childhood, Chaplin fell back, and inwardly, on himself. As a result, he launched into the world at the youngest of ages with a determination not only for greatness and a learned resilience, but in a true sense, artistic revenge. By telling his mother's fall from grace, predicated as it was on mental illness as agent, again and again, Chaplin was perhaps using filmic therapy to exorcise the demons of his own troubled mind. In a just sense, at least from Chaplin's point of view, his childhood poverty was redeemed at the same time by adoring audiences paying him millions.

The influence of a parent with mental illness is accepted as a clinical marker for a latent genetic tendency for mood disorder later in life.[12] The obvious question then arises: was Charlie Chaplin also bipolar? Consider his life's extravagances. One can argue they were to compensate for his severe impoverishment as a child. But it is worthwhile to consider how, while making *City Lights* (1928), Chaplin ran through over $1.5 million, holding his cast and crew on call for twenty-two consecutive months without break. Most of this was spent not on filming sequences, but simply paying exorbitant salaries and preproduction costs while Chaplin obsessively ruminated over his languishing production.[13] At one point, Chaplin delayed filming for over one year while he fruitlessly attempted to devise a plot mechanism by which he could convincingly have a blind girl fall in love with his Tramp. As we will see later, with Francis Ford Coppola's four-year-long making of *Apocalypse Now* (1979), a not infrequent occurrence of bipolarity in filmmakers is an inability to finish their works when they are experiencing severe bouts of manic and/or depression.

Pivoting to his personal life, Chaplin can be assessed, generously so, as a classic womanizer. While this does not confer a diagnosis of hypersexuality in and of itself, his preferred taste for underage women was a constant source of personal and legal entanglements.[14] He was married four times. Russian filmmaker Sergey Eisenstein was impressed with Chaplin's talents before and after they met while Eisenstein was in the United States on a cultural goodwill trip, but he noted that Chaplin was suffering from extreme unhappiness personally.[15] Virginia Cherrill recalled her long tenure as leading actress for Chaplin during *City Lights*'s troubled production as "painful"[16] because it was so clear that Chaplin was unable to achieve anything resembling directorial satisfaction, ordering endless retakes during the film's final count of 179 shooting days. As if channeling his own clinical episode into a script, Chaplin wrote of his own character's role in the screenplay for *Modern Times*: "Charlie [his role] . . . develops a few loose nuts himself and suffers a nervous breakdown."[17] During an IRS audit in which Chaplin was accused of withholding millions of dollars in back taxes, he dropped to 116 pounds in weight and became suicidal. Kono, his manservant, once had to prevent Chaplin from leaping from his Ritz-Carlton suite during this time. Dr. Gustav Tiek was summoned to care for Chaplin and recommended a sanitarium, but fearful of any hint of psychiatric scandal, Chaplin's attorney Nathan Burkan instead took his client to his own apartment for rest until the episode concluded.[18]

Author Joyce Milton succinctly concludes in her exhaustively well-researched biography, *Tramp: The Life of Charlie Chaplin*, "Chaplin suffered from what today would be called manic depression, or bipolar illness. Paradoxically, when his personal life was spinning out of control, he was often intensely creative in his work."[19] Echoing Milton's thesis, film criticism writer Alan Vanneman in a *Bright Lights Film Journal* article called Chaplin a "classic manic-depressive, [who] could never really relax except when he was working."[20] The latter is a hallmark thesis of this book, as the reader will have doubtlessly noted by now, but an important one to reiterate, as it demonstrates the clear linkage between artistic expression and personal therapy. The sufferer is often lost in a mentally confusing maelstrom of inwardly conflicting thoughts, feelings, and desires. The external locus of control offered, indeed demanded, by a complex, multilayered artistic endeavor becomes a form of stabilizing influence in the unstable grip of madness, however contradictory that may seem upon first analysis. The process of constantly facing the shortcomings in the work at hand, and revising them with a new sense of perspective brought on by a recent mood swing, becomes not solely a manner of career achievement, but a form of therapy, in and of itself.[21]

Chaplin was aware of his own instability in this regard. He perhaps unwittingly revealed as much to an interviewer when he remarked how weary he was of performing the Tramp persona to constant public demand, and yet, how addicted he was to the high he achieved each time he challenged himself to go further in the role. But reflecting on his own moodiness, Chaplin remarked, "There are days when any contact with any human being makes me ill. I am oppressed at such times, and in such periods as what was known among the Romantics as world-weariness, I feel a total stranger to life."[22] Chaplin's reference to the melancholia embodied most famously by the Romantic movement of poetry and literature is telling. Among the Romantics were William Blake, Samuel Taylor Coleridge, Lord Byron, and John Keats—all renowned for their writings, but more important for our purposes, now widely regarded as likely manic-depressives.[23] Chaplin's interviewer did not take his subject's downcast answer seriously. He instead reminded Chaplin that his Tramp character was beloved the world over, and therefore, by implication, his creator could never be very seriously sad, at least not for too long.

But such was not the case. Through a lifetime of bad judgment in hypersexualized relationships, often with underage women; in his often tempestuous and iconoclastic artistic and business demands; and in his disastrous political forays, which eventually led to his expulsion from America during the anti-Communist hysteria of the 1950s because of his loudly stated leftist views, Chaplin was far from happy in any continuous sense.[24] In order to self-treat his condition, Chaplin often spent a great amount of his time in his mansion in reclusive self-confinement, reading books and revising his latest creative endeavor, hardly seeking any human contact beyond his able-bodied serving staff for long stretches on end. Then he would cycle up in his moods and become insatiably social, hedonistic, and self-indulgent beyond even his own ability to later rationalize when he was down.[25] He often found himself so "wound up" after shooting a film that he couldn't rest. This lifelong pattern was particularly acute during the 1925 production of *The Gold Rush*. He sat up in bed one night from a troubled insomniac's losing bid for sleep and demanded to see a lawyer, convinced he was dying and needing to correct his will. A doctor rather than a lawyer was summoned the next morning by his staff but Chaplin's hysteria had faded. The examining physician certified Chaplin was suffering from "shattered nerves"—a term for mental illness at the time. As Milton reminds the reader in her book, "Chaplin would recall years later that his main problem was that he kept weeping, about nothing in particular."[26]

This latter detail regarding tristimania suggests Chaplin's moods were probably cyclothymic, or rapid cycling, in nature. Rather than having prolonged periods of depression followed by an exaggerated rebirth in a manic episode, as do many bipolar patients, Chaplin more likely experienced a series of highs and lows, each following the next, without much break. Such instability can be debilitating in extreme measures. Conversely, for an artist with an iron will such as Chaplin possessed, it can offer psychological and emotional insight into the human condition, if for no other reason than one's own unique reality is forever shifting as well. A rapid cycling bipolar creator often is forced to deal with a constant process of realignment. That is, the sufferer must make amends quickly for any transgressions committed during a particular noxious bout of depression or mania, and learn to move on, seeking forgiveness from others who may have been offended even as the sufferer struggles to forgive himself for the latest round of impulsive bad decisions.[27] Such extremes of behavior, in essence, force a form of conciliatory reckoning in the filmic process itself when a bipolar director is in charge. In the chaos that historically is film production, anyone who can pilot the ship through turbulent waters is most often the valued captain who will also gently dock the boat, undamaged and with its cargo intact, at a safe harbor by voyage's end. By surmounting inwardly destructive gales with constant willpower, the bipolar filmmaker places his or her definitive mark on the outcome of the production as his or her crew members and cast look to any guiding light in the repetitive fog that is any movie's cost of making. Surely Chaplin, who maintained almost tyrannical control over every facet of his films' production as soon as he was able to do so, was one of the first progenitors of such a model of film production. In every sense, he was an auteur, if a highly fluctuating one, emotionally. Nor was Chaplin unaware of his emotional illness.

Chaplin once met the celebrity astrologer of popular renown called Darios, who warned Chaplin to be especially careful of his moods during the spring.[28] Normally a skeptic, Chaplin reacted with astonishment. Chaplin confessed that April and May were the two most challenging months most seasons for his well-being owing to his fluctuating moods. Given his mother's mental illness, his own emotional complexity, and his artistic genius, as well as the darker sides of his nature that have been detailed in Milton's book and others, one concludes that one of the greatest early voices in cinema history, so influential in redefining the medium itself that it could after his touch reach previously undreamed of audience numbers globally, was in all likelihood bipolar. Furthermore, his filmmaking was one of Chaplin's greatest tools for self-treatment of bipolarity and maintaining his stability.

As Freud himself concluded in his astute and essentially correct analysis of his meetings with Chaplin: "He is, so to speak, an exceptionally simple and transparent case. The idea that the achievements of artists are intimately bound up with their childhood memories, impressions, repressions and disappointments, has already brought in much enlightenment."[29] It does not take much in the way of speculation, and indeed, one is inexorably drawn to the conclusion, that Chaplin's troubling mood swings were the by-product of both a maternal genetic predisposition and the incredibly stressful life of poverty he endured as a result of his mother's condition. Nor does it deny any of his artistic achievement to attribute his seemingly endless source of creative energy to the profound states of hypomania and mania he suffered with troubling intensity throughout his life.

THE CABINET OF DR. CALIGARI AS SEMINAL BIPOLAR CINEMA INFLUENCE

Because Chaplin's persona on screen was so loveable, and because he was private about his mother's mental illness and his own mood instability, his impact as a manic-depressive is seen more in terms of behind-the-scenes production and artistic creation than on screen and as a subject matter. Throughout the history of cinema in terms of how it is created, and then how it is perceived, bipolar film directors and actors have made profound contributions on both the form and content of motion pictures. Many of the greatest films made by creators on the spectrum of bipolarity have nothing to do with overt manic depression as subject matter. Likewise, some of the best examples of films about mental illness are not made by actual sufferers. But when the creator is mood disordered and the subject matter involves cinematic distillations or representations of madness, the results can be truly spectacular.

One of the earliest films in the silent era to deal with this form of psychological horror and subjective perspective and even introduce the now cliché twist ending as a cinematic narrative device was 1920's hugely influential *The Cabinet of Dr. Caligari*. Though known for its use of strange Expressionistic set designs, weird lighting, and morbid tone, *The Cabinet of Dr. Caligari* deserves long-overdue recognition for another contribution to the filmic arts. For the first time, serious use of the clinical term "mania" is accurately applied in films, thereby distinguishing it as a distant but potent forerunner of a new type of psychological realism that was to follow in more modern films. Rather than hide behind phony gibberish or simply avoid giving a clinical term to the disorder of the depicted patient, the asylum director proclaims via title card (in the Samuel Goldwyn original American 1920 release edition), "At last I recognize his *mania*. . . . Astonishing! But I think I know how to cure him now."

Given there is still no known cure for mania, only treatments and medications with varying degrees of efficacy, this statement also earns a less distinctive notation as being the first on-screen psychiatric diagnosis of mania that was technically incorrect. One will understand the author's noticeable reluctance to assign much historical judgment to the latter distinction, as the film is a sincere attempt by its creators (at least from the writing perspective) to be a first-of-its-kind examination of the terrors of a disordered mindscape. As such, it deserves the benefit of a fresh look, especially given that it accurately distills and introduces many psychiatric concepts and depictions. Many films released the same year were no more accurate in their realization of screen mental illness, and, in sad fact, many simply exploited the distortions and prevailing prejudices in the latest tired incarnation of so-called "maniacal killer" slasher movies. But *The Cabinet of Dr. Caligari* remains, after almost a century of filmmaking, eerily filled with prescience in both positive and negative imagery with regard to manic depression.

There is a reason for the screen veracity. Both of its writers were German veterans of the horrific trench warfare of World War I and met as intellectual layabouts in postwar Berlin's thriving cafe culture.[30] They were not alone, as many soldiers were unable to readjust to civilian life, especially during the inflationary Weimar Republic years when it was nearly impossible to survive even when one was fortunate enough to have employment. Against this bleak societal backdrop, Czech poet Hans Janowitz and Austrian native Carl Mayer, a fledgling screenwriter, used their ample free time to concoct a scenario that would ostensibly be a commentary on the horrors of warfare in terms of psychological costs. Realizing that no one during this escapist era of German filmmaking would attend a morbid artistic movie about the recently ended war, the screenwriters decided to use an abstract approach to depict the authoritarian figures they wished to assign blame to for the ruinous warfare.[31] By doing so, the team of veterans believed they could appeal to some of the more progressive producers who were emerging in the postwar landscape. Many of the new producers wished to see a German cinema free of so much of the mindless fare being imported from America, replaced with a more robust, locally driven cinema that featured varying points of view and new techniques. Janowitz and Mayer conceptually desired, and finally achieved, a film that gave shape and form to the humanitarian insights and soul-crushing nightmares they'd witnessed as combat vets.[32] They figured they would need to enlarge the cinematic language in order to do so, and set out to co-opt many tenets of the burgeoning Expressionist art movement into a film aesthetic as a way of doing precisely that. Their influence is so complete that the film is a rare instance wherein the authors are regarded as being as important to the final outcome as the director, producers, or actors in terms of creative contribution—not an easy task from a writer's perspective in an era sans dialogue and relying on title cards to largely clarify, not layer meaning into, the screen action depicted.

Carl Mayer was on record as noting that one of the key inspirations for him as co-scenarist for the film was an encounter with a pompous military psychiatrist of top rank. Mayer was evidently required against his will to be analyzed owing to some unspecified tendencies as an enlisted soldier.[33] In postwar Germany, many veterans suffering from mental illness as a direct by-product of combat were often forced to fight for their medical benefits against those vocal critics in the Weimar Republic who railed against so-called "pension neuroses." The wealthy private class who did not want to incur the costs of aiding the war-damaged veterans were sadly in alignment with Germany's ascendant class of professional psychiatrists. The German Association of Psychiatry refused to recognize that veterans were suffering from an actual post-combat mental illness. Instead, they maintained that the veterans were only "malingering," or pretending, to be mentally ill in order to be supported by an already debt-ridden state, even as many were clearly worthy of treatment and/or institutionalization.[34]

So if the resulting visualization of the psychiatrist/hypnotist Dr. Caligari as portrayed by Werner Krauss is any indication, there is little wonder why one of cinema's earliest depictions of a medical practitioner of the mind is of horrific, inhumane coldness. With his calculating, bug-sized eyes peering through circular glasses, his white shock of stringy hair, and the massive bulk of his figure enshrouded in overcoats and adorned with a sinister stovepipe hat, Dr. Caligari arrives in the annals of cinema like a spider about to devour a fly, limping along the bizarrely angled streets, entrapped by the surrounding walls that threaten to crush him. With his cane clutched in front of him, like the tapping of an arachnid's leg testing the thread of a web before proceeding, Caligari actually does project the grotesque manner of a human spider, complete with wobbly, side-to-side motion. Even the strange slash marks painted onto the sets seem to be like strands of a spider web, guiding his passage. Suffice it to say, the idea that Caligari's appearance would encourage anyone in right or wrong mind to reveal intimate details of what mentally ails them seems ludicrous beyond the need to critique.

Which is precisely what the filmmakers wanted to accomplish as shock effect. They were perhaps too effective in their designs. So much so that Fritz Lang, who had been offered the film to direct but declined in order to helm another project from his own script, was brought aboard during postproduction by the producers without Janowitz and Mayer realizing it.[35] Lang was tasked with altering the film's basic narrative (for which he received no credit), which as written and initially shot presented a straightforward look at a weird hypnotist by the name of Caligari, and his Svengali-like hold on his sleepwalking accomplice, Cesare. The pair commit a series of murders using a traveling carnival as cover, with the sleepwalking Cesare under the evil bidding of Caligari, who hypnotizes the slumbering accomplice to awake only when doing his master's will. The carnival show setup in the original script basically gives way to a melodramatic whodunnit, even though it is readily apparent that the somnambulist is the culprit behind the unsolved murders from the outset. So apparent, in fact, that the film's producers, Rudolf Meinert and Erich Pommer, as well as its director, Robert Wiene, felt the film's well-being was in jeopardy, owing to the thinly veiled social critique the film espoused. As originally presented, *The Cabinet of Dr. Caligari* made its antiwar sentiment clearly known, and the blame for World War I was lain at the feet of the ruling class and their incompetent generals. As Janowitz characterized his and Mayer's intent, Cesare the sleepwalker was deliberately designed to represent "the common man who, under the pressure of military service, is drilled to kill and be killed."[36] At the end, when Caligari is unmasked by the protagonist, the writers wanted to demonstrate how, again in Janowitz's words, "reason overpowers unreasonable power."[37]

Well and fine, but when the directing/producing team realized as they watched the first cut that such sentiments had been rather too successfully translated into the material, they panicked. Fritz Lang was invited to watch and offer any suggestions. His idea was both simple and economical. Shoot a new scene for the film's conclusion.[38] The new scene would reveal that the entire preceding film was nothing more than the delusion of a madman, and therefore, by definition of society's existing prejudices against such individuals, no one of any power or authority could complain. After all, what powerful figure would imagine himself personified as the mentally ill, when the mentally ill were considered, for all that it mattered, the untouchable class of their respective culture? Better yet, this approach would mean the producers could leave the film intact, without editing to remove any potentially offensive sections.

Lang probably never intended his depiction of the mentally ill as anything less than humane and tragic. This much is evident in his classic treatment of mental illness as played by Peter Lorre in Lang's later masterpiece *M* (1931), and in the sympathetic portrayal by Ray Milland of a former asylum patient in *Ministry of Fear* (1944). Too, Lang should receive credit for accurately showing the asylum as a caring retreat rather than a torture dungeon, as many later screen renditions would favor (not that such realities were not present, as much as they tend to be overly represented in films, favoring as they usually do the lurid over the loving). He also did a fine job of using actual psychiatric jargon and introducing the word "mania" into the cinematic lexicon as an actual clinical disorder. The use of an insane asylum was an easy way to cushion the audience's reception to the material they'd witnessed, Lang probably concluded. The short coda Lang chose—to set the story in wraparound as the ravings of a lunatic mind and against the background of a sanitarium—alleviates the need for the audience to consider the hour's worth of damning screen time that preceded this revelation. Because the filmmaker allows the audience to use its own preconceptions of the mentally ill as unreliable outcasts in terms of societal credibility, he and viewers get to "excuse" all that disturbed them previously and merely shrug it away. *After all*, the hidden implication suggests, what do you, what do *any* of us, expect from a madman but madness?

But Lang's contributions were equally ambivalent over time. For Lang is best remembered as the creative force behind surely two of the

most diabolical portraits of mania as homicidal ever committed to cellu-
loid, and were he not such a talented progenitor of the medium itself,
these negative portrayals would have perhaps not been so forceful.
These include Rotwang the mad scientist in the seminal *Metropolis*
(1927), and the hugely successful Dr. Mabuse serials, also released as
features in the 1920s, which hinged on the unhinged maniac as criminal
mastermind. In these commercial blockbusters of their era, Lang not
only achieved worldwide fame as truly one of the best to have ever
worked in the business, but also was skillful in crafting screen memes of
lasting influence. To this day, Lang's traces on the careers of following
filmmakers are noteworthy. Alfred Hitchcock was an early admirer of
Lang's from Hitchcock's youthful employment at the UFA studio in
Germany, where he watched Lang direct. The sets and attitudes of
ruling-class conflicts from Lang's *Metropolis* weigh heavily in Ridley
Scott's dystopian visionary epic *Blade Runner* (1982), replete with a
plethora of mad scientist stereotypes rather than one. Alas, many subsequent filmmakers lacking the talent and imagination of a Hitchcock or
Scott uncritically recycled the mad genius cliché as shorthand for villain
in their own pale imitations, thus reinforcing a negative stereotype.

Lang's narrative magic worked on *The Cabinet of Dr. Caligari*, and
the film went on to worldwide business, including a ballyhooed United
States release by Sam Goldwyn. But ironically, the film would not entirely escape controversy. The first dispute arose not in Germany, which
embraced it and ignored the anti-bourgeois content, but in America. An
infuriated Hollywood cross-section of the American Legion, the Actor's
Equity, and the Motion Picture Director's Association arrived at Miller's Theater in Los Angeles on May 15, 1921, to protest the showing of
The Cabinet of Dr. Caligari as well as the recent spate of German films
being shown in the United States.[39] Trade protectionists and industry
loyalists first and foremost, some of the more self-aware protestors may
have calculated that the film's very strangeness would be considered
indicative of the whole German output as corrupting to gullible or like-
minded patrons. Whatever their inclinations, they did not escape Upton
Sinclair's sardonic notice. He included them in his novel of 1922, *They
Call Me Carpenter*. Sinclair fictionalized the details, and altered the
protestors' identities as not protectionist and isolationist in origin, but as
day-player goons hired by the studios to protest "Hun propaganda." But
only in order to drum up business for a tepid movie's opening, not scare

it away![40] All of which meant, in terms of historical impact and lingering views of mania and depression, that *The Cabinet of Dr. Caligari* was more widely seen in its release than one might have otherwise anticipated. This is especially true given the anti-German feelings still present among many of the doughboy American veterans. Many of these vets were understandably upset at what they perhaps misunderstood was the glorification of their former mortal enemies on the combat fields of Europe. The irony, of course, is that Janowitz and Mayer were also soldiers who were opposed to any glorification of war. They were also against a foreign country's cinema (for them, it was the American output), which they believed limited the potential of any domestic film to be more widely seen in its own country of origin. And as has so often been the case in film history, opinions were heated and exchanged on all sides of the dispute, but there was no change to the movie itself.

The controversy helped mask the film's less-desirable qualities as progenitor of mental illness realizations in premodern cinema. The most obvious stereotypes one encounters in *The Cabinet of Dr. Caligari* that are notable for their subsequent overuse include the maniacal doctor, more often known as the mad doctor, and the use of the depressive sleepwalker, Cesare, as murderous. Because Dr. Caligari (mania) and Cesare (depression) are joined as partners in crime throughout the film, they remain a pair, rather than discrete, in identity. While they have scenes apart, the magic of the film is that Caligari is never far away from his homicidal human puppet, dabbling behind the scenes, pulling the invisible strings to accomplish Cesare's murderous deeds. The way in which Wiene, the scenarists, and eventually Lang render this codependent quality of Caligari and Cesare, making them doppelganger alter egos, was novel to films in the 1920s.

The sense of power Caligari maniacally manifests is frightening. With his eyes wide stretched and his jaw firmly clenched, he seems perpetually ill-at-ease, a kind of Scrooge with a homicidal rage, ready to strike at any transgressors with his tightly held cane. When the viewer first glimpses him, it is from the artistic device of a widening iris circle. Caligari's eyes and sneering demeanor are all that one sees against a black surrounding void and widening port window into his damaged psyche. He glares at us, as if expecting us and none too happy we have finally arrived. He is malevolence itself, an angry manic ready to snap at the slightest provocation. Caligari is all ego and mania, so much so that when we see him first it is as a floating head, detached from all reality, lost in his raging thoughts, until finally the widening iris reveals that his portly, shuffling body is actually attached to his gigantic face, almost as afterthought. It's a wonderfully accurate moment, true to manic self-inflation of ego as artistic representation and cinematic stylization.

This is also why it has had such a negative, albeit unintentionally so, lasting impact as archetypal image. For at every turn, Caligari acts the unrepentant fiend. A subtle but persistent subtext is established by Caligari's nefarious actions. The manic is dangerous. The manic plots and schemes. He sets himself apart not by mental disorder, but because he is wicked and is afraid of discovery from the "good" people. The manic is gifted in intellectual ability but applies it to deviancy instead of for common good. He uses his ability as a genius not to create but to destroy the reality around him. The manic will even murder and use others to do his evil bidding without any sign of remorse. There is never any other image or shading of mania displayed throughout the film's length that could be construed as positive. Mania, as defined and exhibited by the mad doctor, is a one-way street to self-aggrandizement and self-annihilation. The portrait of the frozen-faced manic masking a raging spite is firmly established and entrenched. Unlike actual mania, which is an event of typically shorter duration, *The Cabinet of Dr. Caligari* suggests it is a permanent state of psychosis without any remittance. This is far from the medical reality.[41] It is akin to portraying someone with an epileptic seizure as never abating from an episode, or a cancer patient never going into remission. Alas, though not guilty of any intentional harm, this inaccurate but persistent screen cliché will come to dominate much of bipolar cinema until many, many decades later.

None of which was completely unintentional, as previously stated. The writers' original conception of Caligari as a mad despot rather than asylum director was transformed by Lang. Janowitz was determined to present the rulers of Germany, and their symbolic stand-in Caligari, as he honestly, some might argue accurately, perceived them: delusional, self-inflated egomaniacs who would sacrifice any amount of humanity in order to accomplish their own diabolical goals.[42] So while Lang later excuses Caligari's rage as madness, rather than entitlement or nobility, as the film's authors intended, he is actually only underscoring the significant depiction of "mania as murderous" that Janowitz, Mayer, and

Wiene had all conjured without disguise in the first version of the movie. Lang doesn't create the screen image, in other words. Instead, he underscores it, and shifts the underscore to an asterisk, which states: the images of madness you have just witnessed are not the acts of your rulers who ruined you recently in a disastrous war; they are merely the damaged fantasies of a deranged mind. Ironically, Lang's ability to so easily mask the blame of the film without alteration of the actual presented content suggests he shared the writers' viewpoint. He must have realized how such institutional insanity as ruling-class privilege was still nothing more than insanity by another name. The next logical step is to equate such bad government to inmates running the asylum, which is what Lang did, following in the manner of Poe.

There was also positive bipolar imagery in *The Cabinet of Dr. Caligari*. Cesare is presented as an empathetic figure under the spell of another, so his killing is tragic and not of his own devising. Cesare (Conrad Veidt) is the classic embodiment of a catatonic depressive,[43] a passive state of being that would not be expected to produce emotion on behalf of viewers, who typically prefer active protagonists to passive ones. In this condition of severe mental illness, the depressed patient becomes rigid, almost lifeless, in posture and position. Such a person can be propped in bed without their assistance and maintain the new posture without demonstrating any cognitive awareness they have been moved. Many severely depressed individuals must be forced to get out of bed and move around for their own well-being as a result of a prolonged episode. In severe depression, even self-care of the rudimentary sort vanishes, temporarily leaving a motionless body where a loving person once resided. Without another human being present to guide and offer direction (to eat, to sleep, to clean, etc.), a severely depressed person resembles the vacant performance embodied by Veidt. Veidt's anorexic, black-clad portrait expressively captures the lumbering gait and self-conscious postures many depressives exhibit during clinical episodes of duress.[44] The contrast of allowing Cesare to occasionally emerge, conscious and aware of the horrific condition into which he is soon to irreconcilably return, further builds audience empathy. The tragedy of a person who is trapped in a depressive state of being, more dead than alive at times, only to have moments of genuine clarity and insight into the drastic nature of his existence, is hard to resist as a model of psychic projection. After all, the tragedy of all mythic monsters, and Shakespeare's best characters, is that they have a flawed nature they must contend with in order to survive. This even as they loathe the Faustian trade-off they strike in order to do so. Cesare has such moments when he recognizes the beauty of the woman he has abducted on Caligari's malignant behest, sparing her and reawakening to his own sleeping humanity as a result. This is in accord with the known models of how many depressives can experience positive therapeutic results from interacting with others when they're not severely down, and drawing inner resilience from their encounters with healthy, balanced individuals whose loving support can alleviate some of their worst suffering.[45]

Cesare is the rare figure in the film who garners empathy, not sympathy. The disturbed, somber, and withdrawn depressives who scarcely populate the asylum's interior hold static positions in the frame's compositions, always looking down and away from one another, and never making or sustaining eye contact. As they sit rigid in frozen silence, faces drawn in private agony, they present a devastatingly accurate portraiture of depression, and all in the opening moments of the film. This creates a mood in the viewer of immediate vulnerability for those shown as afflicted, as well as the ever-present, less noble curiosity factor of seeing The Other which lies beneath many films dealing with mental illness. Lest this seem callous, it is well to remember that as late as eighteenth-century London, the infamous asylums had degenerated into little more that state-sponsored side shows. For only a pittance, anyone could gain admission to Bethlem Royal Hospital and poke the asylum inmates with a provided stick for amusement.[46] One day a month, the doors were opened free of charge as well, for those starved for sadistic thrills but unable to afford them. Against such historical reality, Lang's treatment of mental illness seems positively enlightened in tone, despite the consequential negative impressions that were beyond his ability to control or even predict.

Depression is why Cesare is so willing to be under Caligari's grip and never struggles much with any sense of personal freedom or ambition. Cesare is the slumbering depressive who is amenable to any suggestion, so long as he does not have to originate or be responsible for the consequences. He is not seeking to be evil or harm others. Rather, he is surrendering to the bleak emptiness within which is his truest, deepest nature. By giving over to despair and allowing others to control him,

Cesare is acting like depressives who must trust that their loved ones will take care of them during major episodes. Little wonder depressives often struggle with issues of depersonalization and loss of identity, given that they are required to accept a lifetime of being unable to control their own personal moods and unstable personalities during their disorder's worst moments.[47] For Cesare, it means being reduced to confinement, literally in a coffin. Whereas for the depressive, it most often means being confined to a bed. For Cesare, remission means momentarily emerging from catatonic depression in order to do the bidding of mania's calling, represented by his obsessed master. For the bipolar patient rapidly cycling from depression into mania, it also means doing the bidding of an obsessive thought process, albeit located inside the sufferer's own mind.

Other less obvious but significant clues that demonstrate the creators' familiarity with mood disorders are littered throughout the film. For example, in the opening moments a citizen warns the visiting Dr. Caligari to be careful in dealing with the town's clerk because the clerk is "in a bad mood today." Dr. Caligari is shown with a title card that simply states: "In the grip of an obsession." Later, a character vows to unravel the "psychiatric secrets" of Dr. Caligari. And toward the film's conclusion, Caligari himself is forced into a straight jacket by the asylum's staff, after being revealed to be the madman behind Cesare's murderous actions. In many key ways, much of what follows in film history will but echo, loudly or more softly, many of the themes and soft prejudices of *The Cabinet of Dr. Caligari*.

DR. JEKYLL AND MR. HYDE AND THE BIPOLAR BARRYMORE DYNASTY

While it is undeniably an influence, the 1920 American version of *Dr. Jekyll and Mr. Hyde* starring John Barrymore in the titular twin roles is less a depiction of actual bipolar disorder in the movies than might be first imagined since its emphasis is on the maniacal Hyde, a clear echo of the "dangerous lunatic" cliché already cinematically rampant. The success of the film did nonetheless reinforce the homicidal maniac stereotype because of the manner in which stage-actor-turned-film star John Barrymore realized his screen incarnation of the deranged Hyde.

In part because Barrymore was so convincingly unhinged in a believably crafted performance of insanity, the lunatic as murdering psychopath— as Hyde is shown becoming finally when his dualistic identity is threatened to be revealed by his future father-in-law—yet again is codified into cinema.

Robert Louis Stevenson's 1886 novella *The Strange Case of Dr. Jekyll and Mr. Hyde* explains the display of mania as chemically induced and to be summoned on demand (at least initially). This is why it is less an influence on the depiction of mood disorders in films than otherwise might be expected. This dramatic conceit is antithetical to the actuality of mood disorders, suggestive as it is that mania is a controllable illness, because there is no known cure for manic depression, only treatments that can help alleviate suffering.[48] However, to the extent that *Dr. Jekyll and Mr. Hyde* also reaches a narrative point in its construction wherein Dr. Jekyll realizes he can no longer control the regression to Hyde and the reverse to his normal, civilized self, the film does echo some of the same thematic concerns mood-disorder movies and their makers often share. Here is where Barrymore's portrayal of the foundering good doctor persona at war with his uncontrollable manic side actually does briefly become relevant to showing the wild swings of mood possible during clinical episodes. Patients can actually have mania-fueled outbursts of sudden flight into new territories, wherein they seek the company of strangers, recklessly spend money, and otherwise exhibit behavior they would be mortified to display if they were not temporarily unbalanced.[49] And like Hyde, there can be a quality to the manic's persona that is alluring and seductive, filled as the individual is with the confidence gained from mania's hold.

John Barrymore's contribution to bipolar cinema will be more directly felt in *A Bill of Divorcement* (1932) in the sound era, at least in terms of his screen portrait of a former mentally ill patient attempting to reenter society. But a brief acknowledgment of his and his family's long struggles with mental illness is in order, as they demonstrate the intertwined nature of great acting talent and bipolarity over time. Consider the fact that Barrymore battled with alcoholism as probable self-medication for depression before dying from its effects on his damaged liver. Or that he was married four tumultuous times, as well as had a self-admitted, lifelong hypersexuality (even going so far as to tell the priest as he literally lay dying that he was thinking of his young nurse in a sexual manner).[50] Consider the fact that his daughter Diana Barrymore's own bouts with manic depression and stays for as long as a year at a time in various sanitariums ended with her suicide by overdose.[51] Or that his son John Drew Barrymore became so mentally unstable during his brief acting career that he was nearly thrown out of the Screen Actors Guild for fighting with other cast members and failing to show up as contracted while crews waited. Unemployable despite his name, he became a nearly homeless, penniless derelict for the remaining years of his troubled life.[52] Or that Drew Barrymore, his granddaughter and daughter of John Drew Barrymore, has admitted to her own problems with mental illness.[53] The well-documented connection between genetic lineage and mood disorders[54] is made startlingly transparent in the case of the mighty Barrymore clan in and of itself, and as in other cases of inheritable disorders, theirs is a family tree filled with the creative fruits as well as barren branches of bipolarity.

HÄXAN: MENTAL PERSECUTION THROUGH THE AGES

The Cabinet of Dr. Caligari is the ultimate Expressionist realization of cinema madness until this point. *Häxan* (1922), in contrast, is largely structured as a docudrama, purporting to be a lecture about the true history of witchcraft versus its root causes in persecution of the mentally ill. But like *The Cabinet of Dr. Caligari*, it is equally given to flights of cinematic surrealism. *Häxan*'s imagery is so hypnagogic it is little wonder William Burroughs and friends were able to release it largely intact, with only Burroughs's gravelly narration and a new jazz score added, in 1960s counterculture screenings as *Witchcraft Through the Ages*. To this day, it fascinates modern viewers who are shocked by its frankly lascivious displays of horny devils and lecherous padres, as well as the sexual longing eagerly enacted by its willing female participants. There lingers a perverse sense that the director is implying that the antiquated rites of pagan sex rituals were perhaps a reaction against the strict papal authorities in and of themselves, and that its participants were healthier for having indulged, despite a Pyrrhic cost later at the stakes of the witch burners. Whereas the self-oppressed priests are shown as lip-smacking, voyeuristic deviants, eager to use the devices of torture as much to extract pain from the victims as for pleasure for themselves.

It should come as no surprise that the film was condemned by the Catholic Church and other state censors in almost all countries save Denmark and Sweden.[55] In the latter it was a local hit, earning back its astounding cost of two million Swedish kronors. This made it the most expensive filmic undertaking of its era in terms of cost and ambition to also turn a profit. It was distributed haphazardly and with many cuts in some countries even during its original, largely censored release in some more liberal European countries. The director was quite passionate and dedicated to his cause, buying an old film studio in Denmark and renovating it for the film's sole production. He spent years with the pre-production phase as well, intent on using a scholarly approach to the material, rather than sensationalistic only (though he certainly has both in ample measure).[56] He poured over medieval woodcuts in order to get the precise look for an authentic recreation of the time period, right down to the instruments of torture. The infamous *Malleus Malefi-carum* (1486), the book used by the inquisitors themselves to conduct their ghastly trade, was secured by Christensen in a Berlin bookstore. It became a sort of black bible for the production's art direction and accurate source of historical information.[57]

Häxan is a deliberative exposé of the cruelties of the Inquisition. As such, Christensen forgoes any forgiveness of his intended targets, squarely laying the blame on the Catholic Church. As the UK-based *Electric Sheep* magazine pointed out in its 2007 review of the enduring cult film,

> Through the meticulous recreation of the past Christensen wanted to educate his audience about the consequences of superstitious and intolerant beliefs, demonstrating how they led to the persecution of anyone seen as different. . . . These beliefs were stirred up and influenced by the Church and Christensen starkly denounces the responsibility of the Christian clergy for the burning of 8 million people at the stake (although the scholar Casper Tybjerg explains on the Criterion DVD that the figure is in fact closer to 50,000). In one of the titles Christensen explains that the 'witch madness' was like a 'spiritual plague' that followed wherever the monks of the Inquisition went: the monks were not the remedy as they claimed, they were the disease.[58]

To show this hypocrisy, Christensen first depicts devil worship as one imagines the Inquisitors presented it to their trembling followers in their hell-fire sermons: as cloisters of furtive, secretive loners and outcasts who were doubtless cavorting with devils. How else to explain their often eccentric behaviors, their nonconformity when it was required, and their peculiar beliefs that as pagans they were normal, not demonically possessed, as the Church would later "prove" before setting them ablaze to atone for their imaginary sins? They made easy targets for a Christian religion intent on rooting out The Other wherever such "evil" was encountered. And as *Häxan* graphically demonstrates, most of the damned quickly confessed when put to the literal thumbscrews. Director Christensen even interjects a personal observation in his movie when he shows a modern actress modeling the thumb screws in a supposed audition for his film. He gloats that as soon as the camera was off, she quickly complied with his every request until he released her from her torture. It is both an oddly funny and equally chilling moment in which the seemingly benign modern mind of tolerance is revealed, even by the film's creator, as being far less wholesome once power over another human being is achieved, no matter the cost to the latter.

There is no way to measure the large contribution Christensen made with his epic. That is because the powerfully positive effects *Häxan* could have had upon the world at large in 1922 were denied by censorship and banning. One cannot help but speculate that the film was scorned not merely because Christensen was pointing an accusatory finger at the Church. After all, the medieval atrocities were well known and apologized for as an "unfortunate chapter in an otherwise unblemished"[59] history, which is how religious persecutions are commonly put into historical context. It is true that the nudity and torture scenes were shocking, especially so then, and mildly today, but would one play them as anything but sadistic if one's aim is historical veracity? So, while transgressive, the scenes did not in any way contradict the undisputed facts chronicled in countless woodcuts and published volumes detailing the era's atrocities.[60] Rather, they were objected to because of the imaginative intensity Christensen brought to the accurate details of what really happened during the Inquisition. Part of this accuracy meant the director had to show the victims for who they truly were, as people of their times. They were not witches and warlocks, as it turned out. They were often mentally ill or physically afflicted human beings who, because of their perceived weaknesses, were made sacrificial lambs. Given the enormous prejudice against the mentally ill in the 1920s, Christensen's film was incendiary, shattering such long-held assumptions that those who were bipolar or depressive were demonically possessed, and therefore, deserving of society's contempt.[61] Instead it pivots and says that the Inquisition sadly demonstrated mankind's dark tendency toward long periods of sustained, homicidal mania against its own perceived weakest members. To assign blame not to the mentally ill but to the society around them was perhaps a concept beyond the ability of many to comprehend, let alone accept, in the film's original release time. Thus *Häxan* was first suppressed and then largely forgotten before its eventual rediscovery in the 1960s, because its technique was too far ahead of its time and its message too accusatory.

Christensen's good intentions were censored, supposedly for the betterment of mankind, by its cultural and moral gatekeepers, at least at first. It is ironic in a sad sense, of course, that these were the same descendant forces that centuries earlier tortured and burned the very people the film was seeking to exonerate as victims, not witches. As Dr. Paul Carus wrote in 1900,

> The witch-persecution mania was a general and a common disease of the age. On the one hand, it cannot (as is often supposed) be attributed to the influence of the Church alone, and it would, on the other hand, be a grave mistake to absolve the ecclesiastical institutions of the fearful crimes of this superstition; for the highest authorities of both Catholic and Protestant Christianity not only upheld the idea of witch-persecution, but enforced it in the execution of the law in all its most terrible consequences.[62]

Though it would take decades for *Häxan* to be fully appreciated for its power of vision and audacity of accusation, it is a landmark in its historical importance. For the first time, so-called lunatics were not personified as beneath humanity. Rather, those who held them in sinister contempt and felt morally justified in torturing them were seen as the truer devils personified.

A PAGE OF MADNESS AND
THE NEO-PERCEPTIONIST VIEW OF INSANITY

One of the most unusual, visually dazzling motion pictures that survives amid the immense loss of many Japanese silent and early sound films owing to the devastation of World War II is the masterpiece *A Page of Madness* (1927), or *Kurutta Ippeiji*, as it is known in Japan. A groundbreaking cinematic achievement, it was directed by Teinosuke Kinugasa, a member of the newly fledged Shinkankaku school, or Neo-Perceptionists, as they have also been called. Well schooled in the Soviet advances in filmmaking of his day, and an avid follower of American and European filmic output, Kinugasa was also interested in both surrealism and expressionism as art forms.[63] This is cannily reflected in *A Page of Madness* and its hallucinatory sequences in which cloistered throngs of asylum inmates thrash about in manic epiphany, squirming and screeching in a singular mass of writhing, mentally ill humanity. They begin to resemble the grotesque reductionist displays of woe that one associates with biblical epics by Cecil B. de Mille, typically suffered due to the latest wrath of God. Rarely has screen madness been depicted as such a stylistic assault on the viewer's own mental balance; indeed, it is as if Kinugasa is obsessively trying to induce an inner breakdown in each and every audience member. The film purposely abandons most narrative concerns,[64] hinging its power on the unfolding intensity of the madness portrayed. As languid counterpart, it leisurely unspools a nonsubtitled quasi-plot about a man gaining access to a mental asylum where his wife is being held after she has attempted to drown their child.

The bipolars seen in *A Page of Madness* are in full flights of manic psychosis more often than not. So to some extent, and though it pictures an asylum with far more realism than most European or American attempts at depicting mental hospitals, it does not suggest that mental illness such as bipolar disorder fluctuates in its onset and remission, which is regrettable. But for cinematic realizations of the overbearing nature of clinical mania during the worst of an acute episode, Kinugasa's film is still one of the most powerful ever created. In particular, a woman patient locked in solitary confinement who flutters insistently around a lone light bulb far above her head, arms flapping nonstop like a moth's wings and shaking her head ferociously back and forth as the detached nurses and warden look on, is maniacally perfect in presentation. The woman's escape into her delusional moth display is so complete, so utterly self-contained, and so utterly oblivious to any other who may be watching her, that neurotypical observers find themselves as entranced as a proverbial voyeuristic moth themselves. They are unable to look away from the intricacies of mental illness illustrated before their very astonished eyes.

The clinical detachment comes at great cost, as the staff and doctor later succumb to the frenetic inmates during the film's infamous "dance riot in the asylum" sequence. During the sequence, the inmates, loosed from the restraining cells, flood the small, communal center room and dance with manic fervor. They seem less like dancers and more like possessed bees, throbbing and vibrating with such vigor one fully anticipates they will spontaneously explode at any moment. The manner in which Kinugasa intercuts the baleful doctor with his resistant patients as he is slowly absorbed by their frenetic mass uprising like a twig in the raging ocean, drowned alive in insanity and unable to persevere, is frightening and transgressive. The thin line between insane states of emotional disorder and so-called normal, balanced states of emotional well-being had never before been so clearly suggested, if not outright shown, to be so illusory, so temporary, and so easily displaced in moments of inexplicable human behavior. These horrors of reality are shared by all, mentally ill or healthy, in such dreadful mass-delusional moments as public lynchings and fascist revolutions.

In a pattern that readers will come to realize is oddly persistent, *A Page of Madness* was first believed lost to time, much like the fates of *Häxan* and then, later, the uncut version of *The Passion of Joan of Arc* (1928), until their rediscovery at later dates. And there is perhaps something telling in that three of the greatest achievements in all of silent cinema all dealt with mental illness to varying degrees of verboten frankness. The taboo-shattering nature of their respective presentations of bipolar disorder and other mental illnesses as humane, rather than simply horrific, may have put each at risk in terms of popular and political perception in their respective countries. In Kinugasa's case, the lack of popular appreciation for his attempt to free himself from the commercial constraints of cinema left him artistically despondent and financially bankrupt, as he had financed the film himself at considerable personal cost.[65] It was truly serendipitous that in 1971 Kinugasa found the only known 35 mm print of *A Page of Madness* in his garden shed. Encouraged by the synchronicity of the rebelliousness he saw in the 1960s counterculture, Kinugasa recut the surviving footage for length and released it for a curious public to see what had already been forgotten in Japanese cinema history. As with *Häxan* before it, the startlingly modern style of unvarnished cinema techniques on display were seen in retrospect as revolutionary. Appreciation was reignited for its content (the scenario was cowritten by later Nobel Prize–winning writer Yasunari Kawabata) and its radical aesthetic, though sadly, neither was influential in its era owing to its obscurity. Its later influence, however, is still felt in the echoes of modern cinema. Scorsese's *Shutter Island* (2010) shares a similar plot, in which a husband (this time of a deceased mentally ill woman) attempts to gain entry into a mental asylum wherein he suspects wrongdoing by the doctors. Both bipolar wife characters come complete with a drowning child incident in their respective backstories. While *Shutter Island* is usually much more realistic in tone and style, it also gives way to overtly hallucinatory scenes in which even the supposedly balanced protagonist is no longer sure of his own sanity the longer he persists in remaining in the sanitarium.

THE PASSION OF JOAN OF ARC AND VISUALIZATIONS OF RELIGIOUS MANIA

One last great silent epic worthy of consideration is Carl Theodor Dreyer's *The Passion of Joan of Arc* (1928). Because it touches on many of the same themes as *Häxan*, it can be seen as a spiritual descendant of Christensen's earlier church exposé. The biggest leap forward by Dreyer in his examination of delusional mania masquerading as religious fervor is his choice to center the story not on a romantic couple or a neurotypical protagonist who only must contend with the story's mood disordered antagonists (as in the many lunacy films preceding), but on the actual victim of the clinical mania herself. Even *Häxan*, with all its humanitarian good intent and factual revelations did little to portray the mentally ill as other than harmless kooks and eccentrics who were undeservedly persecuted. *The Passion of Joan of Arc* made Joan herself the front-and-center emotional pathway into the conflict, and by doing so, it established one of the most moving portraits of mood instability in all of film history, silent or sound. What *Häxan* made external in the film's content alone, *The Passion of Joan of Arc* made internal in the film's content and form.

The casting of Maria Falconetti, despite her relative inexperience on stage or screen, was perhaps the greatest stroke of genius. Falconetti's performance is considered by many film critics among the greatest ever given.[66] The stark, almost surreal close-ups of Falconetti as Joan, her face beatific in one shot, eyes glowing with inner light, followed later by close-ups of her face contorted in the burning, inner toil of depression, eyes now bereft of all but the most hollow of human emptiness, defined the film's emotional center. Her amazing ability to transcend any fourth wall and instantly involve the viewer is a testament to her talent as well as to Dreyer's ability to elicit and guide her performance. Indeed, because everyone but Joan seems pitiless and self-abnegating when it comes to admitting, let alone expressing, any emotion that is not scripted or politically convenient, the French martyr comes across all the more empathetic. The pomposity of the assembled group of spiritually dead men who attempt to pass sentence on the only living human being in their presence is genuinely revolting. Their arrogance is the same as the clergy in *Häxan*, but even more resolutely heinous. Whereas Christensen makes them outright lechers and sadistic torturers, Dreyer is much less obvious. His calculating, smug, vain, silly, condescending, and controlling men of the cloth are much more realistic in their respective character pathologies. They are full of preening conceit, smugly self-assured that extinguishing Joan's inner light of religious mania will restore the equilibrium her devout belief has inspired in her fellow countrymen. In order to regain control of the aroused, equally emotional citizenry, and redirect Joan's "passion" back into a dominant male hierarchy, the religious leaders elect to destroy the source of inspiration because it is beyond their control and therefore dangerous to their hold on power. But was Falconetti's acting only a performance?

Dreyer admitted in a *Cahiers du cinéma* interview he gave many years after the film's production that he picked Falconetti for Joan in part because her facial expressions revealed an inner torment she had "suffered" in real life.[67] While the implication is rather cryptic, the admission by her daughter Hélène Falconetti that her mother suffered from mental illness both before and, sadly, especially after this role's rigorous demands on her clarifies Dreyer's deeper meaning.[68] It is hard to imagine the intense nature of Falconetti's range of emotion—in a performance in which she sits mostly immobile during the entire production—without seeing her silently agonizing expressions. She vividly experiences a mental breakdown at the hands of her taunting, shouting, deliberately cruel tormentors shot in grotesque close-up. While the screen is silent, the vindictive nature and destructive tone of their unheard voices is clear enough for the viewer even today, if for no other reason than the devastation their baseless accusations of heresy render on Joan's blank, self-doomed features. She is not merely lost because men of God have abandoned and betrayed her for selfish gain. Nor is she terrified God has abandoned her to her destiny. Joan is a woman whose own mind has abandoned her, and as a result, she cannot even hold steady to her forced confession to save her own wretched existence. In her dying act of self-immolation, Joan chooses to perish with her delusional mania intact. This rather than face a world where her bipolarity and the base nature of her fellow man align to create as byproduct the perfect obliteration of her very soul. It is not a heroic choice, in many ways, because it is foretold, and then circumscribed, by her own uncontrollable manic episode. But given Joan's manic depression, what other choice does the filmmaker posit she has, other than complete and utter self-degradation at the hands of her masters? In a world where the mentally ill can and will be burned at the stake as witches and heretics rather than offered hope and assistance, Dreyer rather bleakly hints that her fiery demise may be the only sane option she has left. In a world gone mad, Joan's madness is the ultimate form of purity, because her insanity is literally and figuratively incendiary beyond reproach. The priestly men of cunning use entrapment and intellectual pretense to gain their desires, whatever the cost to any given innocent. But as Dreyer presents it, Joan cannot be controlled for material gain, and so she is expendable. Indeed, her insular form of madness, in which no one is harmed by her illness but herself, threatens the order of codified sickness with which her world has become infected. And so she is dispatched via flames, her delusions of a just God accessible to any person, rather than only through a paid priest, burned along with her.

Maria Falconetti was not the only one to suffer from mental illness on the set. Antonin Artaud, who plays the sympathetic monk Jean Massieu, was a manic-depressive who had spent time in mental institutions.[69] They have a very famous scene together in which the devastated monk hesitantly informs Joan that she must prepare herself for the ordeal of torture. The look of utter horror and gnostic self-revelation on Artaud's haunted face is remarkable, and as he shares the frame with Falconetti, also suffering from her own private mental anguish, the unspoken but tragic irony of the ordeal to come is silently underscored. That the church feels the moral need to further add to Joan's suffering in order to reveal some unspecified, grander "truth" is beyond either Joan's or Artaud's ability to conceptualize. So they depersonalize, hiding within themselves so deeply that even the inexplicable cruelty they are forced to enact against their very wills becomes an empty theater of farce. The horror of life outweighs their ability to act out, and so they refuse to act at all, stunned into submission. This form of depersonalized behavior is common to manic-depressive illness, a form of avoidance.[70]

There is revisionist history at play in the film. Joan is not a cunning country woman with great political and military skill, as George Bernard Shaw once remarked was his belief,[71] but a manic-depressive with delusions of religious grandeur. With such a curious refocusing of the subject, it probably comes as no great surprise that accounts of Dreyer paint a picture of an intensely private man who was often at war with his emotions. Critic Paul Moor wrote rather disparagingly about Dreyer's moodiness in *Theater Arts* magazine in 1951: "Dreyer's company and crew in Paris regarded him as a combined master, crackpot, and lunatic."[72] Dreyer had a troubled childhood in which he was put in an orphanage and raised by estranged adoptive parents.[73] His biological mother was working class and bore him out of wedlock because her gentrified, higher-class lover could not afford to ruin his marriage. She later inadvertently killed herself while trying to abort another unwanted pregnancy, swallowing a pack of matches in hopes it would cause the loss of the baby. Instead she died a lingering, horrific death via sulfur poisoning. Dreyer recalled his adoptive mother as being controlling, distant in her feelings, and abusive, regularly locking him in cupboards for hours on end.[74] Dreyer's hatred for her was only matched by his love for his missing mother, which is why the news of her death must have taken such a heavy toll on his well-being. Later in his adult life, Dreyer would spend time struggling over his homosexual identity and would have nervous breakdowns on more than one occasion. He spent time with his wife in a sanitarium in Silkeborg during one such episode.[75] This may be why the film has such remarkable staying power, however. The unique collaboration between a manic-depressive director and two bipolar actors resulted in a version of *The Passion of Joan of Arc* not just as historical treatise, but also a historical re-creation of how the mentally ill were treated and even persecuted by a hostile humanity.

The film was thought lost to time in its original, uncut version until it was recovered in an uncensored 35 mm print in 1981. Ironically, at least from this book's perspective, the lone print was discovered in a mental institution in Oslo, where it had resided, perfectly wrapped and untouched in a cupboard.[76] One wonders: was it chance that the psychiatric doctors who ran the asylum felt this particular cinematographic example was so worthwhile as to incur the expense of owning a print of it? And if they did find it of value, was it because they felt the film accurately captured the sometimes slippery diagnostic qualities that make up an episode of clinical mania or depression? No one can be sure, but it seems rather absurdly contrary to suppose that the psychiatric doctors coincidentally had the film in their possession with no real intent of utilizing it. Without ever realizing it, Dreyer and his two spectrum-suffering actors may have unwittingly, though perhaps positively, contributed to the very institutions in which they would seek solace and to increasing the knowledge base for future remedies and treatments of bipolar disorder.

The Passion of Joan of Arc detonated all prior depictions of mentally ill persons as maniacs and fools, instead reversing the perceptions. This enabled the viewer to experience the film in a way such that Joan and the monk Massieu are the movie's empathetic center. The supposedly balanced church officials and the guards who torture for them, some sadistically gloating at their assigned task, become depictions of inhuman intolerance. It had taken a mood-disordered director working with mood-disordered collaborators, but Dreyer had advanced the portrayal of mental illness beyond what could be imagined only a few years previously in film history.

4

1930S: BIPOLAR DISORDER SPEAKS AT THE MOVIES

PETER LORRE AS MELANCHOLIC MURDERER

Humphrey Bogart infamously and affectionately called him "the little creep."[1] He spent a lifetime escaping not only addiction, typecasting, and bouts of intense melancholia, but even the Nazis for a brief period in real life before doing so on American movie sound stages in seminal World War II classics like *Casablanca* (1942). In a lifetime filled with moments of rare artistic and personal triumph but, more often than not, also with pervasive sadness and continuous recovery, Peter Lorre very early in his career came to express, with tragic ramifications for his own mental health,[2] the cinematic epitome of the mentally ill man. He was so aware of his disorder and yet so unable to avoid it or its destructive consequences that an air of noble suffering haunted him in his best, and even least, performances. In so many aspects, Lorre came to embody the perfect distillation of culture, decadence, and fiery intelligence in emotional collision with introspection, doubt, and cynicism. Given the depth of despair his screen characters display, it will come as little surprise to sensitive viewers of his work that Lorre channeled much in the way of personal agony into his mercurial, witty movie roles.

Born as László Loewenstein in Hungary, Lorre had the acting bug early in life, starring in his grade school's production of *Snow White* when he was only eight years old. His passion sustained him through the hardship of the economically devastated Weimar Republic and beyond, catching the attention of German playwright Bertolt Brecht, who was intrigued by the seeming contradictions inherent in Lorre's complex personality.[3] After Lorre became a stage star in Germany, director Fritz Lang decided to cast him as the pivotal child murderer Hans Beckert in *M* (1931), his chilling indictment of both mental illness left untreated and society's hypocrisy in regard to the maltreatment of many underclass children. To say the role typecast Peter Lorre for the rest of his life would be a terrific understatement on a par with the type of droll observation his screen persona often made, as if he were casting an aside to equally bored viewers. "That picture *M* has haunted me everywhere I've gone,"[4] Lorre adroitly summarized in an interview after immigrating to America in hopes of avoiding a legacy of only playing sad-faced sociopaths and deviants.

Though it would limit the roles he was offered, *M* remains a singular testament to the force and conviction Lorre was able to bring to the screen when matched by worthy material. *M*'s Beckert is never said to be a manic-depressive, but rather a psychopathic child murderer. However, Peter Lorre's portrayal is bipolar in its gloomy, self-obsessive tone and emotive firepower. In fact, it is the astonishing range of emotions that Lorre displays that ultimately makes his manic-depressive, rapidly cycling killer so agonizingly human. Against a backdrop of rightfully outraged but stone-faced citizenry hell-bent on prosecuting, if not persecuting, the man whom they know is guilty of killing their children, Lorre's cornered, unstable Beckert becomes a sacrificial lamb for the lynch mob. The mob's ugly faces, devoid of compassion and energized with hatred for The Other, remind the viewer of the inquisitors of *The Passion of Joan of Arc* as they held forth in judgment of their mentally ill object of inquiry, never addressing the imbalance clearly present. They sneer, jeer, and ultimately cheer with each new passing moment of emotional and psychological disintegration and horror experienced by Beckert, their cornered victim, as defendant. He is reduced to a sniveling, whining animal by film's end. Uncomfortable questions are raised as we watch the self-wounded, self-destructed Beckert collapse into a broken heap of sorrowful, untreatable misery. Lang's expert narrative construction, in which Beckert is first shown to be a monster of diabolical cunning luring children to their deaths and then later becoming nothing more than a blubbering, helpless, terror-stricken child himself, combines with Lorre's stunning, awkward, and humiliating turns as an impulsive homicidal maniac. Lorre's Beckert is in constant internal warfare, never stabilizing long in either state. His stable self as shy recluse struggles against a self-loathing, morbidly depressed maniac who cannot function in society. When Lorre sobs that he cannot help himself and delineates the agony of fruitlessly trying to divert each new onset of homicidal mania, though he is powerless to prevent it, the stunned accusers' expressions seem to betray their own inward, silent reflections on their own denied limitations. The construction of The Other momentarily vanishes, replaced by a mirrored image, however cracked, of each mob member as guilty of a form of social injustice themself. Whether it is the fact that they attempt to subvert the law by holding a trial against Beckert, or whether it is the fact they allow their children to freely roam the streets unsupervised and without proper care, or even whether they're morally culpable in constructing a civil society in which the mentally ill cannot exist or will be shunned (or worse) when they do seek help, Lang's use of their dour, frozen faces says it all: each feels a measure of guilt, individually and collectively, albeit mixed with fear and disgust.

Lorre was, by his own admission, prone to bouts of melancholia so severe they made him selectively mute at times. He almost lost the role Fritz Lang was to offer him for *M* when, attending a party being given at Lang's Berlin apartment, Lorre sat alone at the bar, nursing endless drinks, and rudely ignoring everyone, including Lang. *Der Spiegel* recounted the episode in its pages: "Wordless, he sat at the bar. Wordless, he gulped down his cognac, wordless he stared with lost, deeply sad eyes at the guests."[5] Lorre himself often attributed his well-known moodiness to long hours spent working on a multiplicity of projects at any one time. This is a common problem with manic-depressives who use creative forms of therapy. Despite the therapeutic value they derive via creative exhaustion of their energies, the danger is that through overuse the bipolar creator experiences a nervous breakdown owing to improper diet, poor sleep patterns, and constant pressures to successfully complete too many competing projects. The bipolar creator, like Lorre, tends to commit to more than he or she can realistically handle except during the manic or hypomanic phases of the disorder, only to be confronted during periods of noncreative depression by an inability to do even one of them as well or as quickly as previously promised. Lorre rapidly changed moods even during his meeting with Lang at

Lang's apartment that night. He grew animated and excited when discussing the role later that evening with Lang, when just moments previously he had been in a public fit of despondency.[6]

Lorre had addictions to both alcohol and morphine, the latter a habit he acquired after years of chronic pain from a botched appendectomy as a young man. Eventually, Lorre's morphine addiction was an open secret in Hollywood, with producers willingly escorting him on occasion to get his injections before returning him to the sets for filming his scenes.[7] Likewise his emotional instability was diagnosed as early as 1939 by Dr. Louis I. Sokol as "depressive psychosis."[8] In 1949 he voluntarily checked into Wigger's Kurheim, a sanitarium in the Bavarian Alps that catered to those with "inner or nerve sickness."[9] While he was there to hopefully cure his addictions to morphine and alcohol, there is little doubt Lorre's depressive episodes, which he still maintained as work-related in nature, were also treated, given the clinic's emphasis on overall well-being. In fact, years later in Fort Worth, Texas, when Lorre was sent to a sanitarium in order to avoid prosecution for possession of a controlled narcotic by American authorities, the admitting physician recorded Lorre as "giving a history of depressive and anxiety symptoms."[10] Lorre even underwent ECT during a relapse stay at Wigger's Kurheim in 1950, one of which caused his heart to stop and falsely worried doctors he was dying. He was so suicidal that doctors refused to allow him to leave the sanitarium grounds unless he was accompanied by two attendants at all times.[11] Lorre pithily, if tragically, told his friend Joseph Buloff during a drive together in Buloff's car through the Los Angeles Valley one night, "I am a very sick man."[12]

Lorre's contribution to bipolar cinema via *M* is still one of the greatest in terms of its lasting allure to new generations of viewers. His unequivocal humanization of a mentally and emotionally "very sick man" forever smashed the former stereotype of the manic-depressive as a one-dimensional figure of homicidal intent or the butt of mocking jest. By unveiling his own depressive nature and allowing the depths of his despair to flood over into his performance, Lorre rendered an accurate portrait of the many varying, often contradictory, shades of morbid mood instability.

GRETA GARBO AS THE DEPRESSIVE SEX GODDESS

Greta Garbo was, as even a still-awed Groucho Marx recalled decades later on *The Dick Cavett Show* of his first happenstance meeting with her, "the biggest star in the movies . . . untouchable."[13] It took a lot to wow the cynical Groucho by notorious reputation, but his praise was seemingly genuine as he touchingly recounted his chance encounter with the most popular actress in the world (only John Barrymore was her male equivalent). She was first a star in the Swedish silent film industry, and then the American silent film industry, and transcended any barriers her thick accent may have seemingly offered by also conquering the early sound-era Hollywood films of the 1930s. She was unique in her mystique in a way no other star could quite rival in terms of a heady mixture of sexual allure, sophistication, mercurial mood swings, and bored, reclusive distance. Even now she seems an impossibility of contradictions, desiring famously to "be left alone" yet controlling almost every creative aspect during the height of her career, which meant endless meetings. When possible, she would prohibit any of the technical crew to be present beyond the barest necessary to operate the camera and sound gear before she acted her scenes for takes.[14] She rarely socialized outside of a limited circle of narrowly controlled lovers and friends, and suffered from severe depressions as well as sudden swings into mania.[15] She once described in a letter her latest attempt at finding a medical remedy for her manic-depressive nature as "dragging [her new psychiatrist] down into the abyss of pessimism" with her. He in turn saw her as "an interesting case of depression."[16] While she was caustic and self-effacing about her own bipolar nature, she described herself to intimates as experiencing clinical depersonalization episodes to the point of being "a spectator in her own life" emotionally and that her moods swung from "elation to depression."[17]

Garbo never shared her condition with the public, maintaining a strict veil of secrecy over her professional and private matters. It only added to her already potent sense of mystery. Depression-era audiences devoured her poor, blues-prone prostitute turned seaman's fiancée in the 1931 melodramatic film adaptation of Eugene O'Neill's stage play *Anna Christie*. It was billed with the famous tag line "Garbo Talks!" in allusion to the fact it was the first time audiences would ever hear her speak after her stellar silent career. Garbo played the title character as street glamorous, knowing and far from naive, educated to at least the coarser nature of life, however impoverished her educational background. And even though the film is only based on O'Neill's play and not scripted by him, O'Neill's personal struggles with unipolar depression throughout his life[18] color the drab, fatalistic tone of *Anna Christie* from the opening frames of its fog-enshrouded New York City harbor. Only these are not the glam harbors that launch massive passenger liners, as in most films, but the seedier, forgotten back slips where rotting barges tow their daily cargo against whatever the Atlantic throws at them. Against such a bleak background, Garbo's portrayal as angst-ridden but hardened beyond further breaking, is less the conventional "hooker with a heart of gold" and more akin to the girl-next-door turned cynical, self-loathing realist. She plays her climactic scene as a writhing, tortured stand-in for self-agony. She claws at her own taut sweater as if to pull away any last layers of deceit she feels compelled to have worn since her arrival as the supposedly chaste daughter, when in actuality she's been a prostitute. Her catharsis of confession in which the two toughened men of the sea are reduced to quivering blobs of tearful recognition, gripping the table with white knuckles of revelatory shock as if they'll collapse otherwise, is still an amazing tour de force by Garbo. She swears off men as unreliable and, eyes manic with gleam, defiantly informs the only two men in her life, her father and her fiancé, that she was a wharf prostitute for years on end. Her tremulous, back-and-forth performance is the essence of a rapid-cycling mood swing. Garbo adroitly goes from barely able to control herself into later full-on depressive rage, and finally into confusion and emotional despondency by her soliloquy's end. Garbo's volatile emotional nature is on display here in a way that is magnificently groundbreaking in terms of how actual episodes of clinical bipolar disorder are emotionally experienced by sufferers. And not solely by the sufferer, but by the devastated family and loved ones who endure the onslaught of the manic-depressive's verbal attack often characteristic of the disorder.[19] In such episodes, the patient may accuse or defend against imaginary slights or persecutions by family members and loved ones, which may or may not be marginally based in reality. The shifting nature of such an episode, in which the emotional state, if not stability, of the person undergoing manic depression is entirely unpredictable, is not to be underestimated. Startled loved ones are often the only barrier left to protect the sufferer from harm by self or others during such moments of delusional mania and paranoia. They must not only anticipate the delusional patient's next mood, but also plan multiple courses of on-the-fly backup plans in case the sufferer's condition suddenly worsens.[20]

Garbo's intensity in this final scene is atypical of the era's usual static, melodramatic style of acting. Most actresses of her time were favored not for their ability to shift expressions, but for holding one for hours on end as they were carefully lit to achieve certain romantic effects. This fixed style has become synonymous with bad silent-film thespian technique, but in fact, much of the latter is often reduced when the correct, slower speed of silent film productions are restored, eliminating the comical hyper-speed effect. Garbo smashed this conventional, masklike rigidity with her ever-changing, chameleon-like expressions. One moment she is bored, the next interested, the following sexually charged, and then, with no seeming context or subtext presented, she is back to being sullen and languidly smoking a cigarette as if life itself were a burden beneath consideration. This rapid-cycling portrait of a woman was truly revolutionary in many respects. Not that actresses hadn't previously displayed a range of emotions on-screen. But Garbo gave them full range, even as the scene's dramatic beats unfolded, and not just over the carefully measured course of the film's whole. It was as if she were conducting a private symphony and the camera recorded it alongside the other performers, but with a strange, insightful coda all her own in detail and depth, accessible only to each solitary viewer. She performed her own footnotes, as it were, and the audiences hung on every moment. They were enthralled as much by the force of shifting emotionality on display in each passing scene as much as any production values, costars, or clever script scenarios.

It can be difficult to appreciate just how much audiences identified with her depressive soul so trenchantly on display in all she portrayed. She was the classic personality performer whose private persona so overpowered all she ever acted; she was Garbo as whomever in every role, no matter how much she successfully deviated from her own public perception, from drama to comedy, period settings, class milieu, and so on. Her fans followed her from one successful motion picture to the next, seemingly unable to get enough of her sometimes flighty, other times morose, dour-faced nature, as if they were projecting their own worries and angst onto her as they, too, suffered the ravages of the Great Depression. As French film critic and philosopher Roland Barthes wrote, "Garbo belongs to that moment in cinema when capturing the human face still plunged audiences into the deepest ecstasy, when one literally lost oneself in a human image as one would in a philtre, when the face represented a kind of absolute state of the flesh, which could be neither reached nor renounced."[21] She was equally beautiful and distant beyond easy words, which made her a kind of black-and-white motion picture version of the pervasive Mona Lisa smile in moving effect. Her ability to quickly change from sarcasm to joy to doubt in a few lines of dialogue made it possible for audiences to find many faces from which to choose when they lived through her cinematic persona and, by so doing, personified their own insecurities and worries by way of dramatic catharsis. In all probability, her manic-depressive nature of cycling from high to low, repeatedly, is why she was so fascinating to watch as a performer, in that viewers sense how fragile is her hold on her own nervous disposition. It feels as if she is forever in imminent danger of internal psychological collapse. Indeed, in the worst moments, when her illness was overtaking her actual thespian abilities, she was acting her way through bipolar disorder. No wonder she preferred solitude in private affairs and professional settings to the painful scrutiny of others.[22] As Groucho Marx said in one-word summation, she was "shy."[23] In recalling their first meeting, he mentioned that Garbo's aversion to meeting people was so clinically uncontrollable that she had a habit of backing into the elevators at the studio and wearing enormous hats that covered her face so that she would never be recognized.

Greta Garbo's ballerina character Grusinskaya in the Berlin-set *Grand Hotel* (1932) is the epitome of her screen persona as the sexual goddess of melancholia. She is first seen hiding in the dark of her royal suite's bedroom, shut off from the world, wearing blinders and sadly luxuriating, if not slowly drowning, in her bed's sea of satin sheets. When her assistant opens the drawn curtains and allows light into the room, Grusinskaya admits to her elderly matron she was not asleep, merely thinking the hours away, lonely and in the dark. There is a tired, ruffled quality about the manner in which Garbo holds herself and steadfastly refuses to make eye contact unless it is on her own terms that was considered by some as arrogant rudeness or egotistical vanity on her part.[24] This nature suits her well as a royal Russian artiste such as Grusinskaya, who has been pampered her whole existence, and also in other roles in which she played a noble woman of means. They offer a convenient explanation as to why her characters are so seemingly detached and emotionally unstable, attributing it to upper-class status and decorum. But the deeper significance of her avoidance of others, of her withdrawal from all she loves save dancing, and of her ruminative time spent in gloomy, reclusive darkness, is clearly present when one views her performance through the prism of bipolarity, which Garbo is exhibiting.

It is interesting how the film portrays the creative artist as moodily unstable. The basic premise is that Garbo's manic-depressive ballerina would not be able to function were it not for her entourage of professional supporting staff—manager, caretaker, and so on—fulfilling her business and even personal affairs for her when Garbo is having an episode. This is shown from the opening moments and goes throughout the film. Garbo emotionally collapses into self-doubt and negativity, only to be forced to the next stage performance by her hardened support group, each of whom trades weary "seen-it-all-before" glances as the latest crisis is resolved. This very accurately mirrors the way existing bipolar scenarios are handled in order to overcome, and work around, the emotional difficulties of talented, but often troubled, creators and actors of films when they arise. This archetypal image of a fragile but angelic manic-depressive woman as a sexually charged goddess will later be referenced and magnified by such bipolar performers as Vivien Leigh, Marilyn Monroe, and Jessica Lange. But Garbo was truly pioneering the effect in terms of modern cinema with her vulnerable, angst-ridden swings of screen emotion. The only reason Grusinskaya has endured the ravages of bipolar disorder is because she has had the obsession of dancing into which she could pour herself. Facing as she is the end of her all-consuming career and dwindling audiences, Grusinskaya can see no future without the therapy of ballet, and so she slowly withers into suicidal depression.

John Barrymore, referenced above for his earlier portrayal in 1920's silent *Dr. Jekyll and Mr. Hyde* and as a fellow sufferer of bipolar disorder, was costar to Greta Garbo in *Grand Hotel*. He plays a failed baron who has been reduced by circumstances into needing to collect monies he owes, or face death at the hands of his shady debtors. Despite himself, Barrymore as the handsome but aged ruling-class gentleman personified falls in love with the world-weary Grusinskaya, going so far as to hide in her bedroom one night. While he cases her jewelry to steal it, however, she suddenly returns to her room and—in a fit of despondent depression—vows to kill herself, unaware Barrymore is present and eavesdropping. As she grips a sharp object and heads for the bathroom, Barrymore intervenes, startling her into momentarily forgetting her plans. In a remarkable turn of events, the two star-crossed lovers find a reason to live as one, and make ill-fated plans to escape their mutual depressions, vowing to live again. It is the kind of romantic portrait of Berlin one would never really ever see again, owing to the unrest and rise of fascism, and it feels oddly reassuring to see such romp and circumstance, so to speak, on the eve of Hitler's ascension to power and with the knowledge that this was being viewed by Great Depression audiences in America. There can be no better escapist fare, in truth, from the storm clouds of war that were enveloping the world than the goings-on at a posh hotel in the middle of urban decay and upper-class decadence, after all. In this regard, *Grand Hotel* did not disappoint in its ability to open the doors to lighter entertainment. But the darker implications of Grusinskaya's disorder are suggested by the film's gloomy ending. Not only is she deliberately kept unaware by her supporting staff that Barrymore has been fatally shot moments earlier as they depart the hotel, but the implication is clear in the grandiose manner in which Garbo plays her exit: There will be no returns, to stage or life, for this grand dame. If Barrymore's charming, loving baron was the only man who could keep her from previously killing herself, how will Grusinskaya ever survive the loss of him to tragic circumstances even as her own career is closed? The delusional mania Garbo manifests as she's hurried away without gaining the soul-shattering knowledge her lover is dead and in denial that her career is over echoes later in Billy Wilder's caustic *Sunset Boulevard* (1950) and its depiction of a manic-depressive actress fallen into despair, as well as in Blanche DuBois and other such bipolar characters in the screen adaptations of Tennessee Williams.

Greta Garbo would go on to do many other films before retiring into notorious semi-seclusion, to the extent it was possible, as a private but occasionally strolling denizen of New York City. Her work in both *Anna Christie* and *Grand Hotel* distill the essence of what made her such a magnetic screen goddess. When she felt an emotion, it registered not just on her facial expressions, but indeed, throughout her whole rippling body and growling speech, as if she were possessed by the intensity of her newfound feelings to the white-hot exclusion of all others, hers or anyone else's, in any scene in which she acted. She didn't need to be alone in the end, because she always was alone, achingly so, in every screen moment in which she appeared. Whether group shot or close-up, Garbo brooded in an inescapable trap of fluctuating emotions that left her cut off from her fellow human beings for most of her life.[25] "There was a strange melancholy in her, which led one to believe that her marvelous face revealed the secrets of life—both the sorrows and joys,"[26] said Jane Gunther of her friend. Through the magic of the movie lens, her peculiarly sad persona infuses her roles far beyond any apparent calculation and gives them a quality of eternal empathy for viewers. Technologies change, as do cultures, but the universality of human facial and body expressions endures. When bipolar performers like Garbo tap into these deeper truths of our collective nature, they transcend our differences and, in the process, unite us in their singular expression of our shared pains, hopes, and laughter.

A BILL OF DIVORCEMENT AND HEREDITARY MADNESS

Katherine Hepburn plays a young woman who must face hereditary mental illness when her unstable father Hilary (John Barrymore) escapes from an asylum in *A Bill of Divorcement* (1932). Hilary returns to his estranged family home Christmas Eve to elude asylum authorities, remaining in hiding. Sydney (Hepburn) has been told throughout the film that her father Hilary experienced horrors during World War I as a trench soldier, thus leading to his mental illness. She discovers he was actually a renowned composer prone to fits of despondency prior to his tour of duty. Worse, Sydney also learns that emotional instability runs throughout her family, and that the family has traditionally created awkward cover stories to account for what is better explained by a medical condition. Because she has recently engaged to marry and was openly considering starting a large family of her own, Sydney is shaken to her core by the yuletide evening's turn of events and sees in her anguished father a brutal projection of her own potential future if her bipolar illness worsens, albeit with a more manageable outcome because of her youth. Realizing she and Hilary are joined by genetic fate, Sydney chooses to drop her fiancé, remain childless, and release her long-suffering mother from her role of caretaker of her father's memory and failed marriage. Sydney's mother gratefully leaves with her lover to start a life, while Sydney consigns herself to darkness, curtains drawn against her protesting ex-fiancé, who cries her name outside vainly attempting to make her reconsider. Alone with her recalcitrant father, Sydney finishes composing a song Hilary had been working on two decades earlier when Hilary had his last breakdown. Hilary joins her in the effort, and the film concludes.

It is an unsatisfying conclusion in many ways from a modern perspective. Hepburn's dramatic, some might say melodramatic, choice to forgo her fiancé is tragic. No one can accurately predict whether or not a latent manic-depressive tendency will develop into full-blown bipolar disorder or how long such episodes will endure if and when they do occur.[27] To conclude, therefore, that one is unworthy of a romantic relationship during what can be long periods of remission from the disorder is self-depriving, as many successful relationships between bipolar and non-afflicted mates demonstrate. The choice Hepburn makes to not bear children is more understandable, of course, but equally begs the question: if a genetic test were available for detecting bipolar disorder in the pregnancy stage, would humanity as a whole be better served with or without its ultimate expression? A severely afflicted manic-depressive might argue for termination, but those who suffer on the spectrum but otherwise lead productive, even reproductive, lives would presumably argue against. At least for now, there is no known DNA screen to detect any mood disorder, so such speculation remains more fictional than science. The rapid rise in computer-assisted brain imaging, however, along with advances in human genome mapping, will in all probability eventually make this a rather disturbing reality to be faced, rather than merely hypothetical.[28] All the more reason why ideas such as full equality of rights for mentally ill persons should be debated before technology renders the landscape more problematic.

Although it reveals its stage play origins, A *Bill of Divorcement* does offer many new ideas in terms of the portrayal of bipolarity in cinema. The first and foremost is the previously referenced link between insanity and heredity. Although Poe had made this link explicit in such works as "The Fall of the House of Usher" and "The Tell-Tale Heart," the film adaptations of his works rarely made it more than suggested in their cinematic re-creations. Whereas *A Bill of Divorcement* not only makes it textual, but also subtextual, to all that occurs within its framework. Without the devastating news Sydney uncovers about her own heredi- tary bipolar disorder as well as its possibility in any children she might conceive, and her conflict of having to come face-to-face with her refu- gee father, who has already been devastated by the condition, there would be no real story. In past bipolar films, the afflicted person is typically shown for pity or laughs. Here, manic depression is shown as a condition of emotional instability but one whose sufferers are left other- wise intellectually intact most of the time. This is quite novel, even radical, for the era, which favored stereotypes of manic-depressives over substantive levels of characterization. The fact that it was father and daughter, that the explicit dilemma faced by all is the advisability or sustainability of long-term marriages and child bearing, which are core life issues that must be resolved, makes *A Bill of Divorcement* ground- breaking cinema.

Barrymore's portrait of a man haunted by his own sense of preor- dained failure is somewhat like his Baron from *Grand Hotel*, only that character did not survive and live to be remorseful about it for years to come. In *A Bill of Divorcement* he is quite mad, in the sense that he is mercurial, shifting in emotional intensity, first high, then low, endlessly cycling back and forth. But in the film's key sequence, Barrymore actu- ally plays at being manic-depressive in order to convince his wife to divorce him and move on with her new lover. He convincingly tricks the other participants into believing he is having an angry manic episode by summoning from his past experiences and recreating them as distilled essence. In doing so, Barrymore is also showing the audience his own form of bipolar haiku, condensing into the span of a few minutes a rapid-cycling manic-depressive who displays many shades of the disor- der. It is not clinically accurate to suggest a bipolar patient can summon or control his disorder in order to fake or mimic an episode when an actual one is occurring. But no doubt some bipolar patients fall into patterns of dysfunctional behavior wherein they become accustomed to, and exaggerate, their own limitations or perceived limitations, or both.[29] A form of conditioning combines with diminished expectations to pro- duce a self-fulfilling prophecy of despair. So while Barrymore's cunning to stage his own mental breakdown is calculated, it is nonetheless a good cinematic depiction of a manic-depressive facing a moment of persecution delusion and emotional fragility, as well as subsequent feelings of guilt and shame over having had an episode.

THE TESTAMENT OF DR. MABUSE AND GENIUS AS MADNESS

Fritz Lang's earlier contribution to such seminal films as *The Cabinet of Dr. Caligari* (uncredited) and *M* in terms of their perceptions and codifications regarding mental illness have been previously outlined. But his sequel to his own 1922 hit film *Dr. Mabuse the Gambler* (about a criminal mastermind of the German underground who eventually goes insane), released in 1933 as *The Testament of Dr. Mabuse*, is also powerful in its depiction of obsessive mania. The film stars Otto Wernicke from both *Dr. Mabuse the Gambler* and *M*, reprising his role from those earlier pictures as Inspector Karl Lohmann. As Germany's most famous detective crime fighter, Lohmann finds himself having to face the re-emergence of his formerly vanquished foe Dr. Mabuse. Housed in an asylum for the criminally insane, Dr. Mabuse is far from dead. He spends his days and nights writing plans and manifestos detailing how a small class of dedicated hoodlums, by following his every instruction to the letter, could overthrow the government and make Germany a haven for those desiring it to become a criminal empire. Professor Baum (Oscar Beregi Sr.), the head of the institution in which Mabuse is housed, becomes fascinated with the furiously scribbling Mabuse (Rudolf Klein-Rogge) and his prodigious output. In time, Mabuse effects a form of mental possession in which he overtakes Baum's better nature and uses the asylum's director as a shield to mask his own nefarious plot to turn Berlin into a black market mecca. Or is the asylum director merely losing his own sanity and blaming the harmless Mabuse, who is locked away and not having any effect on any reality, even his own? Lohmann suspects Mabuse's unseen influence but lacks proof. The confounded detective races to abort Mabuse's plan to explode critical infrastructure and launch societal anarchy onto a fragile German civic psyche. But how does one combat an unseen enemy, especially one like

Mabuse, a harmless lunatic confined in a sanitarium? In short, how does one fight madness with sanity?

The surreal nature of much of *The Testament of Dr. Mabuse*—featuring gloomy stretches in which a disturbed mental patient's interior delusions are externalized in the form of psychic projections—gives director Lang ample screen opportunity to play with subjective states of mind. The opening sequence alone, set amid an industrial warehouse full of hissing pipes and clanking gears, but no musical score, sets the viewer on psychological edge, forcing the audience to experience the violence firsthand, along with the screen character, instead of with comforting but distancing film techniques such as dramatic music, dialogue, or even narrative exposition (for the scene begins en media res and without introductory setup). It is also a novel use of sound for expressionistic reasons, which would sadly decline in the coming decade as the newness of synchronous sound wore off. The alienated feel that haunts so much of *The Testament of Dr. Mabuse* is unleashed in these opening moments, and though some of the film falls prey to light comedy for relief (particularly with the Inspector Lohmann character), the overall moodiness of the film is remarkable. It is little wonder that when Joseph Goebbels became minister of propaganda in 1933, one of his first acts was to officially ban Germans from seeing Lang's film, even though Goebbels and Hitler were personal admirers of Lang's output. Goebbels perhaps revealed more about his own and the Nazis' rise to power when he said that his decision to ban *The Testament of Dr. Mabuse* was because the film "showed that an extremely dedicated group of people are perfectly capable of overthrowing any state with violence."[30] But Lang was long gone to America by that point, anyway, and the film survived its initial banning by the Third Reich. It is now largely regarded as a key film of its era for its uncanny imagery, which so adroitly parallels Hitler's own charismatic hold over the German people, unleashing master plans to be followed by the obedient, sleepwalking citizens. The historical result was cataclysmic destruction similar to that envisioned by Lang in his opus.

While Lang's commentary on National Socialism has often been the subject of academic analysis, far less has been written about the bipolar aspects of Lang's work, either in this film or others. As with his earlier screen treatments of mental illness, Lang was an inherent investigator by nature. He did research prior to cowriting the scripts by interviewing psychiatric authorities in order to better understand the mental conditions he was so frequently to depict. Indeed, Lang himself characterized his need for clinical accuracy as being "possessed by it"[31] in later interviews. His portrait of Dr. Mabuse as alternately a catatonic, immobile depressive and a maniac filled with the urge to write nonstop, seemingly indiscriminately, as long as he is putting thoughts to paper, is an accurate, if exaggerated, depiction of bipolar patients. Catatonic states occur when depressives become so hopelessly dispirited that they refuse to make eye contact or even acknowledge that others are in their presence. They often sit rigidly and without ability to alter position unless made to do so or until the episode abates.[32] Hypergraphia is the clinical name for the condition Mabuse exhibits in terms of his inability to stop writing. In more controlled fashion, hypergraphia is not uncommon in some well-known authors, such as Edgar Allan Poe, Stephen King, Isaac Asimov, Sylvia Plath, and others.[33] While it is not always concurrently diagnosed with a mood disorder, it is often comorbid, suggesting that for manic-depressives, hypergraphia may be a specific expression of states of fluctuating hypermania and mania, whereas nonbipolar patients, who have only hypergraphia minus a mood disorder, may be experiencing a temporal lobe problem without attendant emotionally affective side effects.[34] The scene in which Lang has Mabuse sitting in his asylum bed, hunched over his note pad, ripping and discarding each newly filled sheet of paper without pause to furiously scribble on a new virgin page, is remarkably powerful even to this day. Rarely has screen mania been so eerily captured. Lang has Klein-Rogge play these scenes absolutely stone-faced, which gives them added visual power. Rather than maniacally cackling or angrily mumbling, Lang goes for the complete and utter absolution of facial catatonia, the alert state of being comatose. Mabuse's eyes are open and concentrated, and yet, they do not apparently see, not even following along with his writing or looking back over what he has written. Rather, he is blankly staring straight ahead, and yet his penmanship is remarkably adept, complete with small illustrations and diagrams when necessary to more clearly elucidate his diabolical plans. The fascination Professor Baum demonstrates in piecing together what the strange, cryptic notes Mabuse produces mean, if anything, is understandable, for if there is ever to be an opportunity to peer "into the mind of a madman," Baum rightfully surmises this is that case. Goebbels must have seen the connection between madness and leadership the film made explicit, too. Baum's possessed, tyrannical despot (complete with stiff-armed gestures as the disturbed mastermind issues forth commands!) was too accurate a critique to allow under the new reign of Adolf Hitler, and thus the film was banned from domestic distribution.

Lang's near inversion of his earlier asylum setting in *The Cabinet of Dr. Caligari* is worthy of commentary. In that earlier effort, it is revealed that a patient's delusions are the source of the screen madness, and that the asylum doctor has only been seen as an evil influence through the distorted eyes of the manic-depressive patient. But in *The Testament of Dr. Mabuse*, the asylum director is unbalanced, and by film's end, is reduced to a quivering wreck of former humanity, much like Peter Lorre's fate at the conclusion of *M*. When Lohmann finds the lost Professor Baum's vacant-eyed remnants in the sanitarium's basement before the end credits, a shocked look of horrified, and then empathetic, recognition spreads across the startled Lohmann's face. He is stunned by the obvious insanity, and then, reconciled to the fact the case has been concluded, Lohmann visibly if sadly relaxes, allowing the tragic irony of the asylum doctor's fate to wash over his large frame. Indeed, as Lohmann quietly intones in the final line of dialogue, there is nothing more that can be done, at least by the police.

Lang also had actor Rudolf Klein-Rogge portray a maniacal genius as lethal in his earlier career-defining film *Metropolis* (1927). Klein-Rogge brought to vivid, mercurial life his diabolical Dr. Rotwang, who is pathologically obsessed with creating robotic life (however contradictory such ambition, at least in semantic terms). Both roles require an enormous level of energy and sustained display of manic behaviors by Klein-Rogge, and he demonstrates ample reason for Lang's loyalty in both roles. But *The Testament of Dr. Mabuse* is more fully centered on Klein-Rogge's bipolar madman than is his Rotwang character in *Metropolis*, who—though he is a major influence on the story—is not as central to its overall impact. The acting theatricality on display by all in *Metropolis*, grandly operatic in tone, helps mask Rotwang's mania, offering camouflage to his disturbing nature. By comparison, Mabuse is full-blown in a manic-depressive psychosis throughout *The Testament of Dr. Mabuse*. Both roles confirm the classic image of the mad genius who is delicately balanced upon the straight razor of sanity. They follow the trajectory Lang has helped define as the essential quality of men of high intelligence who may be inversely low in emotional well-being owing to states of internal mania. His fanatical Supermen of the Mind, as they are shown, are self-absorbed and self-aggrandizing, sure their personal intelligence can bend any human endeavor, be it science or criminality, to the willpower of one powerful, dynamic, and (it is shown to later be) manic-depressive man. An archetypal figure has emerged from clinical portraits of mental illness herein. This archetype will go beyond and create its own subgenre of films dealing with mad scientists and mad criminal overlords who seek to extend their maniacal grip on the world around them, answerable to no one but themselves. For this powerful but typically cliché treatment of mania, often within a science fiction, horror, or superhero setting and with proverbial bad-guy incarnation, entire studies and volumes have been written. But the image of the maniac as a deranged, omnipotent super-mind who controls his cohorts, while not without historical analogy, is clinically inaccurate to most states of mania and depression. Few bipolar patients will remain in any one state of mental being for any prolonged period of time, hence the disorder's perplexing nature in terms of cure or treatment.[35] It is the fact that the patient cannot maintain any one set of psychological realities despite his or her best efforts that is so problematic. In films depicting mad doctors and the like, the mania is fixated, and without abatement. It can be argued these images encapsulate a frozen mask of mania, it is true; but equally true is that they are lifeless to the reality of the actual disorders in terms of the ever-changing quality inherent in mood afflictions. In terms of bipolar cinema examples, they distort the reality of the underlying condition so expertly by the design of their genre that, while they often make superb examples of suspenseful cinema, they are outside the scope of this book's intent to focus upon the real psychiatric disorder via the performers and directors who are themselves bipolar.

5

1940S: THE EFFECTS OF WORLD WAR II ON BIPOLAR CINEMA

ORSON WELLES AS GRANDIOSE HYPOMANIC AND RECLUSIVE DEPRESSIVE

One of the most famous moments in *Citizen Kane* (1941) is Charles Foster Kane's rage-fueled destruction of his wife's property after she leaves him to rot in his stately manor, Xanadu. When the alcoholic Susan summons the courage to abandon the emotionally deadened titan of capitalism, Kane enters her empty bedroom. Alone, he flies into a blind fury after he broods over her betrayal, destroying all that he can get his massive hands upon. It is the amazing, long-take series of low-angle shots staged by Orson Welles as the balding Kane that gives it such cinematic power. Kane begins with his wife's three suitcases, hurling them at her vanity mirror. He rips at her bedspread, pawing it to the floor. He staggers, stiff-legged with insolent hatred like a vengeful zombie, tearing into her bookcases, her dresser, her lounge chair, any and everything that is not bolted to the floor or into the walls, and then, after he's smashed everything not secured, he tears into those as well. Near the end of his manic furor, Kane slams his fists through tiny bookshelves—barely all that remains of the dismantled set—and rips them out of the crumbling plaster walls, unable to contain himself in destructive aggression. When his manic outburst abates, Kane staggers, hunched and heartbroken, down a long line of infinity mirrors that reflect his shattered visage. They metaphorically suggest the endless days and nights he faces henceforth, alone and blindly lurching forward, into a dark hallway that spells certain doom. It's a truly magnificent moment in film history, a baroque symphony of madness, and done all without any dialogue save the one-word utterance that is the hallmark phrase from the film's titular star. "Rosebud," Kane sadly echoes, tears streaming down his face, his destructive urge finally quelled by the familiar snow globe he has chanced upon that was on Susan's dresser and now held in Kane's own round, trembling hand.

Grandiose and self-contained, the sequence is a masterpiece of cinematic construction. It's also a truly spectacular representation on film of the outrageous maniacal energy a bipolar person can unleash without warning. Welles captures this display in a bookended setup and payoff. He first plays Kane as a calculating, controlling man who shows no emotion before his furious breakdown in the middle of the sequence. It is not just masterful, but accurate to actual bouts of bipolar rage. The subject often goes in and out of stability in displays of anger and ability to control it, but the intensity and length of the episode can never be accurately predicted in duration or outcome.[1] As with the fictional Charles Foster Kane, a real-life manic-depressive may give sway to venting the agonizing phases of the depressive disorder in what are tantamount to self-destructive tantrums. The frequent destruction of personal property—either the sufferer's or a loved one's—is intended to externalize the patient's interior pain and hopefully therefore alleviate it. It is a desperate act of insanity when witnessed from the outside, as the viewer does in *Citizen Kane*; it is a wrenching, last-ditch attempt at ridding oneself of unbearable psychic pain when experienced from the inner perspective, as do actual patients suffering an acute episode. Thus, whether intentional or not, Welles as director, actor, and cowriter of this sequence perfectly distills the clinical aspects of a true psychiatric disorder. This is not surprising when one takes into account Welles's personal history and the many reports by those who knew him and experienced his often fluctuating temperament. In this regard, the naming of his New York stage company in 1937 as the Mercury Theatre was perhaps unwittingly appropriate for his own mercurial moods.

Welles was subject to both highs and lows of mania and depression throughout his life, though his ability, indeed charismatic stamina, in maintaining his facade as the gregarious, genius host and bon vivant were legendary. Audrey Stainton, a personal secretary, once described her employer as "a man devastatingly alone. In his good moods in company he enjoyed, no one could be wittier or more charming, but what I remember most are his long silences."[2] Albert Zugsmith, a producer of *Touch of Evil* (1958), recalled that Welles was absent for a month from his postproduction duties on the film, which Zugsmith attributed to Welles having a "month-long psychological bender."[3] His friend, author and magician Bruce Elliott, once wired the errant Welles, querying about the strange distance Welles had suddenly invoked between them. "The atom bomb got you?" Elliott asked in his telegram. "Or is it just your manic-depressive cycle?"[4] As if echoing the famous moment in which Kane transgresses the loving memory of his still-living wife by destroying her every personal belonging, Alessandro Tasca di Cuto, executive producer of *Chimes at Midnight* (1966), remarked on Welles's chameleon-like ability to go from nonassertive when he needed to be (and frequently wasn't to the film's detriment) to behaving like "a bull in a china shop, smashing everything."[5] While making *Citizen Kane*, he would frequently disappear, without explanation or communication, for days on end, suddenly to reappear and resume production on his maiden magnum opus.[6] This life-long pattern of disappearing while others were dependent upon him, as illustrated by the lapses in *Citizen Kane*, became downright perplexing by the ill-fated conclusion of *The Magnificent Ambersons* (1942). Welles basically abandoned the postproduction of the picture, a phase in which he always demonstrated a considerable skill and devout cinematic passion, to the editors at RKO Pictures, while he was in South America shooting carnival footage for his ill-conceived travelogue documentary *It's All True* (1942). Pressed by the studio to complete *The Magnificent Ambersons* in a timely fashion, he issued a series of lengthy editorial notes via telex, which were largely ignored by the irate studio heads, who proceeded to severely truncate the film before dumping it into theaters without backing.[7] On a bitter double loss of credibility as footnote, Welles never completed *It's All True*. It was posthumously released in 1991 as a reconstructed documentary about the film's own failure as motif, a recurrent theme that imbues the Welles legacy.

The perplexing nature of Welles's seemingly self-created conundrum, in which he's first an entirely hands-on filmmaker and then abandons the project for long stretches of time, if not almost entirely, without explanation, is perhaps more germane to his "troubled genius" mantle than has ever been properly accorded. The legend of Welles as a Creative Genius, which he helped create and later was supposedly cursed with, and the contradictory murkier reality in which endless complications and failed or semi-completed movies were the actual outcome may be more closely intertwined than the stand alone reputation of Welles as victim of the studio system. His harsh treatment may have been complicated by his own bipolar nature, which remains unacknowledged or only tacitly implied in most studies. It may well be that the very qualities Welles brought to any project were as dependent upon his mood swings as they were on any studio or other financial backers. Various Hollywood powers were truly opposed to Welles as the creative helm of his and others' projects throughout his troubled career. With an outsized need for creative control typical for bipolars, as well as a persona that doubtless impressed studio heads as arrogant and overbearing, Welles was the ultimate anathema to a very tightly controlled system. He was simply uncontrollable by himself, the studio heads, or anyone else. Welles's outsized need for both the rush of work during his manic and hypomanic phases, and the alternate retreat from it during depressive phases, was surely a contributing influence to his career difficulties, as they are for many on the spectrum. The difficulties of financing independent works outside of the system are legendary, it is granted. But the consistency of Welles's problematic movies—a litany that includes both his studio films, as discussed, as well as outside films such as *The Other Side of the Wind* (1970–1976), *The Deep* (1967–1970), and *Don Quixote* (which incredibly stretched from 1957 until 1972, when he finally abandoned it)—suggests his darker emotional states were an unacknowledged, added difficulty that burdened his creative and personal endeavors. He most likely continuously shot his incomplete epics not because he lacked funding, at least not only, but because it offered him therapeutic benefit to simply make movies, even underfunded ones.

In his own words, Welles felt that when he was depressed, the world was truly a hopeless place in which to exist and that "neither faith nor philosophy" could assist him in his suffering when he was "beneath the ruins."[8] Michael MacLiammoir, a long-term friend, spoke of a brooding shadow within Welles that was always present as a "dark, turgid affair" that "spreads when things go wrong."[9] As if taking MacLiammoir's cue, Welles's daughter titled her memoir of her troubled relationship with

Welles *In My Father's Shadow*. In but one example of how her father's depressions held sway over their familial life, the often estranged Chris Welles Feder recounts how her fiancé arranged to visit Welles in Los Angeles and present himself as a future son-in-law. Welles failed to show and excuses were made about his being in studio meetings, but Feder reveals she later learned Welles "had fallen into a deep depression"[10] and refused to see anyone other than his wife. Throughout her touching, affectionate, and respectful recollection of her complicated life with Welles, Feder notes that from a young age there existed a family support structure that excused Orson's behavior and the hurt feelings they caused because he was "a genius who lived for his work alone."[11] Her disappointments at having her father miss birthdays and being absent from her life for large gaps of time would be smoothed over by concerned relatives who advised her that her father "was not like other men and one had to make allowances."[12] This kind of codependency and mythmaking, however based in true artistic talents, is a not infrequent signature within families marked by twin incidents of creative abilities and emotional disturbances. It is an unconscious form of support designed by family participants to allow the afflicted patient to obsessively indulge in artistic work that others outside the group might find of questionable value in terms of well-being to its creator.[13] Because in essence the family member is utilizing art as therapy, the others in his or her group structure rally to offer sustained support as a way of supplanting having to openly deal with the disorder's darker aspects, as was evidently the case for Welles from a young age. By excusing all transgressions as artistic temperament, one avoids accepting the more clinical diagnosis of manic depression, or at least that the transgressions are only manic-depressive in origin.

Welles has many markers common in bipolar family biographies. The death of a parent at an early age (his mother to jaundice when he was but a nine-year-old) appears in many studies analyzing manic-depressives' backgrounds, and is believed to be a contributing factor in both onset and severity of bipolar disorder in those predisposed to developing it later in life.[14] Never close to his distant father, the death of his beloved mother is echoed in the earliest scenes in *Citizen Kane* in which the soon-to-be wealthy boy Charles Foster Kane is given up by his mother so that he may be educated and raised in the most advantageous circumstances far from his childhood cabin home. As a child, his mother had controlled the young Welles to the point of dressing him in velvet knee-pants and proclaiming his genius to anyone who would listen.[15] Losing her at such a young age dealt a severe blow to Welles's sense of emotional dependency, and possibly influenced the severity of his later manic-depressive episodes. Yet another common denominator revealed by genetic studies of bipolar sufferers is that the disorder is often prevalent in familial histories, and that such a pattern of shared disturbance is, in and of itself, often a good indicator of the possibility of manic-depression as a diagnosis.[16] Richard Welles Sr., Orson's father, suffered from severe depressions and self-medicated with alcohol from an early age, becoming a semi-functional alcoholic by the time Orson was a boy. He died alone in a hotel room, utterly broken and estranged from his family. Welles blamed himself, in part, because he had abandoned his father to his doom while he sought fame and fortune.[17] Richard Welles Jr., Orson's brother, fought a long struggle with mental illness and spent over a decade in the Illinois-based Kankakee State Hospital during one particularly grueling period. He misspent his modest inheritance prior to his confinement and left the hospital with eight dollars as his sole holdings.[18] Orson Welles would also commit himself to a sanitarium for a few days in 1941 owing to nervous exhaustion.[19] Welles suffered from chronic bouts of insomnia, which also rank high on common traits of those diagnosed with mood disorders. He wrote of his condition and its effects on his mental health to a friend in 1941: "My nights are sleepless and my days are tortured."[20]

Given Welles's predisposition toward chronic mood instability, the complex persona he maintained in public and in private company, wherein he often "held forth" in a kingly but gregarious manner, must have taken an enormous toll on his mental health. The nonstop schedule of his earlier career, in which he was shuttling between play rehearsals and live radio broadcasts multiple times daily, required Herculean effort. Most people cannot imagine maintaining, let alone excelling at, such a stress-filled career as Welles as Youthful Prodigy seemed to effortlessly ply. The later image of Welles as tarnished Hollywood angel would cause him to shift his restless urge for perpetual creative motion from the American to the international stage rather than temper it. Instead of going from radio station to playhouse in New York, Welles would jet from one country to the next. He constantly sought financing to complete his latest incomplete work by hiring himself out as an actor on whatever production would pay his acting fees. He lived in hotel suites and in wealthy patrons' abodes and estates, always maintaining the lifestyle of a world-class filmmaker, even when the realities of his directorial career were far less rewarding for his insistent efforts, artistically or financially. The "genius" mantle haunted him so thoroughly, and so early on, that RKO ended their business relationship with Welles with the motto "Showmanship in place of Genius" published in the trade papers as a deliberate insult.[21] Welles's ability to turn the industry's perception that he was a failure into a charming display of feigned modesty deflected the pain he experienced from the criticism. But he struggled to maintain a facade of dignity and self-respect in the face of a preceding, contrary reputation. Like many on the mood disorder spectrum, Welles had to perpetually face his own worst failures and regrets in a Sisyphus-like fashion, continually rolling his personal boulder of sustained critical failure back to the fabled top where he once resided, just to gain employment, only to see it roll down again. Welles worked not just against the vagaries of financial interests and distributors, but his own aging and failing physical and mental health, too.

Many moments in Orson Welles's work capture mania and depression in various guises, both sustained and fleeting. The overt portrayal of madness Welles embodies for his version of *Macbeth* (1948) is illustrative of the range Welles was capable of bringing to a role. His Macbeth maintains an intensity that makes even his most despairing soliloquies seem fraught with manic insistence, and far from depressive in energies. Even when Welles as Macbeth is disheveled and drunken, there is a bearing in his manner that suggests the future king never really relaxes as much as he shifts the steady gaze of his observance, flickering between keen, predatory interest and bemused, distanced blankness. Indeed, Joseph McBride described it in his book *Orson Welles* as being performed in a "transfixed, manic way."[22] While one can argue that Welles is attempting to attribute the mental disintegration Macbeth is undergoing to bewitchment and his darkly hued prophecy, the manner in which he chooses to illustrate this highly strung nervousness is peculiarly manic in its particulars of expression. As a result, the film feels as if one were experiencing it from within the damaged psyche of Macbeth while he's enduring the highs and lows of a rapid-cycling bipolar episode. Though borderline cliché, Welles plays Macbeth as petulantly wide-eyed with emotional instability, at times almost eerily channeling a male equivalent of Marie Falconetti's devastating bouts of actual bipolar episodes captured for *The Passion of Joan of Arc*. It makes his Macbeth a stylized portrait of madness, theatrical but hypnotic.

Another portrayal that bears many hallmarks of manic-depressive illness as embodied by Welles is his infamous Police Captain Hank Quinlan in *Touch of Evil*. Quinlan is obese and rarely without a half-eaten candy bar in his massive hand, limping with a cane, physically slovenly to the point of being repulsive, eyes mere slits behind puffy lids, crusted lips pursed in a perpetual scowl suggesting "I've got you now!" and hat worn low over his balding, sweaty, wrinkled forehead. As played by Welles, he is the distillation of how ruinous low-grade manic charm and charisma is capable of taking an inherently, if only modestly, corrupt man like Quinlan and degrading him even further into an outright swaggering monster of egomania and self-deceit. The very bipolar qualities that make it possible for Quinlan to succeed—his infamous ability to play intuitions in criminal matters and have them later be verified by the collected facts—are in classic, tragic dimensions also the very ones that will bring about his downfall. Quinlan is the bipolar mesmerist whose powers fail, as all powers must do in time, revealing his base nature to all of his shocked, disappointed colleagues. They had invested the police captain with a mythic resonance. When Quinlan psychologically collapses right before them, it is not merely his authority that disintegrates, but the grandiose persona he had projected, which, despite its dictatorial tone, gave many of them a sense of abiding law and order. Quinlan may be corrupt, the tale seduces us to ponder, but in a world full of corruption, isn't the devil who is most charming, most authentically himself, by default the better class of his dark breed? Welles doles out the low-wattage charisma of Hank Quinlan with such obvious relish and regret—both emotions at war—that the viewer finds his pathetic, grotesque lawman empathetic. This is true if for no other reason than he is a formerly great man, or so he is repeatedly told, who has fallen into disgrace while still living, or half-living, to watch it all transpire. "You're a mess, honey," Tana (Marlene Dietrich) accurately surmises when she takes in Quinlan's dissolute bulk toward the film's end. Indeed, throughout much of *Touch of Evil*, Welles seems to be commenting upon his own outrageous public persona as much as he is the fictitious Quinlan. It is not rage his smoldering, tempered eyes shine forth with, however, as Welles had so powerfully demonstrated as Kane during his manic orgy of destruction. Rather, it is the knowing power of astute, and acute, depressive self-entrapment that Quinlan comes to personify by the film's conclusion. He is not merely trapped in his devastated body, confined by Welles's adroit staging to literally bulging out of tight clothes and claustrophobic sets, but equally, his own mind and chronic emotional sickness. By the time Dietrich utters her remark of concern about his physical and mental health, Quinlan has crossed the Rubicon of sustainability. He is living through his own wake and funeral, and he fully knows it. The quiet mirth laced with melancholic regret Welles gives his seedy, heretofore disreputable mountain of a monster in the saloon scene with Dietrich is formidable, and makes Quinlan's demise in the following sequence all the more elegiac.

Orson Welles would portray many more characters whose boisterous, self-aggrandizing style could easily be construed as manic or hypomanic in nature. There is an exuberance to Welles when he is in this stand-by mode of performing that came to be his signature style in later decades of his career as pitch man for various wines and whiskeys. A trademark cigar clenched in hand, sartorial and composed, the articulate, ever witty Welles delighted as congenial host to a secretive party in which you were lucky, indeed, to have been invited to attend. While authentic to his nature, it was also a mask he chose to wear in public, as much designed to channel and dissipate his insatiable, mania-tinged creative energies as it was to prevent anyone from seeing the deep depressions he harbored as frequent interior companion. Long-time friend Peter Bogdonavich revealed how Welles as an older man mysteriously broke into tears of melancholia once after forlornly gazing out the windows of their hotel room. The startled younger director could do little more than gape in surprise at the truer, hidden colors of Welles's troubled emotional life as they were momentarily flown without apology or explanation.[23] In an interview he once gave for television, Welles defended Ernest Hemingway and his choice to suicide, passionately stating that Hemingway was "a sick man"[24] and should therefore not be judged without his mental illness taken into accord, if he is judged, at all. The evident and perhaps bittersweet irony the stone-faced but sincere Welles must have experienced as he stated this lingers in the mind. Was Welles only defending his friend's reputation, or was he tentatively also seeking to advocate for more open tolerance of such afflicted persons as Hemingway, Welles's father and brother, and, indeed, silently for himself? As he remained often obscured behind his own baroque persona throughout his life, so Welles's attitudes toward his and his family's lifelong struggles with mania and depression remain occluded from view to this day. His work, however, is a stark testament to the powers of damage and delight a soul touched by bipolar disorder can creatively bring forth as therapeutic by-product.

GENE TIERNEY AS THE RADIANT MASK OF FEMININE MYSTIQUE

Though her star stature has surely declined in the years subsequent to her 1940s height of popularity with moviegoers, Gene Tierney was once considered the epitome of alluring screen beauty during and after World War II. Her broad cheekbones, flawless complexion, and often impenetrable, almost vacant half-lidded eyes, made her the perfect embodiment of intelligent, reserved sexuality, even if her breakthrough role was as the promiscuous, uneducated, barely clad Ellie Mae in *Tobacco Road* (1941). Though often utilized in strictly formulaic contract films, Tierney's ethereal beauty was used in both *Laura* (1944) and *Leave Her to Heaven* (1945) to stunning impact. In each case, she displayed an icy control over her abilities that refuted critics who dismissed her based on the assumption she was photogenic but unconvincing. Gene Tierney possessed an eerie calm in her manner that made many believe she simply lacked range and depth. While her range may have been limited in part because of her stunning looks—and the bad roles the studio forced her to play—Tierney demonstrates in *Laura* and especially *Leave Her to Heaven* a presence of being that effectively dominated any scene in which she was placed. Hers was an ability to be in eternal fluctuation of emotions on the inside, and yet, to judge by her mask of blank resolve, a person who never bothered to read a disturbing headline even during wartime. But as her crushingly honest memoir *Self-Portrait*, first published in 1978, reveals, she struggled with lifelong bipolar disorder. She underwent frequent hospitalizations and bouts of ECT treatments that left her memory permanently impaired. She had thoughts of suicide even when she was one of the most admired women in the world and was dating such powerful men as Howard Hughes and

John F. Kennedy.[25] As perhaps befitting the severity of her bipolar condition, hers was a lifetime of epic highs and devastating lows, and her genuinely frank autobiography is an early landmark in the now common, but still invaluable, books written by those who have experienced and survived bipolar disorder. Such firsthand accounts may or may not prove beneficial in any medical breakthroughs (though their observational insights are sum positives if for no other reason than they give clinical diagnosticians valuable knowledge), but they provide keen insight into an often mysterious ailment that many in the general public still do not readily understand.

Gene Tierney was discovered in the classic Hollywood sense. Anatole Litvak spotted her in line during a tour she was taking of the Warner Brothers back lot when she was a seventeen-year-old on vacation with her family. She would decline his offer to sign her as a contract player, owing to her father's reservations as well as the fact that she was not yet eighteen. But the impression had been cast years earlier in her childhood when she was an avid moviegoer who kept scrapbooks of her favorite actors and films. Daryl F. Zanuck, the head of Twentieth Century Fox, was equally smitten and described her as "undeniably the most beautiful woman in movie history."[26] Naturally it was to his advantage as the studio head who had her under contract to perhaps demonstrate some bias in his publicly held opinion. Still, her radiant beauty and confidence warranted his public esteem. She appeared first before Fritz Lang's cameras in *The Return of Frank James* (1940), and skyrocketed to stardom in the coming years in top-ranked films directed by John Ford, Henry Hathaway, Joseph von Sternberg, Rouben Mamoulian, William Wellman, Ernst Lubitsch, Otto Preminger, and others. But along the way, she also suffered being voted "Worst Female Discovery of 1940" by the editors of *Harvard Lampoon* magazine, blisteringly negative reviews by some critics, being stuck in formulaic scripts rather than more challenging fare, and even having Fritz Lang call her a bitch in front of shocked cast and crew on the set of her screen debut.[27]

Her childhood was not without medical problems despite her seemingly ideal upscale Connecticut background. Tierney suffered from a chronic stomach ailment that persisted throughout her life, often plaguing her during stressful productions.[28] This history of having debilitating or chronic childhood illnesses prior to the later development of bipolar disorder is not uncommon in patient biographies, many of whom often have suffered from physical ailments that were of enough severity to act as possible triggers in their later expression of manic-depression. Young Gene Tierney's talents for poetry and mimicry of the adult voices she heard and could instantly imitate were not unrecognized by her parents. It has often been noted in various accounts that bipolar patients have a flare for mimicry. Those who are manic-depressive and have demonstrated this ability include Charlie Chaplin, Orson Welles, James Dean, Jonathan Winters, and many others. In severe states of bipolar distress, playful mimicry may give way to echolalia, a compulsive need to repeat what others say or their movements, or word clanging, a frantic need to verbalize alliterative, but not necessarily meaningful, words.[29] The manic-depressive patient who experiences episodes of word clanging may have words become proverbially stuck in their head, endlessly repeating. As the voices of others are likewise often entrapped to endlessly repeat, it is understandable how the bipolar patient has a built-in advantage, such as it is, for mimicking by way of instant mental audio replay. Likewise, the noted connection between melancholia, mania, and poets has been well-established in the works and woes of Edgar Allan Poe, Lord Byron, Samuel Taylor Coleridge, John Keats, and a host of other creators on the spectrum,[30] all of whom may have benefited from the echolalia aspect of their shared disorder. Further evidence of the genetic connection between mood disorders is provided by Tierney's recollection of her clan as haunted by mental breakdowns.[31] One aunt became so mentally ill as a child that she would avoid anyone she saw coming toward her on a sidewalk, crossing a street if necessary to prevent human contact. Her disposition worsened into a form of adolescent paranoia, and she was briefly considered for housing in a sanitarium. Tierney had another aunt who was considered talented as a literary writer but also emotionally flighty, which means she may have been bipolar with hypomanic tendencies. She described her father as highly emotional and charming, two qualities often present in mood-disordered individuals. He also had "his own demons to quell,"[32] a phrase that was the equivalent verbal subterfuge of calling an episode of manic-depression a nervous breakdown. In a perhaps manic-induced decision of desperation, he raided Tierney's life's savings and used the stolen money to pay off personal debts, effectively ending his relationship with his daughter when she discovered his betrayal. As we have read, such cloistering of talent with emotional instability is common in families that have mental illness across generational lines.

Tierney describes her stays in mental institutions with unsparing candor in her book, but her descent into madness was painfully slow before she received any professional help. She began early in her screen career to suffer from depression, finding little that would comfort her during her periods of melancholia. She bought four small homes at one point in the 1940s, personally oversaw their upgrading as she briefly resided in each, and then sold them for a profit. She did not need the money, as she was working full-time as a much-in-demand star, but she needed the additional outlet for her restless manic energy. The fact that she was also romantically involved with Howard Hughes during this time, himself beset by mental illness, probably did not make it any easier for Tierney to relax, even if they shared an emotionally affected kinship. Similarly, her earlier marriage to Oleg Cassini when she was but twenty years old was an emotional roller coaster ride that soon ended in divorce. Her father threatened to have Tierney declared mentally unstable and committed in a failed effort to prevent the proposed union.[33] Her relationships with men were often romantically charged in nature but emotionally incomplete and fraught with a sense of high stakes, as her later affair with the caring but ambitious Senator John F. Kennedy revealed. This series of publicized paramours, and each subsequent tabloid headline of failure, did little to alleviate her intense sense of isolation as her career progressed. The birth of her daughter with mental retardation and the subsequent need Tierney had as parent of a live-in dependent child understandably worsened her anxieties, tipping her into frequent spells of depression.

Her first experience with mental illness in Hollywood besides her own hidden disorder was working with Frances Farmer on *Son of Fury* (1942). She details her shock at hearing crew members conducting whisper campaigns about Farmer's disturbed behavior, including throwing objects at them, exploding into rants on the set, and even snarling at times rather than speaking.[34] Her condition worsened before Tierney's eyes, but what Tierney records as her most horrific impression was not the insanity that Farmer experienced, but rather the cruel indifference and punitive insults of the studio. No one would take care of Frances Farmer as a sick individual in need of emergency medical intervention. Instead, she was cast into the role of veritable but sacrificial Dragon Lady, the proverbial Troublemaker, and allowed to go mad in front of the mystified, mortified production personnel. If Gene Tierney had previously entertained notions of coming forth about her own mental illness, surely her experience on the set of Son of Fury was an eye-opening wake-up call. She sadly wrote: "A very gifted actress had been crying out for help but no one listened."[35] Seemingly unaware of the irony when she wrote this, Tierney may as well have been addressing her own state of psychological deterioration.

Tierney characterized her mental state during her most productive years as filled with an inexplicable fear that was ever present. It abated when and if she slipped into a role, at which point she could relax and the constant sense of being ill-at-ease would temporarily vanish.[36] This is common among mood-disordered creators of all mediums and illustrates the validity of the thesis that many bipolars utilize their respective crafts as much for life-sustaining therapy as for income. Anthony Storr writes about this in his book Churchill's Black Dog, Kafka's Mice and Other Phenomena of the Human Mind. Noting that so many bipolar artists and writers labor in obscurity that is rarely, if ever, transcended in their own difficult lifetimes with recognition or money, he concludes: "Creative work must be inspired by drives which have nothing to do with worldly success."[37] This applies as much for actors as any other profession in which bipolar patients are present. It is not merely that they are anxious between paying acting jobs, as any actor might be, owing to the constant need for money and recognition; the mood disorder may actually make the actor feel depersonalized, lacking an external, fixated identity, such as that offered by an ongoing role in a play or movie that he or she can take on as their own. This kind of coinhabited occupational therapy can be considered akin to a hermit crab's need to find an outer shell in which to make its comfortable home. The actor feels confident and protected inside the identity shell provided by the role, but he falls into introversion and emotional confusion when required to be himself outside of it. It is as if emotionally unstable thespians are seeking to regain control of their internally haywire emotions by imposing, or internalizing, a more effectively dynamic personality construct upon their ineffective, depressive self. Too, by having a large role that lasts in film production for weeks and even months, as well as the enormous amount of time that goes into preparing for the role, the leading film actor is truly getting to "rent a life" for a very intense but sustained moment in time. In essence, the mood-disordered performer is likely using the external mask of the role to simultaneously project a confident persona as well as impose internal cohesion onto his scattered emotional center. This is just what Tierney indicated she did to alleviate her chronic depersonalization, likening acting to "Novocain for the mind."[38]

The tragic dimensions of her illness manifested in one series of humiliations after another once her tumble into the mental health system began in earnest. She started to have rapid mood swings and particularly delusional episodes of mania, believing she had insight into the cosmos that her fellow human beings lacked. She records clearly being able to see evil itself on her toothbrush, and then God incarnate awhile later in a light bulb.[39] Equally alarming was her penchant for sudden bouts of personality change, in which she swung from being outgoing and carefree into withdrawn and anxious in nature, all classic indicators of bipolar disorder in a cyclothymic phase. She experienced an episode of being unable to recall any of the dialogue in a script she was set to shoot that was so severe she contacted a psychiatrist. Ironically, it was the same psychiatrist who had previously treated fellow manic-depressive Vivien Leigh, she was told. Unfortunately, he misdiagnosed Tierney's problem and failed to understand the enormity of what she was describing to him. On the set of *The Black Widow* (1954), she recalled suddenly being unable to recall the faces of people she had known for years, which caused her to further withdraw from social circles.[40] Her decline continued, unrecognized or treated, until she shared the set with Humphrey Bogart in *The Left-Hand of God* (1955). Her symptoms became so severe that Bogart, who had a sister who suffered from mental illness and knew the warning signs, went to the studio heads and convinced them Tierney needed immediate medical help.

Her depersonalization ran deep during this time before her subsequent breakdown. This feeling that one is no longer in one's own body, but somehow detached and even looking down upon the proceedings without emotional concern, is a common marker for those on the mood spectrum.[41] In these states of mental being, the sufferer is like a semicomatose patient who is awake, somewhat cognitive, but also clearly absent from any interior sense of identity. What to the Greeks was known as the Logos, the mysterious sense of inner guidance, is missing. The patient can often functionally maneuver through her day, but ultimately, the emotionally flat affection begins to give her daily routine a sense to loved ones that something is vitally wrong. Tierney likened this time period to watching a silent film in which she was the star, but not really reactive to any of the other players in the scene (a criticism to which she would occasionally be attached as performer, especially in the latter part of her career when her illness was acute). She spent many nights wondering why no one could see she was suffering so much, feeling like she was trapped in a building set ablaze, watching her insanity slowly incinerate her walls of mental stability. The bouts of depersonalization gave way to catatonia. She spent hours sitting in a chair with a book in her lap, opened to the same page, never or hardly ever reading in any sustained manner, or with any comprehension. Soon she was sleeping for days on end and only waking momentarily to eat and use the bathroom.[42] She wrote that she felt like a zombie, underscoring the previously delineated links in cinema between depression, sleep, catatonia, and the gloomy sense the depressive patient may have of sleepwalking through life, as illuminated in such seminal, if highly symbolic, works as *The Cabinet of Dr. Caligari* and *The Testament of Dr. Mabuse*.

Desperate, Tierney agreed to be admitted to the Harkness Pavilion psychiatric facility in New York in 1955 and submitted to the first in a series of electroshock treatments. The early forms of ECT were different from the procedures practiced today, although even modern use of this technique is not without significant controversy. This controversy is perhaps accepted without enough legitimate concern by many in the professional community, as Dr. S. Nassir Ghaemi points out in his book *Mood Disorders*. Still, for those with extreme mania or depression, ECT can be effective in cases where drug therapies and other interventions have failed,[43] though at what ultimate cost to the patient is an unanswered question. For Tierney, however, the answer was definitive. She became a staunch critic of the process, but only after enduring thirty-two sessions of ECT. She lost entire sections of short- and long-term memory and became nauseous and dread-filled before and after each treatment. From her perspective as a patient, Tierney believed her early care was beyond ineffective, that it was actually harmful to her recovery and acceptance of her disorder. She concluded in her book that her treatment in the facility was the worst period in her life.[44] When one considers how Tierney was one of the most famous actors of her time, with the capital to finance her treatment, and yet still endured what she characterized as substandard care for her efforts, the bleaker picture for others in her time less financially and socially fortunate becomes clearer.

She actually made a daring escape in classic fashion from the facility after receiving the first five ECT treatments, convinced her mind was in danger from them. She ran barefoot through the snows of wintery New York wearing only a light cotton dress after managing to escape the sanitarium. She was chased by orderlies and her worried brother (in a scene uncannily similar to one from the dawn of cinema in depicting so-called "escaped lunatics") before being finally cornered in a drugstore. She often became physically violent against the nurses and orderlies, and just as often would have remissions into normal behavior so complete (though not long-lasting, alas) that doctors were convinced she was on the edge of recovery. But such was not the case, and she spent over eight months there before finally being discharged into her mother's care.[45]

Tierney was ensconced at East 57th Street in her mother's four-teenth-floor apartment during this time, coincidentally across the street from where Marilyn Monroe had recently moved into Sutton Place to reside with her new husband, Arthur Miller. In her book, Tierney tells of how she stood on the ledge of the apartment, contemplating suicide until police arrived to intervene. Years later, Tierney would reflect on the tragic irony that Monroe would succumb to her bipolar disorder, at least in large part, while Tierney would endure and survive her own. And yet, for a brief moment in time, both were the opposite sides of the looking glass of mental illness, at least until Monroe's was shattered forever by suicide. Tierney's attempt on the ledge earned her a trip to the exclusive psychiatric Menninger Clinic in Kansas for an extended stay. Already financially thin because of her medical bills, Tierney was forced to pay $25,000 per year in order to be housed and treated, effectively depleting her remaining life's savings.

She had further delusions of grandeur while at the Menninger Clinic, including one in which she believed the Russians were plotting to explode the sun with atomic weapons. Tierney described her prolonged struggles to emerge from the depths of her despair during her stay as "an attempt to climb a greased pole."[46] One treatment she particularly loathed was being strapped to a gurney and then having icy wet bed sheets suddenly wrapped around her entire naked body, from head to toe, in an attempt to shock her from her depressive state. After one such session, she was unable to lower her arms to her sides for days on end, a form of rigor mortis shock having set into her limbs and leaving them painfully dangling uselessly in the air. Further humiliation came from an entire month spent in isolation in South Ward Two, which was normally reserved for violent or hopeless patients. Her room was a brick-walled, walk-in closet with no windows and she was relegated to one brief meeting per day with her guards for human contact. Tierney had only a pencil and a stack of blank paper to occupy her time for the month. By the time the four weeks had passed, she had succumbed to a form of induced hopeless fatigue, compliant but without the will to live. Tragically, she would later realize that her confinement to the isolation room had been based on a misunderstanding by her psychiatrists. When Tierney complained that she heard animal noises at night in her former room, the doctor believed she was hearing them in her head and had her transferred to South Ward Two. Only after Tierney's release did the same psychiatric doctor realize that Tierney wasn't imagining animal noises, but actually hearing them, because her first room was across the street from a municipal zoo![47] Tierney was understandably devastated, further setting back her recovery.

It is interesting that Gene Tierney records in *Self-Portrait* the important therapeutic effect that painting had on her ability to sustain herself during this troubled time. The doctors gave her the paints and brushes, and she believed she found tranquility and a sense of beauty that she could have otherwise never achieved if she were neurotypical in that transcendent moment of artistic clarity. She also believed the counseling and therapy sessions she had there were enormously beneficial in helping her come to terms with her chronic medical condition.[48] During one stay in 1959 at the Menninger Clinic, the destitute Tierney worked for menial pay as part of a therapy-based, prerelease work program at a Topeka, Kansas, dress shop as a repair seamstress. She was recognized by a local reporter, whose story about her misfortunes made national news when it was picked up by wire services. Tierney notes in her memoirs that she was not embarrassed by the event, however, merely grateful that she had an honest job to use as a tool in helping combat her depression.[49] In a life-and-death struggle to maintain her sanity, public exposure seemed the least of her humiliations to endure.

All of her finest moments as bipolar performer are best distilled in *Leave Her to Heaven*. This role was Tierney's own favorite by admission, and the one she felt most reflected her own inner conflicts. What most attracted her to the part of socialite Ellen Harland was the fact that Ellen as a character believed herself capable of fooling all those around her that she was not mentally ill, but completely normal. By maintaining the facade of normalcy at any and all costs, Ellen is willing to forsake and even murderously sacrifice the human life around her, whom she swears to love. Tierney comments that profound denial of the illness is how many who are mood disordered very commonly act in real-life situations, not unlike an alcoholic who denies he is drinking to his family even as he searches for a hidden bottle in his home.[50] The other qualities Tierney believed were in Ellen's fictional psyche—jealousy, sadness, and self-destruction—were also true to Tierney's real-life bouts with mental illness. The need to maintain control for fear of losing all of it if one does not is again a familiar one to manic-depressives, many of whom feel that if even the slightest crack should show in their stone-faced facade, a flood of emotions can, and often does, gush forth. The way that Ellen lies, obscures, and finally begins a systematic campaign against her husband's family in order to be alone with him rather than in their (to her) annoying company leads her to homicide and even to self-inducing an abortion by throwing herself down the stairs. The level of shock and confusion this taboo-shattering role must have caused for post–World War II audiences who were currently engaged in supplying the Baby Boom was considerable, and was one of the reasons the film was one of Twentieth Century Fox's top money makers that year. Ellen is not merely a vision of modern woman as cold and dominating, she is also transgressive, willing to kill her unborn baby so she can keep her husband all to herself. For Ellen, the world is but a playground, and others are to be positioned on it just so. In extreme cases where egomania and narcissistic behaviors begin to manifest during acute manic-depressive episodes, this kind of nihilistic selfishness, although rare, has been recorded among bipolar historical figures such as Adolf Hitler.

Most bipolar patients are not, of course, so clinically unbalanced. But Tierney's real strength in the role lies not in the exaggeration of Ellen's obvious illness, but in her poker-faced ability to convincingly display calm and control to the worried family members around her after each increasingly bizarre behavior or incident. This cat-and-mouse game of secrets and staged meltdowns for emotional gain is a common by-product of families who deal with a manic-depressive relative. Director John Stahl adroitly stages many scenes in which Ellen is playing the inquisitor, gaining information about the family's latest reactions and plans involving her—quite the reverse of the expected situation in which the neurotypical family should be in charge and running the show. Stahl does this by having two shots in which Ellen gazes openly and without being seen doing so by the other cast member, who is typically either looking down or away. This gives Ellen an eerie edge of power over the other characters when she is in her stealth reconnaissance mode and busy laying her latest, unsuspected trap. Tierney takes enormous advantage of this directorial gift, truly imbuing Ellen with a cold pathology that is only matched in more B-movie noir efforts of the era such as *Detour* (1945) and *Gun Crazy* (1950). But unlike the heroines in those crime-spree films, Ellen is not a desperate, shadowy figure of the underworld, maniacally overplaying her manicured hand; rather, she operates as an outdoorsy, all-American blonde beauty with brains and the calm cool that would come to typify Hitchcock's preferred heroines. As played by Tierney, she just happens to be bipolar, and dangerously so. But because she comes from the right side of the tracks and has everything a woman could ever desire by her era's standards—a handsome husband, wealth and status, looks and intelligence—she is above suspicion until far too late. While the cold-blooded crimes Ellen gets away with for so long may seem nightmarish in their melodramatic construction, there is little doubt Tierney's portrayal tragically echoes the kind of feelings she was experiencing as she played Ellen. Tierney was also privately dealing with the "murder" of her own psyche via her undiagnosed and untreated disorder, and likewise, no one was noticing or intervening because she was perceived as ultra-successful, stable, and without seeming worry. Gene Tierney knew all about Ellen Harland's plight in life, even if Tierney's own actions were never as darkly hued. They were Tierney's own, after all, given free artistic expression, in the role of her lifetime. She was deservedly nominated for an Academy Award for her performance in *Leave Her to Heaven*. The impact she achieves is lasting, so much so that modern filmmaker Martin Scorsese cites it as one of his personal favorites. The influence on his own later film *Shutter Island* depicting a bipolar female character who drowns her own children is obvious and heartfelt.

BEDLAM, THE SNAKE PIT, AND THE BIPOLAR AS PSYCHIATRIC INMATE

In the post–World War II years two films in particular are worthy of discussion for our purposes. *Bedlam* (1946) and *The Snake Pit* (1948) both feature extensive and groundbreaking narrative looks at the institutions that house and supposedly care for the mentally ill placed there by society. *Bedlam* uses the infamous and previously chronicled St. Mary's of Bethlehem Hospital in England as period backdrop for largely historically accurate scenes of sadistic imprisonment of the patients. Under the direction of the corrupt apothecary-general of Bedlam, one Master Sims (Boris Karloff), the patients-turned-prisoners are forced at one point to stage a show for Sims's bored wealthy friends, whom Sims enjoys bringing into his asylum after hours to torture the inmates. When an outraged Nell Bowen (Anna Lee) witnesses one performance in which a young boy dies of asphyxiation caused by his skin pores becoming clogged with gold paint he is forced to wear for his part, she demands Sims reform his factory of human degradation. Sims's retort echoes many to this day when faced with the real-world challenge of treating the mentally ill. Showing uncharacteristic alarm, the normally stone-faced Sims replies in no uncertain terms that this is a terrible idea because it would entail having to raise taxes in order to pay for it! While *Bedlam* never concentrates on manic-depressive illness alone, it does contain inmates who are clearly on the traditional spectrum of mood disorders. But because they are supporting players, and not the main focus, *Bedlam* works more as a look at the way institutionalized mentally ill patients are supposedly medically treated, or more aptly, mistreated, in a dramatized, but largely historically accurate, context.

The Snake Pit changes the period to a modern setting and forgoes an obvious villain, instead making its handsome head doctor Dr. Mark Kirk (Leo Genn) the object of misplaced romantic interest for the incarcerated patient Virginia Cunningham (Olivia de Havilland). The setting is nowhere near as odious as Bedlam, but the confinement aspects are similar in psychological toll on the viewer, especially because director

Anatole Litvak (who ironically discovered Gene Tierney) and screen-writer Arthur Laurents (uncredited but known for his construction of the narrative) contrived to have the story unfold en media res, from Virginia's confused point of view, from the opening moments. Coming out of a fugue state and finding herself in the courtyard of the psychiat-ric institution into which she's confined, with no memory of how or why she got there or even who she is, is an adroit use of the same position the viewer experiences when a movie begins and he or she is forced to rapidly digest an appreciable amount of backstory in order to invest in the characters and plot. By having the viewer experience dislocation along with Virginia's character, a truer sense of dread and anxiety is created, which is precisely what a woman who is clinically undergoing ECT treatments in the era would have experienced as she groggily came into clarity after each grueling session.[51] Indeed, Virginia Cun-ningham's fictional experiences so eerily mirror the true ones Gene Tierney chronicles undergoing in her confessional memoir *Self-Portrait* that *The Snake Pit* could easily have been released as a fairly accurate Tierney biopic with minor edits and name changes. The harrowing and extensive montage sequences in which Virginia undergoes one night-marish ECT session after another arguably biased the public against its use as much as later medical and newspaper reports did, which linked it to severe memory loss, broken bones owing to convulsions, and other horrific side effects. Eventually Virginia will be "cured" with a psycho-analytic explanation for her mental woes by the triumphant Dr. Kirk, thus making her diagnosis as manic-depressive highly improbable, but that is where *The Snake Pit* truly breaks from scientific and medical reality in favor of melodramatic expediency. While understandable, giv-en the popularity of Freud in the era, the idea that mental illnesses can be cured at all, let alone with convenient explanations and/or hypnosis, is akin to believing in pots of gold at the end of rainbows. However beautiful the mirage such false hopes bring, the end result must always be the same empty disappointment, as there exists no reliable evidence that serious mental impairments such as bipolar disorder, schizophre-nia, and others are anything but genetic and environmental in nature and expression.[52]

While both films do humanely portray their respective patients as worthy and in dire need of medical help, they also forgo making the illnesses of any one inmate more noteworthy or even better identified than another. Rather than an individual focus on manic depression as theme or patient type, the patients are seen as a larger group of dysfunctional prisoners. Sometimes they appear to have markers known to clinical mania and depression, certainly, such as the patient Hester in *The Snake Pit* played by Betsy Blair, who exhibits catatonia as she sits in her bed, vacant-eyed and unresponsive to her friend Virginia's faithful attempts to bring her back to the land of the living. But for the most part, these bits are kept as background and supporting in nature, rather than driving the narrative. They primarily help illuminate the deplorable conditions too many actual sufferers of mood disorders faced as their grim reality in the 1940s, as far as this book is concerned. So while many audiences were being educated in a dark manner by seeing these films, the societal taboo against mental health was still years away from being lifted.

They are interesting in the sense, as well, that they invert the paradigm of the so-called lunatic as the dangerous element and fully embrace the opposite point of view. In both *Bedlam* and *The Snake Pit*, the audience is moved to feel for the patients as a singular group character, if you will, held against their will by society, whether the society is evil and exploitative (as is *Bedlam*'s view) or well-meaning and kind (as is *The Snake Pit*'s perspective). While this did help humanize the plight of long-term patients in psychiatric facilities, it had an unintended consequence, too. By shifting the "blame" and responsibility from the patient to the doctors and society, the films unwittingly reduced the status of mentally ill people by implying such decisions are most properly made on their behalf, without their consent.

Understandably from the patients' point of view, it is better to act as participants in their care to whatever degree possible. It was not an intended or even provocative slight. Rather, it was indicative of the true shift that occurred in the 1940s, which was humane and compassionate in scope and tone, for the reasons previously outlined in terms of returning soldiers and treatment of posttraumatic stress disorder (or "shell shock" as it was called then). Only in later decades, as people on the mood-disorder spectrum were more accurately portrayed as being quite normal most times but subject to periods of emotional illness, would it become clearer that depictions of manic-depressives as permanently disabled were as one-sided in nature as a manic tirade.

6

1950S: PSYCHOLOGICAL REALISM IN BIPOLAR FILM DEPICTIONS

NICHOLAS RAY AS EXPRESSIVE DEPRESSIVE

Only now is Nicholas Ray's uniquely expressive range of dark-hued cinema gaining a threshold of popular rediscovery. Seeing the disparate subject matter and sometimes morbid self-revelations that fueled the troubled filmmaker distilled with the luxury of retrospection, the underlying psychic qualities that haunt each Ray effort fairly stumble out of the screen's implied proscenium arch and spill into the startled viewer's lap. Here is a body of personal cinema both commercially driven and coded with obvious hidden meanings and cryptic self-mythology. The inherent contradictions in a Nicholas Ray movie in and of themselves are what define the powerful personality that his best works create in the lingering mind of the spectator. They can be bold and achingly heartfelt, and then suddenly shift into camp and sentimentalism, often seemingly without directorial effort or even, occasionally, intent, though Ray was anything but a deliberate obscurer, as some have perhaps misunderstood his approach to filmmaking. If anything, Ray's insistence on creating subjective levels of subtext, some increasingly accessible to none but himself as he aged in the filmmaking process, often put him at odds with cast, crew, and schedules. Therefore, at least some supporting evidence points to a clinically obsessive nature in Ray, perhaps being a defensive means of pouring his rapid-cycling manic-depression energies into an ever-challenging, all-encompassing creative endeavor. These bipolar-tinged qualities in Ray's directorial style are so pervasive that, no matter whether the diverse subject matter was teen rebellion, prescription pill addiction, wildlife poaching, attempted saloon stealing, armed robbery, a Biblical epic, or even homicidal Hollywood, a Nicholas Ray picture was finally best described by ardent fans as "a Nicholas Ray picture." He was the very essence of what the French New Wave critics meant by the term *auteur*, the guiding personality behind each great movie. Godard lovingly said, "The cinema is Nicholas Ray."[1] Given the intertwined nature of filmmaking and bipolarity, as this book proposes, Godard was correct on at least one level of meaning, if not many others.

Nicholas Ray's superb use of composition can be attributed in part to his art school studies with Frank Lloyd Wright as a young man.[2] Likewise, Ray created notebooks and design schemes detailing color codes he would assign for each character's wardrobe.[3] These were not merely for eye-pleasing palette contrasts, though Ray was certainly a master of sublimely beautiful images for images' sake. Ray's approach was meant to subliminally indicate that if a character was wearing one color in one scene, but then changed later, a significant psychological moment had transpired. It was to alert the viewer, albeit perhaps subconsciously (which is where all great art first works upon the viewer), that important character transformation was happening or had occurred, and therefore, to assist with the cathartic experience as cumulative whole. A famous example is when James Dean dons the red blazer specifically designed for a moment in *Rebel without a Cause* (1955). It signals his shift from new kid on the block to a person willing to stand his ground against the teen thugs. This kind of attention to detail based on the externalization of interior states of being harkened back to the expressive use of subjective set designs in *The Cabinet of Dr. Caligari*. Ray subdued his style by burying the intent more into the expressive use of his camera and the creation of moods than in set surrealism, but Ray's intentions—to dramatically render the subjective emotions and disturbed states of mind experienced by characters into the viewing experience itself—were remarkably aligned in spirit.

Like Hitchcock, Scorsese, Kubrick, and Kurosawa, it takes but watching a few scenes of Ray's work to feel the familiar hand of his stylistic touch. Without much warning his velvet-soft fingers around the viewer's throat characteristically go from caressing to a full-throttled choke-hold of expressive overkill. These majestic moments, when they suddenly erupt, are like cinematic seizures, intensely overpowering and never less than startling. Recall Mercedes McCambridge as the gloriously maniacal, appropriately named Emma Small in *Johnny Guitar* (1954), when she sets her rival's saloon ablaze in retributive fury. Ray holds on Emma's black-clad figure in silhouette against the burning flames of the saloon, reminiscent of the witch trials and their outcomes with her puritanical attire and the roaring inferno. Ray has her stagger into the camera's foreground against this fiery backdrop, her back always to the viewer. Only when she is in the close-up does she turn and reveal her evident pyromania. Emma fairly pants with excitement at the sight of the fire, her face sweaty with repressed sexuality breaking through despite the icy facade, her eyes wild with maniacal glee. It is a devastating portrait of madness, a true glimpse beneath the mask of intolerance and cruelty Emma Small has hidden behind until this moment in the film. It crushes with its provocative refusal to exonerate Emma for her clinical disorder even as it cinematically celebrates, even indulges, her insatiable lust for fire-setting. Other examples are the shockingly abrupt gangster deaths illustrated in his underrated *Party Girl* (1958), which were probable influences on Coppola and the manner in which he shot similar scenes in *The Godfather*. The violent criminal deaths enacted by Ray are not the typical suspenseful build-up one is accustomed to in lesser pictures. Ray shatters the calm with suddenly blazing machine guns and jerking, spasm-flung bodies, which often fly across the frame, leaving chaos in their wake, not the glamorized death seen in too many films of the genre.

All of Nicholas Ray's work contains these fitful moments of personal paroxysm, of brooding characters squirming in personal hells of their own private making, only to stagger free in sudden, violent episodes of rage and nonconformity. Picture the glowering, self-wounded James Dean in *Rebel without a Cause*. He's an existential vacuum inhabiting a pair of skin-tight jeans and his aforementioned blood-red jacket, sucking up the malevolent teen angst all around him. Finally he spontaneously ignites like a proverbial phoenix, incendiary in his own fiery sense of avenging self-reclamation. His father and friends literally fall like bowling pins during encounters with the psychologically unstable Dean, toppled over by the sheer force of his pained alienation. Dean barrels first at them, and then through their own weak vanities and petty self-obsessions, shoving all pretensions aside in his fury. Dean's incandescent inability to hide his wounded, confused, embarrassed core being with the usual masks of rigidity society demands leaves the mask holders around him bereft of face-saving fallback. They fumble, they stumble, and always mumble, but the conclusion is always the same, and therein lies Ray's genius: they do not know how to treat such blazing bipolar-induced honesty and maintain the rules of civilized life (which demands anything but truth). So they opt to maintain the latter at the direct, repressive expense of the former. The pressures and expectations of conformity versus the inevitable episodic, reactive breakdowns against it are the central conflicts in Ray's movies. The "acting out" Ray's characters indulge in often catches us off-guard, even though they seem inevitable given the insistent manner in which Ray puts his characters into a perpetual state of uneasiness. These moments are exhilarating to the characters who are behaving badly, even if they usually pay the price for their hubris by the end credits. And these characters equally seem to share a certain self-knowledge that they are The Other in terms of the perception of the crowd around them. This perception further drives them to commit acts of emotional insanity against the tyrannical, hypocritical world in which the usual Ray protagonist is ironically straight-jacketed.

In Ray's greatest films, the narrative construction can feel as if it has been rendered less for logical believability than to emphatically showcase moments of psychological confusion, distress, and deterioration in his bedeviled protagonists. Whole films such as *Rebel without a Cause*, *Bigger Than Life*, and *Johnny Guitar* seem less about plot devices and more about building toward climactic scenes in which leading characters experience uncontrollable nervous breakdowns. So powerful are these scenes of transcendence in Ray's works that they not only stay with the viewer afterward, but often overpower the initial viewing of the film itself. This strange, persistent quality in his works may be why Ray later remarked that he was "the best damn filmmaker in the world who has never made one entirely good, entirely satisfactory film."[4] Ray was far too harsh in his self-assessment, however. What makes his filmography so compelling is that what often supposedly doesn't work in his films is often as mesmerizing as the scenes that do attain great emotional heights of intense melodrama. His way of making movies was such that even the failures were never less than fascinating for what they revealed of the filmmaker's inner, disheveled psyche. His films can startle viewers with their bald-faced contrivances and deliriously over-the-top design schemes, and yet, they also offer a dreamy, consistent state of internal tension. Nicholas Ray was a filmmaker who made movies that may not have escaped his imagination in an always comprehensible fashion, but watching his films, it is hard to argue with the fact that they were at least fashioned with great imaginative passion, however moodily impenetrable at times.

Nicholas Ray's life story follows a typical if nonetheless spectacular rise and fall familiar from so many other bipolar filmmakers and actors. He was raised in Wisconsin in a well-off, progressive family. Throughout his young adulthood Ray joined a litany of socialist groups and "action theater" companies, though his involvement remained characteristically aloof and mainly social in nature. And like many profiled bipolar filmmakers, he lost a parent at an early age; in his case the teenaged Ray watched his father drink himself to death in binge cycles.[5] His stint at the Taliesin Institute, personally run by Frank Lloyd Wright, made a profound impact on Ray's sensibility, especially in terms of composition and color. After leaving the school at Wright's behest because of a growing homosexual scandal involving Ray and another student,[6] Ray drifted without aim and wound up in Mexico, cut off from all friends and family and clinically depressed. He wrote a series of revealing letters to his family describing the desolation and melancholia he felt as a perpetually wandering gringo. Calling these feelings of self-negation and hopelessness his "blue funk,"[7] Ray wrote that he and Mexico were spiritual mates because they had a shared sadness. It was this blue funk, this essential sense of the profound despair so readily visible in the world, always present and seemingly forever in endurance, that moved Ray to feel as if a whole country could personify his own deeply entrenched depression. And it is why his films often feel so gloomy and self-defeatist, as they are accurate if artistic externalizations of the emotional bleakness that was at the heart of Ray's own troubled being.

As with his later films and their elaborate attention to detailed set designs, physical setting was everything to Ray, with an evocative hold on his imagination. He was known for spending long stretches in profound, self-isolating silence, wandering around his sets lost in thought as his bewildered but respectful cast and crew patiently awaited the director's next utterance.[8] These bouts of incommunicado were a life-long source of vexation for Ray, who suffered from what may well have been an undiagnosed case of selective mutism.[9] In layman's terms, it is not unlike a form of pathological shyness, only rendered as a frustrating inability to summon words of expression in any given social setting. The sufferer may remain otherwise in the moment and steadily maintain eye contact, nod, and display correct body language skills, which a typically shy person would not possess during bouts of awkwardness.

Many companions and coworkers noted the mutism in their remembrances of Ray. Some studio heads during the making of *Bigger Than Life* were so flummoxed by Ray's occasional struggles with nonspeaking during meetings that they solicited coproducer and star James Mason's behind-the-scenes assurance that Ray could be trusted.[10] Screenwriter Phillip Yordan recalled that Ray would sit with his back to creative collaborators while looking out a window, even when it was darkest night and there was nothing to be seen. "I would say something and wait fifteen minutes, then Nick would turn around and he still wouldn't say anything,"[11] wrote Yordan. Stewart Stern, writer of *Rebel without a Cause*, said Ray was "in agony, a kind of private hell"[12] during the making of the film. Novelist and script writer A. I. Bezzerides recorded Ray as living in a private world of thoughts.[13] Gore Vidal, calling him both a con man (as Vidal referred to all successful directors) and charming, concluded, "But he was quite crazy."[14] Remarkably consistent in most memoirs in their recounting of Nicholas Ray is a sense of his being almost entirely cut off from the world around him for large periods of time, though he also frequently experienced periods in which he could communicate his artistic desires with complete confidence. Whether it was recorded by a lover, a friend, a producer, an actor, or a former student, the image is of a haunted and self-destructive director not unlike that of later international filmmaker Rainer W. Fassbinder, upon whom Ray's life and work was an admitted influence.

Ray's depressive blue funks drove him from young adulthood through his later years into a continuous attempt to remain intoxicated whether he was working or not. He abused a variety of medications as well as alcohol, marijuana, and other illegal drugs in an attempt to nullify many of his ongoing clinical symptoms.[15] His good physical health enabled him to cycle a lifestyle of toxic chemicals into his body for a number of years before the inevitable damage began to show as residual side effects. As told by an ex-student in the documentary about Ray's later years as college film teacher at SUNY Binghamton, *Don't Expect Too Much* (2011), Ray was once given a joint to sample in the campus theater, where he was perched atop a ladder, surveying the stage scenery below him. After one huge inhale, Ray toppled to the floor, his panicked students rushing to his aid. Ray sat erect as suddenly as he had fallen and, after blinking to regain his composure, asked if the student could buy the sampled weed in mass quantities. In his Hollywood prime Ray was by reputation not just the proverbial last man standing at one of his dusk-to-dawn parties, but the only man left standing by dawn's light, actively conscious, seemingly unaffected, placing a new favorite record on the phonograph, or leafing through a book of poetry, while around him his guests slumbered.[16] While the image is vaguely humorous in a Don Juan way, with Ray as the stalwart party stud, it is actually quite chilling from a clinical point of view. For herein, one sees a rare internal glimpse of a manic or hypomanic mind at work, constantly if restlessly on the prowl, forever shifting over ideas and plans, never settling on any singular focus except for a short bit of time before discarding it for the next set of grandiose visions. The dependency on illegal drugs was a burden on his sense of freedom and finally even in his later filmmaking efforts. This was particularly acute during the troubled making of *Winds Across the Everglades* (1958), which he was unable to complete owing in part to his failing health, physical as well as mental, both of which were compromised by heroin addiction.[17]

While states of mania and depression fill Ray's output, only one film dealt with clinical mania as subject matter. *Bigger Than Life* (1956) is the sobering account of a well-meaning school teacher, Ed Avery (James Mason), who moonlights as a radio dispatcher to make ends meet because his teacher's pay won't suffice. Ed is hospitalized after an accident and during recovery he is diagnosed with a rare, deadly inflammation of the arteries. His doctors prescribe cortisone, a then novel drug, to treat his pain and save his life. The drug works wonders and Ed is soon back on his feet, full of vigor—alas, owing to his growing, secretive cortisone addiction, too much vigor. Soon, Ed is experiencing full-blown bouts of mania, in which he believes his wife is not dependable and that his son is working against the family's best interests. Ed's fluctuating mood patterns of stability and then mania allow him to hide his condition from his loved ones and medical doctors until an inevitable personal crisis explodes, overtaking them all before Ed's breakdown is complete.

Technically, a genetically inherited mood disorder is not on display in *Bigger Than Life*, as Mason's Ed has been given prescription medications that have induced mania as a toxic by-product. Nonetheless, it is a sobering study of how a formerly "balanced" everyman like Mason can find his entire life suddenly altered while under the subtle (at first) influence of a prolonged manic-depressive episode. So delusional is Mason that at one point his doctors actually advise (rather foolishly) that his wife Lou (Barbara Rush) go along with Ed's chronic maniacal delusions at home while they devise a better strategy so as not to further upset him. Clearly a better course of action would have been to seek immediate psychiatric hospitalization for him and safety for her and their son Richie (Christopher Olsen). Melodramatic construction aside, *Bigger Than Life* uses the credulity it spends in this scene to buy emotional dynamism, for soon Ed is demanding his subservient wife Lou join him in a suicide pact. Ed swears they will kill each other and therefore make right with God, just as soon as they sacrifice their willful, unrighteous son Richie first for his spoiled, disrespectful ways. The self-inflated, walled-off narcissism Mason displays as he hurries about ritualistically preparing to slaughter his loved ones, all the while voicing his tortured thoughts with utterances about how he must do these heinous acts as a sign of obedience to God's will, are chillingly believable. The frozen mask of stunned surprise and the perennial look of sardonic bemusement so normally Mason's stock in trade become horrifically magnified, indeed, bigger than life, by his mania. His blustery, erudite delivery only makes his manic psychosis all the more frightening. He acts as sadistic narrator to his own increasingly monomaniacal thoughts of self-indulgent exuberance. Here is a man walking through and actively conspiring to destroy his life's work and loved ones with all the concern he might otherwise exhibit booking a holiday trip online. While unhinged in manner, it is the eerie calm with which Mason almost makes a form of bipolar sense that causes his wife, doctors, and finally the viewer, to give pause. Clearly, Mason is nonchalantly planning his own self-destruction, and yet, he is so lucid, so precise, and so inspired in his delusional mania, that he has a temporary, magnetic hold on his bewildered family and helpers as he unfolds his latest madness. This confuses and confounds them, which leaves them uncertain how to respond with any clarity or reflection.

This is a realistic aspect of actual mania in its ability to manifest itself as charisma. But charisma, of course, is not always applied for positive purposes. Incredulous, even radical ideas and behaviors, can become acceptable when articulated and acted upon with daily fervor by and under the full-court press of a manic's charm.[18] It is much easier to be swayed to a poor idea or product by the use of good salesmanship, after all, or the whole of commercial advertising would not exist. Mason's Ed is a supreme manipulator in one disturbed sense in *Bigger Than Life*. He subverts all that is stable and decent about predictable, if boring, suburban life with his episodic mania, and therefore becomes the grotesque, tyrannical version of his former, meeker self. Whereas Ed was formerly a depressive in personality, in essence self-sacrificing himself by working two jobs and always stretching himself too thin for his fragile emotional state, under the influence of cortisone he becomes an overbearing egomaniac, sacrificing his family along with himself not for God, as Ed lamely submits, but as a testament to his own inflated ego. Like some pharaoh, Ed decides that his family must be slaughtered along with him in order to signify just how great a loss humanity has suffered. The stringent attempt by the manic to weave together all threads into one tightly knit, self-revelatory explanation, beyond the question or critique of any, is again emblematic of the disorder's delusional aspects, commonly known as racing thoughts or flights of ideas.[19] Just as oddly, but significantly, it is this very ability of the manic-depressive to make sense and order from creative chaos that imbues bipolar films with their often eerie sense of enchantment and grip on the viewers' imaginations.

But whether it was the gloomy, manic-depressive glory period of Ray's early triumphant works such as *They Live by Night* (1948) and *In a Lonely Place* (1950), the superstar years of directing *Rebel without a Cause* and *Bigger Than Life*, or subsequently the slow descent—though one still filled with flashes of trailing cinematic imagination—into compromised fare with later works such as *Wind Across the Everglades* or *We Can't Go Home Again* (1976), the one factor that never abated in Ray's life was his bipolar disorder. It waned and tore at him in sometimes chaotic fashion, but it was not only his life's ultimate personal demon to wrestle, it was his artistic muse and imp, both a source of creative passion when his mania exalted his sensibilities, and of lamentable despair when his powers of salesmanship faltered and he remained unemployed. Having seen multiple psychiatrists throughout his life[20] and accepting their easily dispensed yet poorly working prescriptive cures for his perpetual blues, Ray concurrently sought to live his life to the fullest extent possible. He poured his manic depression into moviemaking whenever he could do so as his preferred therapy. He attempted to create a personal cinema of emotionally charged, redemptive self-honesty. The unfortunate characters in Ray's films who blandly attempt to sleepwalk through their lives always pay a huge price. They are destroyed beyond repair, their former masks melted beyond recognition or reclamation, and all because they failed to heed the proverbial "call to action" the siren muses sang in their tone-deaf ears. They must helplessly watch Ray's emotionally disturbed protagonists rail against their shattered conformity in open displays of cathartic self-purging. In the Ray universe, to resist breaking down is to risk being broken, once and for all, with no hope for ascension to follow. Only by letting oneself completely experience the highs and lows can one thrive and survive, Ray's tortured but fleetingly transcendent protagonists proclaim.

Ray would finally find himself in a perpetually sad state of affairs when his old friend Dennis Hopper helped him secure gainful employment as a film teacher in the late 1960s. A staged rescue and intervention of sorts, Ray was by that point an international vagabond, wandering from one semi-completed project to the next, subsisting largely on a diet of Mars candy bars.[21] He was given a small cottage as part and parcel of his tenure as a liberal arts college guest lecturer in residence, which Hopper had originally set in motion. *Don't Expect Too Much* (2011) was largely assembled from the hours of 16 mm and Super 8 mm footage Ray maniacally shot during this period, much of it used and even more discarded for his never completed (at least in his lifetime) film *We Can't Go Home Again* (1976). The title *Don't Expect Too Much* refers to a story Ray often told in which a man for whom life has no apparent meaning searches to the ends of the remote earth, whereupon he finally encounters a truth-telling sphinx. The man beseeches the oracle to bestow but one small bit of wisdom by which he, the lost seeker, can find purpose in life's bewildering fog. The sphinx thinks it over a moment and says, "Don't expect too much." It's readily apparent why the tale was one of Ray's repeated witticisms at this lower point in his once glamorous life, for it renders with heartbreaking clarity how devastating the unending mood swings Ray experienced were upon him as time wore on, and eventually, wore him out.

There is a warm moment in *Don't Expect Too Much* where Ray is blissfully at work/play on his Moviola, that peculiarly romantic, upright editing machine from a by-gone era. Film editors of the day had to handle the bulky, whirring lengths of film they cut, hastily splicing them together and then running them through the clacking editing machine, which offered fully motorized, sound synchronized viewing. As the editor peered into the softly glowing view hood, he pressed floor pedals similar to a sewing machine's that sped the film past the viewing scope and audio heads, offering the cutter a preview of the cut's effect on the scene, dialogue, and so on. Watching Ray become entirely absorbed as he operates the Moviola is revelatory. He is so engrossed, so enthralled, he seems a vacuous shell as mere mortal. He is symbiotically combined with his beloved editing gear, a union of man and machine, for they are as one. Ray, wearing his preferred, if only sartorial, eye-patch, maniacally fixates on the twisting, coiling film strips, so unaware of his surroundings he doesn't notice the two college students over his shoulder. The students trade knowing looks behind Ray's back, and the honesty of their expressions is fascinating. The students are as much awed by the sheer coolness of the legendary Ray as they are mesmerized by the clinical display of mania they are witnessing. There is in their younger eyes the recognition that while what they are seeing is a form of madness, it is being so beautifully controlled, so skillfully self-directed, and to such positive, creative purpose, that they are left giddy, nearly giggly and speechless. Before them, a wizard silently crafts his magic screen alchemy, and they as apprentices can only try to absorb the unguarded mystery before its delicate appearance has passed. This shot is as fitting a tribute in film as any for one of the great expressive stylists of cinema. It is rare indeed to see a master at work with the very elemental tools of his trade. The typical image that comes to mind is of the director on the set next to a massive camera, rehearsing his famous cast. Here it is just a filmmaker and editing machine, and clearly, Ray experienced a genuine state of enraptured ecstasy when he plied his craft, as this scene so movingly reveals. The intensely personal sense of devotion and therapy as sacred approach to living out a troubled life is artfully distilled in this shot of Ray, for one sees both the ruin in his attire, face, and grooming, and yet, the interior glow of a man transformed, albeit temporarily, into a state of complete contentment by his therapy. In this now eternal moment, at least, Ray's bipolar disorder and his very being have become fused, inseparable, and their expression is nothing less than creative bliss personified. Indeed, as Godard concluded, the cinema is literally, figuratively, and even transcendentally Nicholas Ray.

JAMES DEAN AS THRILL-SEEKING, RAPID-CYCLING MOTORCYCLIST

The iconic power of James Dean was uncanny even before his death. Post-burial, his soulful ascension has been even greater. Post-life James Dean has been popularly mourned, biographically laid bare, critically reevaluated, monumentally mass-merchandised, faithfully adored, and culturally enshrined. *Rebel without a Cause* and his incandescent performance have been credited with not merely ensuring his perpetual appeal throughout the ages since its release, but likewise creating the teenage identity movement in a larger context, giving rise to the concept that teenagers were not to be politely ignored, but witnessed and understood with an urgency that caught their elders unprepared.[22] None of which would probably have surprised James Dean had he lived beyond the age of twenty-four. Dean was told by his mother from his earliest memories of childhood that his was a life with greatness as its destiny.[23] It was a prediction eerily akin to earlier profiled bipolar child prodigies such as Charlie Chaplin and Orson Welles, who were also profusely praised by their mothers as young geniuses. Tragically Dean would lose his mother at an early age (again like Chaplin and Welles), but the early death of a parent in childhood is often a hallmark seen in bipolar biographies.[24]

That the impact of his mother's death was tremendous is proven by the fact that family members recalled how James Dean slept with a lock of his mother's hair for the first two weeks after her passing, convinced she would somehow return for him.[25] He was shipped to relatives to be raised because his father felt ill-equipped for the task, a further blow to his psyche that filled him with anger in later years. A natural daredevil, the young James Dean mastered early motorcycle tricks on the country roads of his Indiana upbringing. He would race along a stretch known as Suicide Curve, a winding gravel road near a cemetery, at fifty miles per hour while lying on his bike's seat.[26] He even once bested a rival who raced him in a Chevy in an eerie precursor to a later scene Dean would fictionalize in *Rebel without a Cause* (though in real life, his rival would survive, only rolling his Chevy and crashing it, instead of dying as in the film). Lonely and without a father figure, he gravitated as a teen toward a local guru and pastor, Reverend James DeWeerd. The older man taught Dean that death was but a doorway, and not a coffin, therefore freeing the young actor to take risks and chances others would not consider.[27] After Dean nearly wiped out in a motorcycle accident a week before he was to begin *East of Eden*, his friend, composer Leonard Rosenman, asked him why he was so perpetually suicidal, especially when all Dean had struggled to achieve lay ahead, not behind, him in terms of acting. Dean only mumbled that "death is always there and I want to conquer it."[28]

From an early age, it is therefore evident James Dean had a growing fascination with death and challenging it directly on multiple fronts, whether they were physical, emotional, or creative, such as his early love for acting. He seemed to exist to dispel his own existential despair, as it were, akin to an emotional shark that must remain forever in motion beneath the dark ocean waters lest it die from lack of oxygen passing through its gills. And like that predator, James Dean was an opportunistic feeder, devouring huge chunks of life in fitful gulps, often overtaken by the frenzy of his own feeding and only later succumbing to bouts of rueful guilt and self-recrimination for his selfish, manic behavior. His was a manic-depressive temperament, as was recorded by many who knew him. "He was almost constantly in a blue funk," wrote Beverly Wills. "When he was depressed, he wanted to die."[29] But more acutely, James Dean suffered from a pernicious form of bipolarity known as cyclothymia, or rapid-cycling. It was the source of his greatest acting triumphs and lowest personal agonies, and often multiple times within the same day and night stretch. Like a yo-yo, James Dean went up and then down, only briefly ever hovering in one emotional zone for a brief, tension-filled spell. Next he would be yet again pulled beyond his control into another dizzy, short-lived episode of either mania, hypomania, or depression. He would scarcely be able to gather his wits and catch his breath before the next rapid-cycling episode was upon him. As actor Richard Shannon recalled of their time as young acting buddies in

Santa Monica, "He was like a rainbow. You don't ever see one color, you see a maze of them."[30]

About 20 percent of the patients diagnosed with manic depression were found to be rapid cycling in a 1970s-era study.[31] Technically, a clinical diagnosis of rapid cycling means that the patient suffers from four or more mood swing episodes in a year. However, a more insidious form of this disorder is known as ultradian cycling, wherein the afflicted person may experience mood lability over the hours, as well as ultra-rapid cycling as sub-specifier, which means over the days.[32] Though much rarer, James Dean clearly labored with the more severe forms of his disorder, as the numerous testimonies made by his often bewildered, hurt, and saddened friends and coworkers reveals. He could be funny, charming, and persuasive for the first half of a social gathering, and then sullen, bullying and rude for the latter half. He had a habit of first reaching out to people, and then retreating as they came to know him better. He could rapidly cycle through an entire series of emotions in one night, according to Beverly Wills.[33] She recalled having no better possible company when he was manic, but that he was suicidal in his depressive despair at the opposite end of his mood swings. Barbara Glenn, a former girlfriend, noted folks warned her not to get further involved with Dean because he was to them inevitably "the sickest boy I ever met"[34] in whispered summation. This was a common motif in the descriptions of those who met or worked with him. Others who knew Dean intimately and who expressed a recorded opinion that he was emotionally ill included Elia Kazan, James Whitmore, Marlon Brando, Dennis Stock, Mort Abrahams, Mercedes McCambridge, Lee Strasberg, and many more. Dean was painfully self-conscious of his own misery, as well, as he penned in a letter to Glenn while he was struggling in New York City in poverty, performing on low-wage, live television dramas. "Must I always be so miserable? I try so hard to make people reject me," he wrote. "Wow! Am I fucked up. . . . I want to die. . . . I'm sad most of the time. Awful lonely, too.[35]

"To me, acting is the most logical way for people's neuroses to manifest themselves,"[36] Dean articulately told *New York Times* reporter Howard Thompson. *Neurosis* was a popular term in the 1940s and 1950s media owing in part to the popularization of Freud that had recently occurred in America, especially in Hollywood filmmaking.[37] But it is clear Dean is not referring to a minor if painful psychological problem, but more likely substituting "neuroses" for his own bipolarity. A theater director he worked with named Mort Abrahams recalled that Dean could meld his mood to his performance, and vice versa, with seamless ability beyond anything Abrahams had ever seen in terms of speed and technical proficiency. Dean would alter his entire performance based on the way he felt or the perceptions he supplied to each fellow cast member with each new curtain rise. This naturally caused great tension with the actors, who labored to maintain consistency as their proud thespian tradition. Abrahams recalled how Dean's rapid-cycling moods meant no one ever knew his temperament prior to a scene.[38] Abrahams felt that once one accepted that this was not the spoiled tantrum of a child, but a genuine psychiatric condition, any qualms about his professionalism and amazing abilities went out the window. Sadly, this recognition would largely remain buried with Dean's early stage career once he rose to fame, and would cause Dean countless battles and loss of self-esteem as he encountered studio resistance, frustrated cast members, and misunderstanding directors who were struggling with the troubled nature that was what made him so attractive as a performer. His unpredictability was what made the scenes he fully inhabited so electrifying. It is not that he was a dangerous, violent person that gives his work such fascination, but that he seemed so dangerously perched on the crumbling cliff of his own inexplicable, explosive emotional instability. When Dean tersely sauntered into a scene, there was a sense that the fuse, a rather short one at that, had already been lit and that it was only a matter of time before the sputtering sparks and their inevitable detonation erupted on-screen. The same personality is seen in accounts of his off-screen exploits, thus proving the accuracy of Abrahams's insight into Dean's need to blend his painful disorder with his acting craft in order to transcend his own emotional limitations and find what meaning he could create in his maelstrom of moods.

Dean suffered from terrible insomnia,[39] which is a recurrent hallmark of mood-disordered individuals. It was also perhaps the source of much of his keen love of movies. Unable to sleep in his tiny New York City apartment, he would seek relief at the many movie theaters outside his doorway. He would see three movies a day to escape his tiny apartment off Times Square, even though he was broke and couldn't afford it.[40] He watched the Marlon Brando movie *The Men* four times in a row over two sleep-challenged days and *A Place in the Sun* three times for the same reason.[41] Dean's habit of wrongly giving the impression to all the right people in power that he was arrogant and slovenly may have arisen from his chronic insomnia, although he may also later have developed and suffered from narcissistic tendencies that exaggerated his sartorial defiance. Staying out most of the night with friends and then often playing his bongo drums until the early morning hours in a sleepless daze also meant being late the next day for rehearsals, irritable moods, and unkempt dress and manner. His insomnia may have also fueled his reckless sense of attention seeking. Friends in Hollywood recalled how he once disappeared from a small party without explanation. He was eventually found sitting in the middle of a busy nearby street in a chair, calmly smoking a cigarette and ignoring the swerving, honking cars, until they shouted at him to return to safety. He laughed and chided his friends' ashen expressions, wondering why they never got bored.[42] Perhaps as a result of these incidents, which are numerous from his acquaintances' perspectives, his friends learned early on to separate from Dean when, as photographer and pal Dennis Stock called it, Dean "got into one of his moods."[43] Likewise, Dean sensed their pulling away because of a condition he could not control. The echoes of his childhood loss of his mother with his later adult relationships do not have to be seen in any Freudian light in order to see just how fragile James Dean's sense of well-being was at any given moment. From his wounded self-perspective—the only one we each can see with unfaltering clarity, it seems—if he allowed himself to overcome his doubts that all who loved him would soon abandon him, as had his mother from the wounded child's view, then he exposed himself to their kindness and love being suddenly taken away if he had a foul mood swing. And as he could not but help to have a mood swing, Dean early in his life recognized the impossibility of his position, and that he was doomed to a lifetime of perpetual loneliness. In so many ways, Dean was an eternal child forever being chastised by his emotional caretakers for being a bad boy (and therefore deserving of the silent treatment and all that it implies). Whereas if Dean rejected them outright before they could inevitably leave him, he would, at least in one deeply personal clinical sense, be expunging a repetition of his mother's abandoning death rather than only being beholden to a negative reliving of it. But whether he left his loved ones or they left him, the grueling, endless cycle of cyclothymic attraction and repulsion Dean experienced with each new person who entered his life would always, in the end, leave James Dean alone and wondering why he should continue living. Fame, money, power, sex, and all the other wall trophies a neurotypical might understandably utilize to bolster sagging self-esteem never squelched Dean's restless gloom for very long, but then, how could they? For between the time James Dean had purchased a new sports car to take his mind off his own mental illness and when he later showed up to take delivery, he had become an entirely different personality in mood, and recklessly disappeared into the winding hills of Hollywood's version of immortality.

Among his many personal effects—some of which he had given away shortly before his death, which leads many to speculate he was borderline suicidal in the days before the crash—was a personal scrapbook.[44] It contained articles Dean had deemed inspirational and worth remembering when he was depressed. One article he evidently cherished was written by fellow depressive Tennessee Williams. The Williams clipping was expressly about how important the creative work is to the personality of the person who gives it life. In this sense, as his collaborator and friend Nicholas Ray observed of James Dean during their making of *Rebel without a Cause*, Dean was akin to a starving animal always in search of food in emotional intensity. There was, as Ray, his fellow bipolar sufferer, knew all too well, a mountain of sadness behind the mask of indifference Dean could wear and wear out. "The affection he rejected was the affection that had once been his and found no answer,"[45] Ray summarized. Such is not an uncommon fate for those with rapid-cycling mood disorders. The obvious and understandable toll this disorder causes on loved ones and distressed friends creates a regrettable, but often necessary, distance between sufferer and supporters during acute manic-depressive cycling.[46] Ironically, and tragically, it is when the cyclothymic is often hostile and negative in nature that he needs the unconditional love that he rejects from others. This truly maddening situation is in a sense like being on an emotional merry-go-round in which the bipolar person is forever opposite from family and friends, as they all spin around a central fulcrum of life, unable to overcome the force pulling them away from one another. It is why rapid-cycling manic-depressives must often endure long stretches of social and personal isolation, and equally, why those who are productive but cyclothymic may cherish the intensity and expurgation that dramatic catharsis offers them in lieu of relationships offering the same possibility.

This much was at least true for James Dean, who recognized his bipolarity and his gift for acting in high school and unified them as twin themes in his work with the monologue he chose for a school talent show. Dean took "The Madman" from Dickens's *The Pickwick Papers*, a spiritual descendent of Poe's "The Tell-Tale Heart." The raving monologue Dean delivered has the tortured sufferer bark to the audience at one point, "It's a fine thing to be mad!" His drama teacher, Mrs. Nall Brookshire, was impressed by the mercurial changes of temperament the teenaged actor underwent in the astonishing, nuanced performance he gave that night.[47] Though tragically short-lived, Dean's life can also be viewed as an improbable personal and artistic achievement beyond seeming ability, given the gravity of his emotional disorder. It is possible to see that Dean's triumph was not only over his disorder for short-lived moments of personal ecstasy, but due in no small part because of his disorder, and his need to constantly address it with acting in order to alleviate some of his illness's worst aspects. His innate talent, fueled by true emotional instability, gave rise to what remains some of the clearest, most compelling, expressive visualizations ever yet made in cinema of the ravages and ecstasies of rapid-cycling bipolarity.

HITCHCOCK'S *VERTIGO*: A CASE STUDY IN BIPOLAR CINEMA

Jimmy Stewart was seen during much of his fabled career as the friendly, self-effacing archetype of the American everyman. His comical ability to mask any hint of his characters' dark sides made him seem the perfect embodiment of sincerity and likeability to most moviegoers for decades. But despite this perception of sunny, if cautious, optimism personified, the reality for Stewart as a person was much different. In his own life, he suffered from bouts of depression[48] that became more and more difficult to both mask and overcome as he aged. The tragic death of his son in Vietnam, a war that Stewart vocally, if dryly, had supported in the press, exacerbated his bouts of recurring depression severely enough that he became semireclusive for stretches of time.[49] Two of the greatest film performances he ever gave were in Frank

Capra's *It's a Wonderful Life* (1946) and later in Alfred Hitchcock's brooding *Vertigo* (1958), and both of these performances centered around revelatory sequences in which the usually stalwart, amiable Stewart persona has a nervous breakdown and emotional disorder to the point of suicidal despair. Thus, it is worth considering to what degree Stewart's personal struggles informed and influenced these superb realizations of an individual undergoing an acute episode of severe, sustained depression.

Capra's *It's a Wonderful Life* has been a yuletide holiday tradition in American television programming for decades, and is justly celebrated for its memorable final reel of civic redemption for the maligned George Bailey (James Stewart). But despite the sequences of high comedy and charm, the film has, as its core, a heart of darkness. Stewart is driven by the film's events to actively consider and then attempt suicide as a means of escaping the financial and emotional turmoil of his life one fateful Christmas Eve. Only when the depressed Bailey has leaped from a snow-covered bridge into the icy waters is he miraculously rescued by his guardian angel, shown the error of his ways, and given the proverbial second chance in life. All well and good, but it is during these moments in which Stewart struggles with his sanity and decides that he has lost it, once and for all, that *It's a Wonderful Life* achieves its darkest, and yet finest, minutes of screen hypnosis. Set in the bar where he once found companionship and solace but now feels only personal shame and loss of identity, Stewart's sweating, tension-stretched face is darkly lit to nearly fill the frame, as his rendition of George Bailey gives way to what is surely a co-joined personal revelation of Jimmy Stewart as depressive. Bailey mumbles, biting his lip, his nervous eyes brimming over with withheld tears, a striking, empathetic study in emotional instability. Capra wisely holds on Stewart in lingering, shattering close-up, isolating us with George Bailey and forcing the viewer to experience his inner crisis. It hurts to watch because it is a remarkably factual expression of the psychological torture of acute anxiety and suicidal ideation.

But as darkly insightful as his depressive moments in *It's a Wonderful Life* are, it is his role as Detective Scottie Ferguson in *Vertigo* that truly is a masterful turn in self-restraint as actor. For most of the film, Stewart's Scottie is a carefree, if bored, workaholic, recently sidelined because of clinical vertigo. But halfway through the film, Stewart winds up in a mental hospital, completely catatonic, experiencing a severe, lingering depression for months on end after the tragic death of a woman whom he loved. This exceptionally sensitive sequence is a tour de force for all involved. This is especially true for Scottie's doting female friend Midge Wood (Barbara Bel Geddes), who visits the slack-faced, unresponsive Scottie while Scottie recovers in his private sanitarium room. His depressive downfall is cinematically conveyed by Hitchcock in a brilliant bit of visual conceit in which Stewart experiences a series of unfolding nightmares. The dreaming Scottie sees himself falling to his own death and into an infinitely deep abyss that turns out to be his own grave site before he springs awake, eyes haunted with horror, to so-called reality, which for Scottie has become, from this moment forward, anything but reality, in terms of his sanity. The traditional reading of this scene, in which a lifeless puppet of Stewart is seen falling to its demise, legs and arms akimbo, is that Hitchcock is expressing Scottie's morbid fear of heights. This is certainly true, but equally, Hitchcock is externalizing Scottie's literal fall into deep depression. This is borne out by the fact the scene ends with a fade to black and then a fade in to Scottie already in the sanitarium, thus forcing the viewer to cover much narrative ground that has occurred off-screen (such as Scottie's diagnosis, intake as patient, etc.). The giant, green-tinged, cut-out face of Stewart, rendered in almost Warhol-like pop intensity with garish primary colors, as it plunges into the shaft of a grave, the frozen face flashing in and out of existence, eyes blanked by the terror of nothingness, is as visually literal an expression of the sinking feeling of depression as has ever been rendered.

Midge continues a dialogue with Scottie despite the fact that Scottie sits catatonic, apparently not hearing a word. She attempts a form of therapy by playing classical music designed to spark an emotional catharsis in the afflicted patient. Midge remarks about how the doctors have it all figured now, with "music for melancholics," perfect for Scottie, as it is the one that "sweeps away the mental cobwebs." Alas, Scottie remains motionless, eyes transfixed on empty space, facial expression slack. Despairing at his evident illness, Midge cries, "You don't even know I'm here, do you?" Stewart's portrayal is so spot-on for accuracy one understands Midge's frustrated concern. He feels the heaviness of merely sitting in a chair as intolerable, experiences silently felt agony that overpowers any attempt by loved ones to distract him. Stewart's manner of playing Scottie as a being trapped in his own low-energy life form, unable or unwilling to escape its own psychic imprisonment after being worn down by innumerable, unknown previous failures to do so, is devastating. His eyes remain haunted by a glimpse of some off-screen horror so monstrous, just the thought of it leaves him emptied of any ability to live.

Now consider this sequence of Scottie's catatonic depression in contrast to Stewart's earlier portrait of suicidal George Bailey in his blackest moment of personal despair. Both are laudatory, and both are clinically accurate to the shades of depression. But the differences are what make them so striking, at least seen back-to-back. Whereas George Bailey is riddled with expressive anxiety sweating from his tension-stretched pores, a study in clutching desperation and edged on the pit of a psychological hell to come, Scottie Ferguson is a man already rendered immobile and mute by his excessive depressive episode, who has already seen too much hell on Earth to care what lies beyond nonexistence. His prognosis as told to Midge by Scottie's psychiatrist is not promising. "He's suffering from acute melancholia together with a guilt complex," Scottie's doctor (Raymond Bailey) informs her, further explaining that his recovery is unknowable, but will take at least six months to a year to accomplish if they're lucky. The heartbreaking shot in which Midge resigns herself to the futility of any current treatment lingers after the initial viewing as a moment of genuine, not melodramatic, pathos. It is a moving testament to the many such moments of private agony family members have had to endure on behalf of their suffering bipolar loved ones as they leave them, yet again, in the care of a psychiatric shelter while they return to a home that is not quite home, at least for the time being. Hitchcock holds on Midge as she slowly walks down the long hallway of uncertainty, shrinking with each step as she recedes from the viewer into nothingness (as indeed, does her character from this point forward in the complex narrative). Midge has accepted that while Scottie's recovery may be an uncertainty, it is for certain that any hopes she had of ever loving Scottie as the man he was before are forever gone. This proves to be the last straw for her, and she leaves the film dejected, bereft of hope, again a shattering but accurate portrait not only of the many who have fallen to episodic depression, but also of their fallen loved ones, who have had to endure private heartache for the patient.

The other well-wrought state of alienation shared by many bipolars that Hitchcock renders in *Vertigo* is more commonly known and appreciated. Obsession, and even erotic obsession, is the clear theme Hitchcock is exploring in his relentlessly introspective look at Scottie Ferguson (whom Hitchcock described as "an emotional man")[50] in what is now regarded as one of the more personally laden self-avatars in Hitchcock's body of work profiling disturbed minds. Hitchcock's own well-documented need to control and dominate his self-created Hitchcock-Blonde archetype starlets in reality[51] is mirrored precisely in Scottie's pleading need to have Judy Barton (Kim Novak in a dual role) wear exactly the same clothes and makeup and to walk the same way as did his deceased lover, Madeleine. These obsessive thoughts are expressions of Hitchcock's own compulsion to control the lives of others, therefore controlling his own more completely in the process. This need suggests a profound disturbance in the director's internal emotional landscape. Obsessive thoughts and actions are clinical markers for possible bipolar diagnosis,[52] and certainly Scottie is exhibiting all the signs of an unhealthy mental obsession when he tries to transform Judy into the living ghost of Madeleine. It is a morbidly fixated state of clinical depression that borders on psychosis in its intensity of display by the woman-stalking Scottie. Likewise, by insisting on personally selecting the wardrobe, and even social appearances at times, for such contractually bound actresses as Grace Kelly and Kim Novak, Hitchcock was not merely being professionally diligent, but openly and deviantly acting out his own darker fantasies with reckless disregard for the possible personal and professional repercussions, which is again a sign of possible mental disorder.[53] His emotional fixations spilled over into *Vertigo*, in that he was livid with Vera Miles, whom he had under contract for the role, when she became pregnant before shooting. He subsequently blamed the fact *Vertigo* was only a break-even picture (a failure from Hitchcock's point of view) on Jimmy Stewart being "too old" and Novak's being "a terrible actress."[54] But one hinted reality in his muted comments about Miles implies that he transferred much of his disappointment onto Novak, not unlike Scottie transferring Madeleine's personality onto Judy by proxy in *Vertigo* (and to equal frustration with the results).

While *Vertigo* concentrates its narrative viewpoint largely to the confines of Scottie's vantage point until late in its length, the entire picture is built around Hitchcock's dreamlike cinematic stalking of Kim Novak in her dual roles. Novak's perfectly sculpted beauty, the remoteness in her cool blue eyes, combines with her physical allure and imbues her with a controlled sexuality. Truffaut characterized it a "bestial aspect of hers"[55] which gives her "excitement," as he called it. Reviewers could be far less kind, implying she was simply not emotive in some roles, as Hitchcock's own negative assessment of her talent demonstrates. But time and distance change perspectives, especially when motion pictures are concerned. *Vertigo* is now widely regarded as not only one of Hitchcock's finest films, but one of *the* finest films, ever made. *Sight and Sound*, in a somewhat controversial but refreshing choice, listed it at number one of the "Top 50 Greatest Films of All Time" in a polling of 846 leading critics, toppling the colossus of *Citizen Kane* into second position.[56] Kim Novak is now considered perfectly cast as the self-conscious (but understandably so) Madeleine, a stunning beauty who is unbalanced by fears she is losing her mind. Likewise, when she returns to the picture as Judy, she embodies the uncertainty of a deceptive former lover with a nervous, if irritable, restraint. In its time, her performance was seen, even by its own director, as deficient for its flattened qualities. But with the admission by Kim Novak in 2012 during the taping of a *TCM* interview that she had been struggling with severe bipolarity during *Vertigo*'s production, the admirable stoicism her character exudes, particularly as the mentally afflicted Madeleine, took on new significance in terms of bipolar cinema entries.

"I was not diagnosed until much later. I go through more of the depression than the mania part,"[57] she told interviewer Robert Osborne at the 2012 edition of the TCM Classic Film Festival. She eloquently, though in tears, explained that much of her career was an endless series of painful misunderstandings, both of her by studio executives (who only wanted to cast her as a Monroe copy) and by herself (for she denied the severity of her affliction until much later in her life). Her further admission that the key performances of her career—*Vertigo*, *Picnic* (1955), and *Pal Joey* (1957)—were made under the fluctuations of severe mood disorder make each a unique look into the manner in which bipolarity is manifested not consciously, but subconsciously, by the affected performer. This is because Novak was able to channel her disorder into her acting without any self-awareness that she was doing so (owing to her undiagnosed status).

Novak came from a painful background marked with many of the recurrent biographical similarities we have seen in others who had a parent who was mentally ill. For Novak, it was her bipolar father Joseph who was the source of much childhood unhappiness.[58] Though the family maintained a normal facade, their dysfunctionality was severe, with her depressive father often giving way to rages. She instinctively knew to use this deep emotional hurt in her earliest work, realizing it was the perfect well-spring to release her pent-up feelings, buried in shame since childhood. "I was used to having conflict in the home, so having conflict on a set . . . felt normal,"[59] she explained to Osborne. This was how she was able to sustain the bombardment of massive egos from such directors as Hitchcock and tough studio moguls such as Harry Cohn, to whom she was under contract, and not give in to her own painful episodes of depression and occasional mania. But the overly controlling nature of her overbearing employers wore her down, and unable to keep her sanity and the loss of it secret in a town used to publicizing the slightest indiscretion, Novak fled Hollywood rather than endure a series of humiliating headlines, as had Frances Farmer and Gene Tierney. She has maintained a long-term marriage by living in a rural setting and utilizing painting as therapy. But Novak lamented her decision to walk away from her craft, feeling that if she had only been properly diagnosed while she was still acting, she would have been able to maintain her career.[60] Hers was a case where the trade-off of losing acting as therapy was eclipsed by the need to maintain her sanity without acting's attendant, toxic celebrity-hood.

The case of *Vertigo* as an essential example of bipolar cinema would be incomplete without a final glance at the master of filmic ceremonies. Alfred Hitchcock was fascinated with unbalanced states of psychological being in most of his films. While it is certain that this is in part because Hitchcock realized the keen value of having a complex villain in his pictures (in order to make the threat level seem sufficiently raised against his endangered protagonists), it is also quite accurate to suggest Hitchcock himself suffered from some profoundly darker personal emotions. He once told Truffaut in a series of 1962 interviews about his career that the "fears" one finds buried deeply within *Vertigo* were "probably me, within myself."[61] Whether or not any of them were sufficiently hindering in his life to have warranted a medical diagnosis of clinical depression is debatable, but documented as possibility, especially toward the end of his fabled career. Donald Spoto's *The Dark Side of Genius: The Life of Alfred Hitchcock* is rife with anecdotes from those who knew him and from the master of suspense himself culled from many years of in-depth personal and professional interviews Hitchcock gave during his career that suggest he struggled with depression throughout his life. He admitted in one revealing interview that the single biggest influence he ever had as a young man was the works of bipolar author Edgar Allan Poe, whom Hitchcock felt was singularly superb for evoking states of psychological terror and suspense in his readers.[62] Hitchcock went so far as to say that most of his work was an attempt to emulate Poe, but in cinematic terms, at least as far as creatively instilling the mood of psychological disintegration Poe had so adroitly done in his readers. While most readers who love Poe's work are not on the spectrum, Hitchcock's confession that the attraction was based as much on Poe's melancholic nature as for his deft use of psychological manipulation and literary ability alone indicates he may have felt such profound states himself. "I happened to first read his biography and the sadness of his life made a great impression on me," Hitchcock told an interviewer. "I felt an enormous pity for him, because in spite of his talent he had never been happy."[63] This could almost read as a statement of self-admission given the many accounts of Hitchcock's own morbid state of emotions and dire agitations. Again, Hitchcock's profound love of Poe starts not with the author's works themselves but undoubtedly the leap of identification he had with Poe as a human being with artistic talent who had endured self-tortured states of existence. We note again the unusual influence of Poe on future melancholics who will produce lasting works of cinematic greatness. Surely this is no mere coincidence. It suggests, at the least, that if great minds do not think alike, then disordered ones certainly do.

It is noteworthy that Hitchcock, not unlike Chaplin and Welles, knew emotional hardship from an early age due to a mood-disordered parent. Hitchcock worked from early his teenage years on to support his physically ill father and his mentally ill mother; the latter had succumbed to a lingering state of chronic depression by the time Hitchcock was but fifteen years of age.[64] Recall the treatment of Midge from *Vertigo* as she painfully slinks away when she realizes the severity of Scottie's depression. Or more obviously, in a biographical sense, Norman Bates's browbeaten submission to his beloved but invalid "mother" in *Psycho*. Clearly, Hitchcock's greatest cinematic moments are often tied to examinations of how the mentally ill affect those around them, often to initially subtle but finally debilitating degrees. As previous accounts of mood disordered directors and actors have demonstrated, establishing whether or not a familial mental illness exists is paramount in early assessment for the most accurate diagnosis. Certainly the hardship of his family life was a factor in Hitchcock's depressive temperament. He once tearfully remarked of the aching loneliness of his childhood wherein he felt emotionally abandoned.[65] Toward the latter part of his life, Universal could no longer in good conscience finance his features, but paradoxically felt the need to continue his contract and allow him to work on dead-end projects. This was a fate the industry-astute Hitchcock must have realized was the final curtain to his storied career, akin to receiving the gold watch at a company reception in his honor. Indeed, it was not long thereafter that the morbid director was given a Lifetime Achievement Award by AFI, which must have only aggravated his sense of impending mortality. Hitchcock's behavior became so angrily depressive and then mutely morose that the studio privately worried about his health. They could not keep secretarial help available for him to utilize in story sessions because of his increasingly desperate and illegal sexual advances.[66] Hitchcock's rapid decline without his beloved filmmaking as therapeutic catharsis is obvious subsequent to his being put out to pasture by the studio heads, though blame is hard to assign in retrospect given the severity of Hitchcock's declining emotional state. During his artistic peak years (which were formidable and genre-defining), Alfred Hitchcock explored a range of deviant psychiatric mind-sets, and doubtless at least some of them were personally and profoundly understood. Sadly, after the filmmaker concluded the day's shooting, at least when alone with his own troubled thoughts at home and at night, Hitchcock probably wrestled with mental phantoms. His struggles with his personal demons, however, resulted in surely some of the most insightful cinematic works dealing with mental and emotional disturbances ever made. *Vertigo* is his true crowning achievement, a filmic masterpiece of mordant mood swings, whose key factor of having been made by three hugely talented, bipolar or unipolar depressive creators should not be underestimated in terms of critical evaluation or as a major contributory influence in its production.

LUST FOR LIFE AND THE ENFORCED LONELINESS OF MOOD DISORDERS

Many films concentrate on the manic or depressive aspects of bipolarity without truly delving into the overall cumulative effect of such disorders on the social aspects of their sufferers. As earlier noted, silent cinema was rife with stereotypes showing dangerous lunatics running amok and pathetic depressives sitting alone or in cloistered, lethargic groups in dark sanitarium rooms. Early sound cinema was not much more progressive, with most films showing manic-depressives only during such episodes, not in their calm, rational times. In fact, very few films until the later years of sound cinema, such as *A Bill of Divorcement* (1932), ever attempted to even suggest that a manic-depressive was ever more than constantly unbalanced, and therefore fully deserving of the ill treatment they traditionally received in various screen cameos. What these erroneous visions of manic depression miss, of course, is the struggle that bipolars undergo when they are their "normal selves," and that they often face enormous personal, uphill struggles to repair damaged relationships with business associates, friends, and family caused by their destructive behaviors.[67] Even the most well-meaning and sensitive of bipolar patients in recovery must often resolve the understandable hostility and resentment from those who have had to endure the worst of the disorder's pains directed at them. Loved ones are further called upon to selflessly forgive the afflicted person yet again, excusing the breakdown to the disorder. This eternal cycle of shattering and rebuilding emotional trust typically becomes too self-defeating in feel to endure for most neurotypical persons who are in relationships with bipolars. Thus the sense that many manic-depressives have that they will be soon abandoned by loved ones is, to some self-fulfilling extent, not entirely without truth. And yet, in order to regain emotional health and sustain any recovery, a bipolar in remission needs the same as any individual in modern society, and this does not exclude the necessity of friendships and a sense of belonging to a community.[68] Hence the nature of the tenuous social boulder the Sisyphus-like bipolar must always strain to push uphill, knowing full-well that the inevitable back slide into loneliness and self-recrimination soon to occur will erase many of those hard-fought gains.

This is why *Lust for Life* (1956) is so novel, as it delves into the issues of friendship and loyalty in regard to bipolar disorder with such honesty and relevancy. The biography of Vincent van Gogh was based on the novel from 1934 by Irving Stone, which itself was taken from the candid letters Vincent sent his art dealer brother, Theo, throughout their close-knit lives. Often noted for its largely accurate look into the creation of the Dutch painter's works, *Lust for Life* is also formidable as a screen exercise in bipolar depictions. The manner in which Vincent van Gogh (played by Kirk Douglas) goes in and out of periods of depressive hopelessness and manic artistic fever is fully realized by former set designer turned director Vincente Minnelli. He often incorporates many of van Gogh's most haunting images into the mesmerizing set pieces, bringing them to three-dimensional life. But while it remains faithful to van Gogh's biography in terms of where and when, the revelatory aspects of *Lust for Life* are contained in the way in which it shows van Gogh's delicate, perpetual balancing act between self-sustaining artist and self-destructing madman, particularly as it comes to his stormy, disastrous personal affairs. Vincent is unable to maintain any relationships of any significance, save largely from afar with Theo, whom van Gogh obsessively writes, often when he's in a manic or hypomanic state. Paul Gauguin (Anthony Quinn) stays with Vincent for a brief period in an attempt to offer the lonely van Gogh companionship, but it soon becomes apparent that both men suffer from mental disorders beyond either man's ability to control or modify. The clinging, needy van Gogh (played with superb humility by Douglas) at first smothers the rough-edged Gauguin like a mother nursing a sick child when Gauguin arrives. But in little time, the two are arguing and fighting to the point of threatened, and then nearly attempted, homicide. The tempestuous nature of their on-again/off-again friendship, in which they also occasionally share gratifying moments of quieter elucidation and a profound passion for creating personal art at any cost, is a bravura realization capturing the instability and inherent madness of bipolar disorder. The manner in which Douglas plays van Gogh's growing realization that he is driving away his best and only friend is illustrative. Vincent's sense of abandonment gnawing at his core is bracingly anguished, as he is forced to realize he is himself both the cause of his despair *and* the prevention of his ever being cured of it. Another telling moment occurs when van Gogh attempts to kill Gauguin after Gauguin makes plans to abandon

Vincent as roommate. The seething look on Douglas's face reveals conflicted feelings of depressive self-loathing and manic outward hatred of
others clashing for supremacy. It is as if Vincent cannot decide whether
or not to kill Gauguin first, or not at all, before he certainly suicides. For
sheer pathos, it is unparalleled in accuracy. It therefore makes dramatic
sense when in the next sequence Vincent turns the knife he was to
slaughter his best friend with on his own ear. This scene is thankfully
only suggested by Minnelli, not shown in graphic detail, but actually
makes the impact much more traumatic, in that one must imagine the
event to a soundtrack of Douglas's off-screen scream. Only when confronted with the mutilation does Gauguin begin to understand how
deeply rooted is Vincent's sickness, and he reacts with a stunned sense
of quiet shame. Gauguin realizes his friend Vincent is beyond conventional help, and that even painting may not offer enough solace to
prevent suicide. Implicit in Quinn's Academy Award–winning performance is also the grace note that his own character, touched as Gauguin
is with evident madness, may suffer a similar fate himself. Thus his stay
with Vincent has not been merely a sojourn to paint, but a glimpse into
Gauguin's own possible future. Given that many now consider Gauguin
also bipolar depressive[69] in nature based on his own troubled writings,
albeit more aggressively manic in tone and turmoil than van Gogh's
subdued, depressive persona, the worried expression Quinn chooses for
his Gauguin in this moment of chilling discovery is dramatically, as well
as historically, prescient.

Much of the credit for the portrait of van Gogh's mental illness must
go to Kirk Douglas. His range of emotions is as large as was his character's sense of color and movement in his paintings. But the ferocity and
then tenderness of his mercurially timed performance would not have
worked without Minnelli's sense of pacing and staging. First Minnelli
confines Douglas in a cage of rage when he's housebound and cannot
paint owing to weather or personal frailty, and alternately sets Douglas
free to be wildly manic amid the windswept wheat field workers as the
Dutch artist frantically attempts to capture every motion and movement of the light. This directorial pattern is constructed deliberately
into the narrative. It begins with Vincent's failure in the claustrophobic
coal mines in which he attempts as a wayward member of the clergy to
attend to the needs of the mine's impoverished, grime-covered people.
The task is hopeless, but pious van Gogh cannot help but fulfill the

scriptures he has read and loved in the most literal manner, giving away his clothes to the poor and living in such destitution along with his flock. The visiting clergymen are offended not because Vincent is ineffective, but because his dire personal state of existence threatens the well-clothed church members' sense of worldly entitlement and decorum. Here is the very nature of the tempestuous storm that engulfed Catholicism versus the reformist Protestant religions encoded in a screen conflict—the need to maintain ritual and rich custom over practicality and sobriety—rendered on-screen. It is also a perceptive illustration of religious mania's insistent need to be morally pure at any and all costs, often blindly allowing, or even occasioning, violence to arise in order to stop the adherents' personified evils. It is thematically resonant that van Gogh's approach threatens to undermine the patronage of the priests that for centuries helped keep the very people they supposedly serve in virtual slavery to the mines and their ruling-class owners. For in *Lust for Life*, van Gogh's lust is not merely to realize his will to create over the chaos of his own disordered mind, but likewise to challenge the often calcified moral forces of authority he feels are the root source of his restless resentments. This is a shadow play being enacted by van Gogh, one soon realizes, in that his own bipolarity is larger than any windmills he might eventually slay as self-anointed Don Quixote. But Vincent needs these challenges not because he feels he can actually accomplish them, but as a form of caustic therapy. Only by projecting his own internal giants of disarray and despair onto existing institutions bigger than himself can van Gogh hope to slay them in externalized form. So he targets a negligent church system, or a ruling class who have failed humanity, or a school of self-appointed art critics who keep innovation in painting from occurring, and so on. This psychological construction is nuanced, complex, and ultimately accurate as a portrait of many individuals who are bipolar and politically oriented. Real-life manic-depressive figures of crusading reformation are diverse in example. Mary Todd Lincoln was entrenched in support of her husband—he himself subject to fits of depression—against his many foes,[70] some real and a few perhaps summoned from her manic-depressive paranoia. On the other extreme, bipolar Larry Flynt engaged in his own endless exposés of the latest corrupt Washington figures he deemed personally unworthy of public support in the pages of *Hustler*.[71] It should be noted both figures share one other quality: they were enormously effective in their respective activities.

Such sensitivity to bipolar illness is not surprising when one considers that one of Vincente Minnelli's great loves (and his first wife) was Judy Garland, who was manic-depressive.[72] With six years of marriage before their divorce, Minnelli was Garland's true confidant and loyal supporter. He endured many years of trying times with her well-documented bouts of elation and depression, as well as her disorder-fueled addiction to prescription pills. Likewise, Minnelli himself suffered from bouts of intense melancholia.[73] This was acute earlier in his career when he was unable to penetrate the Hollywood corridors of power as successfully as he desired. Drawing from his perspectives living with Judy Garland and his own blues surely must have influenced his own artistic choices given that in both *Lust for Life* and *Two Weeks in Another Town* (1962), Minnelli explored manic depression with a keen understanding few had mastered in previous films about the subject matter. Both starred Kirk Douglas as a manic-depressive protagonist who actively deals with his disorder by ruthlessly applying himself to the creation of art in one form or another (in *Lust for Life*, it is painting; in *Two Weeks in Another Town*, it is film acting). Along with his sanitarium-set film *The Cobweb* (1955), which is actually a study of the staff rather than the inmates à la 1935's *Private Worlds*, Minnelli was clearly fascinated by the world of mood disorders and their influence on creative individuals.

VIVIEN LEIGH ON A STREETCAR NAMED DESPAIR

English actress Vivien Leigh's famous discovery by David Selznick on the set of *Gone with the Wind*'s fiery destruction of Atlanta sequence and her subsequent casting in the coveted but still unfilled role of Scarlett O'Hara is legendary. Leigh's prolonged battle with bipolar disorder is less enshrined in the annals of filmdom. She won an Academy Award for her portrait of the high-strung southern belle and, in her portrayal, created a definitive turn as a manipulative brat turned lifelong survivor who must overcome a series of painfully failed relationships, the death of her parents, the destruction of her entire way of life, and her own lingering bouts of mood instability. For Leigh imbues

Scarlett not with just all the understandable grace, charm, and arch sense of society her character would have been raised to experience, but with an underlying, impulsive hypomania for grabbing whatever she reasons is hers to take, whether that be power, privilege, or men. When *Gone with the Wind* begins Scarlett thinks of herself as deserving of all good things in her amply rich way of life, with a bland dismissal of "fiddle dee dee!" to any and all of life's profound horrors. In her manic zeal to control her surroundings and the people around her, carefully compartmentalizing each pawn on the grand chessboard for maximum personal gain, Scarlett O'Hara becomes a personification of egomaniacal selfishness. As the film progresses she is properly seen as the epitome of why the South was doomed to lose the Civil War, an emblem of a stubborn refusal to change either customs or beliefs, even in the face of inevitable and often catastrophic reckonings that ensue from such rigid thinking. Despite enormous forces aligned openly against her, Scarlett vows to never be broken, a hypomanic juggernaut of self-determinism. Surely a better distillation of the insidious blindness that the manic and hypomanic phases of bipolar disorder can cause in those under its genetic spell would be harder to conjure in female screen siren form, until perhaps *Sunset Boulevard* (1950). In her turn as reactive agent to each moody turn of tragic events, Vivien Leigh's haughty arrogance gives way to pensive anxiety and even to outright despair with mercurial speed, astonishing the viewer with her sudden range of emotive display. A reviewer who saw Leigh's stage performance in the 1935 production of *The Mark of Virtue* wrote of her magical ability to fluidly alter expressions, noting it as a "lightning change"[74] that came over her face, and this same evident quality is at work in her Scarlett O'Hara creation. It was also the quality that led her to on-set conflicts with replacement director Victor Fleming and co-star Leslie Howard, who reacted negatively to her inexplicable and unknown disorder.[75] Her illness was likely exaggerated by a prolonged work separation from Laurence Olivier, who acted as her stabilizing influence when she experienced episodes. Her fellow star Olivia de Havilland felt the need to defend Leigh against accusations, decades later in Olivier's autobiography, that her bipolar behavior was the cause of many of *Gone with the Wind*'s delays. She denied it and praised Leigh for her professionalism on the film.[76] But clearly, the fact that Olivia de Havilland felt the need to address such rumors says volumes about how pernicious such gossip was, and its prevalence.

It is not merely that Leigh is flighty or manipulative that makes her performance of Scarlett so endlessly mesmerizing, a key ingredient to the film's enduring popularity. It is that she is beneath it all still so supernaturally and calmly in control. She seeks to extend this hard-fought veneer onto such larger-than-life calamities as wars, marriage, and even the death of a child, and that makes Leigh's Scarlett O'Hara bitterly worthy of our admiration as silent observers. Hers is a heroine who is unbreakable not because she is rescued by any gallant gentleman, but because of sheer, dogged ability to survive with her fractured wits by any means necessary. This despite her own worst instincts, which are plentiful and self-ruinous. This was a very personal performance by Leigh's admission, in that she self-characterized her own stubborn qualities as paramount to her joys and sorrows in her personal life. "I cannot let well enough alone," she said. "I am a very impatient person and headstrong. If I've made up my mind to do something, I can't be persuaded out of it."[77] Off-stage her rigidity was problematic, as Leigh's life illustrated, but in her film and stage performances, it added a quality of hypnotic allure. After all, it is hard as an audience to dislike such a strong-willed character unless she is unusually cruel or evil, as we find ourselves projecting ourselves into such shows of character clarity and defiant self-determination much more easily than, say, identifying with a less distinctly drawn character whose conflicts and desires remain non-empathetic. Leigh's winning the Oscar for Best Actress that year was much deserved even in retrospect, a fate not always true for many who remain obscure today despite former Academy Award recognition.

Her love affair with Laurence Olivier would make them one of the most romantically celebrated couples in international filmdom, a constant source of paparazzi delight as they flew back and forth between England and America and paused long enough in each country for the obligatory welcoming shots in the airport concourse. In one such event, they staged a press moment that still exists in photographs, with Marilyn Monroe in tow as she headed to England to work on the Olivier-directed *The Prince and the Showgirl* (1957). In the tarmac-styled snapshot, a mature, bipolar Vivien Leigh smiles at the cameras while a maturing bipolar Marilyn Monroe sheepishly grins, each actress flanked by their famous spouses, Olivier and Arthur Miller, respectively. Olivier remarked at his wife's ability to charm the media even when depressed,[78] and he depended upon her to put on the better face that he himself lacked the grace to necessarily invoke in more private encounters rather than scripted roles. The couple worked together frequently, or as it would later develop, as frequently as Leigh's chronic manic depression would allow her to be dependable. But like many successful performers, Vivien Leigh was able to perform in spite of, and was even enabled by, her disorder more often than not. Olivier recounted years later his first encounter in 1937 with Leigh and her chronic condition. They were backstage at the Old Vic Theatre in England costarring in *Hamlet* as directed by Olivier. Leigh began screaming at him without provocation as he listened on, too stunned to react. She just as suddenly shifted into a nearly catatonic state, silently staring at the dressing room walls and seemingly completely oblivious to Olivier's worried pleading. As if by some miracle, she went on stage in her part as Ophelia moments later and performed it brilliantly and without a fault, leaving him doubly perplexed as to the true nature of his wife's obvious mental illness.[79] Alas, it was but the beginning of a long series of incidents in which Olivier would be left wondering about the hope of their marriage as she succumbed with more frequency into longer and more debilitating episodes of bipolar disorder.

By 1945, the episodes had degenerated into physical violence, with Leigh attacking Olivier during the filming of *Caeser and Cleopatra* (1945) only to break down sobbing on the floor in abject despair.[80] The frequency and predictability of Vivien Leigh's emotional cycles became well-known to Laurence Olivier, so much so that he knew the signs of an impending onset. First Leigh would become obsessively interested in her latest acting project or related endeavor, spending days and nights unable to stop thinking about it. As if an invisible brake were suddenly pumped, she would crash into a deep depression, followed by an explosive outburst in which she verbally, and even occasionally physically, abused any and all in her presence. She would experience fits of cleaning mania in which she could not stop tidying her surroundings even when pristine clean, and shortly before having an episode, Leigh would often divest herself of all of her jewelry as if averse to it on her skin.[81] After an angry tirade, Leigh would collapse into a state of near unconsciousness. She would sheepishly emerge with no recall of her earlier behavior as her mystified husband explained how badly she had behaved during her latest episode. She was filled with guilt and remorse over her inability to control her breakdowns and her tirades against those whom she loved. It sadly only furthered her sense of despair, as there was little Olivier or the medical field could offer by way of hope for effective treatment. She would try shock therapy after being admitted to Netherne Psychiatric Hospital in England after a prolonged period of instability, but the results were horrific to her, wiping out her memory and leaving her, in her own words, "worse than before."[82] She so loathed the facility and the wandering, wounded mental patients that she swore she would never undergo another asylum stay, even though she technically was in a hospital during her treatment.

Olivier's was an admirable and love-filled decision to endure whatever their marriage threw at them until the bitter end because he loved her. But even this remarkable testament to Olivier's true passion for Leigh was finally undone by her illness. As he wrote of Leigh's ability to maintain the mask of sanity to others even as she dropped it at home, subjecting him to some of its worst abuses, "Throughout her possession by that uncannily evil monster, manic depression, with its deadly, ever-tightening spirals, she retained her own individual canniness—an ability to disguise her true mental condition from almost everyone except me, for whom she could hardly be expected to take the trouble."[83] By the end of their fabled marriage, each would be effectively living a separate life, with separate lovers, with Olivier characteristically looking the other way with knowledge as she lived with actor Jack Merivale.[84] Though their failed marriage was a source of tragic disappointment to both husband and wife until their respective deaths, the dignity and discreet handling with which Olivier conducted his and her mutual affairs demonstrates how dependent bipolars can become on those who are their support networks, and vice versa, in both a positive and negative sense. The negatives have been frequently outlined in these pages, but of course the attendant positives of the creatively playful upside of hypomania and less acute stages of mania enjoyed by companions of bipolars, such as a markedly fine sense of companionship, lively ability to discuss and elucidate, and a spontaneity not easily achieved by most more socially inhibited persons are not to be underestimated in appeal. This helps explain why such a man of the world as Laurence Olivier, who had means and moral excuse-making readily at hand to shirk his responsibilities, felt so honor-bound to the Vivien Leigh he adored from their first meeting and working together on the set of *Fire over England* (1937). He loved the part of her that was just as frequently in seeming remission and full of life and happiness as he was crushed by her darker, uncontrollable impulses towards manic fits of self-destructive rage, the latter of which only slowly, if inevitably, took over her health.

The other remarkable portrait of manic depression Leigh bequeathed is the memorable Blanche DuBois in *A Streetcar Named Desire* (1951). The filmic adaptation of Tennessee Williams's Broadway smash was the New York stage cast intact save for the replacement of Leigh as Blanche. It was a distinction that film director Elia Kazan exploited by suggesting to Leigh she play as she was to the other cast members' established camaraderie, that of an outsider who cannot fit in with the assembled group dynamics. His advice seems achingly utilized by Leigh in her nerve-shattering performance, a veritable walk on the dizzying ledge of stability and madness, dressed in fine, if fading, evening clothes and teetering atop high-heeled shoes. Kazan was keen to externalize the state of oppressive claustrophobia Blanche experiences, having the set walls designed in such a way that he could compress them as the film progressed, thus literally creating a feeling in Leigh as performer of the proverbial walls of madness closing in.[85] Combined with Leigh's downwardly expressive spiral into depression, and Williams's eloquent soliloquies dedicated to fading youth, hidden hypersexuality, and implied loss of mental health, as well as the superb cast alongside her imaginatively directed by Kazan, *A Streetcar Named Desire* ranks as one of the finest moments of psychological realism in the movies at the time of its release, and therein lies its enormous impact. It helped establish a new sense of profound naturalism that made previous attempts at madness seem melodramatically dated. This is superbly ironic given how firmly entrenched all of Williams's works remained in the melodramatic form. This movement in which disturbing states of interior disintegration and psychological impairment are not merely vocalized, but equally externalized onto the very scenery of the stage design itself, was novel in the more staidly conservative world of the early 1950s. A great example is in Williams's archetypal *The Glass Menagerie*'s written suggestion to be performed as a "memory play," through varying, hazy veils of gauze, which alternately reveal and then obscure the afflicted protagonists, both as they present themselves to others and drop the facades in private moments of reverie. This moving conceit allowed Williams as playwright to enter into almost mesmeric states of internal confession. Like Shakespeare's finest tragedies, wherein perplexed characters externalize their thoughts via iambic pentameter, a typical Williams lead uses the audience's accompanying, collectively shared silence as group listeners to confess her innermost sins and singularities, as if expecting absolution and catharsis from the stage setting turned public confessional booth.

By creating these dual-edged portraits in mental illness as he so frequently did, Williams was doubtless attempting to wrestle with personal issues germane to his biography, which was riddled with manic-depressive tendencies apparently originating on his paternal side. His alcoholic father was given to bouts of physically destructive rage and depression. His father's fury often involved violence, as when he had an ear chewed off in a bar brawl shortly before Williams's mother moved herself and Tennessee, effectively though not immediately ending their marriage.[86] Like many manic-depressives, Williams's history included not only familial madness, but an extended period of childhood illness, which was a probable influence on the severity of manifestation of his later bipolar disorder. Williams had diphtheria as a child and was severely weakened by the disease, spending a year in bed in slow-motion recovery. He also suffered as an adult from a compulsion to keep moving after too long a stay in one area, a wanderlust mania that helped "divert the downward course of my spirit"[87] as he characterized his moodiness. For Williams, perpetual relocation was almost as effective as writing for treating his intransigent blues. Using any comfort he could find is understandable, inasmuch as he told of one episode of depression which lasted for seven hellish years.[88]

Vivien Leigh had much emotional baggage to unpack for her role as Blanche DuBois, including a potentially scandalous series of past love affairs. She had but a few years prior to the filming had an affair with Peter Finch during an Australian theater tour designed to raise funds for the Old Vic Theatre. Olivier wrote that he had "lost Vivien"[89] at this time, realizing that her mental instability was as much a root cause for her infidelity as anything lacking in their own otherwise loving marriage. Leigh's intense insomnia, so common in bipolar biographies, drove her and Olivier into a slapping match before they took the stage in Christchurch with Leigh cursing him. She would have a period of incoherence and babble without understandable meaning, and then experience periods of lucidity, and by 1948, her condition was so chronic that it was an open secret in Hollywood. David Niven, a friend who frequently looked after Leigh when she was ill, recorded Leigh in this period as "quite, quite mad."[90] Noel Coward recorded in his diary that "things had been bad and getting worse."[91] She worked her way through much of her misery, but in 1953, she had to be replaced by Elizabeth Taylor during the shooting of *Elephant Walk* in Ceylon because of her manic-depressive illness. By 1955 she was cursing cast and crew with such alarming frequency during a stage run of *Titus Andronicus* that Olivier enlisted Leigh Holman, her former husband, in a staged intervention designed to force Leigh to retire for an extended, if not indefinite, time.[92]

But for Blanche DuBois in *A Streetcar Named Desire*, at least, Leigh created the perfect book-end performance to her earlier majesty in *Gone with the Wind*, a height she had never yet regained in her intervening career despite admirable roles. Blanche is a twittering, contradictory mess of edgy nerves, and then steel nerves, as played by Leigh. She is fragile as she famously utters "I have always depended on the kindness of strangers" (a line that would cause Williams to laugh, the only audience member to do so, whenever he watched his play performed on Broadway during its initial run).[93] Leigh's version of Blanche is a woman who is on the run from her own manic depression as much as she is from a past full of shady recriminations and whispered allegations. Blanche is the emblem of denial as the bipolar desperately attempting to imagine away the illness, and offering real-world disappointments as the prevailing reason why she is in perpetual crisis mode. In this lurching from one intense personal drama to the next many well-meaning but self-wounded bipolars have attempted to exhaust themselves as a form of personal therapy, but the problems inherent in such an approach are obvious. Blanche distills the cumulative psychic and emotional cost at the end of the proverbial line for such persons who burn brightest by igniting both ends of the candle at the same time, night and day. She is now the wounded dove who was once and still desires to be the object of adoration and seduction for just one more handsome young man of the evening, forever desiring just one more romantic tryst of all-encompassing lovemaking. *Just one more*, she forever tells herself as a hedge against her encroaching glimpse that it is madness, not her fading looks, that will soon end her sexual life. Blanche DuBois is the realization of nymphomania lost, with the nymph turned into an aged, living statuette in vain tribute to her own former sexual glory. Her sexual fires, a form of intense therapy she once used to temporarily extinguish her smoldering insanity, are ironically themselves now extinguished by her prevailing manic depression. With nothing left to use as an escape, Blanche falls into her own narcissistic web, offering the disturbing vision of the black widow spider ensnaring, and then devouring, itself in its tangled web of unwitting self-deceit. Williams cited her performance on Broadway as definitive, forcing him to see qualities in his creation that Leigh subconsciously manifested, and then magnified, through her own bipolarity.[94] Williams said of Leigh that "having known madness, she knew how it was to be drawing close to death."[95] Indeed, Leigh later attributed her grueling, self-revealing, nine-month stint as Blanche on Broadway as the final straw for her already fragile mental stability, saying it "tipped me over into madness."[96] Leigh's second Academy Award for Best Actress was richly deserved and much cherished by its recipient, a final summit cleared in a career that would subsequently see too many dark valleys and insurmountable peaks, and few chances to ever again effectively use acting as therapy.

THE HIGHS AND LOWS OF AKIRA KUROSAWA

It is not surprising that a director whose translated cinematic titles include such overtly melancholic descriptors as *I Live in Fear* (1955), *The Lower Depths* (1957), *The Bad Sleep Well* (1960), and *High and Low* (1963) suffered from real-world bouts of depression and attempted suicide. Anyone familiar with the prevailing themes of human wreckage and tragic despair in much of Akira Kurosawa's body of work is unlikely to be taken aback to learn that Kurosawa paid a heavy emotional price as he struggled to achieve his artistic immortality. While he was from a relatively well-off and modern-thinking Japanese family, young Akira was somewhat paradoxically expected by his authoritarian father to maintain their conservative samurai lineage, therefore upholding the tradition of their noble ancestry. His influential older brother Heigo, who acted as a silent film narrator of imported cinema from

Europe and America to Japanese audiences, was another powerful lure. Imported films were shown without costly subtitles while a translator such as Heigo not only translated, but also enacted, the title cards. Transfixed by the exotic movies and his brother's personal connection to them, Akira developed an early love of film.[97] He had a dual-edged nature in his early childhood as both a reclusive artistic depressive in temperament, and suddenly a daredevil performer of feats in which he often risked his life to impulsively impress his startled peers.[98] With other admissions in his *Akira Kurosawa: Something Like an Autobiography*, it is speculatively safe to say that Akira Kurosawa may have been bipolar depressive with a tendency toward prolonged episodes of melancholia rather than mania. His psychiatric diagnosis will probably never be known, but there are enough markers in his history to at least legitimately consider him on the mood-disordered spectrum, especially when one considers his childhood, his suicide attempt when filmmaking as therapy was no longer an option, and the themes in his films.

He was obsessively enthralled with movies since an early age, devouring every film, local or foreign, that was shown in the cinemas of Japan. He often traveled great distances alone across vast sections of Tokyo, usually by foot, after school, to see a particular film his brother had recommended.[99] Being obsessed with movies alone is not necessarily a clinical indicator of a possible mood disorder. But taken in conjunction with other childhood memories and emotional tendencies as Kurosawa himself documents in his autobiography, such an obsessive habit does warrant more serious consideration. Early devotion to cinema and repeatedly watching films does occur with remarkable consistency in the history of many manic-depressive filmmakers as part of their evident desire to make movies. It is not merely being a fan of movies, but an excessive sense of belonging that is only acutely satisfied by the actual participation in film viewing, and then later filmmaking. Compulsive film attendance as a habitual form of social, or rather self-social, behavior becomes an uncannily co-attendant detail in the biographies of most filmmakers and actors who are bipolar once cinema became popularized. While many millions of average filmgoers shared a love of viewing films in theaters during this era of movie palaces, the nearly continuous immersion in cinema from around the globe by a total fanatic like Kurosawa, or the earlier-chronicled James Dean, one new film after another and often several viewings per day or night, was a possibility entirely new to Kurosawa's generation. As today's youth know the Internet as an addictive reservoir of unlimited new and old voices and visions, so Akira Kurosawa as a young boy and later teenager knew the cinema as a heady mix of constant imports, domestic films, and classic film revivals. As a result, his own knowledge and vocabulary of world film was already staggering by the time he was accepted as an assistant director in the burgeoning Japanese film industry at the age of twenty-six, after failing to make much impact as a painter despite studying it for many years. The influence would, however, make itself manifest in his painterly compositions and his preference to craft large watercolor studies for key scenes in his films rather than the traditional reliance on storyboards when he became a director.

His childhood was no predictor of his later success. Much like Einstein's biography, there is the story of a late bloomer in Kurosawa's recollection of his life. He was bullied as a child in school, ridiculed for his bursts of tristimania[100] in which he could not stop crying. He was derisively given the nickname Konbeto-san, or "Mr. Gumdrop," because of his childish behavior. In candor, Kurosawa admits he was obnoxious beyond his own tolerance for liking. The sudden loss of his beloved older sister in the fourth grade had a huge negative impact on his emotional landscape. Another was the shattered landscape of the Great Kanto earthquake of 1923, which happened when he was a child. His older brother Heigo took the wide-eyed Akira along as the duo toured the worst-ravaged areas of the former city, reduced to smoking ruins and half-charred corpses from the ensuing fires. Kurosawa recorded in his book that bodies were stacked everywhere he could see, piled high on bridges, clogging intersections and choking rivers. He struggled with the aftermath of what he witnessed, traumatized, though unknowingly so until many years thereafter. "It is a terror that destroys all reason,"[101] he wrote of the impact this hellish tour had on his psyche.

Heigo loomed large in the director's emerging filmic consciousness. Even more so when, after leading a failed strike by the silent film narrators against the showing of sound pictures, Heigo attempted suicide. Kurosawa notes the unhealthy obsession his brother had with a premature death before age thirty. Heigo went so far in his belief of his early demise that he kept a well-read copy of *The Last Line* by Mikhail Artzybashev at hand because its protagonist also believed he would die young. Akira reassured their mother that people who talk about suicide never really attempt it. And then Heigo killed himself a few months later at age twenty-seven.[102] Their father found his bloody body at Heigo's apartment. In shock Akira helped his father wrap the remains in a sheet, and they took it home via cab. He remembered that the corpse emitted an expiratory groan during the long taxi drive to their family's residence, terrifying him with its mordant finality. Kurosawa said he preferred to think of himself as the positive strip of film that developed from his brother's master negative. But whether light or dark, they both shared a profoundly disordered, chaotic vision of humanity as forever teetering on the edge of self-annihilation and egotistical self-need. For Kurosawa, surely a seminal cinematic image is that of human society poised atop the smoldering remains of their forgotten, if still faintly groaning, ancestors. They are tragically lost in their own turmoil, unable or unwilling to even acknowledge the proof of inevitable disintegration that ultimately prevails over the mortal-made sand castles all around them, and that they yet busily refortify without end. This is seen in all of his works, an author's signature of thematic concern, akin in spirit to the socially scathing works by fiction writers such as Kurt Vonnegut and Mark Twain, although minus those authors' penchants for humor. Kurosawa rarely played for outright chuckles, unless they were of the despairing variety, indicating a realization of the foibles of humanity. His was most often a bleak universe, the backdrop for stories about a depressing planet's latest inevitable revolution into madness, murder, and mayhem. Pitted against the very elements of nature and the cosmos, mankind's puny travails never seemed of less significance than against the film worlds he conjured for such existentially fatalistic outlooks as *Rashomon* (1950), *I Live in Fear, Throne of Blood* (1957), *The Lower Depths*, or *Ran* (1985). In citing Kurosawa as one of his favorites, director Alex Cox noted Kurosawa's pervading sense of "epic despair,"[103] which is a fitting turn of phrase for a filmmaker who favored widescreen tragedies involving large scale, often ruinous, battle sequences. There is little wonder therefore why Kurosawa as a child loved the disturbing films of Fritz Lang, as well as *The Cabinet of Dr. Caligari* and the bipolar-influenced paintings of Van Gogh. They were stylistic influences and can be seen in his works in cinematic reincarnations, even literally in *Dreams* (1990), in which he cast Martin Scorsese as Vincent Van Gogh and utilized expressionist sets à la *Dr. Caligari*. In these early seminal film influences, one can easily postulate that he saw the prevailing winds of artistic insanity blowing in them, and they stirred him with their intensity of expression and dreamlike, if not nightmarish, sense of recognition of their, and therefore his own, like-minded moodiness. His love of Van Gogh would support this hypothesis well.

As a young screenwriter trying to make his mark in the competitive film business, Akira Kurosawa experienced swings of elation and hypomania in which he would write multiple scripts for weeks on end, only to finally collapse into crying jags which he drowned out by abusing sake.[104] This happened on more than one occasion in the 1940s. He wrote *To the End of the Silver Mountains*, and then *Four Love Stories*, both features, capping them off with a short film script "One Wonderful Sunday," all in a burst of a few short weeks of sustained creativity. He would then follow these probable bouts of exhaustive mania with missing days of depressive drinking. This yin and yang pattern is entirely consistent with the many other mood-disordered creators in this book. They, too, frequently experienced painful crashes after extensive periods of artistic highs. The highs may only be welcome when set in an artistic, therapeutic context, where they are usually more easily resolvable, rather than solely centered on the depressed sufferer and his more personal, intractable problems. Akira Kurosawa found it too painful to continue his autobiography beyond the year 1950 and *Rashomon*, which is a true loss, as these years would have covered his severe depressions and eventual attempted suicide. Kurosawa merely suggests to interested parties that the films he made post-*Rashomon* themselves should serve as ample evidence of his own struggle to maintain a grip on his mental well-being throughout much of his lifetime as a filmmaker. He states that he believes humans cannot tell the truth about themselves where such dark matters are concerned, apart from in coded, if not therapeutic, form in works of art such as he created.[105]

His silence about his suicide attempt is therefore telling of the probable shame Kurosawa evidently still deeply felt about his act. But in truth, so much of what he had experienced in his life of despondency was only mitigated by the reckless hope his filmmaking inspired in his troubled mind. Little is known of his suicide attempt save that Kurosawa felt zero chance of continuing his work as a film director by the early 1970s, and so on December 22, 1971, he used a razor and slashed himself on his arms and neck.[106] He did not deny the act when questioned by the foreign press during interviews for his film *Dersu Urzula* (1975), but merely repeated his standard explanation that "I couldn't bear to go on living, not for one more minute or second."[107] He would not say what made him so miserable, but the lack of film work was the self-evident answer, as Kurosawa depended upon his film productions to keep his mental illness at bay, or at least keep himself preoccupied with creative tasks so that their destructive voices would not overtake him. As Donald Richie accurately surmised in the documentary *Kurosawa: The Last Emperor* (1999), speaking of Kurosawa's need to be crafting movies as a form of combating his chronic sense of depressive depersonalization, "If he didn't work, there wasn't any Kurosawa around."

There are many movies in his canon worthy of consideration in terms of capturing the expressive range of manic depression in the human heart. His study in middle-aged despair and depression *Ikiru* (1952), aka *To Live*, is a fine example. A bureaucrat who is informed he has terminal cancer and not much time left to reflect on it, therefore does precisely that, ruminating and then attempting to spend his remaining weeks in some meaningful action to make sense of his seemingly pointless existence. It is a sublime study in the effects of depression and social behavior. Prior to his diagnosis, poor Kanji Watanabe (played by Takashi Shimura, body stiff and face gaunt, in a devastatingly accurate portrait of the physical toil depression takes on its sufferers) is already merely a living ghost in his office, hardly noticed or respected, functional at his work but catatonic in his private world. Reacting to his diagnosis, Watanabe experiences life anew. He abandons many of the self-defeating attitudes that have kept him in polite societal check, but likewise in a personal straightjacket of hell. His coworkers cannot help but notice the renewed sense of purpose and dedication Watanabe not only brings to himself and his bearing at work, but after his death, even on their own sense of shame and lack of commitment to their own humanity. Kurosawa carefully peels back the layers of hidden reserve inside Kanji Watanabe as surely as a biologist dissecting a specimen, but with a gaze that is more emotional in intensity than scientific. What is unexpected about *Ikiru* is that it takes Kanji's realization that he is dying to really accept life on its own bleak, existential terms, and then transform them, despite his certainty of death, into something that is lasting for all mankind. In Kanji's case, a civic park project for urban families to utilize beyond his passing is his symbolic final gesture. The irony is, of course, that we are always in the process of dying, to some extent, even as we must re-create to live, to truly *feel* alive, amid this constant presence of death. To our knowledge, we are the only species on the planet that not only knows of its terminal nature, but can self-injuriously obsess and even cause a premature death in reaction to that very knowledge. Kanji Watanabe comes to see that his curse of certain doom is actually a rare blessing in his life, that he has been given the proverbial second chance, however brief in duration, to make amends before expiring. Instead of having to fear an uncertain time and place, he is freed to actually live not just his own death, but in a figurative manner, live beyond it in anticipation of happy families using the park he brought into fruition. A supposedly "small" man who has no significance, either personally or professionally, digs deeply into himself, wrestles his chronic emotional demons, and emerges a bona fide hero of enormous magnitude, at least in terms of the epic story of humanity. Kanji Watanabe, *Ikiru* ruthlessly demonstrates, will be forgotten as soon as he passes, or so it is presumed by the living. Only in death, Kurosawa shows, do the living take stock of their prejudices against the departed (and by implication, themselves). Formerly a slight, depressive figure like the pre-terminal Watanabe is easily dismissed and his painful affliction all but ignored by coworkers and society. But the profound outcome of Watanabe's enormous private battle against self-annihilation, literally metastasized as cancer in the film, is that he not only transforms his own depressive emotional poverty into riches, but in doing so, awakens the neurotypical people around to their own self-loathing and moral hypocrisy. If the least and ignored among them, a person who struggles with an emotional disorder, can triumph over his despair, then what excuses are they left for their own self-negation? Kurosawa's intent is not solely to pass judgment, but to force the viewer to question how easily in our society we dismiss those who present as anything other than "normal" in temperament. As long as Watanabe is meek and accepting of his self-defeating disorder, his place is assured. Only when he questions the place he has both been placed in and then willingly accepted does he become a living, breathing human being again. Only then does he cause discomfort to his social standing, because he does not play his role as assigned. In bitter irony, Watanabe learns that only by engaging his disorder through acts of decency and kindness can he ever overcome the worst aspects of it. He also learns that by therapeutically doing so, he challenges the passive acceptance of his colleagues that one must not try too hard, not push too many envelopes, after all, if one is to "get along" with the crowd. In *Ikiru*, this basic premise is shown to be very short-lived, as short-lived as Watanabe's fated existence. How often must Akira Kurosawa have shared his fictionalized protagonist's sense of uncontrollable hopelessness in the depths of his own real depressions while having to direct the next shot to stay on schedule? And how true to life that the by-products of a mood disordered artist's work can truly heal not only the creator, but vicariously those who creatively participate in them as audiences.

I Live in Fear is even more autobiographical than *Ikiru*. Kurosawa had by this time in his career established himself as an international director of great repute. But in his own native country, he was not as appreciated by the Japanese studios, which shied away from his modernist critiques of Japanese society. As a result, Kurosawa struggled to make films there despite his worldwide acclaim. One of the reasons Kurosawa was great is that he recognized and valued the positive aspects of collaboration, a concept he had to master with great humility as an apprentice to director Yamamoto Kajiro. The musical scores by composer Fumio Hayasaka for the early Kurosawa masterpieces such as *Drunken Angel, Stray Dog, Rashomon, Seven Samurai*, and *Ikiru* were the by-product of an unusually respectful relationship in which Kurosawa not only contributed ideas and reactions to Hayasaka's score, but Hayasaka likewise suggested visual images and metaphors for Kurosawa to use as director.[108] The director became convinced that scores should work in counterpoint to the illustrated visuals as a result of seeing how Hayasaka did not score to the image to bring forth the obvious emotions—as was typical—preferring to offer a musical interpretation (an atonal sound for discordant effect, say, instead of a full orchestral score). These forms of intense director-composer collaborations are historically known as fountainheads for some of the greatest cinema efforts: Hitchcock working as mutual collaborator with Bernard Herrmann, Sergio Leone with Ennio Morricone, or later Ridley Scott working in tandem with Vangelis. The creative synchronization between music and picture never seems more profoundly, irreducibly intertwined than in these kinds of "masters of two fields" blending talents in movies. So it was of course with a momentous sense of loss that Akira Kurosawa

greeted the premature death of his gifted friend and composer to tu-
berculosis in 1955, even before Kurosawa had completed *I Live in Fear*,
which Hayasaka was scoring and which was finished by Masaru Sato
(though minimally so, as the film has very little in the way of traditionally scored music).

In many ways, *I Live in Fear* is nothing less than Kurosawa's attempt
to combine his struggle to accept Hayasaka's slow, lingering death—an
event that must have triggered deeply held, unresolved memories of
losing his sister and brother—with the larger horrors many Japanese
citizens faced as a legacy of atomic warfare. In fact, the script and its
themes were from a series of long conversations the two friends had
while Hayasaka was often in hospital or on the mend.[109] When Hayasaka told Kurosawa that the TB was so painful that Hayasaka could no
longer even summon the energies for his beloved music, Kurosawa was
aghast. He was so dependent upon his own form of catharsis via filmmaking as life process, that the very idea of having to live without it
filled him with despair for his friend and himself. Indeed, it would be
this very same feeling that he could not direct, and so could not escape,
his inner turmoil that would lead him to attempt suicide sixteen years
later as he contemplated facing his disorder without hope of his only
known treatment—making movies. And so *I Live in Fear* is a study of
not the redemptive possibilities of remission from depression, as was
Ikiru, but quite the opposite. It is a study in how a seemingly balanced
man can fall prey to the insidious hold of depression in such a slow-
motion pattern that it is often too late to offer much help by the time
the patient is finally diagnosed. Kiichi Nakajima (played by Toshirô
Mifune) is a wealthy industrialist who faces a moral crisis when he
becomes convinced, owing to his ongoing depression, that the end of
the world via atomic warfare is at hand. Like many equivalent modern-
day "doomsday preppers," who stockpile food, guns, and related survival gear in anticipation of political and religious apocalypse, Nakajima
cannot be swayed by his children, friends, or money men saying that he
is experiencing a bout of clinical paranoia stemming from his melancholia. Before anyone in the scheming family can figure out how to protect
their inheritances from their father's angry outbursts, Nakajima suddenly becomes manic-depressive. He becomes filled with ideas of relocating his family to Brazil so that they will survive the inevitable nuclear
holocaust there at a remote hacienda, fully stocked for enduring the

worst. The spoiled inheritors-in-waiting patronize their father's illness by willfully ignoring and then refusing to participate in his crazy plans, causing a division among them (or is it merely further widening it?). As they squabble over who will get what shares of the family estate even as they have their father committed against his will to an asylum (and therefore stripped of his wealth for them to divide), Nakajima descends into final delusional madness. In an ironic coda, however, we see that Nakajima's fears were not entirely unfounded. There is in his insanity a form of super-clarity at times that is often ignored as just more ranting by his oblivious family members (or, at least, most of them). Thus Kurosawa posits that works of prophetic value are often ironically delivered by unstable minds, however muddled their dire warnings.

Though almost all of his films feature extensive meditations on despair and disintegration as primary themes, *Throne of Blood* and *Ran* have noteworthy sequences involving prolonged bouts of emotional disorder and mental instability. Both are based on Shakespearean plays that also chronicle royalty and madness, with *Macbeth* as the base for *Throne of Blood* and *King Lear* for *Ran*. Both are so skillfully adapted to film that one need not even know the underlying references to the Bard in order to appreciate either movie adaptation (though naturally it adds to each film's impact to marvel at Kurosawa's strength as editor/writer in adapting challenging verbal sources into poetic sequences of moving images). Toshirô Mifune gives another remarkable performance as Taketoki Washizu, the Macbeth character, an ambitious but obedient warlord beholden to his master and ruler in *Throne of Blood*. While the multiple witches from Shakespeare's play are reduced to but one lonely Old Ghost Woman (Chieko Naniwa) in Kurosawa's version, she is of such enormous emotional power that she steals the movie's earliest scenes even from Mifune, surely no mean feat. First she is only heard, or barely glimpsed running supernaturally fast through a dense forest from afar, as she cackles with maniacal glee at Washizu's misfortune at having arrived at her dark place of prophecy. The thunder explodes, the winds blast, and a perpetual bank of fog enshrouds Washizu and his friend Miki (Akira Kubo) as they ride, lost and frightened, through the so-called Spider Web Forest, an intensely claustrophobic network of tangled woods, until they finally arrive at an eerie clearing. In a small, nearly see-through hut, the now nearly catatonic Old Ghost Woman slowly spins a thread on a decrepit loom that clearly represents the ever-turning but futilely cyclic fate of mankind. In a thin, hollow voice barely audible above the stunned silence of Washizu and Miki, Old Ghost Woman hums, "Ambition is false fame and will fall, death will reign, man falls in vain," lest there be any doubt hers is a vision of unending doom. Naturally, and supernaturally, neither of the men present will recall her first warning of pointless aspirations to power. Instead, they greedily devour the private meanings latent in her prophecy about their own personal outcomes. But it is not the depiction of the humans that is so reminiscent of some clinical states experienced by bipolars, but Old Ghost Woman herself. First, she is a maniacally laughing speedster who moves so fast through the shadowy forests, no one can keep up with her. And then, she is a frozen statue, reduced to barely cranking a spinning loom, otherwise unmoving and rigidly unexpressive in her posture. With low, breathy voice and despairing tone, Old Ghost Woman is catatonic depression personified. In a nod to Kurosawa's favorite, Fritz Lang, and his adroit scenes of the catatonic but hypergraphic Dr. Mabuse poised in nearly the same manner in *The Testament of Dr. Mabuse*, Kurosawa skillfully updates and places Old Ghost Woman alongside Lang's Mabuse as one of the great screen visualizations of this perplexing side of manic depression.

Ran focuses on the slow-moving mental disintegration undergone by Lord Hidetora Ichimonji (Tatsuya Nakadai). Meaning well but falling prey to sentimentality possibly brought about by his mental illness and, more specifically, a supposed dream of prophecy in which he unwisely invests truth, Hidetora tragically divides his kingdom before retirement. His wiser, youngest son Saburo (Daisuke Ryû) objects, believing this is not a prudent idea. Familial warfare erupts as jealous brothers fight for power and inheritance, laying waste to the shattered, formerly peaceful countryside. Realizing the error caused by his errant mental condition, Hidetora staggers away in literal tatters into the wastelands of his ruined kingdom, a wide-eyed, nearly catatonic zombie of mute, agony-riddled depression. His only accompanier is his royal fool Kyoami (memorably played by Pîtâ), to whom Hidetora finally and nearly singularly mutters, "I am lost."

What is remarkable is that in all the sequences from *Throne of Blood* and then *Ran* that show manic depression, Kurosawa chose to have the characters immersed in clouds of fog. While this seems literally obvious in retrospect, it is the expressive nature in which Kurosawa utilizes his cloudy mists of obscurity that make them so memorable. These are not merely stage decorations to add Sherlock Holmes–like atmosphere, they are, for all intents, characters, if perhaps a form of Greek chorus. They echo and externalize the lost heroes' states of mental confusion in both films. Indeed, they linger beyond the ability of any natural fog to which cinemagoers are accustomed, apart from later horror films such as John Carpenter's *The Fog* (1980) or *The Mist* (2007). For many amazingly suspenseful moments in *Throne of Blood*, the two horsemen gallop in endless circles, barely perceptible to even one another, hopelessly lost in a thick fog that obliterates all but their shadowy silhouettes. The agony Kurosawa induces by stretching this scene beyond a mere cut or two and into a minor sequence by extending it for what feels like minutes of screen time is extraordinary. It makes sense if one filters it through the filmmaker's own personal moments of depressive hell as influence, too. Herein Kurosawa has symbolically encoded his worst moments of dread and presented them as nothing less than showing an otherwise well-balanced human mind suddenly in the grips of a manic-depressive fear. The stricken figure gallantly attacks the fog of disorder, spurring his steed of consciousness onward in a panic-induced gallop across the cloudy vista of his own mindscape. His efforts result only in exhaustion and further derangement. Meanwhile, the depressive fog encloses him tighter, leaving him further horrified that he is not only trapped, but trapped without personal energies left to fight his enemy. Most tellingly of all, when the figure finally emerges from the fog of mental illness, he will not encounter a world rightfully in its place, but in chaos and disorder. In this sense, Kurosawa posits his own madness, and that of his characters, as being completely mirrored by the chaotic reality they inhabit, mad or not. His perspective is clearly one of non-judgment for his mentally afflicted characters, many of whom remain some of the best in his canon. They inhabit a bipolar universe, he suggests, and so it is only right and perhaps even expected that these disturbed protagonists would reflect a bipolar response to the certain disappointments, despair, and death engulfing them. In crafting these tales, Kurosawa may have been ordering his own place in his personal universe of mood disorder. He may have been attempting to make sense of the seeming conundrum of being an unbalanced artist in an equally unbalanced world. In doing so, he bequeathed a body of work that not merely gazed at despair, but enshrined it as surely as any sacred temple for the weary, bipolar cinema traveler seeking solace and understanding within.

7

1960S: THE LIBERALIZATION OF MANIC-DEPRESSIVE STEREOTYPES IN CINEMA

BREAKFAST AT TIFFANY'S HOLLY GOLIGHTLY AS MOOD SWINGING MODERNE

The cumulative effect of the 1950s' cinema of psychological realism came into full fruition in the 1960s. A succeeding reign of filmmakers became enthralled by new, more realistic ways in which the movies could for the first time more accurately portray unusual, and even clinical, states of mental being. One potent example is the Blake Edwards adaptation of Truman Capote's novella *Breakfast at Tiffany's* into the filmed version in 1961. Many of the novella's darker aspects inherent in Capote's Holly Golightly were leveled into a whispered backstory for the screenplay. In fleeing from her rural Texas background, which is revealed to have been filled with incidents of abuse and neglect, and reinventing herself as the desirable nymph supreme Holly Golightly in New York's fantasy nightclub life, Holly illustrates a common biographic marker in the background of many entertainers. Many bipolar artists will affect masking identities to both actively deny and therapeutically expunge perceptions of themselves from childhood that they feel otherwise powerless to control.[1] Indeed, all of the preceding applies as much to the fictional Holly Golightly as it does to Truman Capote. The fact that so many of the key players involved in the writing, acting, and direction of *Breakfast at Tiffany's* were either manic-depressive or depressive in nature makes it a succinct study in bipolar cinema. As cultural reference point, *Breakfast at Tiffany's* had enormous social impact on young women in its initial release and subsequent enshrinement into enduring classic. It captures a melancholic edge missing in many films that detail the more obviously insidious aspects of manic depression—the rages, the violence, the catatonia, the hubris, the egomania. It also shows a key component of what makes melancholia so beloved in a wistful manner by some of its diagnosed members who do not suffer as from the more negative form of depression. The melancholic phase of the illness is an eternal love/hate relationship for the artistically inclined who have bipolarity, many of whom value the reflective calm with which to create that it provides. This even as they despair knowing the inevitable mood swings that eventually follow will render their creative energies moot or misspent.

Truman Capote was no stranger to spells of depression. "Writing is hard, and you get depressed,"[2] he succinctly said. It says much that one of his most famous lines of fiction is "When you've got nowhere to turn, turn on the gas."[3] He attributed his inner sense of depersonalization and sadness to his troubled childhood, in which his single mother dragged him along to her amorous conquests and subsequent conflicts, over and over again. One night she locked him in a rented room and didn't bother to return until the next morning, having been out for an all-night tryst with her newest lover. Despite wailing in hysteria and banging on the doors, no one in the house ever knocked on the boy's locked door to see if he was okay. The sense of powerlessness mixed with the indifference of the adults who ignored his pleas left him scarred for life. Capote would experience bouts of depression in which he felt helpless when he recalled such horrors. He called these episodes of acute depression his "mean reds"[4] as opposed to the classical descriptions of them as the blues in *Breakfast at Tiffany's*. The author's proxy speech delivered by Holly in which she eloquently summarizes the distinction between the two forms of depression remains artfully relevant for bipolarity. She specifies that the blues are reactive and understandable in nature, often triggered by such life stresses as weight gain and growing old. Whereas, Golightly contrasts in book and film, the mean reds are a persistent, chronic sense of nervous agitation in which one can only fidget in profound agony until the sense of impending doom is finally, inevitably illustrated in the predicted tragic outcome. Again, the nervous state of premonitory exhaustion experienced by many manic-depressives is exactly this in its sense of pervasive emotional fragility, as many await the next unpredictable bout of inevitable mania or depression. This is why Capote's creation of Holly Golightly remains so well observed, for they were, to some real extent, self-observed as he created his feminine alter ego.

Another key influence on Capote's composite character of Holly Golightly was Marilyn Monroe. It was Monroe's life story and emotional disorder that fueled much of his protagonist Golightly's construction. They had met earlier in New York's elite society circle and bonded. Monroe allowed him access to private moments she would have probably blocked from sharing with those to whom she was less trusting. One of the most telling that Capote recorded was when he found her alone, lighting subdued, staring into a mirror at her world-famous reflection in profound silence. When he dared ask Monroe what she was doing, she sadly replied, "Looking at her."[5] Marilyn Monroe's unstable emotional private nature which drove her to seek seclusion, at constant odds with her public attempt to create and then maintain a larger-than-life sex goddess persona that was beloved by all and desired by men of power, is the essence of Holly Golightly's ruthlessly practical side distilled. Hepburn's portrayal is so icily self-controlled (or so she presents and is believed to be by those who do not know her well) that this aspect is less apparent in the filmed version of *Breakfast at Tiffany's*. Written as a form of loving tribute to his mentally ill friend and designed to be the role of her lifetime, Capote felt slighted by the casting of Hepburn. He believed studio trickery was used to pressure the vulnerable Monroe into starring in the ultimately disastrous *The Misfits*, instead of in *Breakfast at Tiffany's*.[6] It is fitting acknowledgment of Audrey Hepburn's talent and poise that she erases much of the Monroe influence on first viewing. Hepburn's vision of Holly was not as merely a resplendent dependent, but as a stand-alone female rogue perfectly willing and adroitly able to manipulate men in the same merciless ways men utilize to dominate women. This seeming lack of vulnerability was the antithesis of Monroe's persona, who was forever at the beck and call of powerful men. This is why the role is so forever associated with Hepburn and her own blithe spirit, rather than the more sexualized but vulnerable form Monroe would have brought to the role.

Audrey Hepburn's choice to play Holly as melancholic stoic rather than overtly flirtatious is befitting her background, containing as it does

Hepburn's bouts of clinical depression, which resulted in an eating disorder.[7] Both conditions were psychological by-products of her early teenage years running from Nazi persecution during World War II. Her mother participated in the underground Dutch resistance movement even as her estranged father kept allegiance to Hitler. Hepburn herself narrowly avoided a Nazi labor camp by hiding in a vermin-infested cellar for a month and subsisting on whatever scraps of food she could scrounge at night. "I forced myself to eliminate the need for food,"[8] Hepburn recalled of this era. A lifelong aversion to food dependency thus developed at an early age and gave the actress recurring bouts of depression as she struggled, and often failed, to control it. Her depressive episodes were exacerbated by haunting images of the terrified faces of family and neighbors who were dragged away by the Nazis in broad daylight, never to be seen again. Her intense survivor guilt fueled her eating disorder and largely contributed to her inability to experience much joy in life.[9] Such a depressive tendency can be an indicator of anhedonia as an underlying disorder, a profound state of clinical depression in which the sufferer can take little or no comfort from the usual activities most neurotypicals find pleasurable. Creative anhedonics tend to obsessively work on their artistic projects as a way of channeling the negative thoughts and impulses arising from their chronic sense of boredom and emotional flatness. They will displace these mental phantoms into, say, fictionalized narrative conflicts for a writer, or emotional back history creation for an actress. Hepburn's depression found creative expression in her portrayal of the grandiose but fragile Holly Golightly, a grand dame in training who is apparently out of her own league in terms of manic self-aggrandizement. Hepburn's studied, bored indifference to any critique of her dishonest lifestyle as a high-class call girl, rather than chic young socialite about town as she feigns, is not defensive in nature as Hepburn plays Holly. Hepburn's delicate performance makes it clear that Holly not only refuses introspection as a means of maintaining her denial, but also and more importantly to keep others at a safe emotional distance. By refusing to examine the opinions and feelings of those whom she feels she must use or ignore to gain her way in life, Holly absolves herself of coming to terms with her own toxic personal choices. This crucial distinction, which Hepburn brings so seductively to life in her subdued acting choices, was actually part of the role's enormous charm. It was liberating to young women who saw, and to some extent still see, Golightly's philosophy of "do unto others before they do unto you" as richly enticing. Holly's attempt to have it all without remorse is heroic in one self-immolating sense. She is stranded on her own island of private emotional turmoil when the film begins, and it is suggested she has not known much remission from her disorder since a trouble-plagued childhood. Her brilliant ability to transform herself despite her psychiatric problems makes her a magnetic protagonist. She is both deeply flawed and all the more human for her refusal to give in to her despair. She instead uses her angst as a private catalyst to reinvent herself as sexual siren beyond future emotional harm or control by others. Like Garbo's defiance in the face of unrepentant male patriarchy run amok in *Anna Christie* (1930), Hepburn's Golightly treads lightly, but firmly, on the conventions of how a young lady alone in the big city should behave. The lasting influence of Hepburn as Golightly is seen in such latent reincarnations as *Sex in the City* and related franchises, though the modern versions typically eschew the troubled mental illness aspects in favor of unadulterated romance.

Capote and Hepburn contributed defining moments of cinematic depression and anxiety with their respective collaboration in the making of *Breakfast at Tiffany's*. But credit is also due to and often strangely withheld from director Blake Edwards, in what was really the first of many mega-hit movies. Never a sure bet for commercial return owing to his willingness to occasionally make bolder choices (such as *Victor, Victoria* and *S.O.B.*), Edwards nevertheless directed many successful Hollywood films in various genres, including his renowned pairing with Peter Sellers in the Inspector Clouseau/*Pink Panther* series. Edwards, who grew up a second-generation movie brat to his father's studio labor jobs, had worked his way up as a handsome young actor into radio and bit parts, such as a small role in *The Best Years of Our Lives* (1946). But it was as director that he took his deepest bows. At the time he was selected to direct *Breakfast at Tiffany's* he was considered a strange choice by many in the film community, in that with his limited feature and mainly television series resume (including the hit series he created, *Peter Gunn*) he did not seem to have the background to direct a delicate story of bipolar love and loss. But Edwards had something better than a resume to draw upon for his directorial choices. He was a lifelong depressive who actively contemplated and eventually attempted suicide at several points in his journey as actor-turned-director.

In a remarkably candid CNN interview with Larry King in 2002, Blake Edwards admitted his lifelong depression with blackly comic, if somber, relish perhaps only the director of such darkly funny films could summon. After a series of taciturn responses to questions about his films and wife, Julie Andrews, and her recent loss of her singing voice due to a botched surgery, Edwards suddenly came alive with the questions asked in regard to Peter Sellers's and Edwards' own depression. When queried about the source of Sellers's genius, Edwards believed it was Sellers's emotional insanity that powered his enormous talent. When King rather blithely suggests that most viewers would conclude looking at Edwards and his estimable career that he has nothing to be depressed about, Edwards sincerely but bluntly retorts that his disorder is clinical, that he has taken and benefited at times from medications to combat it, and that "it has nothing to do with lifestyle and things like that. My depression has been with me most of my life that I can remember. I have spells of it."[10] Sensing journalistic red meat, King next asks without hesitancy if Edwards has ever tried to harm himself. Edwards is taken aback, muttering "Excuse me?" in limp response to the unguarded inquiry. King repeats it, and perhaps to viewers' surprise accustomed to his earlier, evasive answers, Edwards launches into an impromptu retelling of a time he attempted suicide at a Malibu beach home, but was repeatedly thwarted in the effort by his loving dog. Edwards does not skimp on details, rather embellishing his retelling of one of the lowest points of his life with perfect comic timing truly befitting a sequence in one of his movies. And in fact, there are traces of the moment echoed in S.O.B. (1981) with its bipolar director (Richard Mulligan) who wanders his Malibu beachfront in a depressive fugue of suicidal ideation. As Edwards tells it, he tired of his dog and tossed a ball far enough away so that he could buy himself ample time to slash his wrists with a razor blade. However, as Edwards wound back to throw the ball, he dislocated his shoulder, thus postponing his suicide as he hobbled back to his beach house to deal with his excruciating pain. Edwards concludes the tale by adding he realized he'd dropped his razor in the sand, and felt compelled to return to retrieve it before someone stepped on it later. He found the lost razor by stepping onto it himself and gashing open his heel. The wound landed him in the Malibu emergency room suffering from life-threatening blood loss, in another bizarrely sublime turn of irony. As the normally fast-talking King silently fumbles for missing words, Edwards darkly adds, "That was one suicide attempt."[11]

It is just this sort of nonjudgmental understanding on the part of the film's mood-afflicted creators that makes Holly Golightly's bipolar disorder so charming, after a fashion. And fashion is a fitting word choice, for *Breakfast at Tiffany's* use of Hepburn in the proverbial little black cocktail dress set a standard that is still paraded as trendy to this day. Holly has learned to externalize her disorder's most manipulative features—a sense of charisma over others and a maniacal self-control over herself—and embody them as an alluring figment of men's imaginations run wild. Her exquisite sense of tailored chic is part and parcel for her man trap, the fancy outer wrapping around the tasty inner treat. Here is where the Monroe substrata upon which the character of Holly was imagined is revealed again, but with Hepburn's emaciated waif sense of style giving it a more sophisticated air of elegance. Holly's hypersexual need to sleep with one wealthy potential suitor after another, deluding herself that she is really only selectively sleeping her way to the top, is akin to the clinically reported cases of manic depression among those patients who experience increased sexuality as byproduct of their disorder. Many of these bipolars will take risks they would not otherwise attempt while they are in the non-hypersexual phases of their disorder, such as when depressed or in remission.[12] This is how Holly acts, at first manic when she courts danger with men who are not interested in her well-being, and then secluding herself from the world when her depression exerts feelings of guilt and worthlessness. Holly is shown retreating into her darkened bedroom wearing sleeping shades, a reclusive depressive attempt to stifle all intrusions onto her wearied senses. This is the same manner with which Greta Garbo portrayed the depressive phases of her illness in *Grand Hotel* three decades earlier. It is clinically accurate to many bipolar biographies, such as the modeled Marilyn Monroe herself, who often retreated into her windows-blackened bedroom to escape her depressive episodes. Likewise, the rage Holly exhibits when she destroys her room's personal possessions in a manic fit of anger echoes a similar moment exhibited by Welles in *Citizen Kane*, in which he also seeks to obliterate the reminders of his failed relationships. Holly's depressive attempt to abandon her beloved, unnamed cat at the film's climax in a rain-soaked alleyway is an act so cruelly out of character, and so clearly undertaken by a disturbed mind, that the film's hero, Paul Varjak (George Peppard), is compelled to reevaluate her. He is forced to accept Holly as she is, rather than as he would like her to be, in order to completely fall in love with her. Holly must likewise accept that her emotional instability will always be a factor in their new love affair. It implies by the end that she must either rise to the occasion and seek better forms of treatment for herself or risk losing her lover, and her sanity, perhaps forever. For a supposed melodrama with comic touches, *Breakfast at Tiffany's* is still a dour dining experience no matter how bedazzling the setting. Holly explains the rationale, such that it is, as to why she breakfasts at the store. It is because it temporarily abates the "red means" for her. In other words, it is the most effective form of self-therapy she can administer for her depression.

It is no wonder Blake Edwards knew how to evoke the longing sadness that runs like the theme song "Moon River" throughout *Breakfast at Tiffany's*. For, as Holly used breakfast shopping as retail therapy, so Edwards used filmmaking. In the aforementioned interview with Larry King, Edwards gratefully acknowledges how much his desire and drive to make movies helped him endure the worst of his depressive episodes, figuring it was what saved him. "My work has been one of the great therapies of my life," he related in 1989. "Being able to express myself and have it validated by laughter is the best of all possible worlds."[13]

PETER SELLERS AND THE FROZEN FACE OF BIPOLAR MASKING

Though his comic genius is truly beyond any critical reproach or reappraisal, Peter Sellers as human being is one of the saddest examples of a clinically severe manic-depressive attempting to lead a "normal personal life" ever recorded. A driven, compulsive actor whose talents made him a living legend worldwide most of his adult life, Sellers was diabolical in emotional instability. A true enfant terrible in nature, he could be charming and loquacious one moment, only to turn paranoid and withdrawn the next. There were even rare but accompanying acts of physical violence when he experienced acute episodes of delusional mania. While Roger Lewis's scathing biography *The Life and Death of Peter Sellers* is not without critics owing to Lewis's clear dislike of his subject matter (ironically created in large part by the endless lawsuits some of Sellers's relatives threw at Lewis in the British courts in a losing effort to derail its publication), the book is exhaustively researched. It is filled with long, painful remembrances by many who worked closely with Sellers and knew him personally. As a result, it becomes the de facto source on Sellers's darkest hours, of which there were often more than twenty-four in any one given earthly cycle. He was a man on the move, a true global traveler, as he jetted from one country to the next for his latest film production. Sellers perpetually packed and unpacked without end, establishing and then abandoning one temporary domicile after another. He was as emotionally vacant throughout the endless transitions in his own life to friends and family as the character Chauncey Gardner that he played in his well-respected *Being There* (1979). His first wife Anne Levy said watching that particular film was too painful because of its undisguised quality of capturing Sellers's inner sense of being forever adrift.[14] John Taylor, his stand-in look-alike for many films, recalled Sellers was desperate between projects, calling in the dead of night to morosely explain that he did not find it worth being alive without an active film role.[15] Sellers said of his persona outside of any character he was playing, "If you ask me to play myself, I will not know what to do. I do not know who or what I am."[16] He would utter this statement many times throughout his career, with only minor variation in word choice, over decades of interviews. Those who intimately knew him agreed.

How a man who brought so much joy and laughter to so many could survive such a selfish, self-created hell of his own manic-depressive devising for as many years as he did is a mystery even Lewis's insightful biography cannot explain. It does show Sellers's success was often aided by the keen, self-sacrificing support of others on whom he was dependent. Sellers was a force to be reckoned with owing to his insistent self-aggrandizement and self-nurturing talent. He mastered both early in life as a spoiled child of a doting, performing mother. As has been earlier detailed in the upbringing of James Dean, Orson Welles, Charlie Chaplin, and other filmmakers suffering from bipolar disorder later in life, having a mother who recognizes and enshrines a sense of entitlement by genius is a commonality in some manic-depressive biographies. It is not a predictor or causative agent, of course, as there are many such relationships that result in nothing more than dashed expectations for many otherwise healthy children and disappointed stage mothers. The keen similarity with Chaplin is pronounced, in that Sellers's mother was also a dance hall performer. Both comic geniuses were later plagued by grandiose manias and self-destructive depressions, each using their worldwide fame to therapeutically craft movies, but also at times unable to function as creative entities. Like Chaplin, Sellers was enamored of his mother when he saw her on stage as a small boy. One routine his mother performed, in which she was made to appear to change multiple costumes in front of the astonished audience by means of dissolving slide projections cast onto her body (not unlike the classic James Bond title sequences in effect) left a lasting impression. Sellers later recalled in reverential tones how this moment was key in his love of the illusion of multiple character facades he would utilize repeatedly in his best work.[17] It also fit his manic temperament in that no one role could exhaust him as actor before he first exhausted himself with his improvisational mania, which was always at the moody heart of his therapeutic modus operandi.

Sellers had violent impulse control issues early on in his childhood, and was shadowed by them until his death. As a small boy he pushed a woman into a lit fireplace at his parent's home. He did so without provocation when her back was turned, resulting in burns to her hands.[18] Though his young age is within the range of possible explanations, the pattern of exhibiting a willingness to commit such unusual acts of rage-fueled violence against those whom he perceived as deserving would be later echoed throughout his adulthood and into his waning days. Ted Levy had an affair with Sellers's wife Anne which, according to Levy and Anne, Sellers had actually jealously encouraged. Sellers, who had been blatantly courting the happily married Sophia Loren in the press as well as openly sleeping with other women to his wife's hurt and confusion, arrived at Levy's home at two in the morning wearing an overcoat and moving about as if he were armed. Levy certainly felt Sellers was not acting any part, recounting, "I was convinced . . . that he was going to murder me."[19] How ironic that Sellers would not long thereafter play the opening scene of *Lolita* (1962) with the real-life roles reversed and himself cast as the helpless cheater Claire Quilty.

Quilty cowers for his life after James Mason arrives as the jealous lover wearing a long overcoat and brandishing a gun with intent to kill. Another time Sellers brandished a carving knife with the conviction that he should use it to murder his latest replacement nanny. He had deluded himself during a manic fit into believing the poor woman was bewitched. Nanny Clarke escaped his manic attempt to stab her by leaping from a second story window. Injured, she was taken by a concerned neighbor to the hospital. The police were summoned, but after questioning Sellers—who maintained it was the nanny and not himself who had become deranged—no charges were filed.[20] The violence was not only directed against associates and employees. He assaulted his seven-year-old son Michael in front of family and friends when the boy spray-painted Sellers's latest expensive automobile purchase, naively believing he was helping restore some paint damage their gravel driveway had inflicted upon his father's new toy. Spike Milligan, himself a manic-depressive subject to chronic periods of severe depression and a recluse,[21] recorded he felt the need to intervene because Sellers was shaking the boy so violently and without relent that he believed he would kill him.[22] Dinner guests were also frequent targets, with Roman Polanski saying he had to intervene at a dinner party in which Sellers, livid with moral indignation, attacked a fellow guest who was a doctor with whom Sellers disagreed. Polanski records Sellers became "truly demented"[23] and that he and others had to pry Sellers's fingers away from the choked doctor's throat. Directors were not spared his fury either. Joseph McGrath, the unfortunate initial director before Sellers had him fired from the notorious *Casino Royale* (1967), was forced by Sellers to shoot scenes between Orson Welles as Le Chiffre and Sellers as James Bond without Welles. This happened because Sellers felt Welles had embarrassed Sellers at an on-set luncheon earlier in the shoot. The notion that the most important scene between Bond and Le Chiffre would be anything but damaged by shooting the two principals apart in a production already millions over in costs and nowhere near completion is, in and of itself, proof of Sellers's delusional thinking. When McGrath and Sellers retired to a production trailer to discuss the ridiculous nature of Seller's new demand (so as not to argue in front of the demoralized crew), Sellers blew up and swung, hitting McGrath in the jaw. Not surprisingly, this lead to McGrath's quitting the film.[24] *Casino Royale* would see five additional directors before it wrapped ruinously over budget. These included John Huston, Val Guest, and others, as Sellers fired one talent after another, demanded sets be built and rebuilt, and scenes endlessly rewritten, until the whole affair became the epitome of a runaway film production in crisis mode. According to Ken Hughes, one of the replacement directors, Sellers never finished shooting his scripted scenes even with his relentless mania being capitulated to by the film's producers, one of whom suffered a heart attack he attributed to Sellers's destructive behavior.[25] The painful results bear out the notorious status, as *Casino Royale* is one of the worst films Sellers appeared in and his jaded turn as Bond is completely lacking his customary manic charm.

With so much personal darkness haunting his sense of identity, Sellers found no solace simply being himself rather than a character. To alleviate boredom, Sellers expertly developed his gift of vocal mimicry. His chameleon ability forever offered him the possibility of slipping into the latest strong or attractive personality he met or studied from afar. James Dean and Charlie Chaplin were previously noted for their talent in this department, both fast studies in picking up others' vocal tics and mannerisms. This mockingbird aspect of his talent was what led to Sellers's earliest successes on BBC radio and live television such as *The Goon Show*. In fact, to gain early employment when he was desperate and young, he called a top BBC talent producer and imitated a talent scout they mutually knew, telling the producer he would be wise to check out a rising talent by the name of Peter Sellers pretending. The producer was so impressed when Sellers revealed his charade that Sellers was given work.

His ability to recreate any dialect with astonishing veracity while remaining in character, performing subtext and text with great physical dexterity and superb comic timing, made Peter Sellers an international box office superstar early in his career. But even the early BBC shows were pockmarked with signs of his mental instability in hindsight. Particularly notorious was an appearance on a live skit show called *The April 8th Show* in which Sellers, livid because a parody of the prime minister was cut at the last possible second by management, staged a manic tirade under the show's end credits. Berating the BBC's top brass and informing viewers that they were in consort with foreign powers, Sellers's ramble was not only historic, but nonsensical. Whether it was insanely inspired comic satire gone badly wrong or simply inspired insanity manifest, shocked viewers were left to ponder for themselves. A contrite Sellers defended himself in the press furor that developed by vowing to never appear again on the BBC.[26]

Prior to his magnetic turn as improbable comic superstar, his voice mimicry skills made him a much-in-demand vocal dubbing performer, wherein he would often impersonate famous actors' voices and add post-production dialogue over technical flubs and nonexistent sound takes. Sellers did such work for an injured Humphrey Bogart in John Huston's *Beat the Devil* (1953).[27] His star multiple acting turns in *Dr. Strangelove* (1964) as the Canadian-accented Group Capt. Lionel Mandrake, American-accented President Merkin Muffley and German-accented Dr. Strangelove were impeccable, each a lively characterization on its complex own wherein the voice work was but part of the mystical cohesion Sellers achieved despite numerous changes of guise. Sellers thrived on such changes, guaranteeing as they did that he would not be forced to repeat himself endlessly in one role. Kubrick once remarked that Sellers was better in one or two takes, but depleted soon thereafter, and was never an actor one could rely on for technical continuity of performance. But he was brilliant in the flashes wherein he was genuinely in the moment.

Janette Scott, a child star of British films, clandestinely dated Sellers when she was older and recorded that the strain of keeping in mental balance for Kubrick's exacting directorial manner would leave Sellers exhausted and unable to eat afterward. During this time, Sellers was prone to intense bouts of tristimania.[28] She would later be called to intervene when Sellers was hiding in his bathroom and threatening suicide, twice talking him into calmness after night-long cycles of first tears and then renewed plans to suicide.[29] Given that his personal if fleeting happiness was dependent upon having a variety of alternative personalities to inhabit—any but his own morose, ruminative psyche—it made sense that Sellers sought out such taxing acting projects. Without a role to use as mask, Sellers was as defenseless as an overturned turtle, stuck in his own shell, awaiting help via acting in righting himself. Sellers rarely used such moments of personal disability to reflect and reform his aberrant personality issues. Rather he used his sense of growing frustration at being so emotionally unstable and dependent upon others to become even angrier at them, even as he caused their alienation. The singularity of recall in regard to Sellers's acute sense of loneliness that his chronic mood instability caused when he met others is preserved in numerous accounts. Director Roman Polanski recorded his initial impression of Sellers as being a "sad, shy man who hid his essential melancholy behind a fixed smile." Polanski also wrote in his autobiography, "His manner conveyed profound depression."[30] Jimmy Grafton wrote in his biography of his time with Sellers on *The Goon Show* as being a battle of manic-depressive personalities in fluctuating moods, with Spike the most obviously rapid cycling, but with Sellers himself as a more shrewd form of calculating, bipolar manipulator.[31] His first wife recalled that Sellers would melt into manic-depressive tantrums and swear threats of violence against her that would last for hours. One screaming session went on for nearly fifteen hours before Sellers finally collapsed from exhaustion into profound depression.[32] So numerous are these dark remembrances by those who knew him that it is difficult to find accounts of his life that do not concur. If nothing else, Sellers's chronic mental illness was widely understood as a deeply rooted part of his genius, as well as his genius for self-destruction. Too often, the two could not be successfully balanced, but when they were, the results were entertaining beyond measure.

When enchanted with a project, as he was in collaborations with Stanley Kubrick, Blake Edwards, and a few select others, Sellers could summon the personal discipline long enough to sustain production without being a source of its inevitable halting. But the times he seemingly sabotaged a feature film during its production are legendary, even in a town built on them. In addition to *Casino Royale*, he made production extremely difficult on such troubled films as *The Bobo* (1967), *Ghost in the Noonday Sun* (1973), all of the *Pink Panther* series directed by Edwards (despite his fondness for Edwards), *The Prisoner of Zenda* (1979), and *The Fiendish Plot of Dr. Fu Manchu* (1980), to single out but a representative sampling. The recollections from director after director that he worked with, on even the non-troubled films he starred in, paint a portrait of man who is seen by all who worked with him as disturbed beyond repair. Sellers was willing and able to vent rage-fueled behavior against persons he collaborated with and lived with, but he also created brilliant distillations of complicated personalities on-screen with a manic focus of clarity and originality when his clinical disorder did not unhinge him.

The contradictions and conundrums of Peter Sellers's career and disorder were always lived and artistically rendered on the extremes of life's emotional edges, which is why so many of his film characters endure in the mind's eye. His was a life led mainly in his mind's eye, even if his was a case of definitive third-eye blindness, at least as far as his personal responsibilities went. But when he managed to enact and project that cockeyed vision, rather than remain closed off behind and dysfunctional because of it, a spontaneity of insight emerged that was unique and transformational in his performances. By becoming the characters he played so convincingly, Sellers also invited the audience into a private stage play in which they, too, were delighted witnesses to the proceeding's discoveries, along with Sellers, who was always watching himself askance as well. Blake Edwards remarked that the funniest bits of comedy he ever filmed were the out-takes, never seen save by himself and friends, of Sellers in various scenes in which Sellers would break out of character during a take and suddenly, maniacally offer running commentary about the idiocy of his own character's latest actions and statements.[33] The deadly accuracy of Sellers's diatribe would reduce cast and crew to weeping fits of laughter, which only encouraged Sellers to greater manic heights. This ability reveals the underlying hysteria of nature Sellers faced with each new role. He had to inhabit the character so completely that it provoked a form of primal rage in defensive reaction, with Sellers finding each fault of any new character and channeling it into his performance. His was an ability to make performance indistinguishable from pretense, and perhaps only the equally manic-depressive screen comic Charlie Chaplin was ever as adroit in enlisting audience empathy. But whereas Chaplin perfected his persona and mostly played it throughout his career with only minor variations, Sellers would enact an enormous variety of types and personalities from the beginning. Some were inevitably more convincing than others, but all were alive with a restless, nervous presence of truly being there, as it were, instead of only feeling acted. The final negative proof is his atypical performance in *Being There* itself. The complete emotional and intellectual void of Sellers's Chauncey character is so complete, so utter, that the audience is asked to constantly supply meaning and context where he is concerned because none is actually apparent. In strange summation, this was the life story and struggle of Peter Sellers himself, with Sellers desperately using acting as therapy. This allowed him to confront the emptiness of his own inner landscape, for which he could never supply any satisfactory answers without giving into despair. His was a sad case in which the demon that drove him, his madness, alas never abated long enough for him to enjoy the fruits of his therapy beyond the day's shooting. This even if millions of grateful viewers loved his work, and continue to do so, to this day.

STRANDED ON INGMAR BERGMAN ISLAND

Were they not so influential on the world cinema in their era, the complex and challenging films of Ingmar Bergman would be less profoundly relegated to a bygone era than they are in today's cinema of all surface effect, zero subtext. His was a cinema of acute loneliness and private sufferings made external, or at least tantalizingly hinted at being so, despite their surface obscurity. His was an open, but private, filmic world in which the viewing masses could puzzle with wonder, as profoundly as had the director himself, at the achingly universal nature of madness and melancholia. For as the old expression queries, Who does not go mad from time to time, briefly? While social taboos and self-negating attitudes attempt to deny the shared reality of temporary emotional disturbances, each individual will face his or her own lonely vigil in the proverbial tower of imbalance at some point in a lifetime. Whether it is death of a loved one, a divorce, a near death experience, or even "merely" a surprisingly profound birthday reflection that leaves one unquestioningly depressed, states of extreme mental and emotional confusion are not relegated only to those with a mental illness. The afflicted have these episodes with chronic intensity and often without any seeming correlation to any specific external pressure.

That depression is known to all walks of humanity was key to the success of Bergman's films, both in their native country and abroad. His was a cinema in which the depressed tone itself preceded any subject matter or dramatic confrontation. In Bergman's films, the noonday sun was never a source or illumination as much as it was the primary reason for the dark shadows it cast under Max von Sydow's perennially knitted eyebrows. The luminous beauty of the cinematography he and his gifted director of photography Sven Nykvist achieved was otherworldly in impact. Yet there was a pervasive tone in Bergman's movies that God would righteously atone for so much beauty being unappreciated by the selfish, if well-intended, men and women Bergman lamented. He often shows them toiling in virtual blindness to the staggering gifts at their feet even as they trod over them. It's as if we are privy to a creator's point of view as audience members. Bergman's characters wander in and out of ability to be understood in terms of their consciousness by the viewer. He directed his films in this way; the protagonists seemed to be not merely aware they are in a film, but addressing the audience's awareness itself. They do not beg or pray to an omniscient God only, but also to be understood and made whole by the gathered, if unseen, audience. Bergman's characters feel the heat of the voyeuristic microscope they are being scrutinized beneath. Rather than resent or even ignore the intrusion, they welcome the respite from their respective, pervasive states of lonely self-exile. They offer the viewer their soul confessional as if to an unseen priest in a proscenium-bound booth. In many quintessential Bergman movies—think *The Seventh Seal* (1957), *Wild Strawberries* (1957), *Through a Glass Darkly* (1961), *Persona* (1966) and *Cries and Whispers* (1972)—no one is ever free of their intense sense of isolation. They can and do address their alienation with acts of contrition and sacrifice, however, in an attempt to reconnect with their lost inner lives. Perhaps no man is an island, but Bergman shows that many may certainly inhabit one for long stretches of solitude, as they do in his films. And usually, they inhabit islands of their own making, with moats they've created and filled, and bridges they've deliberately burned, long before events unfold. Bergman's characters were very autobiographical in this respect.

Bergman spent many years of his life living on an island, literally and figuratively, as if mirroring his icily remote characters in his real-world domestic settings. Throughout his career, creative bursts of screenwriting coincided with prolonged psychiatric stays for his chronic bouts of depressive, but alternately manic and hypomanic, illness. He wrote his seminal film *Wild Strawberries* while in a voluntary stay at the Karolinska Hospital in his native Sweden, where he was admitted for "general observation and treatment."[34] Bergman resided on the lonely, wind-swept Fårö Island for most of his later years. He maintained a very rigid regimen of daily morning strolling, writing for three hours, and afternoon movie watching in his home theater for maximum therapeutic effect for his bipolarity. He candidly reveals as much in *Bergman Island*

(2006), the documentary about his life he participated in making with filmmaker Marie Nyreröd. The intense sense of isolation necessary for Bergman to create his cinematic masterpieces was perpetually damaging to his personal and professional relationships. But as he detailed in *Images: My Life in Film* (1995), he had no other way of working, needing both the therapy and withdrawal to order his chaotic thought processes. While writing *Winter Light* (1962), a claustrophobic, autobiographic look at faith and despair in the face of religious mania and faithless depression, he chronicled a three-day and three-night, unending marathon of "desperate enthusiasm and exhaustion" which finally concluded with him in a cold "panic."[35] Nor was his mania only confined to his writing. The first night of his first professional directing assignment in the streets of a small village, he became so maniacal his crew threatened to revolt. They demanded he quit shouting instructions at four in the morning, fearing for their safety from the roused, irate citizenry.[36] *The Magic Flute* (1975) was troubled by the director's abuse of cast and crew with "insults and outbursts of rage."[37] He admitted in an interview in *Playboy* to physically ejecting visitors from his sets, ripping phones from the wall and throwing a chair through the glass of a studio control booth.[38] Bergman wrote of his artistic therapy in making movies by comparing it to an ambulance and doctor arriving at the scene of a psychiatric crisis just in time to treat the wounded artist's soul.[39] He declared he would prostitute himself in any way in order to keep making movies as therapy, not limiting himself from betraying and killing his friends, if need be, in his hypothetical scenario.[40] He would later admit he was being at least somewhat facetious in this dark boast. One wonders, however, at the self-evident proof of his troubled mind revealed in even speculating on such a grisly course of last resort, especially as it envisions the demise of his loved ones as premise.

Bergman was the son of a Lutheran parson who achieved prominence in Sweden for his spiritual counsel to royal family members.[41] This access to the inner circles of power made quite an impression on the young Ingmar. Conversely, his longing for spiritual peace within his Christian faith, a lifelong struggle, originated because of his father. For while loving and moral, Bergman's father was also a coldly stern, even abusive, disciplinarian.[42] As a child, Bergman was left with a grandmother who would lock him in a closet for long periods to teach humility.[43] He recalled his childhood home life as "bitter"[44] and withdrew, as have many filmmakers and actors profiled herein, into a richer inner world of private fantasy. When he traded some tin soldiers for a decrepit but functional magic lantern—a forerunner of the later motion picture projectors—Bergman had at age nine found his calling in life. He began obsessively creating stories and acting them out for friends and family with his magic lantern, making all the scenes himself which he then projected on a darkened wall. He acted the voices and sound effects for each character and sequence.[45] The need to escape his private alienation and reach back out to a living, reactive human audience became paramount to Bergman before he was double digits in age. This is another common motif in the litany of many bipolar artists profiled herein.

Bergman's films are largely allegorical in terms of his manic-depressive illness, but he came close to detailing his mental problems in *Through a Glass Darkly* and *Persona*, as well as much later in one of his last efforts, the television movie *In the Presence of a Clown* (1997). Though the diagnosis for Karin (Harriet Andersson), the afflicted young woman patient who has just been released from an asylum in *Through a Glass Darkly*, is technically for incurable schizophrenia, the actual depictions of depression, rage, and hopelessness experienced both by the ill and their caretakers is equally applicable to many cases of bipolar disorder. Martin (Max von Sydow), Karin's caring but conjugally estranged husband, is an aching portrait of the self-sacrificing nature embodied by many who are forced into the role of caretaker for an emotionally ill loved one. As Karin battles to resist giving into internal voices bent on her submission, Martin struggles with the hell of his personal existence, even as he feels guilty for doing so owing to his wife's worsening condition. The psychological tension on display is accurate, and the shifting emotional bonds that occur between characters because of Karin's illness feels dramatically true. The nervous breakdown of an actress was the subject of Bergman's early film *Persona*. Elizabeth (Liv Ullmann) is left mute after her episode of mental instability and must be taken care of by a live-in nurse Alma (Bibi Andersson). As the film progresses, the recovering Elizabeth begins to have an identity crisis in the presence of the strong-willed Alma, finding it a challenge to her own reawakening persona. The film metaphysically deals with issues many bipolar patients confront, especially with depersonalization owing to lingering depression. The desire to rebuild after an episode is often confronted by failed earlier expectations and a sense of the hopelessness of laying a foundation upon emotional quicksand. Bergman demonstrates this in literal fashion as Alma and Elizabeth fuse together on screen in one potently shocking image of identity crisis in full clinical measure. *In the Presence of a Clown* also deals with a protagonist who has been in a mental institution and who struggles post-stay to make sense of a darkly clouded future. Uncle Carl (Börje Ahlstedt) is loosely based upon Bergman's uncle and the diaries his uncle had written, which detailed the familial history of inherited madness. The creepy scenes of Rigor (Agneta Ekmanner) the rigor mortis–faced clown silently taunting Carl in the asylum at night as Carl tries to ignore the leering, grinning figment are horrific. Likewise, Carl's decision to make a movie after his incarceration as a means of healing his mind is autobiographical. "A furious work pace and good professional collaboration can construct a fine corset against the onset of neuroses, threatening breakdowns, and disintegration,"[46] Bergman said of his approach to staving off mental demons by way of channeling his creative energies.

But even though these films deal with mental illness, the reality in Bergman's films is that they're all to one degree or another concerned with the theme of mental disintegration. This is true whether owing to old age (as in *Wild Strawberries*), sudden mortality (as in *The Seventh Sign*), or any number of so-called understandable reasons. Because this was the chronic mental state of the creator himself, Bergman intensely focused on characters who were undergoing psychic crises beyond their ability to comprehend, as he struggled not only to externalize the pain he experienced inwardly, but even to attempt therapy at all in the despairing face of pervasive illness. "The temptation is to resign oneself, to flee into the darkness, into paralysis of non-action, into hysteria," Bergman wrote of his life-long use of cinema as therapeutic model versus his defeatist, depressive tendency toward self-abandonment.[47] His was a triumphant body of artistic integrity, spanning over sixty-seven features, television movies, and shorter works, as well as nine Academy Award nominations, three Academy Award–winning films, and the prestigious Irving G. Thalberg Memorial Award in 1971 in recognition of lifetime achievement. The long list of disciples who praise him as one of the greatest of all time and a major influence on their decision to make films, as well as how they view the possibility of filmmaking as an art form, includes Woody Allen, Paul Schrader, Martin Scorsese, and Francis Coppola, all of whom likewise were sufferers of mood disorders.

FELLINI'S FILMS OF LA DOLCE TRISTE

Federico Fellini's films are remembered today for their sensibility of indulgence and style, surrealistic tone, casts of beautiful people, wonderful photography, and unique sense of evoking all that is universal in the Italian culture he so adored. That's quite an achievement as legacy for any filmmaker. But there was another great quality that was present throughout much of Fellini's august body of work that is not as often critically recognized, and that was melancholia. Whether it was the sad-faced fate of his real-world mate Giulietta Masina as Gelsomina in *La Strada* (1954) in being cruelly married to the emotionally abusive ex-circus strongman Zampanò (Anthony Quinn), or the numerous thinly veiled nostalgic recollections of his childhood memories in such complex efforts as *I Vitelloni* (1953), *8½* (1963), *Amarcord* (1983), or *Fellini's Intervista* (1987), Fellini's was a cinema of intensely private moments of reverie and daydreams rendered into almost embarrassingly revelatory moviemaking. Many directors only hint at a private fantasy life that is dimly reflected in their otherwise pedestrian styles, however successful their efforts. Fellini was incapable of escaping his inner world of imagination and rumination, each at odds with one another, to produce such calculated works of commercial accessibility. Fellini was at his best when they were indivisibly united, such as a love of subject matter with his maniacally expressive style. And more often than not, moments of sustained melancholia creep into some of his most memorable movie sequences, perennially creating a mood of reflective loss and remembrance that is difficult to forget.

Consider Giulietta Masina as the sad-faced prostitute in *Nights of Cabiria* (1957). Her character Cabiria spends long nights in extended sequences walking the empty streets attempting to solicit men amid a dark city landscape. These scenes of urban isolation and desolation, combined with the protagonist's pained forgoing of her own dignity at her sordid circumstances, visually capture the aching sense of alienation many depressives feel while under the spell. It is Giulietta Masina Fellini again uses when he addresses depression and mental breakdown in the haunting *Juliet of the Spirits* (1965), in which the hardly disguised character name Giulietta Boldrini is utilized. Giulietta is the adoring wife of a famous film director. The director has affairs with his beautiful leading women which leaves Giulietta feeling worthless, in a role painfully parallel to the actual marriage of Fellini and Masina. She begins having vivid hallucinations in which hellish visions of her earlier childhood Catholicism and symbolic dream figures representing her emotional conundrum mingle with her everyday reality, making one indistinguishable from the other by film's conclusion. The surrealistic scenes of Giulietta calmly walking amid her own mental delusions as active participant, smiling as if in a private parade staged for her amusement, are justified in the film by suggesting she has fallen under the hypnotic control of a spiritual guru. The more truthful emotional reality in subtext is that Giulietta is having an extended mental episode, involving auditory and visual hallucinations. These are accurate descriptions of manic-depressive illness during more severe phases. In a nod to the master melancholic himself, Edgar Allan Poe (whom Fellini called "a great favorite of mine since I was a teenager")[48], Fellini directed the episode entitled "Toby Dammit" in the trilogy feature film *Spirits of the Dead* (1968), focusing on a drug-addled film star played by Terence Stamp. The common obscuring motif of using hallucinogenic drugs as motivation for the cinematic excesses on display is invoked by Fellini. But another, equally justifiable reading of the segment is that Stamp's character is having an episode of bipolarity, and that he's using the drugs and alcohol as a way to explain his behaviors to others. This is a common biographical element in many shared bipolar histories.[49] The rationale is easy to understand: apart from the relief such attempts at self-medication provide the sufferer, they excuse and mask the erratic mood swings of the underlying psychiatric disorder. This bestows upon their conduct a more acceptable social veneer of lifestyle outlaw, rather than the more ostracizing label of mental outcast. This patterning has been previously chronicled concerning James Dean, Nicholas Ray, Peter Sellers, Blake Edwards, and many others. The increasing social liberalizations of the 1960s in terms of sex and drugs also increased the trend for bipolar actors and directors who will later admit to extensive abuse of both as a desperate means to self-medicate without openly admitting their illness.

The amount of screen time devoted in his films to rumination, melancholia, and attendant bursts of escapist fantasy are numerous. This accurately reflected Fellini, who was as moody and emotionally complicated in his real life as his many troubled protagonists. When one considers the various accounts of his mood and personality given by Fellini and others who knew him, there is a possibility he had an undiagnosed manic-depressive illness with a tendency toward being down most of the time. The possible thesis must suffice because, despite numerous statements from Fellini and cohorts in many interviews and books that openly portray him on the manic-depressive spectrum, Fellini himself rejected any psychiatric diagnosis. His was not an uninformed opinion. He read Jung extensively and publicly agreed psychoanalysis was of enormous value, especially to creative types.[50] Fellini suffered from chronic sleeplessness that often left him depressed throughout much of his adult working life, as it has many profiled filmmakers and actors herein with bipolar disorder. He notoriously quipped in a printed response to Italian film critic Emma Bonino, who had panned one of his films by explaining that it induced sleep in viewers, that even her constant whining about his bad filmmaking couldn't put him to sleep owing to his severe insomnia.[51] On the opposite end of the spectrum, but also indicative of his hypomanic sexuality and partial explanation for his chronic infidelity, Fellini professed to owning a massive collection of pornography stills. He claimed Groucho Marx had given him the photos as a gift after many years of prior personal appreciation.[52] Fellini admitted he had privately utilized and added to the collection over the years. In a textbook example of hypersexuality attendant to some bipolars, he confided he struggled with his constant need for sex daily, and that he had often sought succor for his troubled mind by indulging in nonstop sex until physically exhausted.[53] On the depressive side, Fellini was candidly characterized by collaborator Giovanni Grazzini as being in a constant funk for years on end "unhappy with himself, and the world."[54] So well-known were Fellini's battles with depression among friends and colleagues that Joseph Losey sent him a simple letter that merely stated, "Cheer up!"[55] But for those who have chronic mood disorders, such well-intended, but ultimately unachievable, blandishments are not helpful. They only further remind the patient how little is understood about the underlying medical conditions causing such private suffering.

Fellini was self-consciously aware of how he utilized his illness to fuel his cinema in the later years of his life, comparing filmmaking to an illness that must be worked out of the body.[56] More particularly, he had no doubt there was a link between madness and creativity.[57] He said the filmmaker's pathology "reveals itself as kind of hidden treasure"[58] in terms of how it influences any project. Fellini surmised, blithely but accurately, that the artist for him was "someone who is called by demons and must reply to the summons."[59] In this light, one can view the entirety of his work as a form of intensive personal therapy. That it lasted for most of his lifetime was mostly an achievement in catharsis versus despair. Sadly, toward the end of his life and as his age made directing for therapy remote as realistic treatment, Fellini succumbed to his depression and anxiety. The last half-year of his life was reduced to alternating, rapid-cycling episodes of depression wherein he was nearly comatose, followed by manic bouts of shouting and screaming for his wife by name, even though she was most often not allowed to be by his bedside.[60] This may be the saddest proof that he harbored a lifelong mood disorder that only overtook him in the terminal stages of his life. Though tragic in life's conclusion, Federico Fellini's triumphs are what remain for generations to forever experience anew. During his very imaginatively rendered lifetime, he used first drawing, then writing, and finally directing films as continuous personal self-treatment for his unspecified mental woes. He bequeathed a legacy of still unmatched visual lyricism and expressiveness in cinema. The fact that his style has been so little copied when so many of his contemporaries were mined ad infinitum is testimony to the unique power of vision Fellini possessed. He worked in a fevered state he described as a seizure,[61] allowing it to creatively overtake him, however delusional the visionary outcome. This is very akin to the way visionary manic-depressive artists work, as has been previously detailed. Fellini's films and statements about his prolonged periods of mood instability contribute to a body of work that is ripe with expressive moments echoing bipolar cinema's major themes and imagery.

8

1970S: THE MANIC-DEPRESSIVE TEMPERAMENT DEFINES NEW HOLLYWOOD

The French auteur theory was lionized by many influential young American filmmakers and film critics in the late 1960s and early 1970s. The radical notion that a director was the key author of a motion picture (as opposed to the more inclusive view that of equal importance were a screenwriter who presumably wrote the script, the actors who performed it, and/or a producer who often hired the writer, cast, and director in the first place) created a generational devotion to the new possibilities of a deeply personal, yet paradoxically commercial, filmmaking style that could be widely released. While the horizons were truly vast, the sad reality is that the artistic results achieved in the era of so-called New Hollywood cinema were very short-lived and practically negligible in terms of cultural impact in America by the early 1980s. They were, in large part, steamrolled by the Reagan-era corporate takeover of the industry. But while under the thrall of such grandiose wishful thinking, namely that the new auteur theory would finally represent an ongoing challenge to chaste conventional studio filmmaking, some lastingly great movies were made. Some were arguably the best ever made in the American studio system, if not the medium itself.

How else other than the auteur theory to account for this rare, unparalleled creative time in American cinema? If one forgoes the influence of auteur theorists such as Truffaut, Andrew Sarris, Pauline Kael, and their like, then dependent and subsequent works such as *The*

400 Blows, Bonnie and Clyde, 2001: A Space Odyssey, Easy Rider and *The Last Picture Show* would likely never have been realized. Under the control of the studio heads and appointed lot producers prior to the rise of the auteur influence in 1960s Hollywood, these films would have been radically different. *Easy Rider*, would have featured tons of rear projection screen footage of Captain America and Billy on stationary motorcycles à la Brando in *The Wild Ones*. That is, without auteur-enthralled director Dennis Hopper insisting the picture be shot on the road minus the usual studio lighting. Kubrick's *2001* would have been another space opera with tail-finned rocket ships sputtering exhaust sparks, bikini-clad Venusian women in need of Earth spacemen for crossbreeding purposes, and the inevitable, slinky-armed, clunky silver robot. That is, without Kubrick's ability to exploit the auteur theory for all-encompassing artistic control over the production process. Bogdanovich's *The Last Picture Show* would have been in glossy color, filled with teen roles acted by thirty-somethings, and luridly akin to *Losin' It* or countless other so-called "virginity" genre movies. That is, had the auteur-obsessed director not insisted on keeping the adult sexuality of novelist Larry McMurtry's source novel and shooting with a young cast of relative unknowns. Of course, it is more likely these films would not have been made at all, given their subject matter, mature natures, and directorial visions, without the protective shield of the auteur theory. Perhaps the best, if saddest, evidence supporting this generally accepted historical view of 1970s New Hollywood cinema excellence as exceptional is today's anemic output. The auteur theory finds as much sustained belief among today's studio power brokers as would global warming inside an oil conglomerate's ruling echelon.

Thus the key films of the 1970s can be viewed as a collective body not because of similarity in themes and styles, but by the one, overriding belief that unites them all: the director is, and acts as, god. These influential movies shared a self-defining aesthetic. This aesthetic insisted that all key creative decisions were significant to the director, and they were made with as few compromises as possible to his or her vision during the production process. To this end, the auteur's cast and crew needed to rise to the occasion and embrace the new creative freedoms offered by having a director on the set guide the process, and not studio executives imposing decisions via memo from on high. Whereas one well-staffed but regulated department was anonymously assigned to the latest studio product in the preceding system, New Hollywood cinema set in motion a series of revolutionary practices in filmmaking techniques and methods of production behind the cameras as much as in front. This meant a greater stake in the creative outcome for collaborators. They were now freer to suggest and contribute to the integrated vision offered by a central figure, the auteur director, rather than hoping someone in the proverbial front offices would care about anything other than their respective department's bottom line. This is perhaps why such rich collaborations emerged in the astonishing array of films made under the auteur rubric. There is a general misunderstanding about the "director as author" concept in the era since its untimely demise, best distilled as the image of a tyrannical director insisting on complete control and obedience to his absolute dictation. The flowering reality was just the opposite in actuality. Each director empowered, and some might say stranded, on Auteur Island quickly realized that no director alone could make a masterpiece. The filmmaking process was and remains so technically and economically challenging that only a collaborative auteur had any real chance of achieving greatness. The director imposed a singular vision, but used his vision as guiding light for others to bask in as well. In some ways and despite the contrary image, the auteur director was even more dependent upon his collaborators than his previous studio brethren in the craft. The New Hollywood cinema required a more personalized approach to each production, wherein the director had to assemble each new movie almost from the ground floor, instead of waiting to be assigned his cast and crew by his studio bosses. However messy at times, this enforced a more democratic tone in many of the auteur-directed movies and resulted in a more diverse, complex cinema wherein each movie more often bore the psychic imprint of its auteur director as a result.

    This level of directorial control would ultimately prove a bridge too far for sustained Hollywood blockbuster moviemaking of the type George Lucas and Steven Spielberg soon popularized with such movies as *Jaws* and *Star Wars*. Such efforts and their later adherents were more stringently calculated than the auteur-driven efforts. This is not a value judgment, save to recognize that the value of box office grosses grew larger and faster in direct proportion to how much a movie preshrank its premise and execution in terms of viewer challenge. As a direct consequence, the more personal visions of Martin Scorsese and

Francis Ford Coppola, two filmmakers whose auteur works had come to define what made New Hollywood cinema such a watershed, were slowly driven from the marketplace. They were replaced by the less sophisticated thrill ride movies, which had the bonus of favoring sequels, prequels, and mass merchandising. Additionally, the boom in 1980s multiplex cinema construction also lowered the overall quality of movie production in terms of narrative complexity. Multiplexes demanded a faster turnaround on opening night (and therefore more gimmicky high-concept ideas over plotted stories). This soon ended the more traditional model, which allowed for a film's grosses to grow over time by holding it at a sustained location to build audience awareness and interest. The hit-or-miss mentality meant that if a picture failed to make money on Friday, by the following mid-week plans were already underway to substitute in its place the Next Big Thing. The mantra was quickly established: reduce risk and increase returns. The promise of a cinema experience with dozens of new films on a theater's multiple screens rapidly degenerated. Against an offering of variety as spice, the blander taste of tent-pole cinema prevailed. New franchise pictures such as *Indiana Jones and the Temple of Doom* would occupy five or six screens during its opening sweep. Too often, the rest of the multiplex offered nothing but leftover studio fare that too often already had the newly emerging cable and home video markets stamped on them as ultimate destination. The one-two punch was a lethal knockout as far as the dying auteur theory and quality-conscious American filmmaking were concerned.

In fairness, the other forces contributing to the rapid decline in Hollywood narrative excellence are numerous beyond the mere overbuilding of movie screens. The aging boomer population, which had funded the art house cinema movement (always an important epicenter of talent discovery and critical opinion, both of which were necessary to sustain the auteur theory as reality) began to stay at home with children rather than attend lengthy double-bill evenings of subtitled, imported movies (with attendant costs of dinner, parking, and babysitter). Alternative venues that formerly offered challenging cinema from around the world folded in all but the largest urban American centers, thus shrinking the available fare from which discerning critics could discover cutting-edge films. Faced with a marketplace filled with movies of an increasingly commercial-only nature, and witnessing a global art form slowly being replaced by homogenized global "product," American film critics turned from championing the latest new import and instead lamented the passing of an era—if they bothered to comment upon the decline at all. In this light, it comes as no surprise that the in-depth arguments of passionate cineastes who once followed each new rising film director or movement with ardor soon devolved into the "thumbs up/down" mentality of film discussion embodied by *Siskel & Ebert at the Movies* and the like. As any attendee of a dinner party gone awry knows, when the conversation lacks a congenial but spirited airing of ideas, the conversation turns to self-conscious, reductionist statements such as "I liked it," or the converse. But given that the films themselves had begun to shed all semblance of artistic, rather than brutally commercial, intent, any other cultural outcome seems unlikely. For how were fans of the New Hollywood cinema to sustain their own admittedly often self-aggrandizing, but equally artistically inspiring, critical chatter if the directors, writers, producers, and actors themselves had fallen by the wayside? As went the auteur-driven movies, so went the once fostering critical response, into mutual obsolescence.

We recap this monumental movement in filmmaking not to bury Caesar, but to praise him, so to speak. For it is truly a fitting analogy to say that the Hollywood director of the 1970s who worked under the auteur framework found the same fate as the imperial rulers of the glorious days of Rome. And this is why the auteur is so critical to our review of bipolarity and its influence on filmmaking as an art, as well as artistic therapy, by its creators. Some of the most influential filmmakers of the 1970s—Francis Ford Coppola, Peter Bogdanovich, Woody Allen, Martin Scorsese—who powerfully defined New Hollywood cinema, were also mood disordered. Mania and depression run throughout their biographies as surely as does cinematic greatness. The singular fact that each of these auteur practitioners can claim to have had nearly complete artistic control over his creation (at least as truthfully as can any director of a motion picture), and then later received universal accolades for the visionary aspects of their works, even while they were all suffering under the vagaries of mental illness, is some of the most convincing proof of this book's central thesis. To suggest that this rich output of creative genius was only coincidentally made by mood-disordered directors during the 1970s and that their illnesses had no expression in their works, when each admitted to his personal mental health

issues in countless interviews and accounts later given by working associates, and when each stimulated the others with their compulsive com-
radeship and obsessive natures throughout the era, and when the films
in question were undoubtedly made under the auteur theory and therefore by definition self-revealing with director as author, simply begs
credulity. It is therefore worthwhile to examine each of these key filmmakers in some depth, as their singularity and persistence as individuals
is just as revelatory when seen through the perspective of bipolarity and
the arts as it is through auteur theory.

FRANCIS FORD COPPOLA AS
BIPOLAR ARTISTIC VISIONARY

Francis Ford Coppola knew early childhood setbacks attributable to ill
health as part of his psychological makeup. As many psychiatric studies
have concluded, early adolescent stressors of an unusually intense variety (the death of a parent and/or incapacitating illness) can be later
contributors to the severity of bipolarity,[1] at least in those who already
probably have a genetic latency for it. Coppola was stricken with polio
when he was eight years old. He spent over a year and a half in bed with
his legs paralyzed. As a result, Coppola's formative years were largely
housebound. He faced emotional duress both overcoming the illness
and then undergoing the painful physical rehabilitation for his affected
gait. Coppola also did it alone, as the neighbor parents, fearful their
own children would contract polio, forbade visitations to the bedridden
boy.[2] He was by self-admission forever the new kid in the class owing to
his family's constant moving due to financial constraints, relocating over
thirty times during this tumultuous period.[3] Like many profiled bipolar
filmmakers and actors, he spent many lonely hours as a child forced to
fill the void with mainly his expansive imagination. Coppola escaped via
nearby movie palaces in his boyhood cities of Detroit and New York
when he was physically capable, and spent a great deal of time watching
early television's insistent replaying of classic movies as a means of
obsessive study. "A lot of my getting into the movie business stems from
me feeling this isolation,"[4] Coppola commented. Like many in his generation, he saw filmmaking as a profound possibility that was unrealized
too often by the mundane, factory-styled Hollywood epics of the early

1960s. Beginning as a screenwriter and then graduating into the ranks of writer and director for cinema outlaw Roger Corman's own perverse cadre of young talent eager for experience, Coppola's rise to stardom as auteur would come to define all that was revolutionary about New Hollywood. It all was seemingly possible because of the liberating power of auteur theory in practice, just as surely as Coppola's personal and financial plummet after the fiasco of *One from the Heart* would seal his fate as a failed visionary as the 1980s progressed. His manic heights and epic lows were not only part of his legendary status as genius filmmaker with a flair for grandiosity, but equally the driving force behind his tortured creativity during the 1970s. It is staggering to think that in the span of seven years, Coppola wrote/co-wrote/produced/directed such successive classics of American film as *The Godfather*, *The Conversation*, *The Godfather Part II*, and *Apocalypse Now* in surely what is one of the greatest-ever runs of artistic and commercial success in Hollywood's admirable roster of stellar over achievements. Nor does this filmic string of pearls include only its own strand. Coppola also helped launch many filmmaking careers during this incredibly fertile, if often deeply troubled, period of his bipolar-inspired career as producer. George Lucas and Walter Murch profited as younger protégés who had mega-careers of their own in part due to Coppola's patronage. On the other end of the spectrum, an elderly Akira Kurosawa saw Coppola as kindly benefactor (along with a by-then wealthy George Lucas) for funds to complete *Kagemusha*, enabling the film to get theatrical distribution in the United States when such imported releases were a dying breed. But though brief in duration, in his rebellious reign as auteur and visionary, Francis Ford Coppola *was* the prince (however Machiavellian), and some would argue king, of New Hollywood cinema. But finally, the very strain of madness that imbued his masterpiece works with achingly melancholic tones tipped over into the constant battle for his own personal emotional sanity. Thus ended his incredible record of artistic triumph in the face of, and briefly over, chronic mental illness.

Eleanor Coppola, his wife of many decades, recorded her encounters with her husband's bipolarity in her autobiographical account *Notes: The Making of Apocalypse*. In one vivid remembrance, she recalls a forlorn 1970s evening at New York's trendy Elaine's, frequented by the profound and the powerful. Francis and Bernardo Bertolucci were dining, each looking, as she recalled, severely depressed. Eleanor describes Bertolucci as a mirror image of her husband in terms of devastated facade, with Coppola's droopy eyes haunted and devoid of his normal energy. She contrasts this dinner to an earlier encounter the two previously shared in Italy many years earlier. Then Coppola and Bertolucci were manic in their giddy enthusiasm over life, loves, and their mutual admiration for cinema, literally dancing through the darkened Italian streets late into the night with glee. But as the two formerly magnetic screen legends sat before her at Elaine's and dejectedly picked at their uneaten food, Eleanor Coppola wrote how she began to see the profound disparity so inherent in manic-depressive illness, at least as far as world-class filmmakers who labor with it are concerned. As if to add a downcast coda to the joyless meal, Bertolucci recounted how the prolonged filming of his epic *1900* (1976) was in large part because of his nonproductive depressions, during which times the producers shut down filming until he recovered. Bertolucci concludes the grim memory by stating he became a temporary hypochondriac in order to complete the film and save face with his bewildered but loyal crew, who knew nothing of his mental illness.[5]

As if on strange, synchronistic cue, Eleanor Coppola next noticed Woody Allen also was in the restaurant, sitting alone and looking miserable, what she described as "a caricature of a lonely little man."[6] To make her *Twilight Zone*-styled encounter with mental illness and directorial visionaries all the more complete in one horrific evening, she unbelievably then saw Bob Fosse, clearly depressed, hiding away in a dark corner booth behind clouds of chronic nicotine and surrounded by sycophantic floozies. Eleanor reflected that success had done nothing to alleviate the mental illness present in Fosse, despite his maniacal attempts to work himself to death. She concluded in her journal later that fateful evening the following entry: "Francis and Bernardo had shadows of some personal lingering depression. Woody Allen looked miserable. I hear Marty Scorsese is not well. What is happening to all these directors?"[7] And the answer, of course, was clinical mood instability. Be it from excessive, prolonged hypomania or mania followed by the inevitable exhaustion of depression, or from drugs and/or alcohol fueling their natural bipolar or unipolar states, or from the pressures of constant scrutiny and paparazzi pursuers, or the escalating film costs and therefore critical expectations, and/or all of these and other intense stressors, the unequivocal conclusion to Eleanor Coppola's rhetorical question

was: *they were all under the influence of mania and depression.* It was
the only unifier between them that bound them and their boundless
energies, and lack thereof, together as a band of brethren.

The works of Coppola during the New Hollywood cinema are the
best source to understand Coppola's intensive struggle with his own
manic-depressive tendencies. Think of the withdrawn persona of Michael Corleone in *The Godfather* (1972) as eerily personified by a sul-
len-eyed, stone-faced Al Pacino. With his compartmentalized, secretive
nature, Michael is the embodiment of a highly functional but emotional
depressive. When he ruthlessly acts with diabolical genius during the
baptism of his own son to murder his rivals all at once in a maniacal
display of absolute power, he is acting out a classical bipolar stereotype
of criminal madman. While it is true Michael is not wearing a white lab
coat, or holding a screaming victim at bay with a knife to her throat, he
is nevertheless a distillation of the criminal mastermind à la Dr. Mabuse, but recast as a Mafioso overlord. But did not Dr. Mabuse equally
run a secretive criminal empire issuing orders for his henchmen to carry
out under the facade of normalcy, as does Michael as head of the
family? Likewise, the hot-headed Sonny (James Caan) seems on the
spectrum, barely in control and with a propensity for manic-laced behaviors, such as his hypersexual affairs and explosive, abusive rage. Indeed, the tragedy of Sonny's character is that it is precisely this, his
innate propensity to give in to his own instability, that is used by the
family's rivals against him. They use Sonny's incipient rage to fatally bait
him in the film's memorable tollbooth assassination. Older brother Fre-
do (John Cazale) appears to have mental issues beyond bipolarity alone.
He nevertheless exhibits a chronic sense of depression and fatigue in
most scenes, and has been excused from the family's dynastic politics
for this largely unspoken reason. Patriarch Don Vito Corleone (Marlon
Brando) suggests the apple indeed rarely falls far from the tree, at least
in terms of his passed-along genetic predisposition for depressive behavior. Vito spends most of his days in dark, shuttered rooms, privately
ruminating in silent agony over the tragedy of his own criminal life,
even as he hopes to redeem his sons' fates before he dies. Vito is also
inarticulate to the point of mumbling, so personally painful are his
bouts with depressive fatigue. He is the sluggish personification of
weariness, and though his life of crime is contributory, Vito suffers from
lingering depression. It is clear to everyone that Michael is Vito's favor-

ite son, but it is not only because Michael has, when the movie begins, seemingly managed to escape the clutches of Vito's failings. There is another, more subtle suggestion that Vito senses Michael is more like the old man than even Michael yet understands. The father knows that his son's darker, depressive mania can, and perhaps will, drive the younger man to commit acts of revenge and murder currently beyond the son's reckoning. Vito's hopes are not only for his son to escape a life of savagery for profit, but likewise, to escape the clutches of a haunted sense of self-alienation that the father's own depression has created as vacuum in his life. So when therefore Michael acts to avenge the attempt to assassinate Don Vito, the tragedy is heroically delivered, thus temporarily deceiving the audience. Michael is acting in the best interest of his family to protect them, and yet, conversely and tragically, is falling prey to his own latent homicidal mania, which in time will lead him to murder even his own brother. The heavy sense of portent and latent doom Coppola creates in his claustrophobic masterpiece of human darkness is grandiose in the best sense of the term. The dirge-like theme that accompanies Michael on his depressed, nearly catatonic rounds as an angel of death to those he encounters is a subtle depiction of the aimless restlessness manic depression can induce. Michael is too often remote, keeping himself distant, withdrawn and, by the second film's conclusion, almost reclusive. Only his piercing eyes, boiling with cunning and intent, betray the poker face he perpetually wears as dour mask to conceal his bipolar depressive rage. His estranged wife Kay (Diane Keaton) will grow to see through his mask of calm deception, as do all others who grow close to Michael, to the destructive, vengeful, tormented soul hidden deeply inside. By *The Godfather Part II* (1974) their estrangement is perfectly captured by Coppola without a word, as Michael unexpectedly arrives at the family's Lake Tahoe compound. He strolls around the empty house finding no sign of Katy until he happens upon her upstairs in their bedroom, silently if morosely sewing, alone in her thoughts. He stares at her from the hallway without announcing himself, too depressed to initiate conversation, and clearly further saddened by her own obvious self-entrapment. He finally walks away, and in the minute that has elapsed without dialogue between his arrival and non-announcement to his wife, Michael's dour expression silently conveys all of his internal misery. But as with some undiagnosed bipolars, Michael cannot admit to his morbid condition. He thus dooms himself to be forever controlled by it via his own denial, just as he denies his involvement in his murderous deeds.

Things fare equally badly for Coppola's next alter ego protagonist Harry Caul (Gene Hackman) in his depressive masterpiece *The Conversation* (1974). An expert in audio surveillance with a shady past, Harry buries his chronic depression with non-stop work, avoiding at all costs emotional attachments to other people. His is a bachelor life lived without adornment, designed to avoid self-introspection by negation of personal effects. Indeed, as Harry tells his landlady during an annoyed phone call with her, he is without a sense of personal needs. "I would be perfectly happy to have all my personal things burn up in a fire because I don't have anything personal," he coldly tells her, adding, "Nothing of value." But as Harry will come to learn when his own amoral spy games are turned on him, there was one quality of life he had of value that he denied until it was forever gone. And that was his peace of mind, his inner sense of solitude, his private reservoir of lonely pain. It is finally destroyed in him by the film's end when he realizes his privacy is but a sad illusion maintained for the vanity of the next highest bidder. In his desperate depressive fortress of solitude, Harry is made to see even personal despair cannot shelter one from life's darker forces when they are intent on seeking one's weaknesses out. His only form of therapy, his work, loses all meaning, and he's reduced by the last shot to desperately playing music in order to wrestle with his inner turmoil.

Gene Hackman's physical portrayal of Harry Caul is remarkably accurate to many depressives, complete with his rumpled overcoat which he seems incapable of taking off. He lives a severely restricted life of not interacting with other humans, preferring to hide behind an endless series of gates, locks, bars, and electronic surveillance. He is the perennial key master, forever selecting which small area of his life to allow, or deny, access to others. Harry is clinically accurate to successful depressives who learn to mask their downcast natures by sublimation into their work, the proverbial workaholic, and by compartmentalizing their relationships so that no one person has any real hold over them. Much like the depressive salary man in Kurosawa's previously referenced *Ikiru*, Harry buries himself in his workload, which is forever expanding, and in his fascination with the latest technology that will, ironically by film's conclusion, be utilized against him.

Harry's choice of occupations is shown to be no coincidental matter, but as all things in Harry's life, meticulously considered and then controlled. Even his name has a literal pun in it. A "hairy call" is slang for precisely the kind of sinister warning telephone messages he receives as the film progresses in which he is anonymously advised against taking any actions that might save the lives of his recent surveillance suspects. Likewise, Harry spends his days and nights in his master control room inside caged rooms, obsessively reviewing the latest voices on his surveillance tapes in order to filter out hidden meanings, playing the ghostly conversations over and over. In many ways, Harry hears voices both in and out of his head. The outer voices are echoes of his own interior monologue, which is a depressive mantra never far from Harry's besieged conscience. He uses his own form of audio therapy to attempt to relieve the inner voice of certain doom that plagues his waking state, only to ironically find that he has projected his fearful thoughts onto his latest case to tragic ends. *The Conversation* makes it painfully clear, to viewer and protagonist, that depression makes Harry his own worst enemy, because it isolates him from humanity and from seeking help for his chronic loneliness. Depression also fuels his latent paranoia with well-earned guilt at the moral implications of his work, therefore making him mistrust even his paid mistress. She laments that he always opens a locked door quietly and then quickly enters, as if he's going to catch the person in some shameful act. At every turn, Harry's paranoia, already raging quietly beneath his calm exterior, threatens to overwhelm him and his unwavering loyalty to his secretive trade. As if to accentuate this hiding-in-the-shadows quality about Harry, he is most often photographed slinking in the background of a scene, or hovering in a darkly lit corridor, or even sitting in a dark city transit bus at night and never turning on an overhead light. He prefers to remain incognito in silhouette, even in his own life, when he's not on the job. But as Coppola elegantly shows, set to a musical score of downbeat notes that promise to crescendo but always instead seem to fizzle out into a depressive coda of failure, Harry cannot survive by hiding from himself, or his disorder, without horrific consequences.

If these three key films—*The Godfather* and *The Godfather Part II*, along with *The Conversation*—constitute the bulk of Coppola's definitive examinations of depression, then surely *Apocalypse Now* (1979) is his best artistic statement about the unchecked ravages of clinical manic

depression. A bona fide masterpiece in the sense that it truly represented the ultimate example of synthesized auteur theory and Hollywood
blockbuster, *Apocalypse Now* also managed to offer some of the most
shocking images of bipolar-inspired madness ever committed to cellu-
loid. The multiplicity of manic-depressive characters is truly an accomplishment. With his wife's unblinking journal about the making of the
film, there can be no doubt that Coppola was at both his manic creative
best and depressive own worst enemy in the four years the legendary
film took to complete, nor can there be doubt that he was intimately
incorporating his own psychiatric illness into the film's very themes.
Eleanor Coppola recorded in *Notes* that for Coppola, the line between
screenwriting and his state of bipolarity was rarely disjointed, and that
for most of her years married to him prior to *Apocalypse Now* the
process was agonizing, self-tortured, and never without costs to his
emotional well-being.[8] During the extended production of *Apocalypse
Now* he extensively rewrote the script, often to fill time between jungle
monsoons that made shooting impossible for weeks on end, experiencing insomnia and falling into, by his wife's description, "a black depression."[9] Part of his agony was that, as she explained, Coppola insisted on
always working out current personal demons as he wrote rather than
examine already resolved conflicts with dramatically licensed hindsight.[10] So the resultant scenes of internal emotional confusion, self-
aggrandizing egomania, and destructive rage present in *Apocalypse
Now*, as well as behind the cameras, are entirely predictable based on
Coppola's need to use his screenwriting not only for commercial consideration or even artistic clarity, but a personal sense of resolution. It
was this need he had during this period—to pull off the ultimate hat
trick of box office popularity, cinematic excellence, and art as therapy
for its maker—that defined the essence of New Hollywood filmmaking.
Because Coppola's struggle was with manic depression, and because he
utilized his characters to express the various shades of bipolar behaviors
he had personally known, *Apocalypse Now* (perhaps one of the most
self-revealing film titles ever, as Coppola certainly underwent life-altering revelations during its making) is a definitive look at the eternally
conjoined nature of the arts and madness.

The film opens inside a delusional episode of manic-depressive recall as experienced by soldier assassin Captain Willard (Martin Sheen)
in which memories of napalm jungle clearings, fiery temple facades of

forgotten gods, and Willard's own dark history as an elite forces killer combine in one hellish nightmare montage of personality disintegration. Willard recalls his dissolved marital ties, remembering his last visit stateside was nothing but prolonged depression and selective mutism. "I hardly said a word to my wife, until I said 'yes' to a divorce," he flatly tells the audience. Willard is shown retreating from reality via a weeklong drinking binge that seems unending until headquarters has need of his services. In a drunken stupor of dulled senses and simmering, repressed violence, and glaring at the seedy room where he has endured his depressive episode, Willard says "each time I looked around the walls moved in a little tighter." This remains one of the more expressively apt lines ever written for the movies describing the debilitating boredom so often experienced by the depressed. Fueled by a growing mania for action, Willard explodes in a stylized kabuki version of his own disorder's worst aspects. He attacks a full-length mirror while naked, ramming his fist into the panes of his own reflection, and then falls beside his bed, spent and weeping with depressed agony. His bloody hands grasp his sweat-stained bed sheets, as he uselessly wraps them around his heaving, destitute form like a baby attempting to comfort itself with a favorite blanket. In the opening minutes of *Apocalypse Now*, the audience undergoes a vivid episode of manic-depressive psychosis with its beleaguered bipolar protagonist. Willard is not only unable to escape his own racing thoughts, but witnesses the devastating loss of all hope and identity that accompanies a severe episode of mania and depression.[11]

If Willard as functional manic-depressive, as the film's opening moments suggest, is at least a debatable thesis, then Col. Kurtz (Marlon Brando) is the end game of bipolar dysfunction, a true madman in all senses of the word. Where they differ is the expression of their shared illness. Willard is reserved, a hider, a true killer when provoked, but otherwise in control of his latent homicidal mania, using alcohol as self-medication and coping mechanism for his depression. In some aspects, Willard is a continuation of the flat emotive qualities (clinically a marker for potential mood disorders) seen in both Michael Corleone and Harry Caul as the preferred style of Coppola protagonist. Beneath the depressive facade in all three characters lurks barely checked maniacal anger, but the stone-faced mask each wears attempts to deny their inner conflict to outsiders, and tragically, to themselves. Kurtz is fully lost in his insanity before the film even begins, already another in a series of ghostly voices (like the couple's voices in *The Conversation*) in Coppola's films who haunt each new listener. Via recorded radio broadcasts earlier made by Kurtz, Willard hears Kurtz openly speak of his mental illness as akin to being a snail and "crawling, slithering, along the edge of a straight razor . . . and surviving." There seems implicit in the commanding officers whom Willard must audition for in his assignment to "terminate" Kurtz a complete disregard, even mild disgust, for Kurtz's descent into madness. Only Col. Corman (G. D. Spradlin, in a clear namesake nod to Coppola's mentor) expresses mild, if condescending, patronage at Kurtz's plight, wearily resigned after numerous failed assassination attempts that Kurtz is a dead man walking. He even goes so far as to refer to him in the past tense even before Willard accepts the job to "terminate with extreme prejudice." The prejudicial aspect is not only in terms of saving face and avoiding public war crimes trials, but also against the mental illness Kurtz is exhibiting. No documents in the many numerous private papers Willard studies in regard to Kurtz's past urge Kurtz to seek mental health treatment, even as he undergoes an increasingly erratic, mood-based series of personal and professional decisions potentially manic-depressive in nature. The horror of his slow, grinding descent into insanity is delineated with clarity. Conversely, no clinical or humanistic understanding of the agonies detailed is ever made, or successfully comprehended, by those who encounter Kurtz's bipolar illness until long after the fact of his having lost his mind. Indeed, a worried, manic photojournalist (Dennis Hopper) who has fallen into the jungle cult of Kurtz babbles to the imprisoned Willard that no one will ever understand Kurtz as the "great man" that he was, owing to Kurtz's madness. There is an understandable recognition herein by Coppola of a fear inherent to all artists who work the edge between stability and beyond, spoken by the photojournalist. Will the work be judged by its own integrity, or will the creator's illness work against its later, objective appreciation? For as much as bipolar disorder may confer some creative advantages, it surely exacts a toll, as the prejudicial nature all mentally ill patients face is still rampant in society. Thus many artists eschew acknowledging their painful personal disorders so that it will not interfere with the perception of their produced visions. It is, of course, an enormously private choice to disclose or not, and no negative values should be placed by those outside the one having to make such a measured, often agonizing, decision.

Kurtz was a very personally painful stand-in for the troubled Coppola, as his wife wrote. She noted the parallels between them in their shared manic exhilaration of indulging in risky behaviors as a bet against the onset of the blues, with a willing blindness for understanding the possibilities of personal ruination as a result.[12] As we have seen in a previous account with Nicholas Ray and his gambling debts, this is not uncommon bipolar behavior. One night as the torrential Filipino rains poured, Coppola crawled atop a lighting scaffold and lay there, moaning. When Eleanor joined him, he begged her to encourage him to quit the production and return home, lost in depression and panicked at his need to continue despite himself.[13] He would rocket up into hypomania and become prone to rages, such as when someone made an off-hand comment during the projected nightly rushes of the day's shoot. During such fits of rage he would scream and break whatever object first came into focus of his blazing eyes. He threw a two-by-four piece of lumber at producer Gary Frederickson during one tempestuous outburst.[14] Once when a helicopter pilot refused to transport Coppola out of the jungle owing to an approaching storm, Coppola responded by grabbing his newly purchased Nagra miniature sound recorder, a marvel of design and expense, slamming it to the tarmac and grinding his heels into it. He scooped the pieces with immediate, childlike remorse as he broke into tears, realizing what he had done.[15] These kinds of heartbreaking displays of self-destructive behavior, in which bipolars wreck their personal belongings as a form of self-immolation, are sadly common, particularly during acute episodes.[16] As puzzling and unpreventable as such manic rages are, they nevertheless capture the disorder at its most indefinable paradoxical nature. Such film sequences as those in Welles's *Citizen Kane* in which Kane rips apart his former wife's bedroom as artistic representation distill the true pathos of a destructive bipolar rage.

Mania is also full-blown in Lieutenant Col. Bill Kilgore (Robert Duvall), with a focus on the charismatic quality it bestows upon leaders, motivating their followers to often seemingly impossible feats. Coppola also shades it by way of criticism that it is used just as often by the charisma-charged alpha male for personal narcissism and childish power brokerage. In a self-referential nod to his earlier Academy

Award–winning screenplay for *Patton*, Coppola stages Kilgore as more a garden variety charismatic career officer turned carny pitchman, half-charlatan and half-genius. He suffers from clinical delusions of grandeur brought about by mania. Kilgore is obsessed with all the bravado of a helicopter-flying John Wayne, whom Duvall seems intent on physically channeling with such Duke trademarks as hip-swivel swagger and perennial ascot. Willard belatedly appreciates Kilgore's beaming charisma, concluding in the voice-over that "he was just one of those guys with that weird light around him." This is a typical descriptor made by those closest to manic-depressives who are in the up phase of their cycle and who possess latent charisma.[17] Fueled by mania and with a willing audience eager to absorb each new idea, charismatic bipolars account for many real-world leaders. This is why Kilgore is so self-parodying and generates the most audience laughter of any sequences Coppola ever directed. The viewer recognizes in the gargantuan overkill of Kilgore's self-magnifying persona so much of the mindless, but mind-numbing, platitude masking as rational thought one encounters in interviewed military leaders. At least, of the kind who are eager to divert attention with double-speak and defensive posturing during losing or prolonged conflicts. Kilgore is about the style, not the substance, of his acts of atrocity against mankind. As long as he can surf his beloved waves and maintain his American gung ho diet of steaks and beer, Kilgore is a-okay with slaughtering civilians and profiting from his actions. His moral center is a bipolar-magnetized needle that spins on a dime's notice, depending entirely upon his mood. When he is pliant and agreeable, as when he has taken a beachfront from the North Vietnamese and turned it into a party zone for his men, Kilgore is deftly manipulated by the watchful Willard, who patiently awaits his chance to gain favor with the unstable Kilgore. Later when another landing zone is still hot with enemy gunfire, Kilgore will make his famous insistence that the beach is safe to surf, not because it is, as witnessed by his terrified men being blasted out of the waves, but because his mania has declared it so. It induces laughter, but again, it is not without reason that Willard screams a rhetorical question of "Are you crazy, goddamn it?" when confronted with Kilgore's actions. His question is received with snarling indictment by Kilgore, who again proclaims the beach's safety and angrily strides into incoming fire without a nick to prove his point (and, unintentionally perhaps, Willard's point). Kilgore's constant use of urgent manliness to cover his mental illness is sadly revealing. In a key moment, he regrets the inevitable end of the Vietnam War not because of the countless lives wasted, but because it will, in essence, leave him with nothing with which to occupy his disorder after the war. The look of pure resignation on Kilgore's face shows forlorn distress as he contemplates a future without his daily regime of therapeutic geno- cide. In a moment of unguarded manic-depressive panic atypical for a bipolar character otherwise entrenched as a take charge persona, Kil- gore's ego deflates. As a result, it is almost the only truly poignant moment in Duvall's otherwise blustering performance. Even though his narcissism is as pathetic as his willing mania to murder on a mass scale, Kilgore feels empathy for at least one human being, himself. It hu- manizes him for a briefly shining, if selfish, moment, before Kilgore resumes his arrogant posture as inhuman killing machine. Such mercu- rial shifts themselves are indicative of probable cyclothymia.

And though it is but a brief cameo, Coppola's own Hitchcockian insertion of himself into the landing zone sequence in which Willard and crew accompany Kilgore on his village airborne raid one morning is interesting to note, too. He is standing beside his 16 mm camera opera- tor in battle fatigues and sunglasses, shouting directing tips above the din of exploding shells and the screaming wounded. He yells for the bewildered Willard to move along for his camera as if nothing were unusual. Coppola's alter ego is a raving maniac whose voice is miracu- lously heard above the surrounding sounds of warfare. His emotionally laden insistence for the actual soldiers to play along, as if they were not in harm's way but pretend actors on the back lot, is indicative of clinical mania. In a film filled with manic-depressive archetypes, it is only fit- ting Coppola rendered himself in miniature performance as a delusion- al filmmaker lost in the making of his latest cinematic opus, as he was in actuality during some of its production and post-production history. For as Eleanor later described it, Coppola cycled up and down to greater heights and worsening lows than he ever had before in their marriage, and much of the worst of his bipolarity was manifested in the prolonged editing of the film. Jerry Ross, a sound editor on *Apocalypse Now*, complained the entire sound crew would spend as long as three months waiting for an editing directive from the absent director, only to receive a cryptic note from his penthouse that was beyond decoding.[18] He would occupy the screening room by himself, smoke marijuana, and

endlessly watch the six-hour rough cut with various self-supplied musical cues, while his bewildered editors passed their time wondering what
had gone wrong with him. Toward the end of the ordeal, Coppola
suddenly appeared in the edit bays and, driven by uncontrollable mania,
began an impromptu, hours-long critique of the current edit of his film,
insisting on radical changes beyond the crew's endurance.[19] One fired
editor became so hostile he stole the final reels of the film in rough cut
form and reportedly sent Coppola a mailed envelope each day filled
with burned film ashes. Coppola finally broke down into paranoia, accusing his editing team of being against him and his vision. Via phone
Warren Beatty evidently recognized the symptoms when Eleanor described them (possibly from working as far back as 1961 with Vivien
Leigh in *The Roman Spring of Mrs. Stone*), insisting she needed to get
Coppola immediate medical help. Coppola went on lithium for four
years after his 1979 breakdown, but was on record as not liking it. He
would complain to his doctors, but they insisted he needed it as a
precaution against suicidal behavior.[20]

Today Coppola's style of narrative filmmaking, and therefore influence, has waned to the extent that it is difficult to properly understand
the full context of the auteur kingdom he once briefly, if creatively,
ruled. Coppola helped transition a mordant Hollywood style of studio-
bound production into a new sense of reality-influenced filmmaking
that was still as dreamlike as the best of the studio system's output in his
milestone 1970s works. Then he led another, apparently less successful
revolutionary movement into "electronic cinema," as he dubbed it.
Coppola's flagship example of the new aesthetic of filmmaking was the
disastrously received flop *One from the Heart* (1982). But consider the
gallant effort on its own merits, rather than assignment of critical blame
or box office returns, and one immediately sees Coppola was again a
radical visionary. For everything that he attempted in the creation of a
new studio system based in high-definition video production that was
dismissed in its era as so much delusional egomania has become the
latest visual cliché at the local cineplex. Today's cinema is nothing but
high-definition video and chroma green screens, computer-created
backgrounds and, increasingly, actors, all directed by a nonentity from
on high, more akin creatively to the way an animator approaches making a film rather than the classically set-bound director. These were
precisely the technical means Coppola outlined as the future of film-

making in 1980. Coppola saw the possibilities of cinema unlike any other in his generation. His manic-depressive temperament was key to his ability to be unique and authoritative even as he was inventing a new way of filmmaking within the confines of the American studio system. If today's movies have only sadly taken the technical means, and rejected the narrative aspects Coppola advocated, it is not the fault of the visionary who ushered it in. Rather this dubious distinction belongs to the adherents who selectively choose ease of production over complexity of vision when both were and are achievable. They need only have the artistic resolve to explore the visionary aspects of the medium as ruthlessly as they exploit the bottom line. Such creative epochs are rare in Hollywood's century-plus history, and are always driven by exceptional visionaries such as Coppola who are often on the mood-disordered spectrum. As *Apocalypse Now* co-screenplay writer John Milius once told a college film class I attended, such visions never come from the front office "bean counters" who insure profits at all cost, particularly the audience's, at the direct expense of originality.

THE LOST PICTURE SHOWS OF PETER BOGDANOVICH

If Coppola is unfairly negatively characterized for championing auteur theory, it can be perhaps attributed to his own penchant for making self-aggrandizing statements to friends and media. Like many talented bipolar actors and filmmakers, modesty can be sometimes notably absent amid manic self-inflation. One of the main, if generally friendly, acknowledged rivals to Coppola's title as best commercial filmmaker in New Hollywood cinema was Peter Bogdanovich. Bogdanovich also amassed a reputation within Hollywood's power elite as a true enfant terrible during his head-to-head struggle with Coppola to be crowned king auteur. Screenwriter David Newman accused him of having a monstrous ego that people loathed, and talent agent Sue Mengers described him during this era as "rude" and "cavalier."[21] In startling contrast, he could be generous of spirit, as demonstrated by his befriending Orson Welles, or his tireless devotion to cinema as historian of often overlooked figures worthy of praise. His attitude was sometimes characterized as arrogant and dismissive, and yet his films of this era are intimate and unguarded. Like his competitor, Bogdanovich was under the influence of his own bipolar disorder during the key peak of his creative output in the 1970s. His influential films of this time have always been noted for their melancholic tones.

Bogdanovich was the second generation son of Serbian parents who had fled their Belgrade roots to avoid Hitler's rise to power in the 1930s. Destitute, tradition-bound, and unable to easily adapt to New York City's polytheistic culture, Borislav Bogdanovich, Peter's father, struggled as a manic-depressive painter of landscapes in an art world obsessed with more modern styles. Unable to sustain himself or his family, Borislav finally had a nervous breakdown in 1948 and was hospitalized when Peter was but ten years old. Borislav would never fully recover, being subjected to ECT when his morose depression would not abate after other treatments.[22] From the earliest age, Peter Bogdanovich knew the firsthand reality of the illness and the huge toll it took on family, friends, and professional ambitions, as he slowly, inexorably watched his father's descent into insanity. In doing so, Bogdanovich also shared another common childhood marker common in bipolarity with his future rival Coppola: each had experienced a major childhood stressor before later developing manic depression as adults. Coppola's stressor was polio and isolation, while Bogdanovich's was his father's clinical mania and depression, which meant many painful episodes witnessed by the bewildered young Peter. This profound early shock was doubtless a driving force behind Bogdanovich's early need to seek the relative emotional stability, and fantastic escape, offered by each new feature at the local movie palaces of his youth. By his own accounts, he obsessively attended movies from a young age, claiming that he saw over 400 films each year. Those who knew him in the era never disputed his claim owing to his impromptu encyclopedic knowledge of movies. He was a programmer and wrote the well-regarded critical notes for the first major Orson Welles and Howard Hawks retrospectives at the prestigious Museum of Modern Art in New York City when he was only twenty-one, helping to elevate the aging filmmakers' fading status among the influential cineastes of the early 1960s.[23]

As we have previously seen with Marilyn Monroe and James Dean, and with directors such as Francis Coppola and now Peter Bogdanovich, ritualistic, precocious attendance at movie theaters is a common biographical marker in bipolar filmmakers and actors. Given that the 1940s and 1950s cinemas of their youth showed movies all day and into the night for very low admission rates, this is somewhat understandable. Film attendance in that era was a much heavier percentage of the general population than it is today. That stated, the unusual devotion to seeing hundreds of movies per year as many of these chronicled persons did is staggering even when one accounts for increased film attendance in prior times. This is especially true when one considers how much more effort anyone, let alone a child or preteen, had to put into actually seeing a movie back then, as opposed to now, where one is hard pressed to find areas of the globe where movies cannot be instantly viewed on demand. This obsessive devotion to cinema itself often lurks in the background of many bipolar directors and performers, and it is not difficult to speculate on reasons why the connection to film viewing is so fanatic. The best Hollywood films have traditionally offered a sustained emotional arc, complete with a dramatic catharsis for their viewers. Unlike a stage play, the same moments with the same performers can be repeatedly, and therefore reliably, experienced ad infinitum by re-peat viewings. Those on the emotionally disturbed spectrum perhaps find comfort in participating in experiences that offer predictable, com-forting conflicts and outcomes in comparison to their own unstable, moody landscape. This is not to say that bipolar viewers prefer safe or predictable cinema. Rather it is that the overall sense of being able to trust the Hollywood formula film to deliver the goods, as it were, ena-bled manic-depressive viewers who heavily attended movies in the era the ability to expunge their pent-up needs to cry, or growl, or even scream, in a socially acceptable manner. It was a form of semi-private, low-cost therapy. Of course, many otherwise healthy viewers also rou-tinely participated in movie-watching marathons, but for these profiled manic-depressives, the allure of repetitive watching may have been more internal. The ability to repeat watch the same movie as such mood-disordered viewers did also meant they could undergo a kind of emotional baptism. The same set of intense emotions could be endless-ly called forth in stylized participation, over and over, but predictably so. For many healthy viewers, such repeat viewings, back-to-back, would quickly induce boredom. But bipolar attendees probably craved the emotional stability presented by the repetition, as it offered them at least a semblance of such continuity while their own emotional states were more highly fluid. It is true watching the same movie is easily done today in smaller settings, if not alone, on private viewing devices.

All the more reason the idea of figuratively "escaping to the movies" had a resultant bigger psychic and cultural meaning when Coppola and Bogdanovich were impressionable youth. Such experiences were done in darkened movie caverns and mostly, if not totally, in the company of strangers. If one wanted to participate in the film's deepest levels when these future auteur directors were young, one had to commit to regular movie theater attendance as part of the only critical ability available to study the art form itself.

While melancholic themes run throughout much of Bogdanovich's work, *The Last Picture Show* (1971) is as definitive an expression of depressive alienation in American cinema as ever made. The cover of banality provided by the dreary, rural Texas locales of author Larry McMurtry's childhood does little to alleviate the horrific sense that boredom, not money, is the root of most evil. The bleak, despairing tone, set forth from the opening shots of the windswept streets of the forgotten little town and the decrepit movie theater in particular, seem to be commenting upon all of cinema to this point in weary time. It's as if the filmmakers were invoking a funeral service in an abandoned cathedral for film itself as redemptive art form. This evocative, bravura tone of elegy and hopelessness is so adroitly handled and maintained throughout the movie that it is easy to appreciate even after decades of repeated viewings why audiences in 1971 were so mesmerized by *The Last Picture Show*. It casts a lingering, hypnotic stare at a small town's hidden sexual and social moreys. In doing so, it reveals a suggested prevalence of mood disorders in many of the characters across a wide range of ages and backgrounds, none of whom seem even aware they are suffering from mental illness, let alone ever having sought any form of clinical treatment. The film is not merely about characters with depression; it is depression personified, and every low-energy angle, every moody line of dialogue, and each darkly lit black-and-white scene is designed to induce a kind of voyeuristic coma in the viewer. In a word, *The Last Picture Show* casts a spell, and it holds until the final bleak moments when Ruth (Cloris Leachman) breaks the reverie with her sad utterance to the depressed Sonny (Timothy Bottoms), "Never you mind, honey. Never you mind." She may as well be speaking to and for the audience as she blows out the dim flame of flickering humanity Bogdanovich has so expertly rendered before the final existential fade-out.

Several characters in particular stand out as being on the mood-disordered spectrum. Sonny is a shy, downcast, awkward young man given to going along with whatever life throws at him in order to avoid confronting his own depressive nature. But his hang-dog look of perpetual confusion and inability to articulate his deeper, repressed feelings mark him as having an early onset of clinical depression. His spiritual godfather, Sam the Lion (Ben Johnson), is a sad preview of Sonny's own coming decline into perpetual blues, and Sam seems to recognize a kindred spirit in the forever sighing Sonny. Until his untimely death, Sam tries to steer Sonny to follow his passions and not give in to the small-town skepticism and self-defeatism all around the young man. Sam's eloquent scene at the fishing hole wherein he laments his early "craziness" over a lover he lost, and how he misses being crazy in love with her, is one of the film's highlights. Bogdanovich very simply shoots it as a long, slow dolly in, and then out, on Johnson's wistful, craggy face. He lazily rolls a smoke and allows the years of depressive misery to devour his stone face, even as his eyes twinkle with dim satisfaction when he recalls earlier days when he still had a reason to live, and love, life. Ruth, Sonny's older and married lover, is expertly played by Leachman as suffering an extreme episode of depression that only abates whenever Sonny distracts her from the crushing boredom of her empty life. Her stiff, awkward movements and plain, pained features give her a tragic dimension that Sonny is too oblivious to understand until he later experiences a clinical depression himself. And Lois Farrow (Ellen Burstyn) is presented as a functional depressive who hides behind alcoholism, fading memories, and shopping sprees to Dallas to mask her ongoing disorder. Thus, many of the townspeople of *The Last Picture Show* are in obvious, desperate need of mental health intervention, but in a dying town where even the movie theater is closing, what hope do they have for a psychiatric doctor to open a residency?

Peter Bogdanovich once spoke at the UCLA film school after a screening of *The Last Picture Show* in the 1980s in which I was in attendance. One of the first questioners from the audience was a young man who confessed he was from a small town eerily akin to the one depicted in film, and further, that he thought Bogdanovich had done the finest job of any movie the student had ever seen in capturing the bleak reality of such an existence. Bogdanovich adjusted his trademark ascot, stared blankly for a moment through his oversized glasses, and drolly replied, "God, I hope not. No town should be like that. It's just so . . . *depressing*." His dry response generated laughter, but there was a knowing sense in his reply that more was being alluded to than was being acknowledged. It was telling, perhaps, that he did not mention the major contributions of Polly Platt, his first wife, whom some consider a codirector of *The Last Picture Show* in terms of her shot-to-shot contributions behind the camera in consultation with Bogdanovich. Ben Johnson certainly thought so in interviews, flatly declaring she directed much of the film albeit through suggestions to Bogdanovich.[24] Others, including Platt herself, were less accusatory, implying that the creation should, at most, be looked upon as an intensive collaboration between herself and Bogdanovich, but with Bogdanovich rightfully credited as director.[25] The point is not to stir waters best left stilled with Platt's passing, but to introduce a very probable reason why the depressive themes resonate so well in *The Last Picture Show*. For Platt herself suffered from chronic spells of depression and hypomania, and she freely admitted to abusing alcohol throughout much of her life as self-treatment to prevent suicidal thoughts.[26] She and Bogdanovich fell in love and married in 1963 because both loved movies and knew them as few others did, but likewise, they shared the bond of familial instability. Polly Platt's mother had suffered a nervous breakdown and was hospitalized when Platt was a young girl. This gave her a childhood stressor as clinical marker that she shared with her first husband, Bogdanovich, that of a mentally ill parent. She also coincidentally shared another key stressor with Francis Coppola when she was also stricken with polio in her childhood. Platt recalled the ordeal as being isolating because she was left alone in a sick ward for months on end. Her unstable mother never visited her, emotionally abandoning Platt at age eight to face her fate and recover alone. Although she recovered from the polio, she was not as lucky concerning the sense of abandonment her mother's rejection caused.[27] Given that both Bogdanovich and Platt were emotionally unstable at times in their lives, and that both were so intimately involved in the translation of book to film, it is only fitting that *The Last Picture Show* is still considered a classic of melancholic cinema. Both of its major creative contributors knew from personal experience the soul-burdening challenges of loving, and living with, someone with manic-depressive illness. They used the barren landscape and defeated characters of the film to sketch their intimate view on depression in bold, clear strokes.

Hollywood would not be as kind to Bogdanovich as it was to Platt in later years, but both managed long careers in an industry in which it is difficult to ever successfully maintain steady employment. Bogdanovich never really matched nor topped his early 1970s entries, though there were many admirable efforts. *Saint Jack* (1979) in particularly warrants mentioning for its melancholic undertones. Jack Flowers (Ben Gazzara) is a charming, manic American pimp hustling in Singapore who dreams of one day owning his own brothel. Key to the film is Flowers's friendship with depressive British accountant William Leigh (Denholm Elliott), a middle-aged man pensively poised on the edge of a perennial nervous breakdown. The project was a collaboration between Gazzara and Bogdanovich, with Gazzara even cowriting the screenplay with the director. Bogdanovich recognized the pangs of suffering in Gazzara and tailored the role for him to reflect it. While Bogdanovich characterized Gazzara as the type that could make a scene of himself telling a story in a restaurant while in his up phase, Gazzara struggled with depression much of the remaining time. "I could see he was very depressed, but he gave a great performance," Bogdanovich later wrote in a memorial to Gazzara's passing. "It was quite evident he was suffering."[28] Bogdanovich's tragic relationship with Dorothy Stratten, and his subsequent, prolonged depression over her heinous murder, was in part the subject of Bob Fosse's *Star 80* (1983) and Bogdanovich's autobiographical book about his downward spiral after her homicide, *The Killing of the Unicorn: Dorothy Stratten, 1960–1980* (1984). His tragic loss overshadowed Platt's own brand of loneliness, particularly after her third husband, Anthony Wade, died, a death she attributed as a catalyst to one of her severe depressions later in life.[29] And while it is a far cry from film art like *The Last Picture Show*, Bogdanovich perhaps fulfilled a deeper purpose when he appeared as host of a two-part instructional video in 2000 for pharmaceutical giant Eli Lilly called "Achieving a Balance: A Beginning of Hope for Patients with Bipolar Mania," and "Achieving a Balance: Tips, Resources, and Strategies for Patients with Bipolar Mania." Both were designed to highlight the benefits of Zyprexa, a medicine used to treat the manic phase of bipolar disorder, for which Eli Lilly holds patents.

WOODY ALLEN AND THE
DEPRESSIVE NEUROTIC ARCHETYPE

Woody Allen, born Allen Konigsberg, began life with an innate sense of how to entertain. He performed magic tricks to amuse older relatives and neighbors, and was, according to his mother, an outgoing, socially well-adjusted boy who showed great promise at an early age given his self-confidence. And then, for reasons not understood by anyone, including Allen himself, he experienced his first excruciating clinical episode of anhedonia at the age of five.[30] As a result, his personality rapidly changed from easygoing into withdrawn and melancholic. He spent most of his time engaged thereafter in creative solo activities, often alone in his room, a habit he has largely kept to this day. He developed many deep-seated fears during this initial phase of his ongoing depressive state that would haunt him in his adult life: of death; of being in the dark alone; of imaginary abductors; and of mechanical transportation, especially via ship, aircraft, and elevators.[31] Indeed, so rooted is Allen in his disorder's identity that the working title of his masterpiece *Annie Hall* (1977) was "Anhedonia." He wisely changed it when in test screenings of the film the audiences' only negative reaction was to the title.[32]

The anhedonia Allen experiences is a form of depression that is largely limited to the pleasure-directed centers of the brain. The anhedonic state is often characterized as a chronic restlessness in which the sufferer cannot easily find remedy because such typical mood-boosting activities as eating a fine meal, visiting with friends, having sex, or related intensely social interactions prove emotionally deadening. Individuals afflicted with this profoundly alienating disorder struggle to find meaning in the very concept of social existence.[33] They experience an often acute sense that they are cut off from the busy social world constantly going on around them, no matter their best attempts to reconnect with estranged friends and other relationships. As an episode of anhedonia wears on, sufferers may simply avoid seeking relief via others altogether and isolate themselves in private activities, especially if they are lucky enough to have a creative or therapeutic outlet to alleviate their painful withdrawal. Alternatively, after enduring agony over their inability to connect with pleasurable activities, anhedonics may shatter their isolation by throwing themselves into new activities with goal-directed plans that force them into contact with other human beings.

More often than not, however, and dependent upon the severity of anhedonia, such social redirections are short-lived. The anhedonic needs to withdraw to lessen the self-consciousness of his inability to talk or exchange physical cues with others when experiencing an acute episode.[34] This aspect of Allen's own depressive nature is constantly referenced in his films and characterizations, such as the lonely, recently divorced film critic, with the barely disguised name Allan, in *Play It Again, Sam* (1972). Allan finds dating again almost as unbearable as his collapsed marriage, which has largely dissolved owing to his obsessive movie watching and inability to lead an emotional life outside of his devotion to films. As he painfully attempts to find a significant other, Allan must confront the fact that his own innate neurotic nature acts as a natural repellent to members of the opposite sex. He must also work through his own anhedonic personality, in which he can find little relief from life's endless series of disappointments. His only effective coping mechanism lies in escaping into delusional fantasies involving movie icons, wherein no less than Humphrey Bogart circa *Casablanca* appears to give Allan personal dating direction. While it is pathetic on a blackly comic level, the portrait of Allan as an emotionally unstable man with a need to draw upon fictional screen personalities to sustain his own faltering ego is a realistic aspect of the depression of many others chronicled herein. Another is the obsessive need to continually watch favorite films because of the delineated emotional catharsis they always deliver upon each subsequent viewing. For a personality like Allan's, which is always on the verge of depersonalization, a strong-willed, never-yielding tough guy persona like Humphrey Bogart's understandably represents the ultimate wish-fulfillment fantasy.

It is worthwhile to also point out that while anhedonia and manic-depressive illness share some commonalities, they are also clinically quite different. An anhedonic who impulsively seeks out social contact with others may be acting in response to his mental condition, but he tends to be less beholden to his condition during the process of actual socialization itself. The neurotypical aspects of such a person may remain otherwise balanced, and such a sufferer may in fact make otherwise healthy choices even while nervous or not severely afflicted. A manic patient who is acting under the influence of his disorder in a like manner may have no basis other than grandiosity or delusional thinking as his rationale for interaction. While an anhedonic will typically be shy and less than the center of any gathering, a manic can often be charming, talkative, and charismatic, with the hallmark that the self-aggrandizement is often tinged with delusions and distortions.[35] An anhedonic state does not necessarily mean one is having an episode of mental impairment that affects judgment, whereas a bipolar patient experiencing clinical mania can, and most often does, lose objective mental balance. But, this distinction noted, and it is more than a fine one, the two states of emotional disorder share depression as their common denominator. Expressions of depression are often a hallmark in cinema made by artists on the mood spectrum. It is why, beneath every well-timed and keenly observed joke, there is in Allen's oeuvre the lingering doubt that comes with living with a clinical mood instability. "Many times, I've gone to sleep at night, and it wouldn't bother me for a second if I didn't wake up in the morning,"[36] Allen told Roger Ebert, lamenting the pointlessness of life from his perspective. He told interviewer Robert E. Lauder as late as 2010 that "existence is a brutal experience to me. . . . I'm really impotent against the overwhelming bleakness of the universe and that the only thing I can do is my little gift and do it the best I can,"[37] adding that the gift of filmmaking was "cold comfort."

The various dark shades of clinical anxiety and depression are so numerous in Woody Allen's work, however veiled with grim humor, that he seems to be obsessed with exploring them. One only has to conjure the befuddled Alvy (Woody Allen) in *Annie Hall* and the numerous scenes of Alvy's fears, such as the freeway ride at high speed with his convertible-driving buddy and manly alter ego Rob (Tony Roberts), for the laughable side of his neuroses. The constant use of psychiatrists as a necessary evil hovers throughout much of his 1970s work and is also an indication of his decades-long dependency on therapy. A childhood friend who ran into Allen early in his career was startled that Allen confessed he'd found a psychiatric clinic with a sliding-scale fee and, as early as the 1960s, was seeing the therapist there five times per week. Allen characterized his need for treatment to his former classmate as an attempt to rid himself of "a continual awareness of seemingly unmotivated depression."[38] At times, his heavy feelings of depression have tipped his films into nearly hermetic efforts that can leave some viewers too distanced, such as with *Interiors* (1978), *September* (1987), and *Another Woman* (1988). *Interiors* is noteworthy in that it focuses on an aging woman protagonist named Eve (Maureen Stapleton), icily controlling matriarch of her dysfunctional family. Eve has a past history of sanitarium stays and ECT treatments for her recurrent clinical depression, and eventually suicides because of her inability to avoid relapses. As if in reaction to the relatively cool, if not negative, reviews and tepid box office results of these grimly serious efforts (in which he usually does not appear as actor), Allen generally prefers to craft his more accessible films with a comically endearing perspective on his hopeless situation (for anhedonia has no known cure, only treatments, like bipolar disorder). In this way, even those not afflicted by a mood disorder find his flailing, often fruitless but heartfelt, stabs at personal happiness empathetic and entertaining.

It is illustrative to view his vast body of moody cinema through the lens of bipolarity in order to fully appreciate how Allen captures realistic states of manic-depressive illness so truthfully. Key to Allen's clinical understanding of bipolar disorder (besides his own depressive tendencies) was his second marriage to actress Louise Lasser, a diagnosed manic-depressive who shared Allen's deadpan sense of comic delivery. Lasser's own mother had committed suicide after failed bouts of ECT, a situation that Allen used in *Interiors*, much to Lasser's chagrin.[39] Lasser was so manic-depressive that she had daily telephone calls with her therapist and was heavily medicated to the point of sleeping throughout much of her day. As Allen lamented to Lasser's friend Eric Lax, she went from having remission and stability for weeks out of each month to less than a couple of good days per month toward the end of their marriage.[40] As chronicled in Marion Meade's *The Unruly Life of Woody Allen* (2000), their mutual disorders resulted in many days in which the depressive Lasser retired to her bedroom for solitary confinement, while a frustrated and helpless Allen retreated to his study to immerse himself in his writing. While this action by Allen may appear callous and abandoning, the reality of their life together was such that there was little Allen could have done other than sit by her bedside and passively watch her suffer. His underlying anhedonia would have likely skyrocketed in response to her amplifying depression had he chosen a less therapeutic path of inaction, and a vicious cycle would likely have ensued. Instead Allen poured himself and his despair into his work in a form of self-obliterating catharsis. As Allen said of his disciplined need to work through his depressive state of mind, "I can go into a room every morning and churn it out."[41] *Interiors* was a first stab at delineating the emotional roller coaster ride that comes with every relationship with a bipolar person, but in the 1980s with *Stardust Memories* (1980) and *Hannah and Her Sisters* (1986), Allen would more fully explore his time with Lasser as his suffering manic-depressive wife with even more candor and revelation.

As his work demonstrates over decades of constant refinement and achievement, Woody Allen is anything but a commercial hack. This despite the fact that he has remained a safe financial bet for most of his career and has had several movies defy their modest budgets to become lucrative hits. As his career skyrocketed, however, Allen remained self-isolating. Although he had many collaborators, upon whom he was creatively, if sporadically, dependent, he was largely without friends. And even the intense daily interactions in his filmmaking were not without anhedonic side effects for those who intimately worked with Allen. Ralph Rosenblum, the editor who cut such films as *Annie Hall* and many others before his professional falling out with Allen, said of their remote, decade-long collaboration, "We've never shared a heartfelt concern, an uninhibited laugh, an open display of despair or anger."[42] Nor are such accounts of his solitary nature infrequent. Recall the earlier quote by Eleanor Coppola describing Allen as the embodiment of loneliness in the public setting of Elaine's Restaurant. Such stringency and distancing even from those closest to the sufferer is again typical of the anhedonic disorder, in which the afflicted seeks to minimize involvement with others as a form of self-defense against experiencing deeper bouts of anxiety and depression.

As suggested, most of Allen's films, to some degree, deal with characters who are either mood disordered and/or are involved romantically with such characters. Whether bipolar, unipolar depressive, or other psychiatric illnesses, Allen's filmic universe is one in which every newborn's umbilical cord is attached not to the birth mother, but to an "infant care" psychiatrist. Alienated and aware of it, the typical Woody Allen protagonist struggles to find a stable sense of identity. More often than not, these Allen avatars wrestle with a malingering sense of doubt about any number of obsessive negative ideas, including the value of life itself. They throw themselves into new romantic entanglements without much thought. Only later do they come to find they're stuck in a resultant quagmire of doubt and self-recrimination as their latest ill-advised, compulsive affair stumbles, then crumbles, before their bewildered, bespectacled eyes. Allen's nebbish hero is forever awakening as if from the dream of perfect romance into the nightmare of human needs such as loyalty and questioning, or faith and doubt. He attempts to pair with equally complex, saddened loners who are also struggling, and usually failing, to be joiners and not withdraw from their reality. In a pattern that also mirrors his autobiography, Allen will seek the object of his affections with ruthless intent, only to abandon them as soon as he feels he has achieved his goal, rather than work through the difficult emotional terrain long-term love relationships inevitably demand. With characteristic turns of petulance, flashes of anger, and whining but brilliantly acerbic self-commentary, the usual Allen screen persona will blatantly use doses of despair and manipulation to uselessly try to avoid the coming catastrophe of dashed hopes and acrimony. He always takes the first train leaving town when the going gets too demanding. But if the Allen stand-in protagonist can be narcissistic and self-alienated, he is at least being truthful to his disorder's darker, relationship-destroying nature. Woody Allen once told an interviewer in 1980 that he had spent almost a decade never dating anyone for more than two months despite his best efforts.[43] His marriages successively failed in time, culminating with his bitter estrangement from Mia Farrow over Allen's sexual affair with his adopted step-daughter Soon-Yi Previn. As recently as this book's writing, new allegations have emerged in the ongoing saga.

As suggested, Allen's more specific contributions to manic-depressive cinema will arrive more fully distilled in the 1980s productions of *Stardust Memories* and then *Hannah and Her Sisters*, the latter of which features two protagonists with bipolar disorder. But his personality-driven, auteur-devised filmmaking from the 1970s is key, along with contributions from Coppola, Bogdanovich, and Scorsese, in defining the very essence of mood-disordered cinema. Allen has always professed a devotion to the films of Ingmar Bergman. One sees Allen's desire to chronicle the states of misery, alienation, and longing in his largely depressive characters as an insistently repeated subtext, much like in the work of his bipolar mentor Bergman. Here we see how the influence of one generation of mood-disordered filmmakers and actors has a direct, substantial impact on those who follow and their cinematic legacies. But despite the clear Bergman influence, there is in Allen's body of work a cohesion that is self-defining. His trademark simple title cards, jazzy scores, claustrophobic interiors, large ensemble casts, im-

peccable set designs, and predilection for showing his alter ego protagonists in an unflattering, embarrassing light add up to something unique
in American filmmaking. As Walter Bernstein once pointedly quipped
of Allen's films, "He's made his lunacy work for him. It takes a special
kind of genius to successfully use your insanity."[44]

UP AND DOWN THE *MEAN STREETS* WITH MARTIN SCORSESE

The rapid-fire delivery of real-life director Martin Scorsese and the
fictional characters that he has machine-gun pressure-speak in his alter-
ego movie roles is a defining signature touch. As a result, it is easy to
conjure scenes from his films that are nothing but manic-laced banter
between two or more protagonists who will endlessly repeat, parrot,
and mock one another in a verbal joust of willpower. The stakes are
usually about who will prevail as alpha wolf in status, even if only for the
momentary length of a snarling argument, in a dog-eat-cowering-dog
world. Think of the pre-brawl trash talk that goes on between Johnny
Boy (Robert DeNiro) and Joey "Clams" Scala (George Memmoli) in
Mean Streets (1973), where the two engage in a form of violent foreplay
by questioning the very ground rules of their conflict a priori. They
debate whether or not it is acceptable under the rules to call anyone a
mook, before they bloodily drag one another around a dive bar, demol-
ishing it in the western saloon tradition, if with an East Coast knock-
about twist. Or the sinister interrogation Sport (Harvey Keitel) subjects
potential trick Travis Bickle (Robert DeNiro) to in *Taxi Driver* (1975)
before allowing Travis to use Sport's underage hooker. He lays out the
disgusting ground rules and knowingly tweaks the fidgeting Bickle with
suggestions that Travis is actually an undercover cop. Or the maniacal
way in which Jake LaMotta (Robert DeNiro) needles his squirming
brother Joey (Joe Pesci) in *Raging Bull* over whether or not Joey is
having sex with Jake's wife Vickie (Cathy Moriarty). Jake repeats his
ugly, unfounded allegation with the most crude terminology possible
and in a low, threatening tone of voice promises violence as response to
any "wrong" answer, which causes Joey to finally explode and accurately
accuse Jake of being mentally sick. Or the manic stand-up comic monologues with which Rupert Pupkin (Robert DeNiro) slowly tortures all

who fall within earshot of his desperate need to be heard, not even understood, by any fellow human beings in *The King of Comedy* (1982). Or the gun-wielding Italian gangster Tommy DeVito (Joe Pesci) in *Goodfellas* (1990) and his demand to know in a maniacal tirade whether or not Henry Hill (Ray Liotta) "amuses" him "like a clown?" in a menace-laden game of blink-first-or-die. In film after film, Scorsese uses speech to overpower the target person into whom the pressure-speaking protagonist discharges his automatic verbal weaponry. In the world of threat and malicious revenge that dominates the brutal, but perversely lovingly crafted, screen worlds Scorsese creates, words are not used solely to intimidate a friend or foe, as much as they are to buy the speaker time to decide if a more violent means of retribution is necessary by argument's end. Dialogue tends to drive even emotionally bound characters away from one another in horror in the typical Scorsese picture, rather than create bonds, bring catharsis, and lead to recovery, as it does in many other conventional Hollywood efforts. Talk creates tension between participants in his movies, tension that they will usually struggle to later resolve with nonverbal, destructive means. In so many ways, his prototypical protagonists are emotionally and mentally unstable, many of them well-meaning, but most morally conflicted, and this consistent screen archetype coincides with the biographical realities of his troubled young life growing up.

He was born during World War II in the Queens area of New York City and lived on the Lower East Side for much of his youth. Living so close to the infamous Bowery district (which during this time was overrun with the city's homeless and mentally ill) had a profound impact on the filmmaker's view of humanity. The grinding poverty, the prevalent mental illness self-masked with alcohol and street drugs, the easy lure of crime to seemingly solve all problems and supply the addicted, and the unending parade of suffering and betrayal he witnessed in the tough streets outside the windows of his tenement bedroom fortress of solitude made the sensitive, asthmatic creator feel at once frightened and intrigued. He lived in fear of the violence and the daily degradation of spirit he saw as bullies and gangsters ruled the neighborhood over any who would rise against them. But as a weakling with asthma who perceived himself as such, he secretly admired the liberating swagger and sense of group loyalty and identity gangster life promised to those willing to risk their lives climbing its underworld ranks. He characterized the mean streets of his upbringing as a make-or-break reality;[45] one either gained favor with and for the corrupt power structure already firmly in place or one vanished into the night without farewell.

The emotional damage was not confined to the exterior asphalt. Scorsese's living room was frequently a nightly scene of angry diatribes and accusations, courtesy of his otherwise quiet father, who argued over family choices and history with disturbing menace. Scorsese's older brother was made the butt of much accusation by his father until the brother was finally driven out of the home. As he was the youngest member, Scorsese felt compelled to bottle his reactions and not speak up against the abusive tone. He attributes his inability at times to easily articulate his feelings on the sets of his films with his actors to this history with his family.[46] These formative years from six to fourteen years of age were, as he says, "really, really tough for me."[47] The future filmmaker took shelter in local churches, libraries, and movie theaters for temporary escape from the perpetual East Side ugliness of his reality. Noting that the appeal of cinema was that it induced a waking dream-like state, Scorsese conversely appreciated the church and the library for their calming quietness, a quality his chaotic, noisy environment rarely allowed. Although he witnessed much violence in the streets, if from above through a protective window (not unlike a balcony seat in an old movie theater), and emotionally experienced it with passive acceptance in his argumentative family structure, Scorsese describes his childhood as sheltered.[48] This was because he spent so much of it alone and endlessly watching syndicated movies such as *The Shanghai Gesture* (1941) and *Of Mice and Men* (1939) which played constantly in syndication on the early New York television stations. He absorbed every nuance he could in terms of their lighting, their camera angles, and other technical factors.[49] When healthy and able, Scorsese would haunt the movie palaces and see first-run debuts of personally influential movies such as the Hollywood ode to filmmaking *The Bad and the Beautiful* (1952) and James Dean in *East of Eden* (1955), often accompanied by his movie-loving father. Scorsese identified with Dean heavily in that film, feeling, as he did, that he was also the outsider and younger brother who was overlooked by a dominating father in a turmoil-fueled household.[50] Another film Scorsese deemed influential that he saw when he was ten years of age was Michael Curtiz's *Bright Leaf* (1950), a study in revenge in which the audience does not realize that the leading character portrayed by the vengeance-minded Gary Cooper is emotionally unbalanced until deeply into the film's narrative.[51] As early as eleven years of age, Scorsese would make elaborate storyboards on pretend 70 mm format paper strips and project them onto his bedroom walls, imagining himself directing an elaborate biblical epic, which were so fashionable in the 1950s. So specific was Scorsese's early passion that he even gave his pretend productions titles, such as with his hand-drawn "The Eternal City," with imaginary cast members Marlon Brando, Richard Burton, Virginia Mayo, and Alec Guinness in key roles, right down to their sketched likenesses.[52] Remarkably, even these surviving early remnants of his lifelong obsession with filmmaking show an innate talent for composition and kinetic flow of imagery. These qualities will later help to define his expressive style as director, as well as prefigure the epic style of filmmaking he would helm as director of such religious spectaculars as *The Last Temptation of Christ* (1988) and *Kundun* (1997). Nor has his obsession with delineating every framed shot with meticulous, privately coded storyboards abated since childhood. Indeed, so specific is his creative compulsion that he insists on using only one sketch pencil to create his storyboards: the Eberhard Faber Ebony, Jet Black, Extra Smooth, 6325, which he has used since his boyhood days visualizing *The Eternal City*. When the pencil recently went out of general production, he bought the last boxes of existing stock on eBay.[53]

Scorsese relocated from New York to Los Angeles as an editor-for-hire in the early 1970s, in part after acclaim and support from filmmaker John Cassavetes, who encouraged his nascent talent. But the cultural relocation was not an easy one for the New York–reared Scorsese to make, especially since he lacked even the most basic skills for living solo, such as cooking, cleaning, or even driving, having only lived at home up to this time. He watched his other New Hollywood associates, such as Coppola, Lucas, and Spielberg, direct their early features while he was still cutting other people's movies for a paycheck, which fueled his desperation. His early-adult onset of chronic mood disorder left him so depressed that friends and associates of the young wunderkind openly worried. Concurrently, he would experience manic highs while working, often staying up all night and sleeping most of the day. He was nicknamed Dracula by friends in regard to his chronic insomnia and the way he painted his Hollywood rental home's windows black to keep out the daylight while he slept.[54] Scorsese later admitted to interviewer Richard Schickel that the early 1970s in L.A. was one of the most painful periods of his entire life, one of three "bad times"[55] as he labeled his chronic mood-disorder biography in which he had fallen into depression. When he finally sought treatment, the psychiatrist medicated him and Scorsese slowly recovered his nerves. Cassavetes took him into his home and helped the troubled young man, even securing editing work for him on *Medicine Ball Caravan* (1971) to help speed Scorsese's healing. But Scorsese's attempt to seek help did not come without familial cost. Sandy Weintraub, Scorsese's former lover at the time, recounted how Scorsese's father was visiting the West Coast to check up on his depressed son. When Scorsese explained he was doing much better because he had seen a psychiatrist and taken medication, his father exploded in rage, accusing his son of not being a man and needing to grow up.[56] Little wonder the troubled Scorsese had experienced inhibition against previous medical intervention, given such harsh parental objection. But the nonstop high pressure and demands placed on him by Hollywood, such as in his post–*New York, New York* (1977) phase, left him depressed. He was unemployable by his own lack of interest until Robert De Niro basically rescued Scorsese as Cassavetes had, by helping guide *Raging Bull* to completion, thus giving Scorsese a creative therapeutic focus.

His best New Hollywood films, such as *Mean Streets* and *Taxi Driver*, reflect the constant state of alternating depression and manic overdrive he experienced concurrent with this first great period of mainstream productivity. That Scorsese managed to create such a bipolar masterpiece as *Taxi Driver* while suffering from an affective illness is a testament to his ability to channel his driving manic energies into therapeutic art rather than self-immolation. Scorsese has characterized the intense feelings of mania he experiences as a "frantic voice in your head"[57] that is unbearable to the point that he feels as if he's going to explode. He said he related to the rage he saw in fellow manic-depressive Paul Schrader's horrific screenplay and experienced bouts of what he called "extraordinary depression"[58] while shooting *Taxi Driver* and working in hellish 42nd Street and Harlem locations at night during the grueling heat of a New York City summer. Scorsese has cited the troubling scene in which Travis ill-advisedly attempts to open up about his racing thoughts with Wizard (Peter Boyle), an older man with a sense of

hard-earned street wisdom, as key to the film's overall theme of alienation and depression.[59] Travis realizes his own manic-depressive psychosis is reaching a point of acting out, but when the moment comes to talk
himself out of his bad thoughts, Travis cannot articulate his inner feelings of rage and destructive paranoia. He remains frozen with a pained
expression of loss, unable to speak. In this tragic instance, if only Wizard had possessed the sensitivity and foresight to see and feel beneath
Travis's facade, the filmmaker suggests, there might have been a ray of
hope for Travis to transcend the gulf of dead feelings that forever separate him from the rest of humanity. But as Travis falters and fails to
communicate, and as Wizard uncomfortably offers a self-serving platitude of "you'll be alright" as prescription for Travis's metastasizing pathology, the violence and bloodshed that follows is all but guaranteed. It
is a chilling reminder that we are all our brothers' keepers, however
much we deny the responsibility, especially where mental illness in our
fellow citizenry is concerned. The catastrophic unintended consequences of denial and self-willed ignorance can only be measured later
by moral approximation in the latest mass shooting at a mall or movie
theater. Wizard is a proxy for society's inability, and even unwillingness,
to acknowledge that the stigma against mental illness leaves the sufferer
with no recourse save to deny and mask his own medical malady and
prompts the repressive neurotypical world to look the other way with
embarrassment when the subject is broached. The portrait created
herein as easily fits Arthur Bremer, the mentally unbalanced man who
shot presidential candidate George Wallace, whose memoirs Schrader
drew upon for *Taxi Driver*, as it does recent Navy School Yard mass
shooter Aaron Alexis. Alexis was also a troubled young man who, like
the fictional Travis and real-life Bremer, sought, and tragically did not
find, adequate help for mental illness.[60] Bremer and Alexis were suffering from probable missed diagnoses of a schizophrenic-related disorder,
given their paranoid delusions and hearing of voices commanding them
to take violent action, rather than manic-depressive psychosis. Nevertheless, the moody behavior, emotional instability, and depressive social
withdrawal Travis Bickle experiences, along with his sudden, manic-
driven change of plans that involve suicidal thoughts of a blood-soaked
redemption, suggests Travis experiences many bipolar symptoms. On a
more chilling hypothetical note, he may even be in the unfortunate
minority who have bipolar disorder and schizophrenic comorbidity.

Though Scorsese would experience other terrible depressions throughout his life, the 1970s were the beginning of his many episodes in mental hell. They became his baptism in the purgatory of his own lapsed Catholic faith, battling internal demons far more real and soul-destroying than any biblical creations. Through clinical episodes of anger-fueled mania during this time, Scorsese periodically punched holes in the walls and ripped telephones from their wiring.[61] He wore white gloves to prevent himself from endlessly chewing his fingernails and brandished lucky charms around his neck to ward off evil spirits.[62] He abused prescription drugs such as Quaaludes and street drugs such as cocaine, and had delusions of seeing things that were not present even while not taking drugs.[63] Yet, despite these enormous personal obstacles, he also managed to make a series of films so original in vision that they were a key influence on the New Hollywood cinema in perhaps its most lasting manner. For they made the entire New Hollywood output street real, not in the Cassavetes mode, but in a dreamlike, fugue-state kind of filmmaking in which the audience is watching the movie in the director's head as much as the actual movie unfolding on the screen. In no uncertain terms, Scorsese wedded his own despair and depression with a maniacal passion and feverish imagination for cinema that transcended all of his key influences, and made his a style and signature all its own.

His feelings about his condition have always been somewhat guarded, despite his candor about his struggles with depression, rage, and having racing thoughts. He has also attributed his rapid-fire speech to his use of cortisone asthma inhalers since childhood. These may be a contributory influence on his underlying pressure speech, but, of course, not the only cause of his manic tendencies. It is also worthwhile to note that cortisone can trigger mania in some patients, a fact bipolar director Nicholas Ray used to great dramatic effect in the profiled *Bigger Than Life* (1956). While he avoids any admission to a particular psychiatric diagnosis by clinical *DSM-V* terminology, Scorsese has admitted to taking lithium to help prevent his violent outbursts and stabilize his combustible anger, as well as to treat his chronic depression. He has also praised the field of psychiatry and its many advances, particularly for the benefits he has received from both talk therapy and the use of mood-stabilizing medications. His constant battles to maintain a mental equilibrium have cost him dearly, with failed marriages and lost friendships, but have left him, by his own admission, with at least his therapeutic directing ability intact. The payoff for his struggle in terms of legacy has been truly astounding. With continuing contributions to bipolar cinema, Scorsese's influence goes well beyond the New Hollywood paradigm and well into the present day.

PAUL SCHRADER AS GOD'S LONELY MANIC

Any appreciation of *Taxi Driver* that did not give proper credit to the suicide-fixated, manic depressive author of its script would be incomplete. Paul Schrader was born into a Dutch Calvinist family in Grand Rapids, Michigan, with a history of abuse and suicide as its core legacy. When Schrader was six years old, his uncle committed suicide. Half a decade later, the dead uncle's eldest son committed suicide on the anniversary of his father's death. This grisly pattern was unbelievably carried out again, five years down the road, when a second son of the dead uncle killed himself on the same calendar day. The horrible reminders of self-termination were not yet done, however, because twenty years later, a third cousin unsuccessfully attempted suicide.[64] The cruel realities of Schrader having to emotionally resolve the continuous impulse toward self-negation which he witnessed in his uncle and cousins were only matched by his own family's admonitions to never discuss the sad heritage of suicide so clearly manifest in Schrader's blood line. Worse still was his own troubled family dynamic, which included multiple instances of physical and emotional abuse from both his father and his mother.[65] As has been previously noted, such early childhood stressors are often present in the biographies of adults with mood disorders.

Schrader, along with his older and only brother, Leonard, was forced by his tyrannical father, Charles, a fervent devotee of the Christian Reformed Church (a fundamentalist splinter group from the Dutch Calvinist tradition), to every week get dressed in their Sunday best an hour before attending services. This just so Charles could seat the family at the front in the same pew, week after week, in a show of righteousness. The father brooked no dissension from his cowering sons, who dutifully submitted for fear of their father's frequent beatings. Most of these whippings were for nothing more than maintaining a human existence in the Schrader household. According to Leonard, any perceived slight or fault resulted in having to remove their shirts, lean over a kitchen table, and endure Charles wailing on their backs with a cord, which left their shoulders and mid-sections bleeding with tiny holes.[66] This happened almost every day of their lives as children with few exceptions. Charles was also quite sadistic, telling the boys the precise number of lashes they would incur with never any show of mercy. Once he announced sentence, he was all too eager to carry out the order precisely as prescribed. His mother Joan was only marginally less abusive, stoically going along with her husband's sickness. She would sometimes break down in her own resentful rages, at which times she beat the brothers with a broomstick, going so far as to break the handles on their backs. Yet another time she suddenly drove a needle into young Paul's thumb as a warning of the painful consequences of eternal damnation.[67] In such a bleak household gripped by unending despair and religious mania, there is little wonder why both brothers would grow up fixated with the idea of suicide. They were forbidden the usual teenage escapes to vent their building rage and horror, such as dating or attending movies. Paul Schrader was seventeen years old when he secretly broke his family's religious prohibition against entering any satanically controlled movie theater. He was already prone to visual hallucinations since before he saw his first movie, *Anatomy of a Murder* (1959), a sensationalized Otto Preminger courtroom thriller that dared to broach such then taboo subjects as rape and repeatedly used the word "panties" for the first time in an American motion picture. The scintillating nature of the mature movie sent the teenaged Schrader into a clinical episode of delusional mania in his theater seat. He claimed he witnessed white lights, descending angels, and even the Lord Jehovah himself, on the theater's darkened ceiling, all aligned against the young sinner and intent on sending him to hell.[68] So intense and disturbing was his apocalyptic hallucination that Schrader ran from the theater for six blocks before slowing down to see if his Maker and company were still after his soul. He slowly realized after catching his breath that he had experienced an episode of religious mania, so he hurried back to his empty seat with humiliation, determined to at least earn his eternity below by seeing as much of the remaining film as possible. Given his background and that he saw the creator of the universe at the first film he attended, it is understandable that Schrader equated movies from that point forward in his life as something akin to religious in nature.

His new passion eventually led him to abandon Michigan and his restrictive religious upbringing, relocating in the turbulent late 1960s to Hollywood, where he studied film production at UCLA for a while. He later worked as a professional film critic in the style of influential film reviewer Pauline Kael, who actually helped him gain admission to UCLA and a job at the *L.A. Free Press*. [69] He actually failed his course work at UCLA and transferred into the school's film history studies, which proved fortuitous, demonstrating as it did his talent for writing analytically about films. Schrader also lost his job at the alternative newspaper because he wrote a negative review of *Easy Rider*. Just as well, for his early shot at success lay with the strength of his original scripts and their intensely nihilistic themes. Such revenge dramas as *The Yakuza* (1974) and *Rolling Thunder* (1977) proved with Schrader's spare, if brutal, writer's touch to be definitive, if dark, examinations of male camaraderie and the gulf of silence keeping them emotionally distant in the New Hollywood cinema. But his pseudo-confessional work on *Taxi Driver* is what propelled him from the ranks of interesting screenplay writers into an auteur scriptwriter, then auteur director, in later years. Without Paul Schrader's rambling, keenly observed sense of nervous compulsion and alienated distancing, Travis and his endless nights spent trolling the worst streets of New York City would have been nothing but seedy travelogue footage. Schrader's layering of Travis and his insidious, manic-fueled monologues being delivered over the montage of decay and depression Scorsese summons as visualizer makes *Taxi Driver* play as a surreal, interior-driven film. It is a study in claustrophobic spaces and dead-end emotions, as if the viewer has climbed into the driver's seat with Travis and is experiencing the events through his mood-disordered psychosis itself. Colors become visual smears as fire hydrants spray Travis's windshield and reduce his (and our) visibility to a fragmented swirl of reds, blues, and yellows. Motions are constantly slowed down when seen from Travis's distorted perspective, as if to illustrate the paranoia he is suffering by way of prolonging certain agonizing moments. A great example is when he watches a black man in an all-night diner balefully stare at him with silent accusation, tapping his fingers on the grimy table top. These slow-motion fragments are meant to visually express the same sense of inner fragmentation Travis is undergoing as his depressive psychosis worsens. The chronic loneliness Travis endures as a result of his unending mood instability is adroitly illustrated when he attempts to reconcile with Betsy (Cybill Shepherd) using a pay phone in a tenement hallway. Scorsese pans away from the stumbling Travis as he pathetically fails at his goal, and instead holds on the empty hallway with Travis stuttering off-screen. The effect is to reduce him and his pain to empty space personified, and it works well. "I'm God's lonely man," Travis elsewhere bemoans, but the comment is externalized with aching clarity in this shot. None of these cinematic moments, however, would be as electrifying were it not for Schrader's complicated protagonist. It is one that, by some accounts, was actually in part a thinly veiled realization of many of Paul Schrader's own unstable mannerisms and inner torments when he wrote *Taxi Driver* in the spring of 1972.

The image many initial and subsequent viewers maintain as the essence of Travis Bickle is his signature ex-vet Army surplus jacket, tight jeans, and combat boots. This look was actually based on the style maintained by Paul Schrader when he first arrived in Los Angeles.[70] As he was socially connected to such young rising stars as Martin Scorsese, Steven Spielberg, John Milius, and Brian DePalma, Schrader's well-known nervous tics, such as mumbling owing to a slight speech impediment and shyly casting his eyes downward when he spoke, were also a source of probable inspiration for the visualization of Travis Bickle, as Robert DeNiro knew the same group of young creators. Nor was it only the look of the bipolar Schrader that influenced the final screen images of Travis Bickle. John Milius told Scorsese a true story in which Milius had taken then neophyte gun fanatic Schrader to a sporting goods store to purchase a .38 handgun. As the clerk and Milius looked on, aghast, Schrader aimed the empty gun at an unsuspecting woman playing tennis nearby and, drawing down on her as he squinted for accuracy, clicked the trigger a few times.[71] Scorsese was so chilled by the account he had De Niro recreate it in the truly repellent scene in which Travis buys his illegal street weapons in a seedy hotel room and likewise sights unknowing civilians walking down the street through the windows. Equally influential on the future depiction of Travis as a gun-obsessed manic-depressive were the open displays of Smith and Wesson handguns Schrader maintained, keeping one .38 beside his bed for all to see, and showing friends another he kept loaded in his car's glove compartment.[72] The painful opening scenes of *Taxi Driver* in which Travis Bickle confesses during an interview with his future employer that he needs the work because he can't sleep, as well as the shy Travis spending his lonely after-work hours in seedy X-rated theaters, were also identical to Schrader's biography. Perhaps most disturbing of all, the barely teenaged prostitute Iris (Jodie Foster) was visually modeled on an actual encounter Schrader had one night in which he realized the young hooker he had brought to his hotel room was underage.[73] In another instance of Schrader's own manic-depressive struggles influencing *Taxi Driver*, Schrader insisted Scorsese meet with his real-life Iris the next morning. The meeting was impressionable enough that it resulted in Iris's on-screen attire and street smart mannerisms being largely based on it.

"I fell into a state of manic depression,"[74] said Paul Schrader when describing the restless insomnia he endured one spring that would soon lead to a fast two-week first-draft screenplay of *Taxi Driver*. He became obsessed with delusional, self-destructive revenge fantasies of harming himself and others.[75] Unable to sleep at night, Schrader would leave his apartment at sunset and go on an aimless drive through the infinite urban and suburban landscapes of Los Angeles in his battered Chevy Nova, which he thought of as a "metal coffin."[76] When trolling without purpose failed, he would visit bars and drink alone until they closed, silently stewing in his cynical, racing thoughts. At which point, he would visit peep show theaters and porn shops until dawn, when he would finally be tired enough to sleep the day away, only to start the same vampiric cycle yet again with the setting sun. Compare this to Travis's monologue in *Taxi Driver* in which Travis relates that "the days go on and on. . . . They don't end." Schrader's self-described "abnegation"[77] lasted for weeks without end and landed him in the hospital with an ulcer and still experiencing severe manic depression. He claimed the script emerged fully formed in hypomanic flashes of insight as he recovered with nothing else to occupy his racing mind. When he was discharged, he wrote the script in two weeks, and then went on what he termed a "suicidal road trip"[78] across the United States, driving aimlessly without destination. Despite the thousands of miles he blurred beneath his straining vehicle in a wanderlust of failed self-therapy, his undiagnosed bipolar episode continued unabated. It would take several years before the admired, but seemingly impossibly dark, screenplay would be finally realized as a film, and to critical acclaim as one of the best New Hollywood ever made.

According to Penny Marshal, who knew him at the time, Schrader was obsessed with suicide, constantly talking about how to end his own life with the least amount of carnage left behind for others to clean up.[79] His ex-lover Beverly Walker remembered him as literally threatening to kill himself with believable intent if she did not invite him onto the set of *American Graffiti* so that Schrader could network with its creative talents such as Lucas and Coppola, whom he was trying to meet.[80] Religious guilt seemed to be a driving source of much of his suicidal ideation. Schrader sometimes wore a brass crown of thorns at home, which left pinpricks of blood on his forehead, and read the church bulletins his mother insisted on mailing him for each week that he missed in his hometown worship service while in sinful Hollywood.[81] She added handwritten reminders that she and his father would surely regret the absence of their son's company in God's kingdom, as Schrader would, she sadly implied, be somewhere else. As if to show his contempt for their religious piety and in a probable bout of manic grandiosity, Schrader arranged along with his brother for the two to purchase a gaudy, expensive Hollywood Hills mansion. The act seemed carried out in order to impress his visiting parents, who came to see their errant sons one Christmas holiday. The following spring and in the ensuing post-manic depression, Paul ordered Leonard to list the property for sale, its seeming and singular purpose having been accomplished.[82] Schrader's bipolar extremes of self-inflation and self-destruction would finally result in a hot tub game of Russian roulette in which Schrader pulled a loaded gun's trigger while pointing the barrel to his head. His psychiatrist arrived not long thereafter, insisting Schrader surrender his guns or face involuntary incarceration for suicide prevention.[83]

With these episodes in mind, one thinks of the haunting image of Travis, blood-soaked from his mass murder spree and left with no bullets in his gun, slowly placing his crimson-coated finger to his temple and feigning to blow his brains out, whispering the sound of exploding bullets—one of the most powerfully expressive scenes in all of bipolar cinema. For Travis's devastated eyes do not merely signal self-termination, they hold the gleaming realization that he has lived beyond his failed suicidal attempt, and now must face even more mental terrors, as well as the societal consequences, for his rampage. That he is turned into a vigilante folk hero is, of course, an ironic coda. But this salient image of Travis Bickle, experiencing a form of cathartic release in his pretend self-immolation as he uselessly pulls his own trigger finger, is at the heart of Paul Schrader's struggle with suicidal fixation, and why the image's power is so radiantly provocative to viewers. In writing *Taxi Driver*, it is as if every moment, every line, and every emotion has inexorably led, as Travis laments in his deadpan voice-over, to the final moment wherein Travis commits virtual suicide. "Now I see this clearly," Travis says. "My whole life is pointed in one direction. There never has been a choice for me." The sick, but wizened, grin that slowly devours Travis's face after he makes his symbolic gesture of self-extermination is the proof of the emotional release Bickle experiences at having finally taken action, even if it was the worst possible, rather than remain beholden to the torture of unrelenting mental illness during an acute episode. Sadly, Scorsese hints in the final frames that Travis's remission will be short-lived. Travis madly glares at his own red-tinged eyes in his car's mirror as if recognizing the subtle sign of an oncoming episode (itself an echo of Humphrey Bogart's similarly haunted eyes in his car's mirror in the opening titles of Nicholas Ray's *In a Lonely Place*). *Taxi Driver* was, and remains, an unsettling, but entirely accurate, summation of the state of mental illness in America, and the subsequent blow-back neglect and ignorance foster as the inevitable outcome. Travis emphatically states to the viewer that "I don't believe that one should devote his life to morbid self-attention, I believe that one should become a person like other people." But as his chronic episodes of depersonalization owing to his manic-depressive psychosis grind on, Travis tragically fails to do precisely that, instead falling into his illness with fixated thoughts of homicidal intent, surely the ultimate form of morbid self-attention.

Paul Schrader's contributions to mood-disordered cinema continued throughout the New Hollywood era, especially apparent in his biographically tinged study in depression *Hardcore* (1979). The central figure of the repressive widower Jake (George C. Scott), the Calvinist single father whose only Grand Rapids–raised teenage daughter disappears during a field trip to Southern California and winds up being exploited in the porn underworld of L.A., has obvious parallels to Schrader's own stern, disciplinarian father and the way he expressed doubt about Schrader's immoral career. In a veiled way, Paul Schrader is the real-life doppelganger of the fictional missing daughter, who has all but abandoned her father and his religious views for the earthly pleasures of Hollywood and pornography. When Jake must enter into the hellish subterranean lairs that constitute porn production in the late 1970s, from sordid motel rooms to S&M dungeons, and spiritually attempt to save his offspring's soul from the venal horrors of debauchery, Schrader is perhaps vicariously living through a stylized persona projection of what his father must have felt about his errant son's lifestyle. Likewise, the depressive rages Jake experiences as he is forced further into the lower depths of Hades in his quest to rescue his daughter, and his explosive willingness to use violence when he can no longer control his rage, are reflections of the manner in which Schrader's father would treat Schrader as a growing boy. It is also interesting to note that Schrader experienced other bouts of clinical bipolarity in the 1970s while making films, including during the directing of *Blue Collar* (1978). At one point three weeks into the shoot, Schrader underwent intense, uncontrollable tristimania to the point that it temporarily affected his ability to work.[84] As has been previously shown, Charlie Chaplin, James Dean, Marilyn Monroe, Francis Ford Coppola, and many others on the manic-depressive spectrum have also had debilitating episodes in which their melancholia led to long durations of uncontrollable, seemingly unmotivated, weeping.

RAINER WERNER FASSBINDER AND KLAUS KINSKI: A STUDY IN BIPOLAR CONTRAST

A world away from New Hollywood, but equally relevant to any discussion about bipolar disorder and filmmaking, was the New German film movement. The New German films, which had their roots in the same European political uprisings of the 1960s that inspired Truffaut and others in the French New Wave, really came into their own in the 1970s in terms of international acclaim, eerily mirroring, and sometimes actually influenced by, their New Hollywood counterparts. The 1970s German domestic political tensions, fueled by leftist radicals who used terrorist acts to achieve notoriety in mainstream media, were a continued deterioration of the failed 1960s first wave of protests and power struggles, turned lethal and self-destructive. The divide between the older, more conservative German citizens, who favored forgetting World War II and its atrocities, versus a more youthful generation, who sought social justice and were openly critical of the prevailing power structures, presented an opening for young filmmakers willing to make daring exposés and class warfare studies from the proletariat's point of view. Because there were suddenly devoted, if small, art cinema audiences for radical movies by new German talents, as well as German cable outlets funding nontraditional, more personal filmmaking projects, visionaries such as Rainer Werner Fassbinder, Wim Wenders, and Werner Herzog emerged as important voices rallying for a more robust, engaging cinema language. Coincidentally, Polish born but German-launched actor Klaus Kinski would mark his greatest successes collaborating with Herzog, in a pairing similar to such other cinema director/actor teams as Kurosawa and Mifune, Scorsese and DeNiro, Fellini and Mastroianni, and Truffaut and Léaud. While Kinski had achieved acting success prior to his work with Herzog, it would be his breakout roles in such New German Herzog films as *Aguirre, the Wrath of God* (1972), *Nosferatu the Vampyre* (1979), and *Woyzeck* (1979) that truly elevated him to international box office star status. And in a strange but perhaps inevitable reflection of New Hollywood and its bipolar-influenced filmmakers, New German cinema also had bipolar illness as a source of creative inspiration in two of its key artists: both Fassbinder and Kinski were subject to chronic, often agonizing, episodes of manic depression. As we will see, they make for an illustrative contrast in how bipolar disorder not only manifests itself in terms of symptoms and lifestyles, but also informs the afflicted creator's work itself in varying, and radically divergent, tones, themes, and styles.

Rainer Werner Fassbinder was born in 1945 into an emotionally distant, but financially comfortable, middle-class family in Bavaria. He was surrounded by books and paintings provided by the income of his father, Helmut, a successful doctor, who was aided in his practice by Fassbinder's equally well-educated mother, Liselotte. Fassbinder spent his earliest years indoors, largely unaffected by the surrounding devastation of post–World War II Germany as a sheltered, lonely, only child, content to stage pretend radio plays using his father's tape recorder and precociously to read the intellectually challenging books in the family library. But when Fassbinder reached the age of six, Helmut and Liselotte divorced, and he was largely left in the care of his mother. Without the financial support of his absentee father, Lisolette was forced to move into more modest living quarters in Munich with her son. She began translating English texts for German publishing houses in order to support them. Because she could not concentrate with the noisy, self-stimulating Rainer in their small apartment, Liselotte would give her son money to attend the cinema houses nearby as a means of having privacy while she worked for long stretches of time.[85] Like many of the other bipolar filmmakers profiled herein, Fassbinder was soon a child-hood devotee of the cinema, seeing at least one movie per day, and sometimes more, a streak that he continued into his teenage years. Fassbinder even boasted in his diary during his youth that the number one achievement for the year 1961 was that he "saw four films every single day that God made."[86] Not unlike Kurosawa and Fellini, Fass-binder preferred the American studio output to most of the other world cinema, and gravitated toward their dream-like style and larger-than-life melodramatic narratives—even if he resented their obsession with happy endings and false promises of material security as he became more radicalized in the late 1960s. But Fassbinder's angry young man phase seems to have started in his earliest years and never abated. This may be an indicator that he was afflicted with an early onset of bipolar disorder and that his notorious personal animosity originated from his chronic mood instability and its resultant irritability and hostility. He was regarded as a self-aggrandizing cultural poser by many rivals, and ex-lovers and estranged colleagues bemoaned his excessive, self-indul-gent egomania. As if to prove his critics correct, Fassbinder listed him-self as number one in an article he penned called "The Ten Most Important Directors in the New German Cinema," as well as placing many of his own works under such headings as The Best, The Most Important, The Most Beautiful, and even The Most Disgusting.[87] As we have seen with Francis Coppola and Peter Bogdanovich, who also shared Fassbinder's penchant for grandiose self-inflation and personal extravagance at the expense of their own critical and commercial suc-cess, manic tendencies toward delusional self-beliefs, such as having special hidden talents, an ability to communicate directly with God, and other irrational, mystical ideas, can be as much a source for ruinous mistakes as they are creative inspiration in the afflicted.

"I'd say I'm manic-depressive, and I just try to be depressive as seldom as possible,"[88] quipped Fassbinder about his prolific drive. He added that nonstop work helped abate his blues. Hence his frantic desire to almost never stop creating, whether it was writing the latest script, directing the newest low-budget feature or television project, editing a film he had recently completed, or penning a film essay for a magazine. Fassbinder was always in medias res on some film or script, and as a result, from the moment he created and starred in his first low-budget feature *Love Is Colder Than Death* (1969) until his overdose in 1982 while completing *Querelle*, he directed over thirty fictional feature-length films (writing, cowriting, or adapting many of them himself); two different television series, including the epic miniseries *Berlin Alexanderplatz*; several short films; and even live theater plays. That so much of his prodigious output remains accessible and entertaining is a testament to his genius for artistically challenging himself even when many critics of his era dismissed him and his cadre as so much failed pretentiousness masquerading as social statement. His personal lifestyle choices, including supporting radical leftist causes, intermixing his cast and crew with his sex life, abusing cocaine and alcohol, and then finally losing his gay lover to suicide in their shared flat,[89] all took a heavy toll on him. But given the enormous stress of his medical condition and nonstop professional activity, it is perhaps harder to understand how Fassbinder had any time left for such personal relationships at all than why almost all of them quickly became acrimonious. The lonely, moody boy who had to learn to cope with his isolation by ignoring his need for friendship would never recover. Even though his bipolarity would give him charisma and an insatiable desire to direct as he matured from childhood, Fassbinder never overcame his manic-depressive need to surround himself with others whose task it was to fill the infinite void of his childhood existence, or at least momentarily alleviate its lingering memories of sadness and abandonment. What he offered in return, he once said, was a sense of creative possibility for those who fell into orbit around his magnetic star, a feeling that he, the creative genius, could be relied upon to mutually advance all of their careers, thus making them dependent on, not coauthoring, the decisions Fassbinder would make on his and their behalf.[90] The strategy was doomed to repeatedly fail Fassbinder and his dependent friends, but therein may lie its deeper significance, as it enabled him to continuously act out and expunge a cycle of need, loyalty, and betrayal that he experienced early in life with his parents' emotional distancing. As witnessed in the accounts of other bipolar patients who tried similar coping strategies of leaning upon codependent relationships, such as James Dean, Marilyn Monroe, and Peter Sellers, however, the outcome was predictably too self-alienating, precisely because it was so overly controlling, and therefore negative, in the long term for either the bipolar patients or their enabling helpers.

Fassbinder would profile this tension between visionary leader and resentful cast and crew members in his bitter take on the perils of low-budget filmmaking *Beware of a Holy Whore* (1971), a film whose title sums up the film's cynical attitude about the nonstop infighting accompanying any pressure-filled, collaborative creative act, but especially independent filmmaking. In a *Waiting for Godot*–styled setting that induces claustrophobia, a film crew is stranded in a seedy hotel on location awaiting the late arrival of their notoriously bipolar director, who is by rep a cruel, manipulative egomaniac. Fassbinder casts himself not as the director, but a creative member of the crew, thus allowing himself to talk about the film's fictional director, who is a thinly veiled alter ego of Fassbinder, with complete disregard and utter contempt for one and all, especially himself. Fassbinder's great accomplishment here was to display the enormous psychological stress caused by his chosen profession, while slyly critiquing his own manic need to be working at all times as contributing to his chronic state of misery. It was at once autobiographical and darkly entertaining, a brazenly honest look at the sheer pettiness that devours the creative energies of a film production, which would be better utilized by being poured into the film. But like most of his works, it remained essentially a chamber piece in conception and execution, an inward-directed, self alienated look at the world, a viewpoint coming from wounded intellectualism and a failed sense of humanistic idealism. There are outbursts of sheer emotional desperation in this film and others by Fassbinder, but these typically come after his suffering, repressive protagonists endure endless screen reels of small humiliations and huge disappointments in turn, before they finally implode, as embodied by the title of his feature *Why Does Herr R. Run Amok?* (1970).

On the other end of the class spectrum, yet on the same shared spectrum of mood disorder by way of bipolarity, was Klaus Kinski. Born in a Polish ghetto almost two decades earlier, in 1926, he was a child of stunning poverty. Though viewed skeptically by some reviewers owing to its hyperbolic writing style, Kinski claimed in his scandalous *Kinski Uncut: The Autobiography of Klaus Kinski* (1996) that his childhood was a living hell on Earth. He and his family would go days on end without food or any heating in the dead of winter in their non-insulated, vermin-infested apartment (in which the former tenant had killed himself), afraid to complain to the landlord for fear of overdue rent monies being demanded. He had a borderline incestuous relationship with his mother,[91] and despised his underemployed father, who was a failed pharmacist turned day laborer or store clerk when he could find the work. Kinski's mother would explode in hate-spewing rages while his depressed father looked on, silent in self-recrimination and unable to help his manic-depressive wife until she finally collapsed in exhaustion from her tirade.[92] As all family members had to scrape for whatever income they could manage, Kinski had a gruesome assortment of numbing childhood jobs, including as a rug beater, a coal lugger, washing corpses at a funeral home before burial, and even disposing of medical waste for a hospital, including amputated limbs. Kinski was so emaciated that he was once accidentally dragged by a passing motorcyclist who snagged him in the street, his unprotected head bouncing on the asphalt for over thirty yards. Unable to feed him, his mother sent him to a children's home, believing there he would at least be temporarily fed. But Kinski vomited on a caretaker and screamed as loud as he could for hours, deliberately driving them mad, until his humiliated mother was summoned to permanently remove him.[93]

Obviously his childhood poverty and dysfunctional family were major stressors in Klaus Kinski's later descent into full-blown manic depression. He spends many paragraphs and passages in his book cataloging the abuses and deprivations he suffered, always with the tagged admonition that he swore he would one day be wealthy and free from the horrors of poverty. To his credit, given the enormity of his psychiatric illness, Kinski actually achieved his plan in terms of making a lot of money, even if he maniacally spent much of it as fast as he could. But the amount of venom he summons to characterize his loathed childhood is revealing. Like other profiled bipolar film actors and directors, Kinski's bouts of chronic anxiety owing to his family's dire poverty were clearly markers on his way to developing later full-blown manic-depressive illness. What emerges from the depths of his Sade-like autobiography, and from eyewitness accounts and interviews with coworkers, is one of the most compelling, and yet clinically disturbing, of all the film artists examined herein. For Klaus Kinski suffered not merely for his art, or because of it, but from his unrelenting, rapidly cycling episodes of manic homicidal rage and depressive psychosis. From late childhood into his young teenage years, Kinski reveals in his exposé that he was subject to chronic insomnia, destructive anger, hypersexual thoughts, delusional obsessions, sudden tristimania, uncontrollable wanderlust, and anxiety-ridden depressions. All of his clinical symptoms would worsen in time and with fame, and many others even more troubling would emerge, resulting in a tortured life story. It defies credulity if one considers the Kinski's accomplishments, personally and professionally, while struggling against a ravaging case of untreated bipolar disorder, which frequently left him facing courts, paying fines, running from his latest ex-lover, yelling at audiences, and fighting with directors.[94] Though extreme in the manner of Peter Sellers when violently unstable, Klaus Kinski's chronicle of his struggle is a sobering reminder of the enormous personal suffering many afflicted with manic depression must endure due to their disorder, whatever the positive gains as a result of its creative influence as potential compensation.

After being drafted into the depleted ranks of the German army shortly before its surrender in 1945, Kinski survived being bullet-ridden by liberating English soldiers after he went AWOL from the Nazi forces. He was later released from a British POW camp and haunted the theaters of Berlin, living in poverty as he sought acting work to validate his childhood dreams of stardom. During this time, and whenever he would get a small or large role, Kinski would lock himself away for days on end in whatever hovel he inhabited at the time, refusing all human contact as he studiously created his character for later unveiling on the stage.[95] Just as suddenly, he would be prone to a form of ambulatory psychosis, in which he could no longer remain in self-confinement. During these episodes of wanderlust, Kinski would bolt from his living space and walk without direction through the city's many parks and endless boulevards for multiple day and night cycles. During such phases and surely of later benefit in his portrayal of a melancholic vampire in *Nosferatu*, he would visit cemeteries in predawn hours and enter marbled tombs, vainly listening for ghostly voices coming from inside sealed crypts.[96] The often sustained, destabilized periods of self-isolation were also not without incident, as is revealed by Werner Herzog in his documentary about his complex relationship with Kinski called *My Best Fiend* (1999). Herzog tells in his film of how the young Kinski, only thirteen years old, was renting a room in the Herzog boarding household and had a prolonged fit of agitated mania that lasted for days on end. During this time, Kinski screamed at the top of his lungs, and smashed everything in his room he could lay his hands on until Herzog's frantic mother summoned the police. Nor was Kinski's spontaneous need to run away without explanation when emotionally overwhelmed atypical, as when he first attended an exhibit of van Gogh original oil paintings at the Haus der Kunst.[97] After seeing van Gogh's work, Kinski left the exhibit and dashed through the streets in tears, unable to stop his wailing even as onlookers stared in bemused bewilderment at his distraught condition. Perhaps the bystanders would have been more understanding if they had been privy to Kinski's empathetic catharsis at the exhibit engendered by his sudden realization of the mental horrors he shared with van Gogh. As has been previously underscored, tristimania is common among bipolar patients.

Klaus Kinski's insatiable sexual mania was actually the inciting reason for involuntary confinement at the infamous Wittenauer Insane Asylum on September 5, 1950, under the name of Klaus Nakschinski, his birth name. According to Kinski's autobiography, he fell in love with a psychiatrist named Dr. Milena Bosenberg, a woman two decades his senior, when he was twenty-six years old. She became one in a series of female lovers and temporary caretakers, allowing him to stay with her on cold nights so he wouldn't freeze when he was between shelters and sleeping in city parks, in exchange for Kinski's self-described inexhaustible sexual ability. Kinski claimed he accidentally swallowed poison he believed was medicine from Bosenberg's clinical practice, without her knowledge, to self-treat a persistent gall bladder infection. He nearly died until his stomach was pumped in the emergency room, and he soon found himself committed to the asylum for observation and treatment. According to Kinski's version of events, he wound up in the sanitarium because Milena refused to admit to authorities that she "whores around with me."[98] The official medical records released to the public in 2008 reveal a quite different version of events. In the declassified documents as reported in the German newspaper *Bild*,[99] Dr. Bosenberg, engaged to another man, stated she had only matronly feelings of concern for Kinski, although her admission to financing his acting career, as well as sheltering him at times, must have raised eyebrows. The asylum doctors concluded Kinski was clearly a madman, actually misdiagnosing him in all probability in his initial admission file with a "preliminary diagnosis" of schizophrenia, with a conclusion of "psychopathy."[100] The report also included a claim that Kinski had twice attempted suicide, first with morphine tablets, and then an overdose of sleeping pills. Kinski denied this in his memoir. Dr. Bosenberg further detailed in Kinski's file how he was prone to sleeping on her balcony and breaking into her apartment when she was not present. He also destroyed her flat and then attempted to strangle her in the altercation that led to Kinski's arrest by the responding police. Doctors concluded in the once-sealed file that Kinski was "dangerous" to the public and showed signs of "severe mental illness."[101] The same anonymous psychiatrist noted in his assessment that Kinski was delusional in that he hadn't acted in over a year, but still maintained an unshakeable belief that a new film in which he would star was just around the corner. Of course, given the competition for roles for all actors in any era, one wonders if, using only this criteria, all actors would not be judged mentally unstable, given the need to maintain determined self-belief between acting jobs. The clinical report also detailed that Kinski was "violent" and "incorrigible," and that he was deluded by a paranoid-fueled belief that he alone was the balanced person in a world gone mad around him. At its heart, this is the same worldview that his demented, power-grabbing conquistador would years later act out in *Aguirre, the Wrath of God*.

His probable misdiagnosis, which Kinski also rejected as inaccurate, was not uncommon for manic-depressives in that era, as they were often under clinical states of delusional psychosis when finally admitted for observation. In this scenario, and especially before the differential criteria distinguishing schizophrenia from bipolar disorder was better understood, the two maladies were often mistaken for one another by even trained psychiatrists.[102] In rare cases, a lone patient can be diagnosed as bipolar comorbid with schizophrenia, further clouding an easy initial assessment. And in fact, both schizophrenia and manic depression produce many shared states of mental confusion and outwardly similar signs, despite vast differences that make them quite distinctive.[103] But such acute, shared symptoms as paranoia and delusional ranting are difficult, if not impossible, to distinguish when a new patient with no prior history of mental illness is admitted into an emergency health care facility. As a result, well-meaning doctors often attempt to classify based on the limited markers they can accurately observe. The very same records that definitively notate Kinski as mentally ill also reveal a more sinister side to the story of his incarceration, and one that tends to more fully support Kinski's admittedly biased perception that he was mistreated during his stay. For despite being on record in the report as protesting his confinement as unjust, Kinski was subjected to insulin treatments as therapy against his wishes in both accounts. Insulin shots were usually reserved in the 1950s only for schizophrenics and manic-depressives in severe, unresponsive episodes of distress. According to Professor Peter Bräunig, a chief doctor of psychiatry in Berlin's Vivante Humboldt Clinic who reviewed the Kinski file in 2008 when it was made public, while the practice was considered cutting edge in the era, it was actually a life-threatening one by modern standards that should not have been attempted given the high risk that it could lead to coma or death.[104] Though unconfirmed by the records, Kinski also claimed he was subject to prolonged submersion in ice-cold bath tubs until he quit raving, as well as treated to electroshock therapy and solitary confinement. These were then standard bipolar treatments worldwide, as witnessed by the fact Kinski's therapy is nearly identical to what Gene Tierney underwent in the same period in America. The official report that stated Kinski was released on his own recognizance after three days of confinement would tend to put in question that enough time had truly elapsed for as many treatments to be attempted as Kinski claimed, however, in a clinical institution not known for its reputation for high-quality care. Kinski remembered how he was forced to share a large common room with a hundred fellow inmates, all of whom were unstable to the point of wailing, soiling themselves, screaming, rocking furiously, and blindly stumbling around in semi-catatonic states, offensive in their unwashed stench. No one could sleep for the mournful cacophony, and many died in confinement. Such horrific images of neglect and institutional abuse recall the tragic conditions of other notorious asylums that engaged in inhumane treatment of the mentally ill, such as the Paris-based Charenton and the New York–based Bloomingdale. Kinski recalled it as "true hell."[105] He was finally forced to sign an affidavit in exchange for his asylum release in

which he cleared Dr. Bosenberg of all responsibility for his incarceration and promised never to bother her again. Though this signed statement was not included in the released documents, it stands to reason
that Kinski was indeed required to affirm such legalities, especially
given the staff's observations that he was a continual menace to himself
and others when agitated. But it equally begs the question: if Dr. Bosenberg was not romantically involved with Kinski as he claimed, or at
least had aroused suspicions as such by the board of directors, then why
would an asylum release him after only three days if, as their doctors
concluded upon review, Kinski was a menace to society left at large?
Such contradictory conclusions leave a cloud of uncertainty over the
motives of those involved, at the very least, however delusional might
be Kinski's paranoid belief that the doctors were deliberately toying
with his mind. In a reprise of the old saying that just because you're
paranoid, it doesn't mean they are not out to get you, Kinski may have
arrived at the truth, however distorted, as to why he was shown the exit
as fast as he was initially straight-jacketed into admittance. This early,
bitter experience with psychiatry left Kinski forever hateful of the field,
and thus unwilling to seek further clinical help throughout the rest of
his deeply troubled life.

Despite their age differences and polarized backgrounds, Fassbinder and Kinski shared many personal indulgences as manic-depressives.
They were each hypersexual, although Kinski's nonstop need for sex,[106]
to the point of hiring many prostitutes in one night in every city in
which he found himself temporarily employed, or maniacally having
marathon, sadistic sexual sessions with his current longer-term lover,[107]
reads as manic self-debasement bordering on sexual psychosis. The
constant recalling of his sordid affairs in his book seems to imply a need
to relive them with his own perverse mental imagery imposed on each
conquest. When Kinski begins detailing each new depravity with passionate devotion, it is not unlike the dark writings of confessed serial
killers, albeit with sexual partners as willing victims substituted for hom-
icides. Obvious labels such as "misogynist" and "sexist" vanish into easy
distinctions as one delves into Kinski's autobiography, in which long
passages read as if penned by a pornographer, but taken one objectionable step further. In fact, and indicative of the many legal troubles he
endured throughout his life owing to his erratic mental state, the first
editions of Kinski's memoirs were retracted by the European publisher

because of threats of libel. Fassbinder equally faced many legal and societal rejections of his open preferences as a bisexual male who mostly preferred gay sex. This was especially true among the conservative elements of the repressive new German republic, who rejected his leftist revolutionary political and radical artistic stances, which Fassbinder rarely failed to espouse in interviews and feature in his proletariat-centered universe of lonely, broken characters. Fassbinder and Kinski each viewed themselves as artistic renegades in their chosen professions, and above the normal considerations of their industry peers owing to their self-nurtured genius status. Their shared manic self-aggrandizement made each unafraid of demonstrating utter contempt and even hatred of their viewing public, either in their work or interviews. Their shared malady also fueled their perfectionist drive to make each creative moment they participated in come alive in its best form, if for no other reason than to alleviate the physical tedium of film production itself. Each lived apart from society like a rock star, basking in media appreciation and equally in conservative contempt. Each worked excessively in order to combat the magnifying effects of being unemployed with no creative therapy while undergoing a bipolar episode. Each dealt with lovers who either killed themselves, or attempted suicide, at some point in their personal lives.[108] And each finally succumbed to heart-related failures before old age, in large part due to the destructive manic-depressive lifestyles each led.

But while they were bipolar similar in many respects, they were also bipolar opposites, too. Fassbinder, for example, poured his manic energies into his writing and directing craft. Rather than utilizing the modest profits he made from each new independent movie to buy expensive material goods, Fassbinder would often invest his money in each new production. He did this in order to get it started and/or finished if completion funds were not forthcoming toward the end of the film. And while he began to become excessive toward the end of his life in terms of wasting his income as he became further addicted to cocaine, he was remarkably frugal for most of his career, which helps explain how he was able to produce such a large body of work with often meager means of capitalization. Fassbinder no doubt had the artistic soul of his studio idol, Douglas Sirk, but he also possessed the same successful low-budget exploitation filmmaking skills of Roger Corman, preferring a "grind-them-out" mentality rather than attempting to make each movie definitive and stately in nature. In contrast, Kinski lived a life of excessive materialism whenever he could, which was frequently, given his admitted ability to be hired by virtually any filmmaker provided the check arrived ready to cash and attached to any offered screenplays. Kinski was not about quality, but the money, by his own admission. He once turned down Fellini after being personally courted by him because the monetary offer was so low, wiring back a simple telegram of "Fuck you!"[109] Likewise, he told Spielberg no to a villain role in *Raiders of the Lost Ark* and no to Claude Lelouch's *Les Uns et les Autres* for monetary reasons. Others Kinski deemed not worthy for lack of paycheck heft included Ken Russell, Pier Paolo Pasolini, Lilian Cavani, Arthur Penn, and Luchino Visconti. Instead, Kinski, whose view of his industry was that every project he worked on was drafted from the utter dregs, even the admired ones, quit reading each new script. Using this method of career choice, he would move from one set to the next, rarely with any sustained break. He was once simultaneously working on three movies, capitalizing on a salary of fifty thousand marks per day at his career height. His gambit worked, at least in terms of keeping him forever working, and therefore forever grossing, money he quickly spent. In various manic sprees, not unlike Peter Sellers, Kinski bought almost two dozen expensive cars, such as Ferraris, Rolls Royces, and Maseratis, wrecking many of them. He kept a permanent staff of seven on hand to run his chalet, devoured caviar by the spoonful, and had a custom, thirty-foot trailer made (outfitted with silk walls, teak and gold interior finishing, private dining, and separate kitchen) to haul to each new location. It was staffed for Kinski's ease with a permanent chauffeur, manservant, and cook.[110] Where Fassbinder was careful and methodical, Kinski was careless and spontaneous. Where Fassbinder maniacally planned for each new movie, Kinski forgot each new assignment as soon as the shooting day was done, if not sooner. Both used the film process to exhaust their manic-depressive energies, but to greatly opposite artistic results.

This disparity is magnified in their creative output. A typical Fassbinder film is moody, introspective, and full of stone-faced characters who only seem to frostily come alive when they gaze into mirrors. Kinski and his portraits, on the other hand, tend toward wild, manic exaggerations and snarling, depressive retreats, intertwined and inseparable, a yin/yang flow. If the average Fassbinder protagonist is inwardly directed and an emotionally rigid depressive, the average Kinski role is, via bugged eyes, bared teeth, and hysterical screaming, manic external- ization personified. Fassbinder's films are intellectually challenging and often complex in terms of levels of meaning, feeling as if the filmmaker is holding back. Kinski's film portraits are impulsively alive and contra- dictory, messy in their desperate, selfish grabbing at life's bounties. There is a quality of Gollum and "my precious" in Kinski's screen man- nerisms, as if he is afraid his secretive bipolar talents and treasures will be stolen by the camera. Fassbinder dryly examines the alienation in- herent in manic depression in movies such as *Despair* (1978), wherein a man experiences such depressive depersonalization he forgets his past and social identity, and *Fear of Fear* (1975), focusing on a lonely house- wife suffering from depression who studiously avoids her apartment building neighbor rather than befriend him because the neighbor is clearly mentally ill, too. In contrast, Klaus Kinski's greatest screen crea- tions are never intellectually achieved, but expressively captured. This is perhaps why his best work was always with Herzog, the self-described intellectual, as Kinski's chameleon ability to shift moods during his per- formances gave Herzog's non-descriptive protagonists a sense of unpre- dictable menace otherwise absent. Likewise, Herzog's intransigent na- ture on the often remote, primitive locations where they filmed offered Kinski a perfect artistic foil, supplying a firm, steady hand to Kinski's tendencies to become overwrought and/or dismissive of the work at hand. It also kept Kinski from his otherwise morbid need to vanish into the sex and drugs underworld of any nearby teeming metropolis by night. Though they would alternately love and hate each other, and threaten to kill and physically attack one another, Kinski and Herzog worked brilliantly together to achieve a body of work that remains some of the most impressive in all of bipolar cinema.

Not that the performances Kinski gave to Herzog's visions were easy on him. In fact, they were among the most difficult in his career of over 135 feature film credits. Much of the blame he attributes to Werner Herzog, whom Kinski describes in the most unflattering terms in his book. While Herzog has claimed some of the hyperbole was a prank he and Kinski agreed to foist upon an unsuspecting public as a private joke, it is hard to believe Kinski was not sincere in at least some of his ventilated rage. He paints a picture of Herzog as having "a toad-like indolence" and his endless talk made Herzog "a very slow blah ma-

chine."[111] Kinski accuses Herzog of having megalomania, delusionally
believing he is a visionary. Kinski insists he's never met a more depressing individual in his lifetime. Adrift together for two months in the
jungle locales of *Aguirre, the Wrath of God*, Kinski and Herzog begin as
tentative collaborators, only to end with Kinski threatening to leave the
picture shortly before completion. Herzog responded by promising to
first shoot Kinski, and then save the final bullet for himself. Despite
being estranged after *Aguirre*'s tortured production, they worked together on successive pictures, each more grueling on Kinski's mental
health, if not Herzog's. By the time they made *Woyzeck*, Kinski recalled
spending his nights banging his head against his trailer's walls, fighting
to keep his illness at bay long enough to complete shooting. His recovery afterward, always slow where Herzog's tasking productions were
concerned, dragged on for months, leaving him subject to fits of
screaming and brief periods of visual hallucination involving demonic
creatures clawing at his brain.[112] Kinski laments the agonies of his mental illness with unrelenting clarity and descriptive fervor throughout his
memoir, which provides a final study in contrast between himself and
Fassbinder.

Fassbinder, typical of his icily observant but moody body of work,
approached his own clinical bipolarity with a sense of ironic self-detach-
ment, if not even alienated self-enlightenment, rather than rage against
his madness as did Kinski. Fassbinder wrote of the need for hopeful
characters in his cinema, especially those who suffered from madness.
He likewise opined in another critique about the "land of madness"[113]
as a potentially positive state of emotional anarchy. Of Douglas Sirk's
films, Fassbinder also advocated a running theme showing insanity as
hopeful, as the only cure for those suffering from the cruel vagaries of
the so-called normal world. Such statements suggest Fassbinder held
his own manic-depressive tendencies at arm's length when he was capable of doing so, especially where the rigors of maintaining his self-
discipline in terms of sheer output were concerned. Further, it hints
that Fassbinder realized his abilities were bipolar driven to the extent
that he probably would have otherwise never attempted to be a director, which was his lifelong dream realized. Even with his many cinematic disappointments and personal failures, Fassbinder mostly found a
hopeful redemption with his directing-as-therapy. Kinski's dreams of
fame and glory as an actor were shorter-lived, if only rarely aspired to

by the actor himself, and therefore Kinski treated his career, and those who enabled it, with utter contempt. He bitterly complained his directors were all garbage collectors who pilfered from the dumps of prior cinematic outings.[114] He only worked for the money, and even more importantly, for the distraction it offered his restless, manic-fueled mind. Kinski summed it up as a battle to remain alive fighting his own demons of mental illness, staying employed without a break at whatever artistic cost to himself. It was this, or an even darker world where he had to patiently await only quality projects with prestigious directors and would likely have killed himself in the interim. The troubled actor concluded his book with no apology for his many inexplicable and harmful actions, given that he existed in a personal reality wherein no one ever offered him any help, any solution, that ever worked for him. He committed to his craft not for respect, but for absolution from the agonies of unending manic depression. As Kinski wrote by way of attempted rationalization, only by expunging his mania through acting could he momentarily slip free from his "chains of torment."[115]

9

1980S–1990S: THE BURGEONING DIVERSITY OF DEPRESSIVE EXPRESSIONISM

A sea change occurred in Hollywood studio filmmaking in the 1980s that would subsequently impact American bipolar movies and their mood-disordered creators. Powerful conglomerates funded by Wall Street, which had formerly avoided Hollywood's endless production money traps and incalculable fluidity of box office results, took over and transformed the business. The corporate culture would soon come to be reflected throughout the production process. Concept-driven projects with lucrative toy tie-ins became the predominant philosophy. Young executives who steered the next graphic novel adaptation or hot spec script sale into a sequel-friendly franchise series stood to become millionaires, while those championing character-centered, auteur-driven projects aimed at smaller audiences were shown the studio exits. Much of the individuality and humanistic vision so vividly on display in the 1970s New Hollywood filmmaking was left behind. Newer, more globally minded movies featuring action, special effects, and less need for dialogue translation in order to be effective in all markets replaced the former paradigm. Though it has undergone permutations since this transformational period in the twenty years that encompass this chapter, the corporate mentality arising from this period of back-to-back reductions in risk-taking and quality of output endures to this day. That is why studying the arc of bipolar cinema throughout the two decades is revealing. It shows the narrowing of gains of realistic portrayals of bipolar disorder that were achieved in the prior decades. It also indicates a healthy, often independently financed or non-studio-influenced counterreaction to the corporate takeover of global cinema was alive and well. Many of these efforts would not succeed in altering monopolized media ownership by an ever-shrinking handful of powerful players. Yet they did maintain a brave attempt to further the portraits of manic depression in the face of film markets that increasingly resisted sensitive dramas in favor of mega-budgeted, violent action movies. It became a time of limited artistic success in terms of larger studio products, but varied, and sadly variable in their necessarily sporadic output, individualistic efforts that kept alive and carried forward bipolar cinema.

THE *RIVER'S EDGE* OF INSANITY

When first released in the enchantment years of the Reagan revolution, *River's Edge* (1986) stirred critical interest for its generational portrait of teenagers moved far beyond rebellious boredom and descended into indifferent, homicidal tribalism. As a movie, it was styled as a neorealistic update of *Rebel without a Cause*, but with a grittier, grunge-flavored nihilism as if directed by Alex Cox. It is a nervous, edgy film filled with many grotesque moments of black comedy and then strident melodrama. Many of *River's Edge*'s characters are in need of psychiatric intervention, at least based on the depicted course of their actions over one long, twenty-four-hour period. Foremost among them is Samson "John" Tollet (Daniel Roebuck), a brooding hulk of a high school dropout in training. When we first meet Samson one gray dawn, he is sitting beside the corpse of his former girlfriend, Jamie (Danyi Deats), whom he has killed and left nude by the edge of the river. He surveys the horror of his actions and blankly decides to score a six-pack of beer before school, channeling an emotional void of feeling that accurately represents episodes of post-psychosis. The fact that he can commit murder and then not miss the tardy bell for school within the same hour of the morning is indicative of Samson's deeply troubled psyche. His disturbing inability to emotionally process his own psychotic actions, and his subsequent cloud of denial in pretending he will not be the obvious suspect, is suggestive that Samson has undergone an episode of impulsive homicidal mania. Sadly, such accounts of loved ones becoming the victims of manic-depressive rage are not entirely rare, but neither are they as likely or common as many movie depictions falsely indicate.[1] Samson's moody instability, in which he's a docile, subservient man-boy in one moment, a rage-filled alcoholic masking his inner torment the next, and finally murderous in rare, uncontrollable violent breakdowns, does suggest the possibility of a bipolar diagnosis. But the severity of his afflictions, and inherent psychopathic nature, suggest other, comorbid latencies for personality disorders are perhaps better clinical probabilities as explanatory or even concurrently present.

Samson indicates many mood-disorder markers with his biography alone. He lives solely with his invalid grandmother. This paradigm establishes Samson's chronic sense of loneliness, as well as suggests he has lost his parents either via neglect or in an unspecified tragedy. Such tragic backgrounds in early childhood are common in patients who are later diagnosed with bipolar disorder. Samson is very deferential to his grandmother's off-screen presence, serving her dinner and attending to her simple needs. But he feels overwhelming shame and guilt at having to be her constant caretaker, which he cannot express to her. During these moments, his demeanor becomes introverted and depressive, his voice lowered, head bowed and body movements stiff and awkward. Later, when he boasts of his slaying with callous indifference to his astonished friends, Samson foolishly exhibits hypomanic delusions of grandeur, acting as if Jamie deserved her fate for daring to displease him. Still later, when he confronts the older man Feck (Dennis Hopper), Samson deliberately pokes at the unstable, gun-toting Feck using a manic rant so vile, the wounded Feck believes killing Samson is the only way to end the relentless diatribe. Samson exhibits many other signs of psychiatric illness apart from possible bipolarity alone. But whatever his diagnosis, it hardly matters as far as the film is concerned. Samson winds up the next body to be found, not far from his original victim. He becomes yet another undiagnosed mentally ill teen ready for the exploitative headlines as post-mortem fodder. Even more grimly ironic, the fictional script was loosely based on a real life Milpitas, California, high school murder case, sadly proving the point before a frame of film was exposed.[2] There is little, or no, preventative care suggested as having occurred from anyone involved in *River's Edge* prior to Samson's explosion of violence and death, even though the warning signs are abundant. Whether it's the torn families patched together to dysfunctional effect, the working poor backgrounds that makes them view ascendency as beyond their grasp, or the overcrowded school rooms filled with too many students simply being passed along or dropping out, *River's Edge* posits an American suburban dystopia teetering on the constant edge of implosion. The unbalanced teenage protagonists become stand-ins for the absentee parents and authority figures, who seem to be hidden away in another, parallel cinematic world for most of the film's running time. Like *Lord of the Flies*, it views all of humanity's darkness by showing the adults' reflection in the mirroring eyes of their confused children. The teens of *River's Edge* act not as much in defiance, as in absence, of rational figures of any moral authority to guide them. This is indicated by the stance of a history teacher in their school who is the lone voice of reason, and who challenges the students to drop their masks of cynical apathy in order to make a difference in their own, sleepwalking lives. His interdiction, though seemingly a fool's errand, leads to at least two of the film's characters realizing Samson's murder of Jamie must be reported to the police, even if it means risking being labeled a fink for having done so by their peer group.

The peer group is dominated by a manic-depressive named Layne (Crispin Glover), a pseudo-punk, Gothic-dipped hipster afflicted with self-aggrandizement. With his fingerless gloves, wool cap, and tight leather jacket ensemble, and an unnerving sense of how to exploit anyone's perceived weakness for mockery or personal gain, Layne is a bipolar study in teen angst, narcissistic egomania run amok. It is difficult to intellectually distill the astonishingly self-fixated quality Glover brings to his over-the-top performance. While it plays as exaggerated camp in some moments, owing to its outrageously mannered style, it concurrently captures the underlying rampant nature of mania when it becomes enraptured with its own beatific essence. Layne's bipolar viewing of himself as a de facto leader beyond question, mixed with his spur-of-the-moment, often hare-brained, actions, collides with the stark realities of police detectives investigating Layne and his group for murder. Layne models his grandiosity with a hyper-self-consciousness in his body movements, as if he were a preening peacock on a punk rock runway. Already hyperactive and jittery owing to his chronic moodiness, he cajoles his friend Matt (Keanu Reeves) to drop by old man Feck's

house and score weed before school. He also suffers from blatant persecution mania, as it was once termed. The moment he sees anyone is his
subservient camp display independent thought, Layne's ever-present
paranoia takes over, leading him to persecute the heretic with the threat
of banishment from the inner circle. His need to control others in this
manner by deciding who is, and who is not, a part of their small tribe is
very much akin to portraits of leadership mania previously reviewed,
such as Michael Corleone in *The Godfather*. When Layne sees that he
alone must lead his tiny group out of the danger, he suffers from a
delusion that the events are transpiring as if in a movie. He even reca-
pitulates the plot in a postmodern soliloquy about how their friendship
since second grade is being tested, which ironically is also the plot of
River's Edge. Layne shudders with manic glee and sheepishly adds, "It's
kind of exciting. I feel like Chuck Norris." For Layne and his upside
mania, which rarely, if ever, abates, the death of their friend and the
need to supposedly protect Samson from the authorities acts as a mechanism to engage his mania for fantasy-laden acting out. As a result,
Layne uselessly spends all night cruising in his car in a losing quest to
orchestrate reality to his own inner, manic-driven plans for societal
control.

Feck is a seedy study of unkempt depressive furor unleashed by
Hopper with characteristic bombast, even if he is restrained for most of
River's Edge. Hopper's Feck is a flighty, unstable ex-biker with physical
disabilities who prefers the companionship of his inflatable love doll to
humans. His chief demeanor is one of defeated depression, with a
heavy self-medication reliance on pot, some of which he freely gives to
a group of high school sycophants. While the young cast sets the energetic tone of *River's Edge*, it's Hopper's melancholic turn as Feck that
gives it the deeper pull of melodrama. He is reclusive in his depression,
unable to form lasting relationships with outsiders. His projection of
erotic needs onto Ellie, his love doll, is beyond pathos and into pathological denial. Feck contends he is fully aware Ellie is not real, even as
he bonds with her as if she were alive when others are present. Feck
also suffers from sudden onsets of paranoia in which he believes the
cops are closing in on him for the murder of his former lover, a young
woman Feck admits to having shot to death with a gun he still bran-
dishes. In fact, Feck and Samson will briefly unite in the film's final
moments over the fact each has murdered a woman. Their understand-

ing lasts until the older Feck, who has murdered out of a delusional, misogynistic moral authority that pronounces all women evil, is repulsed by Sampson's amorality, for what Samson has randomly done without supplying any internal meaning to his killing. In his final scene, Feck is booked for the murder of Samson, sadly confessing in his holding cell that "I'd like to leave now. Very tired. Sort of depressed." The grim irony is that Feck has been clinically depressed from the film's opening. The sickening events that unfold around, and later engulf, him are completely out of his control. From the outset, his bipolar illness has rendered him symbolically impotent against others who manipulate him for selfish gains. Feck is a town fool in the classic sense of bipolar antiquity, laughed at by all, taken advantage of by many in turn, as they celebrate their superiority to the poor idiot. Layne is so bold as to ridicule Feck's endless talk about "all women are evil" even as he pressures the old biker for free weed. In short, Feck's mental illness is ignored because it provides a means to control Feck by using his own bipolarity against him. His mental condition is self-evident, but his fellow citizens look the other way in this regard, acting to Feck's face as if his mental illness is completely normal, and his paranoid seclusion justifiable. Rather than advocate or administer help, they use Feck's illness to extract from him what they need. A black comedic tension is created by this see-saw of pretense in *River's Edge* whenever Feck is present. The other characters must act unnaturally stiff and overly friendly whenever they deal with Feck, for fear Feck will drop his friendly facade and mercurially switch to his belligerent side. They tiptoe around his insanity like mice attempting to steal cheese from the trap. They are always keenly aware that Feck's fickle nature may manifest a threatening demeanor if they so much as utter the wrong word, or give a condescending look, after his latest manic diatribe about the evils of the modern world. But such is their need for free marijuana to dull their chronic pain that the teenagers who frequent Feck's den of iniquity will gladly risk their bored lives to score even a few loose joints, if for no other reason for the cheap thrill of having survived.

Some films have a melancholic overlay that is palpable to the senses. These kinds of studies in dejected states of being often feature lonely characters, repressive social milieus, and expressive visual styles. *River's Edge* is classical in this regard in bipolar cinema, even as it breaks new ground with the blasé indifference to the human misery it chronicles.

The callous disregard for life and accepted level of dysfunction on display are not novel to films featuring manic-depressive characters and
themes, and earlier groundbreaking bipolar films such as the studio
works of Nicholas Ray are particularly influential on *River's Edge* in this
regard. But Tim Hunter's bleak look at existential teenagers in crisis is
still an original, moodily observed affair. The storm-soaked Pacific
Northwest settings with dreary, overcast skies and raindrop-sprinkled
windshields give the film a depressive pallor. The restless characters are
never shown relaxing at home or enjoying a social scene; rather, they
are always hurrying from one moment of emotional crisis to the next. In
the bipolar down view of *River's Edge*, most people are alienated, but
the few that are not are just as likely victims of social cliques that pit
members against one another to alleviate boredom. The depressive's
need to withdraw from society at times, especially when combined with
psychiatric illness such as Feck suffers from, becomes more understandable in the face of the ongoing petty jealousies and cruel mental
games. Blanche in *A Streetcar Named Desire* "depended on the kindness of strangers" in order to avoid the worst aspects of her manic
depression; the bereft protagonists of *River's Edge* are dependent on
the kindness of supposed friends and family, but they too are strangers
in this movie, although some are friendly strangers who can, from time
to time, depend on one another to form alliances, if only temporarily.
This is a bipolar point of view in terms of narrative construction, in that
many who are manic-depressive drop in and out of relationships owing
to episodic behaviors.[3] Thus many bipolar patients are constantly seeking to renew old, perhaps strained, friendships, however short-lived
they may be in the final sum.

MEL GIBSON AND THE DARK SIDE OF MANIC RAGE

Given the severity of his rage-filled bipolarity seen in anti-Semitic remarks made to arresting police and physical abuse of ex-girlfriend Oksa-
na Grigorieva,[4] it is sadly ironic that Mel Gibson first became internationally famous for his role in *Mad Max* (1979), in which he plays an
upstanding, moral police officer who seeks to protect his threatened
wife from harm. Gibson's biggest early commercial success, however,
was as the manic-depressive police detective Martin Riggs in the *Lethal*

Weapon series, which seems prophetic in hindsight, in that Riggs's depression, alcohol abuse as self-medication, suicidal thoughts, outbursts of anger, and reckless risk-taking are all bipolar symptoms Gibson would experience in real life.[5] His manic depression was privately known to him early on, but he was only diagnosed decades after his fame. Gibson experienced what he termed "really good highs but some very low lows"[6] in his college years spent at Australia's National Institute of Dramatic Art, which would seem to imply the onset of his disorder. But it would only be after moving to Los Angeles and becoming one of the most successful leading men of the 1980s and then commercially reinventing himself as a maverick director and producer in the 1990s and into the 2000s that his bipolar-fueled rages would finally break the surface of underground gossip and appear in tabloid headlines. This forever altered his previous media image as a happily married, religious family man.

His unfortunate fate would be to wear the mark of Cain within the studio system after an arrest for drunk driving in 2006, when he uttered the widely disseminated comment that Jewish people were the cause of all warfare.[7] His comment was particularly insensitive, given that he had directed and produced the controversial *The Passion of the Christ* (2004). It had grossed over $600 million in global revenues—all outside the traditional releasing structure of the Hollywood studios—but had also been condemned as anti-Semitic by the influential Anti-Defamation League. Studio heavyweights such as Amy Pascal and Ari Emanuel wrote open letters in trade journals demanding a boycott of all Mel Gibson movies in protest of his bigoted rant, as well as for his fellow actors and crew members to refuse to work on any production with him.[8] Robert Downey Jr., himself no stranger to damaging headlines, would openly advocate for Gibson to be forgiven,[9] and Jodie Foster as director would cast Gibson in a biographically tinged story of a successful bipolar executive who experiences a career-ending manic-depression in *The Beaver* (2011). Of his performance, Foster, a longtime friend, called it "one of the deepest performances Mel's ever given and the most true to who he is," in behind-the-scenes interviews for the film's DVD release. But his career would never be the same after the scandals. Gibson continues to work to this day, but the audience perception of his rants originating in intolerance, rather than at least par-

tially from behind the mask of bipolar illness, has been widely attributed to his commercial decline.

The ultimate struggle of the bipolar is to control his own worst
enemy, namely himself, when he is ranting hateful bile. Perhaps more
than any other filmmaker profiled, Mel Gibson and his inability to manage his lifelong bipolar disorder, particularly his screaming diatribes,
raises serious questions about the structures of morality and decency
that manic-depressives sometimes mangle during episodes of madness.
The ability to control one's own biases and fears versus the need to
remain civil and observe the social contract is a theme that reverberates
throughout all arts and literature, particularly in Western variations. It
is readily understood that neurotypical protagonists often succumb to
their repressed, base natures. Tragedy as a dramatic form is based upon
this basic tenet, as any number of doomed protagonists from the Greeks
to Shakespeare vividly demonstrate. When one adds the factor of madness to the difficult proposition of resisting one's own worse instincts,
the struggle becomes unsustainable, at least during acute episodes. In
addition to the duress of life's ordinary pressures, the bipolar patient
must concurrently navigate the extraordinary headwinds of manic depression. As this book hopefully reveals, many afflicted filmmakers have
prevailed against the inner mental storms that often threaten to wreck
them. But the reality of life is that even the strongest among us are only
human. We erect enduring myths to deny our inevitable fallibility, but
they are merely sources of comfort and inspiration, not actual confer-
ment of immortality, despite how often they address such themes.

Mel Gibson's angelic ascent to stardom and sudden fall from its
graces illustrates this reality as succinctly as any other icon. Bipolarity
does not excuse or negate prejudices and private mythologies. Quite
sadly the opposite, it can inflate them and seek to project blame onto
The Other with a manic intensity in some. This inability to resist manic
rants, spewing racial and sexual stereotypes as well as making obscene
threats of violence against his ex-girlfriend,[10] has been enormously destructive for Gibson in all aspects of his life. What is often overlooked,
however, is that these failings originate in the same qualities of bipolarity that he has also channeled into his tense, hyper-emotive directorial
style, producing some of the more visually exciting cinema sequences of
their era. In such hyper-kinetic, suspense-laden films as *Braveheart*
(1995), *The Passion of the Christ*, and *Apocalypto* (2006), Gibson as

filmmaker has shown genuine talent for crafting sustained sequences of hallucinatory power, often blood-soaked affairs with more than a streak of sadomasochistic violence. Somewhat akin to how Leni Riefenstahl's works must be footnoted with their Nazi origination as balancing consideration, Mel Gibson's ability to focus his maniacal energies into his therapeutic filmmaking must be viewed against the excesses that have led to his public humiliation. Caveats aside, Gibson as auteur exhibits an obsessive quality of intense focusing on camera technique and almost obtrusive observance of the actors, distantly similar to the mannered style of Martin Scorsese. Both favor nervous, unpredictably moving camera shots, sudden intrusions from off-screen into the frame, and a mesmerizing fixation on the minutiae of enacted violence.

A brief study in contrast between Martin Scorsese, the mood-afflicted Protestant who directed *The Last Temptation of Christ*, and Mel Gibson, the mood-afflicted Catholic who directed *The Passion of the Christ*, is as revealing for their similarities as differences. This applies even to their respective narratives' embodying an alternative thesis regarding the life of Christ. Some in religious communities disagreed with Gibson's interpretation, as they likewise did with Scorsese's movie. But Scorsese's more meditative effort lacks the expressed need for blood redemption as supreme sacrifice, which is visually illustrated to the point of grotesque, though some might argue realistic, detail in Gibson's *Passion of the Christ*. A strong sense persists of the director forcing the viewer to experience in microscopic intensity each and every excruciating act of defilement undergone by Jesus during his darkest hours. The pain is never merely physical, but also spiritual, with a concentration on the leering faces and humiliating taunts that accompany the physical abuses. In these hideous moments, Gibson evocatively captures a true paranoid state of consciousness. The viewer identifies with the belittled protagonist, all alone against a violent mob intent on seeing him first horribly suffer and then later slowly die. There will be no last-minute rescue by the Roman cavalry, or any others, not even by the hand of God. Gibson, unlike Scorsese, is not focused on the moment of existential abandonment, in which the Christ questions aloud his fate before he expires, but on the slow ride into Christ's personal hell in which he will endure the literal tortures of the damned, but never break nor bend his will to them. Gibson's manic-depressive need to drag the viewer along is what distinguishes his best work from the more pedestrian Hollywood fare. Most mainstream efforts would only suggest, not openly parade such depravities as Gibson does in his directorial efforts. *The Passion of the Christ* is not a somber, intellectual exploration like Scorsese's movie, but a visceral endurance test designed to separate the faithful from the damned. His film seems more like a Christian haunted house designed to "scare straight" attendees as much as produce any emotional catharsis. This is backed by the fact that so many screenings of the film were staged in large-arena church auditoriums during its independent release to enthusiastic crowds and huge financial returns. In *The Passion of the Christ*'s self-sealed cinematic world, the viewer arrives already believing in the events, and all that follows after the opening credits is a litmus test; to wit: if you cannot withstand watching a movie version of these events, then how can you even imagine the horrors Christ underwent at his death? There is a Hammer Films tone of lurid color use and moral abandonment throughout *The Passion of the Christ*, and equally, a pervasive use of gore and blood to shock. These cinematic obsessions run throughout *Braveheart* and *Apocalypto*, too.

It is during these moments of abandonment that Mel Gibson is most clearly indulging, and then expunging, his manic sensibility, and it is what fuels his best sequences with passion. As director, he seems intent on punishing the viewers for their sins, which are never specifically charged by Gibson, though he frequently characterizes his protagonists as lacking in some crucial spiritual aspect. In *Apocalypto*, Gibson as storyteller distills this thematic obsession when the tribe is told a story about a human who was so melancholic, all the forest animals gathered around the destitute man and whispered to him their condolences. When this failed to rouse the depressed man, the animals next gave him special powers, such as wisdom and strength. But even these failed to inspire the catatonic human, who sighed as he stared into the abyss of his campfire. The animals leave, perplexed as to why such sadness should exist in the face of so much splendor, until the owl tells them this is the nature of mankind. "It is what makes him sad, and what makes him want," concludes the owl.

Surely this story relates to Gibson's own manic-depressive nature as much as it more generally covers the lot of humanity. For if any human being was ever blessed with the proverbial All, it is Gibson. His net worth can be more fully understood when one considers that his ex-wife

Robyn took half of their joint estate with an estimated $400,000,000 in their divorce settlement. Even with fame, good looks, wealth, and creative control in an industry that rarely grants it, Mel Gibson still plunged by 2011 to a status where *The Beaver*, a modest film made for $22 million, would only gross $958,319 in U.S. admissions, and have a disastrous non-opening weekend gross of $107,577,[11] a staggering failure given Gibson's former box office dominance. Though no proper accounting of both the favors and damages bipolarity can bring its afflicted is ever able to be fully calculated, at least the contrast is stark when one considers Gibson's status prior to and then after his public infamy. *The Passion of the Christ* made $320 million in the United States prior to any public problems owing to his bipolarity, while *The Beaver* made less than $1 million at the American box office after his personal debacles became widely known. It is true that the tone and genre differences between the two movies are part of the explanation, but the numbers are so vast, and Gibson's output so diminished subsequent to the negative public perception, that the argument that his disorder has cost him hundreds of millions of dollars is at the very least defensible. Conversely, one can say his fortune was amassed in part because of his bipolarity, as his brooding, self-conscious intensity in such films as *The Road Warrior* (1981), *Gallipoli* (1981) and *The Year of Living Dangerously* (1982) were key to his early charismatic appeal with fans worldwide.

Gibson's directorial work is filled with characters who have religious insights, sudden epiphanies, and emotional fits, all of which Gibson has personally experienced. His films are filled with heroes who face dissolution and disaster on every level, but especially from outside societal forces. In Gibson's movies, the external world is typically disintegrating, and the internal mechanisms of his protagonists must be activated in order to survive the onslaught. In *Braveheart*, *The Passion of the Christ*, and *Apocalypto*, the Gibson avatar fights not merely for his masculinity, but to prevail as a sovereign entity versus a horde of ugly aggressors. Whether they're invading Brits, invading Romans, or invading Mayans, they are amassed and intent on forcing Gibson's heroes into groveling submission. If viewed through the prism of Gibson's bipolar disorder, it is revealing as life metaphor. Gibson posits his own conflict of moods into the framework of his stories, portraying those events that seek to oppress an individual's liberty as externalizations of his own manic depression. His protagonists who must struggle against such forces of disintegration are projections of his own inner need to maintain personality stability against the ravages of bipolarity. His paranoid-laced studies in xenophobia are like a visual tell in a game of cinematic poker, in which he constantly, but perhaps unknowingly, reveals his inner states of misanthropic anxiety. There is an uncomfortable sense that much of the degradation Gibson so insistently inflicts on his viewers is, for but one example, akin to an episode reported by Joe Eszterhas. Eszterhas wrote that he witnessed Gibson chasing guests around his private villa island in the middle of the night during a violent fit of mania, all the while threatening them.[12]

There is a feeling in many of the scenes of violence and suffering in Gibson's films that he is vicariously inflicting pain on audiences, as well as excusing mankind's own worst instincts, if not his own. That he shows himself in an anonymous cameo in *The Passion of the Christ* as one of the Roman soldiers eager to pound nails into Christ's palms is indicative of his ambivalence toward his own role as either savior or sinner. It is this sense of internal struggle in his movies that imbues them with an uneasy tone of tense conflict and non-resolution. It is as if each has been pried from the grips of his madness, as wholly intact to his bipolar phantasms as he can render them without compromise. His uncontrolled mania has cost him dearly. But his pugilistic technique has produced some nightmarish flights of bipolar cinema as by-product of his wrestling with insanity.

THE SAD BALLAD OF JOSEPH VASQUEZ

On the bipolar opposite end of the fame and fortune experienced by Mel Gibson, fellow manic-depressive filmmaker Joseph B. Vasquez toiled during his time as independent filmmaker virtually unnoticed save for scant critical praise for his bold visions. He was of mixed Puerto Rican and African descent, and both parents were addicted to heroin even prior to his birth.[13] Dolores and Fermin Vasquez gave Joseph and his siblings to Bertha, his paternal grandmother, who lived in the South Bronx of New York, and rarely saw their children thereafter. His father overdosed in 1985, by which time he and Joseph had ceased contact. Bertha's recollections of Joseph's neglect by his mother meant his lot in

life improved with his relocation. Though lonely, he found a new passion when he borrowed a relative's Super 8 camera at age twelve and
began making movies. He would recruit neighborhood friends to play
the key roles, and then invite them to see the results at his grandmother's apartment later. His dream from that point forward was to be a
professional filmmaker. [14] His grades, which had been declining as he
toyed with dropping out of school, improved as Joseph began to study
harder in order to apply to a college-level film program and further his
ambition. Setbacks were still a common reality in his life, including the
suicide of a beloved cousin who was only thirteen years old.

His efforts were rewarded when he was accepted into the film department at City College of New York. After completing his studies in
1983, Vasquez embarked upon his first feature film in 16 mm made for
$30,000, *Street Story* (aka *Street Hitz* as it was later known in a home
video release). Never shy of exhibiting his manic propensity for talent,
Joseph wrote, directed, edited, produced, shot, worked sound, and even
cut the negative himself. He hustled the completed maiden effort to
any and every film distribution company with which he could finagle a
meeting, but with little success. Undeterred, Vasquez finally managed
to raise $320,000 to finance *The Bronx War* (1989), another examina-
tion of the harsh realities lensed in his beloved South Bronx locales.
This time the use of violence would be even more explicit than in *Street
Story*. Vasquez had apparently been made aware by his inability to
release his previous film that screen violence would help sell distributors on releasing it. The film opens with a surprisingly tense sequence
in which a rival gang of black drug dealers makes a hit on a Puerto
Rican family that deals on the same turf. Rather than play the action out
in the streets for more visual impact, Vasquez keeps it all interior, with
claustrophobic effect. The family is crowded into their tenement apartment, arguing and abusing drugs in order to escape the monotony.
Vasquez intercuts their domestic boredom with the silent gang of killers
exiting their sedan and silently making their way up the dimly lit stair-
wells. A crescendo is achieved as the guns inevitably open fire, leaving
the carnage on display. It has an *In Cold Blood* feel to it because of the
assault on the family unit, but as if directed by Abel Ferrara circa his
more sacrilegious period, such as *Ms. 45* (1981). The movie is full of
raw, crude power tinged with a sense of transgressive outrage at the
conditions it accurately depicts. In a bizarre looking-glass manner, *The*

Bronx War is like an old 1930s piece of Warner Brothers social realism, only updated. Instead of the Dead End Kids, Humphrey Bogart as hoodlum, and well-lit back-lot sets, Vasquez stages it against hardened, second-generation immigrants, with himself as Tito the drug dealer, in the dark pools of actual South Bronx locales. As a result, the clichés gain new urgency, cast as they are in the opening slaughter inside a supposedly safe domicile. There is another touching moment wherein Crazy (Miguel Sierra), a troubled wannabe gangster, with bewilderment in his eyes explains to a girl in a bar that his nickname is not merely decorative, but clinically accurate. It is interesting the way Vasquez casts himself as Tito, the sleepy-eyed depressive hero, playing against Crazy's hypomanic hounding for attention. Vasquez invokes both extremes of his own manic depression on-screen in these split, polarized avatars, and the tension is palpable, as if as writer he was battling with his two opposing sides in his conflict-ridden screenplay. Though the final effort is not entirely successful as commercial exploitation fare, it shows the talkative, languidly kinetic style that Vasquez would better demonstrate in his next signature production.

New Line was impressed with the results of Vasquez's second independent feature and financed him with $1.9 million to make *Hangin' with the Homeboys* (1991). The trailers would market it as a hard-edged look at urban gangs like *Boyz n the Hood* (1991), but Vasquez's third narrative played closer to a South Bronx *American Graffiti*. In fact, the opening scene parodies the sense of menace urban black males routinely express as rap media stereotypes. Aboard a New York subway, a trio of young street toughs picks a fight with a lone black male, holding him down as they assault him. The white, mostly middle-aged riders are shown reacting with fear and silent judgment, retreating to the safety exits but never offering a hand or uttering a sound to stop the violence in progress. The black "victim" suddenly laughs, the trio of thugs help him to his feet, and a loquacious Tom (Mario Joyner), a prankster with acting ambitions, deeply bows. He formally thanks the astonished riders for "attending another performance of ghetto theater" before Vasquez playfully cuts to the rousing opening title credits.

Much as in *The Bronx War*, Vasquez halves his bipolarity into two different stand-ins with *Hangin' with the Homeboys*. Johnny (John Leguizamo) is a clean-cut, self-conscious stock boy who is stuck behind his dead-end job in a neighborhood grocery store, despite his clear intelligence and abilities. Vinny (Nestor Serrano), a Puerto Rican whose real name is Fernando but who pretends to be Italian because he envies their higher-class acceptance, negatively describes Johnny before he is introduced as "always being depressed." Johnny describes himself this way when he declines to go out with Vinny and best friend Willie (Doug E. Doug), although Willie convinces the downcast Johnny to give it a chance to improve his mood. Vinny is a loud-mouthed, pressure-speaking hypomanic who has delusions of grandeur as a womanizer even though he rarely has any conquests to show for his talkative efforts. He overplays his Italian role so that his real racial identity will be masked. This manic self-aggrandizement to hide low self-esteem is not uncommon with some bipolar-afflicted patients. Vasquez himself would often face angst over his conflicting cultural affinities, even as his cinema would provide a rare biracial, cultural bridge between the two separated Bronx enclaves. Vasquez would experience spells of hypersexuality as well, also a marker of bipolarity. [15] This is illustrated in Vinny's annoying, and yet alternately appealing, chatter, forever eager to strike up a flirtatious conversation with any female passerby. It is telling that Vasquez wrote the role of Vinny for himself before agreeing with great reluctance to New Line's demand to instead cast Serrano, in order that Vasquez could concentrate fully on directorial chores. Given that his Tito in *The Bronx War* is a depressive, and Vinny is clearly a manic, one can see that Vasquez's desire was probably to create a book-end set of performances, studies in manic-depressive contrast based on his own unique temperament.

The film was a surprise hit, owing to the fact that it was actually more aligned in tone to *Diner* (1982) than to gangster melodrama. Basically a four-character study with supporting players, *Hangin' with the Homeboys* is a slowly unwinding "night in the life of" look at its urban players, with a sweet-natured goofiness that redeems its meandering pace. Producer and friend Michael Lieber commented on the speed with which Vasquez worked. He wrote the first draft of *Hangin' with the Homeboys* in three days without sleep, [16] lost in a manic cloud of creativity. Rather than grasping the seriousness of Vasquez's disorder, which Vasquez seemed fully in creative control of during this period, Lieber and colleagues were instead understandably impressed with Vasquez's amazing display of talent. But like almost all other aspects of his life, bipolar disorder would come to dominate not only his rational and private sides, but his creative energies, too. In many ways, the high point of *Hangin' with the Homeboys*, which won a coveted screenwriting award at the Sundance Film Festival the year it showed, would come to represent an unrepeatable zenith in Joseph Vasquez's career and life. Perhaps no other omen marked the tragedy to come more than when Vasquez was attacked by a homeless man during shooting of *Hangin' with the Homeboys*. The man slashed Vasquez's face and caused a scar that Vasquez felt ended any hopes he ever had of acting again. His mood turned sour on the set from that point forward, and he bitterly fought with cast and crew.[17] Many were unsettled by the change, since he had been so positive on the set previously. But the results he was producing in the dailies were undeniably positive despite his new moodiness. By the time the film was shown to a gathering of New York City film critics in June of 1991, however, Vasquez was displaying signs of increasing instability. He arrived disheveled for the affair, angrily claiming he'd been accosted by the police in a case of mistaken identity. He asked the assembled critics in a hushed tone to enjoy the film and then left without further comment among astonished whispers.[18] Inasmuch as the press could either make or break his directing career based on such a screening, one can easily understand how the burden of responsibility he felt, combined with his growing mood disorder, defeated any chance he had of representing himself well that pressure-filled evening. But if anything, Vasquez's street credibility may have risen with his seeming indifference, signaling an underlying rebelliousness that was authentic. He began attending screenings and saying more provocatively outrageous things to the press with a straight face. He thanked New Line Cinema for not only producing the film, but also supplying the best drugs in the business during its making.[19] The comments were often taken at face value, which was ludicrous, as Vasquez maintained a personal drug-free policy, probably owing to the horrific impact of his heroin-addicted parents. But suffice to say such public comments did not endear Vasquez to New Line, which was eagerly trying to position itself as a growing center of influence in mainstream Hollywood.

Vasquez was not immune to the call of tinsel town. He would move there to try and capitalize on *Hangin' with the Homeboys* and its limited, albeit critical, success. But subject to increasingly longer, more destructive bouts of mania, he would fail to achieve much in the way of measurable success, turning down more projects than he ever managed to direct. He developed ideas during an unending series of creative meetings with studio executives, but nothing ever came from the pitch sessions. Ideas that never saw the light of day included a gender-flipping *Hangin' with the Homegirls* semi-sequel. One closer to Vasquez's heart called *Writing on the Wall* was about three racially mixed teens who must confront their own prejudices because of a homicide. His deterioration would worsen as the endless talks proved fruitless, providing him no therapeutic outlet. His hypersexuality was never secretive, but Vasquez did not let most friends or associates know he had developed AIDS, afraid it would hurt his chances to be hired to direct. [20] Unable to get a project made in Hollywood, Vasquez went to Puerto Rico and independently lensed *Manhattan Merengue* (1994), a strained attempt to cross the dance musical genre with an immigrant love story. While this worked wonders for *West Side Story*, Vasquez's modest film was sold only to home video markets in Spain and France, and was never released in the United States. Vasquez was beginning to succumb to manic delusions of grandeur and their subsequent fall-out. Having predicted to everyone he knew in the film business that *Manhattan Merengue* would make him a millionaire when it became a huge hit in the United States, only to watch it be buried alive, may have been the final straw for Vasquez's weakening hold on reality. Vasquez would soon be restrained by authorities and placed in a mental hospital for observation after running naked through his apartment building and proclaiming he was Jesus Christ reincarnate. [21] His psychiatric evaluation suggested Vasquez be held for several months of recovery and observation, so severe was his manic psychosis upon admittance. But California state law prevented his being held unless he consented, and Vasquez was eager to leave. After his release, his religious mania worsened. He rented a house in the Hollywood hills and brought in a variety of prostitutes and beggars whom he allowed to feed in his kitchen and sleep on mattresses he had scattered in various rooms. He referred to himself as Jesus and the hookers as his wives, and he gave away his worldly possessions. Soon the money he had earned was gone, and he was teetering on the edge of financial ruin.

Miraculously, given his advanced manic state, Vasquez convinced a few independent producing friends to finance a few days' worth of shooting for a new horror project called *Devil in the Hellhousein*. But his career ended when he brought a loaded gun to the set and began brandishing it as he yelled at the bewildered cast and crew.[22] Within two days, the crew had deserted the shoot, the producers were forced to call it quits, and a lonely Vasquez was faced with the end of his life's dream to be a filmmaker. Michael Lieber recalled Vasquez called him during this period, clearly having crashed into a severe depression, and full of remorse and mystery at the idiotic choices he had made while in his manic delusional state.[23] He would turn the guilt and shame into the writing of one of his last screenplays *The House That Jack Built*. In a fairy tale of childhood reunification and urban dysfunctional reality, a Puerto Rican drug dealer named Jack buys a tenement building and fills it with his estranged family, hoping to regain the deep sense of belonging they all once had in earlier times. Much like Vasquez and his messianic attempt in real life, his fictional Jack's foray into beatific mania does not end well. As his AIDS worsened and his financial realities surfaced, Vasquez was forced to move into a small apartment with his mother in San Ysidro, California, which sits on the Mexican border. His mother, then sixty, had kicked heroin and lived alone, and was eager to have a last chance to right any wrongs. But the task was not easy, as Vasquez was subject to intense episodes of tristimania when left alone while his mother ran critical errands.[24] Though impoverished and living in a subsidized unit, she insisted on taking Vasquez to a nearby free clinic and getting him medicated. Vasquez had briefly tried lithium for his manic depression, but he forsook all drugs whether legal or not and reconciled himself to death. He was thirty-three years of age when he died on December 16, 1995. The few who knew him in Hollywood and the Bronx were saddened by the news accounts of his passing, but most of the industry's eyes Joseph B. Vasquez had only barely emerged into the limelight before he disappeared from it.

Vasquez was prone during his troubled, turbulent life to self-aggrandizement as are many bipolar patients. But even he perhaps could not have imagined that his script *The House That Jack Built* would be made almost twenty years after his passing. Producer Lieber kept a death-bed promise to Vasquez to get the script made. He utilized the Kickstarter website to fund and complete a 2013 feature version. It played at the Los Angeles Film Festival that same year in an act of spiritual completion for the deceased Vasquez, whose own Hollywood Hills episode of religious mania had inspired it. For a mixed-race child born into poverty and addiction in the South Bronx, whose own severe mania and depressions sidetracked and train wrecked his daily stability, Vasquez accomplished more than even he gave himself credit for, save perhaps in his most narcissistic moments of grandiosity. Producer Janet Grillo, who worked on *Hangin' with the Homeboys*, showed insight when she once remarked that looking back on the acute nature of Vasquez's bipolarity, it was a miracle he ever got one film made that showed such coherence.[25] Ironically, as Vasquez was facing his own mortality, Mel Gibson's public displays of mania were grabbing headlines, even as his films were grossing hundreds of millions. If Vasquez ever contemplated the situation, it must have seemed grimly humorous in juxtaposition, for Vasquez was neither rich nor had any fame or power. What Joseph Vasquez had heroically done, however, was to mount a valiant, if finally unsustainable, charge against his own fortified walls of madness. Just as with Gibson, Vasquez's sporadic, even shabby films were created as self-defense against his own uncontrollable disorder. But while Gibson's films and battle for mental health were framed against a canvas of vast creative power and lucrative pay, Vasquez's films and struggles were staged against backdrops of staggering poverty, racial injustice, childhood abuse and neglect, drug addiction, and violence. To compare Gibson and Vasquez is not to suggest either is lacking or lessened vis-à-vis the other. Rather, the point is readily made: though his success and fame were microscopic compared to Mel Gibson's cinematic legacy, Vasquez overcame greater odds against perhaps a greater degree of madness, even if he is only generally remembered now for making one minor cult movie.

TIM BURTON CINEMATICALLY CELEBRATES PERPETUAL MELANCHOLIA

While there is a manic, concurrent uplift in the movies of Tim Burton, the underlying sense of Gothic melancholia also present is the dark well from which he seemingly draws more deeply. The hyper-kinetic, visually expressive sequences that marked his earliest screen works and defined his pop-kitsch sensibility, such as in the fast-paced *Pee-wee's Big Adventure* (1985) and *Beetlejuice* (1988) with the maniacal Michael Keaton, gave way beneath the cultural psychic shock waves of his darker, depressive visions in *Batman* (1989) and *Batman Returns* (1992). The impact of Burton's *Batman* films and their phenomenal success would be so greatly felt as to later redefine the superhero cinematic genre. The bright colors and upbeat tone of films such as *Superman* (1979) and even the earlier, campy *Batman* (1966) were replaced with tech noir shadows and mentally unstable characters as heroes and villains. While the works of Alan Moore and Frank Miller in the graphic novel form are correctly credited for much of this visual influence, and the contributions of production designer Anton Furst in the first *Batman* are not to be underestimated, Tim Burton nevertheless was the commercial instigator of this trend. It continues into the new Batman reboot and the admittedly parodying excesses of countless caped clones to this day. But though his works often celebrate the gloom-laden twilight of borderline depression, they also rarely dwell too directly upon its self-negating injuries. Rather, there is in the prototypical Burton protagonist and film project a sense of belated self-acceptance as the Outsider and the Other. It is an understanding that while one may be in the rejected class of society, it does not by default mean one would wish to join the ranks of the so-called normal. Johnny Depp wrote of Burton's "profound respect for those who are not others,"[26] even as he correctly characterized the director, and quite lovingly despite the satirical rhetoric, as "a pale, frail-looking, sad-eyed . . . hypersensitive madman."[27] There is a palpable reaction in the movies Tim Burton creates that is akin to the climactic refrain from *Freaks* (1932), wherein the outcast denizens of the sideshow yell in unison "One of us! One of us!" to mark their unity as an excluded minority. It is not merely a posturing, or pretense, of angst, but the full-blown expression of the rejected without apology or shame. The trappings are pure Hollywood propulsion of glitz and style over latent substance, but the darker subtext is always lurking in abundance. Burton himself has remarked on the source of this "freakish quality"[28] as his own morbid personality type. Yet in the same interview, he calls his alienation "a sad kind of freedom"[29] because others leave him largely alone to create his outrageous visualizations as a result of his disorder.

Burton's imaginary worlds are often decay-filled, routine-choked affairs in which sensitive, moody souls struggle to find a sense of belonging in any larger group. There is an anhedonic listlessness to many moments in his films. It is as if even the director himself were bored with the material and is eagerly seeking to break sacrosanct rules of perceived mainstream directing. He is not known as an actor's director, though Martin Landau won an Academy Award for his frank, heartbreaking turn as Bela Lugosi under Burton's direction for *Ed Wood* (1994). Conversely, even though he unleashed the Batman anti-super-hero film meme, Burton has never been critically lauded for his urgent sense of action or pacing. His storytelling skills were always singled out in negative reviews, and Burton himself has admitted that narrative is not the primary concern that motivates his desire to make movies. What drives him and his best movie moments are pure, unfiltered expressions of mania and depression, which bubble from his subconscious when he works, without breaks and without too much in the way of overt contextual analysis on his part. He is a supreme visual stylist above all else, attracted to stories that offer rigid aesthetic challenges versus working out dramatic beats with his lead actors in lengthy rehearsals. He has described himself as a "happy-go-lucky manic-depressive"[30] and this upside beat to his downside nature is what gives much of his work a sense of innocent beguilement, not unlike a giggling child who prods an animal corpse with a stick out of primal fascination. Like much Gothic fiction and filmmaking, Burton celebrates his own mordant awareness of his perpetual strangeness to, and estrangement from, neurotypical reality, including his own viewing audience and any expectations they may harbor. He told *Newsweek* during his first rush of fame that he often questioned why he bothered making movies, in that he could never sit with an audience as they watched his work, as it gave him no joy, only misery.[31] This quality of self-deprecating charm combined with daredevil effrontery became his signature in key works in the 1980s and 1990s, creating a strong sense of identity around the director not unlike the director-as-superstar model constructed by Walt Disney and Alfred Hitchcock. This kind of market-ready directorial identity was unusual by the 1980s in corporate-settled Hollywood, and executives were quick to realize Burton could be branded for his very peculiarities. Burton represented a change to a new generation that was virtually unrecognized at the time and only later came to be known as Generation X. Astute execs reasoned there were likely many moviegoers who felt as unrepresented and abandoned as Burton did. Like much in Burton's ironic, contradictory world, this was actually debatable, as Burton was born in 1958 and therefore part of the boomer generation. Thus he had a foot firmly in the *Leave It to Beaver* land of American suburbia and Universal's classic horror monsters as a defining influence, and the other foot planted forward into an emerging nexus of underground comics, punk rock music, and supposed junk fodder like drive-in movies that was more reminiscent of 1970s culture.

Unlike Spielberg, who idolized suburbia even as he hinted at its darker aspects, Burton both detested and was held spellbound by much of what he witnessed growing up in Burbank, California. Despite its proximity to Hollywood, Burbank offered a very quiet, self-contained existence for the young boy, quite apart from any glamorous notions of filmmaking, which largely lay beyond its interstate-proscribed boundaries. Unlike its flashier cousin Hollywood, with its red carpet roll-outs, Burbank was a sleepy hub of anonymous warehouses and bland supporting businesses. One could grow up in Burbank and hardly realize Warner Brothers lay within its confines. The stifling boredom and chronic depression Burton felt from an early age drove him to escape into monster movies, television cartoons, and endless drawing. It is very reminiscent of Woody Allen's biography in some aspects. Burton reported he never felt like a child, a teenager, or even later, an adult, in the respective eras of his life, but instead wrestled with a sense of fluctuating depersonalization, marked by long periods of reclusive retreat and excessive anxiety. Capturing the manic-depressive contrast so often at play in his work, he described his childhood as a "surreal, bright depression,"[32] and characterized the myriad back alleys, concrete cemeteries, and abandoned lots he explored throughout Burbank (when he wasn't in his cramped bedroom obsessively leafing through *Famous Monsters of Filmland*) as a "visually wonderful, hellish place."[33] Despite his Gothic self-therapy, it was not an easy existence, and he experienced constant tension with his parents, particularly his father Bill. Bill attributed much of his son's resentment to internal strife that Tim brought upon himself.[34] Burton was unable to cope with the pressures of his family's domestic life, and moved in with his grandmother during junior high and part of high school, already estranged from his only brother Daniel and mother Jean. Given that his parents were American suburban success stories, with Bill a former minor league baseball player turned Burbank Parks and Recreation worker, and Jean the curator of a cat fancier's emporium known as Cats Plus, Burton's rebellion against all things middle class is understandable. From his wounded, beleaguered perspective, movie marathons of Godzilla, Vincent Price, and Ray Harryhausen were preferable to the blandishments of baseball and felines. This suburban angst shows up in many of his visions, but especially in *Edward Scissorhands* (1990), which he has described as one of his more personal works.[35]

He caught the eye of Disney talent scouts early in his student work at the California Institute for the Arts. Burton was soon working as a conceptual artist for *The Black Cauldron* (1985), though little of his creative work was actually utilized in the final film. He suffered hypersomnia as a result of his schedule, feigning to be awake whenever anyone was present at his work place with him, and then closing his eyes with his head still raised to sleep on the job when alone. He began sleeping over fourteen hours per day, four at work and ten at night, to get through his ongoing depression. He would crawl under his desk to vanish, or sit alone in a closed closet while he continued to draw.[36] Fortunately for Burton, Tom Wilhite, a creative head of development at Disney, and Julie Hickson, a producer on lot, noticed his talent, ignored his depression, and groomed him for a career. The result in 1982 was their funding *Vincent*, a short film written and directed by Tim Burton, and narrated by his childhood hero, Vincent Price. The fable told the story of a depressive child of suburbia more at home with creating Frankenstein monsters in his basement lab than playing with the neighborhood kids (unless it is to lure them to their doom). *Vincent* was an announcement that a major talent had arrived in mainstream filmmaking, bearing a new sensibility that was both mordantly witty and touchingly melancholic. The Edgar Allan Poe influence was completely on the surface. Burton has admitted his love for the author, recalling his own childhood as one in which his bedroom's windows were mostly obscured so that he felt joyfully buried alive.[37] In many ways the purest expression of his own bipolar alienated childhood, *Vincent* is a remarkable distillation of its creator's personality and perceptions as much as its fictional namesake.

This penchant for having a supposedly difficult personality was brought home to me when I asked to interview Tim Burton about *Vincent* in the fall of 1982 for Frederick S. Clarke's seminal publication *Cinefantastique*. I was warned after Disney arranged the session not to expect too much from Tim, in that he often had problems articulating his point of view, especially under duress. Having also suffered similar problems during acute episodes, I readily understood the task at hand and was relieved to hear such a talented person I had never met was, after all, also human. During the tense period in which *Vincent* producer Rick Heinrichs and I awaited a tardy Tim to show for our scheduled interview, Rick warned me that it was entirely possible Tim would never arrive. As if on cue, Tim entered, hair a-muss and disheveled in his rumpled, oversized black clothes. A stiff, worried look between Rick and myself, a hurried introduction, and I peppered questions at Burton's passive, hangdog countenance. Without much success I watched him squirm with each inquiry I made about the film's technical factors, its budget, how he had convinced the notoriously tightwad Disney to finance a $60,000 short film when there was no apparent market, and related industry topics. Tim showed no enthusiasm at all for anything I had asked until I desperately blurted out how much I had loved the film, explaining that it reminded me of the classic Rankin/Bass stop-motion efforts such as *Rudolph, the Red-Nosed Reindeer* (1964), *Mad Monster Party* (1967), and the like. Suddenly the withdrawn, socially awkward figure before me came to life, eyes sparkling, as if someone had stoked a furnace in him, his voice newly urgent with passion. We began trading favorite moments from cherished childhood memories, shared ones at that, almost talking over one another in mutual manic enthusiasm, even though we had never met before. They were the memories of endlessly watching televised kiddie fare, especially our beloved Rankin/Bass. The transformation I had witnessed from shy, introverted depressive into radiant, expressive manic was like human alchemy, the spark being our mutual love of stop-motion. Tim warmly gave me a personal tour of the modest production offices in South Pasadena he and his partners had rented. The topper was when he showed me the walls of storyboards for a project that would, many years later, become *The Nightmare Before Christmas* (1993), though as a much different, nonmusical visualization when I was lucky enough to preview it. I could not help but notice the astonished side glances I was getting from Heinrichs as the interview stretched on. Our meeting ended with a sudden reversion by Burton to his former, distant self as he politely thanked me for the first-ever interview of his career. He then disappeared from view before I could thank him for allowing me to give the first-ever interview of my career as writer as return compliment. Alone with a surprised Heinrichs, Rick privately remarked how fortunate I had been to be able to draw Burton out, as this was far from the usual case. But I rather believed, and still do, that it was our mutual appreciation for Harryhausen and his ilk, if not our shared bipolarity, that was the catalyst. When Tim was enthusiastic about a subject he knew and that was dear to him, he became almost a different person, laughing with ease and nodding his wild mane of hair in agreement. This description could fit the author in certain moods, as well, hence a natural affinity.

Alas, in many ways his path forward, while legendary in terms of career fame, would be fraught with the perils not only of navigating Hollywood success, but of recurrent manic depression at the same time. While the money and power would help him choose virtually any project he wanted, the limitations of his own disorder often took as much as they gave in the succeeding years, always coloring, if not discoloring, his own perilously changing attitude, and love/hate affair, with corporate culture production. His productions of *Batman* and *Batman Returns* are worthy of some consideration, in that they hallmark many of the ups and downs of his illness, and how it affected his choices, and their results. These are also the movies that launched him beyond merely director into the more rarefied heights of cultural icon, even if his ambivalence about his association with the series has always been present in public comments. But just as Vincent and Edward Scissorhands act as doppelgangers for Burton, the Batman films offer a screen stand-in that Burton readily identified with, owing both to Bruce Wayne's depressive seclusion and his alternating, mania-driven compulsion to act out in a cape. If Pee-wee represented the lighter, airier side of Burton's mania, then Batman captured his depressive need to deny friendship, suffer alone, and take ill-conceived risks to free himself from the grips of his manic-depressive slumps. Bruce Wayne would hide behind his money and fame to keep people out, just like Tim Burton would do in short order. Batman would keep to his own nocturnal schedule and mysterious ways, answerable to no one in terms of his creative focus, just as Burton would shortly order his own career. It is easy to see why the character galvanized Burton. When asked what *Batman* really meant to him, Burton told an interviewer he never considered the project as a story about a hero saving a city, but instead, as a look at a person who is "completely fucked. . . . It's about depression."[38]

Burton attributed his fascination with the dark knight in part to the fact that Batman is not "integrated" as a personality,[39] which Burton has struggled with all his life. This lack of integration is a form of clinical depersonalization common to manic-depressives, and earlier detailed in the entries about Nick Ray, James Dean, Ingmar Bergman, Paul Schrader, and others. Burton has complained that he cannot stabilize his own self-image and inner knowledge for long stretches of time, instead fragmenting into a complicated mental state of being full of crossed signals, split possibilities, and confusing interpersonal dynamics.[40] He retreats into his art as therapy, using the externalization process of sketching and visualizing his latest project as a means of controlling, or at least alleviating in part, his mood disorder. Yet conversely, he has told numerous interviewers the actual production process is always trying for him beyond measure, each time resulting in serious illness and prolonged post-movie depression.[41] During *Batman*, his sickness reached fever pitch, as his raging bipolarity clashed with the enormous pressures of pulling off what would essentially be the make-or-break moment of his career. He was dysfunctional at times, once experiencing tristimania so acutely he fled from the set, unable to stop crying as his stunned cast and crew looked on. Producer Jon Peters was able to finally calm him and Burton returned to finish the scene. Burton felt as if he were a somnambulist through much of the grueling shoot, which saw constant changes in the script to the point Burton felt he had lost control of the production.[42] Luckily, he had found a rare friendship with Anton Furst, the talented English production designer who had so memorably transformed Kubrick's English locales into a convincing scene of Vietnam war atrocities in *Full Metal Jacket* (1987), and who had also brought alive the fairy tale aspects of *The Company of Wolves* (1984) for Neil Jordan all within the confines of studio sets. Furst designed much of the Oscar-winning look of *Batman* in collaboration with Burton, especially the *Metropolis*-esque vision of Gotham City. Furst created not just a labyrinthine look, but also backstory, envisioning New York City, circa 1900, but absent any of the progressive reforms to building and zoning laws that would occur in the twentieth century to make it a livable space. During at least the chaotic preproduction and production phases of *Batman* (which Burton would later characterize as torture[43]), Burton and Furst were a dynamic duo of their own, each suffused with artistic hope for what they could achieve working together. With talk of an inevitable sequel, given how the unreleased film was testing beyond frenzied with anticipatory audiences, it seemed as though they would team again in the near future.

When Burton moved back to the United States, it would not take long before Anton Furst, riding high on the insider buzz from his eye-popping work on *Batman*, but from afar in England, would choose to relocate to Los Angeles, intent on starting his own career as director. After over a year of touring the executive suites of Hollywood, Furst found that initial promises and story meetings never progressed beyond talks and lunches. He was a talented production designer, they agreed, but no serious offers to test his mettle as a director were ever signed, merely hyped as in motion, always tantalizingly vague for actual specifics. He tried to reach out to Burton to seek guidance and solace, but true to his lifelong form, Burton was experiencing a clinical need to retreat from others. This process of cutting off all communication was in part because of his deep depression after the completion of *Batman*, which he has expressed is usual for him after a film finishes.[44] Unknown to Burton, Furst was suffering from his own chronic mood instability. While never publicly acknowledged as such, Furst clearly suffered from a mood disorder. Numerous colleagues recalling his intense passion, his manic ability to drive himself long hours, his genius talent, and his darker side when his moods turned sour.[45] Furst lived in fear of winding up like his father, a mentally ill man who died from alcoholism when Furst was twenty-one years old and became addicted to Valium to control his chronic anxiety. Though he was quick to praise Furst for his contributions and ease of collaboration, even Burton described Furst as "a delicate person"[46] to *Premiere*. So it could not have helped Furst's despair when he learned that he would not be needed to design the sets and look for *Batman Returns*, with Burton failing to return Furst's frantic phone calls wondering why he had been sacked.[47] It was a final straw of seeming pointless futility Furst felt had become his life since moving to Hollywood. Despondent and suicidal, he agreed a few months later to check himself into a downtown Los Angeles psychiatric facility. He jumped to his death from an eighth-story parking garage adjacent to the facility when family and staff were not looking.

Furst's death sent shock waves throughout Hollywood. The impact on Burton was incalculable, and he grieved publicly and privately for months on end. He was unable to rationalize the loss, or his own genetic inability to sustain or nurture friendships. Burton also blamed much of Furst's demise on Hollywood's ego-driven system which was from his perspective as dangerous for the overly heaped praise as the critical lambasting it routinely administered to all within its employment. Both praise, then punishment, were designed to break individuality and make the artist dependent upon the studio, he once explained.[48] It was not as if Burton's mental health had readily improved for all the trappings of fame and fortune, either. Nathan Stein, who had a minor role in *Batman Returns*, told of dropping off his resume and head shots to Burton's production bungalow one day. To his surprise, as he left, he glimpsed Burton in his office, propped behind his drafting table, eyes open but unseeing, "shell-shocked to the point of catatonia."[49] In many eerie ways, this is almost identical to the manner in which Burton dysfunctionally operated during his first stint at Disney. Unable to cope with the pressures of celebrity and directorial responsibility as they magnified beyond proportion, Tim Burton again retreated into himself. This time he went so far as to drop all professional obligations, including to valued colleagues such as Henry Selick, Rich Heinrichs, and Danny Elfman. He drifted into what he called chaos, letting his Hollywood deals go unattended as he refused to even acknowledge that his company, and his many professional associates who worked for it, was still an ongoing entity.[50] Henry Selick said in plain summation of this time that if one went to work with Tim, one would get "bloodied and hurt and bent out of shape"[51] as a probable outcome. But as the lonely childhood and friendless young adult years of Burton amply show, he really never had any real choice in the process, as much a victim of his own condition in this regard as were his disappointed acquaintances. He rarely retained friends, feeling as if he floated through his own life's events as a teenager, retreating into grindhouse triple-bills to alleviate his loneliness. "There's enough weird movies out there so you can go a long time without friends,"[52] he both offered, and lamented, in reflecting on his upbringing.

JESSICA LANGE AND THE STRENGTH OF MANIC-DEPRESSIVE FRAILTY

Jessica Lange's work in two movies of this era warrants discussion. Her portrayal of Frances Farmer in *Frances* (1982) is a devastating portrait of the ravages of untreated, and then mistreated, manic depression. Likewise, her Marilyn Monroe-tinged evocation of hypersexual bipolarity as Carly Marshall in *Blue Sky* (1994) offers a study in contrast to *Frances*. *Blue Sky* is soaked in Carly's need and hypersexual vulnerability, whereas in *Frances* Farmer is remote, when not engaged in fits of rage and anger. Each distinctive, yet polarized, performance was drawn from Lange's own interior emotional landscape. She has admitted to chronic periods of depression in past interviews,[53] just as she has chronicled how difficult drawing from such deeply personal wells of darkness can temporarily exhaust her as performer.[54] "I've always had a place in my heart for the madness in people,"[55] she said in explaining what she personally appreciates in some of the roles of manic depression she has inhabited. "The rational and the reasonable, that stuff doesn't interest me as much as the emotional frailty or borderline madness,"[56] she further elaborated. With this in mind, it is easy to understand that her empathetic command of the screen as Frances Farmer and Carly Marshall is then, in essence, an expression of the so-called frailties of her own disorder. These frailties, under the steely determinism she exhibits in both roles, threaten to destabilize both protagonists over the course of their respective stories, but her fiery demeanor prevails with varying degrees of hard-fought success until the breaking points finally, inevitably occur.

Frances received much critical acclaim during its release, capitalizing on Lange's previously lauded performance in the remake of *The Postman Always Rings Twice* (1981). It was loosely based upon the real life Frances Farmer (earlier covered in the Gene Tierney overview), a young studio-contracted actress from Seattle who was institutionalized for manic depression. *Frances* took many liberties with the biography of Farmer; nonetheless, as a moody study in extreme states of melancholia and rage, *Frances* is an effective evocation of bipolarity, especially in Jessica Lange's ability to freely allow herself to become unhinged so brazenly in scene after scene. The manner in which Lange fixes her inscrutable eyes on those she taunts while in states of manic anger is chilling, almost like a taut, hovering cobra preparing to strike. Whenever anyone blithely ignores her menacing look, Lange verbally bites, injecting as much emotional venom into each victim as her acid tongue will supply. Whether it is in the guise of a local gossip wag who questions teenaged Farmer's atheist status, a sexist studio bigwig who controls her destiny, or even an asylum psychiatrist in charge of her mental health, Lange's Farmer cannot resist engaging in a manic game of one-upmanship with any authority figure who wields power over her. It is as if she is drawing an invisible circle around herself in her portrait of Frances Farmer and daring anyone to cross it. Only her lover, Harry (Sam Shepard), will ever be allowed inside with her broiling madness. After witnessing her first inexplicable episode of bipolar behavior, Harry mutters with a profound, caring mystery, "Frances, you're crazy." She does not argue, merely implores him to not tell anyone, partly in comic pretense. But even Harry will be eventually excluded, along with the rest of humanity, when Frances becomes institutionalized beyond redemption via a lobotomy, lost in her own thoughts.

In reality, Farmer faced legal consequences for some of the acts she committed in her bipolar episodes, which is sometimes true for manic-depressives, particularly those subject to intense states of hypomania and mania.[57] *Frances* depicts a true ordeal in which Farmer was arrested while hiding out during a bipolar episode at the Knickerbocker Hotel in 1943. Rather than serve legal notice via her attorney, the paparazzi arrived outside the hotel door as police officers took her against her will into custody. The photographs of the snarling, disheveled Farmer as she was dragged away became nationally sensationalized, forever tarnishing her already shaky career. But while this incident was one of the truly most deplorable she endured while in Hollywood, it provides Lange with one of her most brazenly defiant scenes. Held before an arrogant arresting sergeant and queried as to her occupation despite his clear knowledge of her celebrity status, Lange slyly grins and ironically answers "cocksucker." She snarlingly laughs in manic supremacy at the shocked gasps by the assembled media, and, in another often tragic reality for some bipolar defendants, casts aside all concern she is damaging her already fragile case further with her outbursts. Lange's stridency provides a cold rebuke to the face of displayed public hypocrisy, especially considering that the law ignores Farmer's distressed mentally ill status, even as she is paraded before cameras for public exploitation. Lange's self-annihilation in this degrading scene is heartbreaking. It is a measured performance of unraveling layers amid downbeat moments of slow realization that she is losing her battle for sanity but is unwilling to admit it to her assembled persecutors. It is not unlike watching the sacrificial Joan of Arc turn on her demeaning inquisitors and unleash a stinging critique of their transparent double standard. Given how often real life and screen bipolars endure deplorable outcomes in matters involving police and courts,[58] Lange's short-lived moment of radiant self-release is all the more rare in its poignancy.

An interesting footnote to the passion Lange's engrossing performance engendered in some viewers is that it led to a renewed interest in the real life of Frances Farmer. This led to many corrections of the flaws depicted in *Frances*, which was based in part on erroneous data in the 1978 biography *Shadowland* by William Arnold. Chief among the new details to emerge in light of the film was that the transorbital lobotomy that is shown being given to Farmer when she is deemed incorrigible by asylum doctors was entirely fictionalized. The extensive use of ECT as shown in the film is also untrue, as the only reliably uncovered records suggest Farmer only underwent moderate sessions once in 1945 during a relapse.[59] As researcher Jeffrey Kauffman's exhaustive work has established,[60] Farmer recovered for long periods of stability after her various institutional stays from 1943 to 1950, even managing to retire to a relatively quiet life with a new husband in Indianapolis, Indiana. While she did have occasional lapses of manic behavior and self-medicated with alcohol to control her depressions, Farmer was anything but a mental vegetable post-institutional life, as wrongly depicted in *Frances*. Whatever the biographical liberties, however, it is the singular manner in which Jessica Lange embodies Farmer's moments of manic-depressive psychosis that transcend any of the film's potentially melodramatic shortcomings or issues of veracity. She is a study in cold, manic fury, tragically misunderstood and self-alienated.

Blue Sky's Carly Marshall is the antithesis of Lange's earlier bipolar portrait. Farmer rejects the rampant sexism and crass objectification of her body and looks over her talent and intelligence in *Frances*, but Cold War era military wife Carly Marshall craves the attention of every male within eye-shot, which is plenty given her husband's career base hopping in the Army as a nuclear engineer. Carly is subject to fits of delusional self-aggrandizement in which she imagines herself to be, and often acts out as, the literal belle of every social ball, no matter how inappropriate her lewd attire and suggestive behavior. She is very much in the mold of Marilyn Monroe in physical make-up and body language, a coiffed, seeming innocent whose sexuality is overpowering, and who nonchalantly uses her naive facade to manipulate desirable men. Her Carly is a classic home wrecker from the point of view of the other enlisted men's wives, and when the film opens, she and husband Hank (Tommy Lee Jones) are relocating with their two children in part to keep hushed Carly's last indiscretion at their last base of residence. The dynamic between Hank and Carly is what drives the film and makes it interesting, as the plot mechanics fall flat at times, especially the politicized ending. Hank is a willing if quietly embarrassed cuckold to some degree to Carly's hypersexual ability to attract other men, which he finds exciting despite his jealousy and ire. Likewise, Carly pushes the edge of any situation in which a male lover is possibly present in Hank's company, flirtatious and signaling to her stewing husband her mutual desire to any new paramour. Theirs is a classically codependent relationship. Even their daughters precociously note as much in a kitchen scene after enduring the latest manic-depressive cycling of their mother, and the inevitable tension and reconciliation it produces between their warring parents.

Lange's breathless, sinewy embodiment of Carly's overheated imagination and oversexed state of constant arousal, combined with her emotional instability owing to manic depression, give the performance a dynamic that steamrolls over every other character. Like Monroe at her sexually fragile best, Carly steals the viewer's eyes at every turn, dominating the screen in all her scenes. This is in part because Carly constantly uses her beguiling manic tendencies to sweet talk her way into various socially upward settings, which fulfills her vain need not only for social status, but likewise for a hunting ground for future lovers. Earlier manic-depressive portraits such as those given by Monroe, and Hepburn as Holly in *Breakfast at Tiffany's*, are being subtly drawn upon in terms of female bipolar archetypes, but Lange uses alchemical charm to mix them into a new concoction that is far more revealing than previous screen incarnations. Lange's mercurial changes of mood are so clearly delineated on her face and in her swaying, languid body movements that often other characters seem rigidly fixated in reactive response, silently watching her out of the corners of their eyes in mute judgment. This directorial stratagem by Tony Richardson gives Carly's admittedly grating, high-flying manner a softer side of pathos, as the audience is left to feel Carly's sense of justifiable outrage with the chronic boredom and inhumanity their stressful military life produces as by-product. Her good-willed acceptance of their latest move with her family in the opening scenes, only to slowly dissolve into depressive anger as she witnesses the poverty of their new living arrangement, is deftly handled by Richardson as a quick series of cuts. Carly's face nervously twitches as she is seen behind the windshield of their car, downwardly adjusting her already modest expectations as each new shock of decrepitude fills the family's horrified field of vision. By the time the family arrives, nerves shot and tensions running high, Carly stages her usual depressive rant, railing at Hank for the abysmal conditions of their bungalow and retreating into her sadness with utter clinical accuracy. Another moment that accurately captures the codependent nature of Hank and Carly as partners is when she experiences a depressive breakdown and runs through the rain in the streets of the small town they inhabit, causing Hank to chase after her. He eventually corners her in a supply store and calms her down, forcing her to accept she is lost in a mental episode and to admit quietly to herself she needs his help in order to cope.

The quiet resolution in her eyes as she allows Hank to take the psychiatric steering wheel, after she has steered herself into the ditch of depression, and guide her by his side to safety and recovery are among the most moving scenes in *Blue Sky*. In terms of authenticity, even though it is not evidently based upon it, the screen event is similar to one reported by Gene Tierney in her autobiography, in which she fled an asylum dressed only in a thin gown and ran barefoot over the snow, only to likewise be finally calmed inside a store. Lange's character is a woman who lives with a disorder that threatens the only love and support she has in the world because the illness drives her to infidelity, and she is sadly all too aware of her inability to change her fate beyond a bittersweet self-acceptance. Lange won a deserved Academy Award for her portrayal of Carly Marshall. It still ranks as one of the greatest in all of bipolar cinema for accuracy and, perhaps more importantly, emotional honesty.

While she has publicly stated that she has never tried therapy and does not believe in it for her own problems, Lange nevertheless has admitted to maintaining a constant vigilance to keep mentally balanced and "not go in that downward spiral."[61] Her work is a form of therapy, but equally, it is a pressure from which she feels the need as a clinical depressive to retreat and recharge between acting roles. To lessen the chances of depression, Lange lives in the rural areas of New Mexico, Virginia, and Minnesota, where she admits to feeling enormous calm between the stormy realities of cinematic collaboration.[62] But it has been a lifelong struggle to keep her work and her mental health simultaneously in accord.

10

2000S: BIPOLAR CINEMA FULLY EMERGES FROM LINGERING SHADOWS

Growing economic inequality in America was readily apparent by the beginning of the new millennium. It was only a matter of time before a match was lit that would ignite the long-ignored realities of untreated mental illness in large numbers of Americans without access to health care. On September 11, 2001, the world witnessed fanatic religious mania transform into delusional martyrdom in the attacks on the World Trade Center and Pentagon. The wars that would ensue and engulf America would lead to soldiers returning from prolonged stays of combat with posttraumatic stress disorder (PTSD) and other psychiatric illnesses in numbers not seen since Vietnam.[1] Many were survivors in combat zones (who would have been killed in an earlier era) owing to the increased armor protection, high-tech fighting equipment, and rapid medical intervention and recovery treatments (that is, for physical injuries). But this also meant many thousands of veterans would survive with severe brain injuries, only to return to America to face an underfunded health care system overwhelmed by their sudden, critical psychiatric needs.[2] As the wars in Iraq and Afghanistan dragged on for over a decade, the ranks of veterans with mental disabilities grew, even as Congress enacted budget cuts for civilian and military health delivery systems. On the civilian front, many were blatantly denied coverage because of a so-called "pre-existing condition" if they had a history of mental illness or were only offered plans that were unaffordable for all but the elite, resulting in the increase in untreated mental illness by default.[3] Far too many community mental health centers were closed owing to budget deficits, leading to swelling homelessness and dire poverty for their former patients. Lack of employment opportunities meant no chance for employee-provided health care, further dooming more Americans to suffering from untreated mental illness.[4] In a pattern we have witnessed ebb and flow throughout history, the mentally ill were largely abandoned to their fates by society, left to cope as best they could, and without permanent medical assistance. Or so it seemed as the new century initially unfolded.

But the national dialogue revived around the topic amid growing concern over former soldiers suffering from PTSD and multiple incidents of unstable shooters committing mass atrocities with unrestricted firepower, moving the conversation away from the idea of ignoring, but instead treating, the larger social problem. Economic pressures during the Great Recession further widened the gap between the wealthy and the struggling, and took their toll on barely surviving families. Health care for the uninsured mentally ill became a signature reform goal of the hotly contested Affordable Care Act. President Obama's signing of it in 2010 abolished the discriminatory policy allowing insurers to decline them. But even as of this writing, the controversy is alive, with many proposing to roll back the law to allow insurers the ability to once again choose who will be treated and who left untreated. Numerous polls have revealed that Americans favor the ending of such exclusionary policies, even by as much as 99 percent of polled respondents.[5] The nation thus has apparently progressed in its view of the mentally ill as full and equal citizens under the law—a change that continues to be nationally significant in the second decade of the twenty-first century.

The bipolar-themed movies that have emerged during this time, which illuminate and examine these profound changes of attitude, are in some ways as diverse as the varieties of affective disorders themselves. Given that the earliest screen depictions of the mentally ill often involved grotesque stereotypes with little concern for distinguishing between the various conditions, this in and of itself is a tectonic shift in favor of public understanding and clinical accuracy. Another factor influencing twenty-first-century bipolar cinema is the ease of use and affordability of new digital technologies. Documentaries and features are created across a wider spectrum of tone, style, and ambition. And they are not coded in the language of shame as many former bipolar movies. For the first time, many are less about pleading for acceptance and more an outright depiction of the reality of mental illness. The dam of self-censorship has broken, allowing a torrent of creative bipolarity to gush forth with some of the most accurate movies portraying bipolar disorder ever crafted.

HEATH LEDGER AND THE SARDONIC SMILE OF MANIC DEPRESSION

Though he's admired for other roles, such as his lonesome, closeted gay cowboy Ennis Del Mar in Ang Lee's *Brokeback Mountain* (2005), it is his eerie, desolate performance as the Joker in *The Dark Knight* (2008) for which Heath Ledger is most famously known. This is partly attributable to the sad fact that Ledger tragically died prior to the film's opening, but also to the raw audacity of his portrait of Batman's most delusional nemesis. Much like Dean's triumphant postmortem turn in *Rebel without a Cause*, Ledger's incendiary acting abilities were on full display in his grotesque characterization of the evil Joker, perhaps weirdly aided by his premature death. It is not an exaggeration to say that his Joker is the darkly beating heart of *The Dark Knight*, for without Ledger's leering madman, the film would lack the onerous aura of clinging psychosis that his quivering performance injects into it. The added note of Ledger's personal tragedy cannot but elevate the sense that the Joker's troubled, unforgiving hold on Ledger's psyche may have contributed to his death via accidental overdose. But the deeper truth that was never widely revealed during his lifetime and known only to his family was that Heath Ledger was bipolar,[6] with a tendency toward depression. It was a lethal combination of pharmaceutical drugs (including Valium, Ambien, and Xanax, which are all commonly prescribed for treatment of affective disorders and their associative symptoms) mixed with cold remedy medications and Oxycontin that led to Ledger's unintentional death, according to the New York City Medical Examiner's Office autopsy.[7]

His childhood was set in pastoral Perth, Australia, but troubled by the bipolar episodes of an uncle as well as the tense divorce of his parents when he was still a boy. Ledger's paternal grandfather, Colin, experienced sudden episodes of tristimania, whereupon he would retreat from company, unable to control his tears. His resilience during even modest setbacks in life was low, and he often felt alone in his peculiar emotional states. Though Colin would never seek medical help, owing to the rigid macho culture of the family and surrounding community, most within the family privately considered him a depressive.[8] Heath Ledger's uncle Haydn had been diagnosed as bipolar by a psychiatrist, which brings in the distinct possibility that Colin Ledger, though never clinically evaluated, may also have been bipolar, but with a propensity for depressive episodes. This type of behavior aligns with a bipolar-II diagnosis, in which the afflicted person typically only experiences hypomania, rarely full mania, and many more episodes of lingering depression.[9] As we will see, it also fits Heath Ledger's mood instability by his own description. The more salient point is the illustration yet again of the genetic aspect of mood disorders. In families where relatives have experienced affective disorders, the likelihood of offspring having the same malady is greatly magnified. So with one diagnosed bipolar uncle and one undiagnosed depressive grandfather, the young actor was clearly at risk of inheriting some form of affective illness.

After his passing, Ledger's friends and loved ones noted his inability to sit still for long. Ledger was variously described as being restless, hyperactive, and nervous.[10] He was also very shy in most social gatherings, unless he knew someone who was present and/or was keenly interested in the topic or event. He was not aloof or pretentious, at least by Hollywood standards, but rather self-effacing in nature. By his own frequent admission, he was very hard on himself, rarely, if ever, pleased with a performance. This sense of relentless perfection as guiding instinct can also be indicative of bipolarity, the flames often roaring beneath the mantel of bestowed genius. His wife, Michelle Williams, noted that while his energy was a blessing for his acting, when he was without his preferred method of therapeutic creativity, it could be a challenge for him and his friends. She said his mind was always "turning, turning, turning"[11] with too much energy, which is a very accurate description in other words of the hypomanic condition known as racing thoughts. This led to chronic insomnia, which was often at its worst later in his life as he worked overnight hours on the grueling, back-to-back, post-sunset scenes of *The Dark Knight* and *The Imaginarium of Doctor Parnassus* (2009), the latter of which he did not complete before he died. He told interviewers in the weeks before his death that he was only sleeping two hours per night because although his body was exhausted "my mind was still going."[12]

The actor quickly came to dislike the rootless international travel made necessary by his career. Vast amounts of time in his young adult life were spent in spare quarters, living out of a proverbial suitcase, away from family and loved ones.[13] He attempted to settle into a domesticated life with his wife, Michelle Williams, and their daughter, Matilda Rose, for a brief time, but the pressures of his career and the need for constant travel alienated him from them.

Ledger's use of marijuana to alleviate his nervous condition and lift him out of his depressions, which he had used since he was a teen, smoking five joints daily as self-medication,[14] led to legal jeopardy. Con artists intent on extortion once set him up and covertly videotaped him at the Chateau Marmont attempting to buy marijuana.[15] His paranoia constantly being justified by acts such as this and by the hounding paparazzi, there is little wonder that Ledger felt besieged by the fame and demands of his career. He began experiencing anxiety attacks and morbid ideation,[16] and took to wearing unkempt clothes that did not go together and sunglasses at night and indoors, often showing up to parties and events thus oddly dressed. While notoriety for attire is hardly news in Hollywood, Ledger's bizarre thrown-together outfits suggested a darker reality for the star, who spent much of his private time secluded from fame. Shortly before his death, Ledger visited the Beatrice Inn, an exclusive dining club in New York's West Village frequented by celebrities looking to socialize with some assurance of privacy. He was wearing a ski mask with makeshift eye and mouth holes and a hoodie. He refused to remove any of this garb, even when indoors, and remained aloof, seemingly depressed.[17] Once during a studio meeting Ledger excused himself and went into the adjacent bathroom. He began hyperventilating after banging his head against the bathroom wall and uncontrollably sobbing.[18] This incident mirrors the behavior attributed to Ledger's grandfather, showing the familial continuity of the disorder.

Watching his pressure-speaking Joker, one feels that somehow Heath Ledger was attempting to distill all that was hideous, all that was selfish and uncaring, about his manic depression in his self-loathing creation of the unkempt domestic terrorist. This bizarre passion to act out his feelings and thoughts, no matter how clinically disturbed, is at the center of Heath Ledger's interpretation of the Joker. It is what places his Joker so far apart from other screen renditions. With a tweedy lisp, greasy hair, and black-encased, glaring eyes that appear to have been clawed out of his skull in recalcitrant defiance, the Joker is horribly disfigured, and yet ironically covers his scars with white clown greasepaint to draw attention to them. It is interesting that whenever the Joker makes a sudden, unexpected appearance in the film, he launches into a different telling of how he came to be scarred. None of these stories match, and in fact, they openly contradict themselves. Is the Joker merely a pathological liar, or is there a deeper meaning to his cryptic stories? If there is a coherent thread, it is that all of his biographical sketches involve his either being abused or victimized first by others. This offers moral justification, or at least convenient cover, for his own sense of divine retribution. What is germane for this study is that the unusually stressful or tragic childhood so consistently seen in mood-disordered patients is not only verbalized by the Joker as causative to his disorder, but is actually mocked as being therefore responsible at the same time. The stereotypical Joker usually deliberately overplays his own maniacal fiend role, pointing out to Batman how self-deceiving the neurotypical citizens are in their obliviousness to the pain of such outsiders as himself and the Dark Knight. Thus the Ledger incarnation alters one of the oldest clichés in bipolar cinema history, that of the diabolical madman. While the Joker is still intent on subverting order, and it is indeed very much to his own dark vision, he is no longer driven by the idea of being in the top position on the dung heap of humanity, as he sees it. Instead, Ledger's Joker embraces chaos theory, believing destruction alone will bring about his domino effect of citizen vs. citizen, and the collapse of the old order of things. For the nihilistic Joker, anarchy is hell enough to be his eternal heaven, and so he unleashes the full measure of manic genius for destruction on Gotham City.

It really is, with all due respect to the other creatively involved players, Heath Ledger's conception of the Joker, at least from an actor's point of view, that so propels his mesmerizing hold over the film. Obviously, the character had been done before, and clearly, some had difficulty believing that anyone could top the iconic performance given by Jack Nicholson in Tim Burton's *Batman*. These included even those cast alongside Ledger: Sir Michael Caine, for example, whose skepticism gave way to belief the first moment he saw Ledger take command of the scene in a performance he deemed "terrifying."[19] Gary Oldman, himself no stranger to playing dark roles, was equally stunned, comparing Ledger's work to Nicholson, only this time in *One Flew Over the Cuckoo's Nest*, not *Batman*. He also detected a subtle bit of Malcolm McDowell's Alex from *A Clockwork Orange* in Ledger's first day of shooting, sharing that as a compliment to the flattered Ledger, who admitted he had been watching the film that very morning in his trailer. Oldman called the turn Ledger gave as one of the most frightening he'd ever seen in a film.[20] Their advance praise, based solely on what they'd seen on the set, was deserved, and born of hard work on Ledger's part. For while many of his earlier roles reflect his talent range, none until the Joker were truly his own to craft from scratch, without predetermined variables such as realism, period detail, and so on. Indeed, director Nolan (who claimed he cast Ledger because the actor "had serious nuts"[21]) started meeting with Ledger as long as a year before a script was even fashioned, allowing Ledger to privately work out the characteristic nuances that make the Joker so memorably creepy. Ledger was intimately invested in the entire process, from wardrobe to makeup. He nearly vanished for a month prior to shooting and lived like a recluse to perfect the Joker's aching sense of chronic loneliness and psychotic alienation.[22] He kept what he called his "Joker's Diary" during the process, detailing with photos, sketches, and handwritten observations the Joker's inner turmoil, which helped the actor distill the character's nature. All of these commitments to his craft resulted in a perfectionist's realization on the set, but also left him emotionally and physically drained to utter exhaustion by the time of the film's completion. Ledger limped into his next role never fully recovered, and then expired during its making.

What is it about the Joker as maniac that gives him such a fascinating hold on modern audiences? The magnified images of maniacs in film, so reductionist and clichéd, have been excluded from this examination beyond noting their importance to early depictions of bipolarity. Their inclusion would both quadruple the page count and offer little insight. Most of these images are stereotypes of blood lust and power grabs by monstrous, dehumanized egos posing as characters. Such images may have some clinical accuracy to mania in its more excited states, but they rarely show the disorder's permutations over time. Instead, it is usually shown as a sustained mania from which there is never any remission. The Joker is the antithesis of this premise. Instead of gloating power, he is a voice-clenched, barely functional psychopath who struggles merely to remain in the presence of other human beings, as their proximity alone invokes a primal sense of misanthropy. To be around them is to feel an unwavering need to taunt them, to manipulate, to reduce them to his own level of depersonalized madness. But tragically, being around others also reminds the Joker how truly alienated from any sense of love and friendship he has become, and this further spurs his retributive anger. Like Lucifer in the rays of Jehovah's heavenly light, the burden of jealousy as the Joker watches others form relationships while he is forever shut out is too intense to bear without gnashing of teeth and rending of garments, both of which Ledger enacts as the Joker.

This sense of hidden private agony is primal in Ledger's approach, especially in the staccato voice laden with hints of coming pain and suffering. There is a pressure-speaking that is very accurate to true hypomanic and manic speech in Ledger's performance, a sense that *every . . . single . . . word . . . is . . . being . . . deliberately . . . exaggerated.* This manic intensity, in which the speaker loses the ability to emphasize the words that are important to underscore, and thus decides to simply underscore them all, is again accurate to bipolar rants.[23] One thinks of the way in which Hitler did this when he was agitated beyond control by his own public-speaking tirades, each word being hurled at his adoring audience with rapturous pause and inwardly weighted significance. But Ledger's lip-smacking, lisping fiend is forever emerging as a wounded wastrel, astonishing viewers that such an obvious monster who should be easily despised, is difficult, if not impossible, to glance away from. Ledger uses a diabolical uncertainty in his manner that, while in control of others, at the same time, is at odds with its internal sense of itself. The Joker, as Ledger realizes him, is a depersonalized soul, clinically depressive to the point of utter invisibility when he is not fantastically, utterly present while committing acts of maniacal but criminal genius. The Joker hides himself away like many classic depressives, only to emerge radiant in the flush of mania as he extracts his revenge on a society he deems barely worthy of his contempt. It is a form of psychological transference that many who fit a societal ideal of The Other fall victim to self-inflicting, even as they seek to inflict it on others in retribution. This sense of being forever outside any possible hope of reconciliation with one's community is what seemingly drives the Joker, though he never dilutes the operatic high of his epic displays of egomania with any clear statement of his grievances. His evident sense of manic self-aggrandizement, tempered with his melancholic knowledge that he will also always be depressive, imbues the Joker with a tragic element. The sad implication is that there is a formerly loving, caring human being inside the fleshy gargoyle that is the Joker, but untreated mental illness, physical abuse, and other acts of darkly alluded to degradation have left him an incandescent flare of his former self. Ledger plays him as a burning apostle of repressed vengeful animus, fully intent on extracting every painful ounce of suffering from the citizenry that he feels they have inflicted on him prior to his rise to power. Ledger's Joker is a visceral summation of fear and loneliness personified by mental instability and personal despair in a society that just doesn't care.

There has always been a hint of suicidal desperation in the Joker character, both in the comics and other film portrayals. While the maniacal laughter and diabolical mental states of excited depravity are emphasized, in an actual diagnosed manic-depressive these are rarely attendant without the accompanying depressions afterward when the bipolar afflicted cycles down.[24] So while the movies and comics rarely show the drawn, depressed side of the Joker, it was surely present, if not motivating him, at least in terms of any verisimilitude with real-world mania and depression. Ledger wedded his own morbid, racing thoughts to the role, filling in many of the gaps without any need of exposition as to why the Joker was so pitifully damaged. There is such self-loathing in Ledger's clenched vocals one feels as if the actor beneath the role is going to collapse under the weight of the mask itself. Never has a supposed villain in a superhero movie seemed so fragile, so devastatingly self-injured, so clearly mentally deranged. This is the ultimate unmasking à la the Phantom of the Opera. The audience is left holding the mask of hate the Joker wears and staring aghast at the naked face of his insanity writhing beneath. It is ugly, fearless, and damning as a performance, and the sheer bravado of it renders the other actors in his scenes, many top-billed as well, as virtual extras. The Joker's bipolarity is being expressed as a manic self-appointing of social hierarchy organization via intellectual and emotional terrorism. Like the bipolar self-aggrandizement Malcolm McDowell imbued Alex with in *A Clockwork Orange,* it is shown to be devastatingly effective when applied to the weak of mind and willpower. The threats are not merely hinted, for the actual dark card the Joker carries up his sleeve is always suicide as first resort. The Joker crashes a crime lord meeting wired with explosives that will self-detonate if he is shot or harmed. The Joker taunts the crime bosses' inability to call his suicidal bluff, blatantly murdering one of them as the other kingpins look on, infuriated but helpless pawns in the Joker's deadly game of ultimate chicken. Because they are presented as sociopaths in their criminal activities but otherwise neurotypical, the crime bosses feel vulnerable to the psychotic superiority the Joker wields over them, cowering for their lives in silent but obedient rage. The brutal reality is that some bipolars, at least those with a negative proclivity for power and politics, can use their disorder to charm, coerce, and even terrorize others, and it is vividly captured here.

Heath Ledger seemed to become unbalanced beyond his control during the last weeks of his life. Some on the set of *The Imaginarium of Dr. Parnassus* claimed that Ledger became "unhinged"[25] at times in his constant need to avoid the paparazzi, and others noted his worsening insomnia, which left him perpetually exhausted. The insomnia may have also triggered his mania, as one extra described him as appearing "dirty, wired and manic"[26] during the last week of the shoot and having three nonstop days of wildly energetic displays. He had before his death expressed a passionate interest in making a biopic about the obscure English rocker-turned-suicide Nick Drake, possibly even as a director. Ledger was haunted by Drake's somber lyrics and spare recording style, going so far as to self-finance and direct a rock video set to Drake's song "Black Eyed Dog." The title was a reference to bipolar Winston Churchill's famous quote about depression being a black dog, one both Drake and Ledger appreciated. In the video, Ledger disturbingly stages himself drowning via suicide in a bathtub as the final shot, as if in homage to Drake. Though his death was officially ruled as accidental, the fact that Ledger died in large part from an overdose of antidepressants, just as Nick Drake did, does explain why some were reluctant to believe he had not taken his own life. Whatever his intent, Ledger's death was a blow to those who knew and loved him. Christian Bale, who had told interviewers previously he had experienced bouts of insomnia and blue funks in his own past,[27] became close to Ledger during the shoot, and was devastated by the loss, falling into a lasting depression. Ledger's family was equally stunned by his passing, choosing to withdraw from the public eye and for the most part mourn their loss in private. Though his death forever marks his career as tragic in destiny, Ledger's work, particularly as the deeply depressed, world-weary Joker, is a transcendental turn in bipolar expression. Similarly to Peter Lorre's performance as the guilt-ridden child murderer in Fritz Lang's *M*, Ledger as the Joker now invokes the modern covert sympathizing with devils, especially figurative devils of the mind caused by mental disorder, while we dream awake at the movies. We all can feel reduced and worthless in the current techno-obsessed climate, but few of us can imagine giving in to our despair and hatred on the level of dissolution as has the self-imploded Joker. Thanks to Ledger's willingness to dredge the worst pathologies of his own troubled being and display them as his character's behavior, his anarchy-loving Joker literally staggers onto two wiry legs just long enough to achieve lasting cinematic fame as an ultimate embodiment of maniacal delusion, before self-exploding into incandescent evil from his own internally fueled rage and loathing. It is an incendiary performance, one of the great depictions of the psychotic state of degradation a bipolar person can endure, and sadly inflict, over a lifetime of abuse, failure, and regrets, propelled forward against seemingly impossible odds by a will to prevail over, and in spite of, the underlying psychiatric illness.

THE DEVIL AND DANIEL JOHNSTON

As can be seen in the legal limbo entanglements of such films as *Titicut Follies* (1967), documentary cinema in even relatively recent times was not the ideal choice for exposés about the treatment of the mentally ill. Such films often involved challenges to existing laws and risked the rights of housed patients being violated, however inadvertently, by the filmmakers. But when the subject of the documentary agrees to open himself and his clinical bipolarity to scrutiny for the filmmaker and audience alike, even exploring the pain and harm he has unwittingly inflicted upon others in moments of clinical madness, the former, legalistic documentary worries cease to exist, as the subject has entered into a form of self-confessional with the audience. *The Devil and Daniel Johnston* (2005) almost singularly encapsulates and dramatically illustrates many of the recurrent themes of this book. The particular symptoms Daniel Johnston exhibits in his personal expression and experience of bipolarity are unique to him. But the universality of the themes his mania and depression force him to dwell upon, such as love, loss, and self-damnation, make this unguarded look at the history of bipolar disorder in one young artist's life emotionally understandable to all who encounter it in a profound, nearly primitive way. There is a raw, untarnished power of self-expression in Daniel Johnston's songs. They most often consist of the sparest of musical accompaniment and his plaintive, pained voice cracking under the sheer weight of expression. Both combine with his devastatingly honest, lonely lyrics to evoke the common woes shared by us all. Like a blues artist from the 1930s, Daniel Johnston's garage-recorded works have transcended the modest recording techniques he has utilized to create his best work, including recording to cassette tape when he began in the 1980s distributing his music for free to anyone who would take a hand-out.

His life is an almost perfect distillation of many of the qualities that previously profiled bipolar filmmakers and actors have experienced, and whose biographies also mirror the same profound sense of alienation and anxiety Johnston felt as a child. According to *The Devil and Daniel Johnston*, he was a proverbial outsider from birth among his traditional, religious, West Virginia family members, who openly regarded Daniel as weird, arrogant, and conceited, yet never attributing his odd behavior to possible mental illness. This owed mostly to his peculiar obsessions with music, movies, and comic books, all of which he voraciously devoured as a child with early onset bipolarity. His inability to show any interest in church, school, sports, or other social activities other than his established obsessions, led to frequent battles of will with his obstinate mother during his childhood. She unsuccessfully attempted to coerce her son into taking control of his laziness, as she called his mental illness, not through medical treatment, but via dutiful prayer and hard work. When this strategy failed, his mother would accuse his endless supply of popular ephemera and records of being devil-possessed and posing a mortal risk to his already troubled soul. Daniel Johnston understandably retreated into living in the basement early in his conflicts with his family, preferring the isolated mad lab feel of his dark, subterranean lair to the painfully revealing rays of noonday sun and his family's living room. As the film also reveals, Daniel Johnston lived in his elderly, retired parents' basement to the day of the documentary's production. They dutifully express to the camera at one point their concern of what will become of their dependent son with their passing. His remarkable arc from a child with bipolar obsessions and delusions, mixed with a latent talent for making original music, short animated films, and his own comic books, to his later phase as the young artist who achieves recognition only to fall prey to his disorder's worst symptoms before he can truly capitalize upon his break, and to his middle-aged years filled with both the highs of international fame and critical respect, mixed with a lifetime's lows of regrets owing to lost opportunities and failed relationships leaving him virtually alone, is epic in human endurance and heartbreak.

The Devil and Daniel Johnston is a testament to tenacity in showing how Johnston dedicates himself to his outsider work as musician, artist, and filmmaker, even in the face of chronic, debilitating episodes of manic depression. As such, it is the quiet triumph of the human spirit against improbable odds, along with the inevitable failures that must ensue, that makes the film so especially insightful to many viewers. Director Jeff Feuerzeig takes the necessary time to explore the full range of stories and myths that have arisen around the legendary but notoriously self-effacing subject, and separate them, at least as much as Daniel's own damaged memory will allow. His impairment grows from episodes of delusional psychosis while living in Austin, Texas, as a young man, which blocked many memories of this time for him. During this phase of his life, he recorded some of the most influential music of his troubled career. He was at the same time reduced to shouting about a coming apocalypse while standing in the water fountains around the University of Texas campus, until he was finally checked into a mental hospital for acute religious mania. The extremes in his life continued, reflecting his disorder, during his twenties. He improbably appeared on MTV's show *The Cutting Edge* in 1985 as representative of the emerging folk sound coming from Austin, giving him overnight national exposure and boosting his reputation among the city's cultural elite. Yet some years after this shining moment of personal triumph, Johnston would attempt to kill himself and his father, Bill, while Bill, an experienced service pilot, was flying them both in a small airplane. At the time, Daniel Johnston was experiencing a delusional psychosis in which he believed he was Casper the Friendly Ghost, and could fly the plane without the need of the plane's ignition key, which he threw out the window in midflight. As the teary-eyed Bill recalls the story in *The Devil and Daniel Johnston*, he was only able to land the plane in the dark Texas woods through sheer luck. He and his son escaped with only minor injuries in a miraculous turn of events, though the plane was totally lost. Daniel was involuntarily committed to a stay in a sanitarium after this incident, the first of several such unfortunate trips. The years would pass, and largely pass Johnston by, his unique signature voice and output quelled by long stays in psyche wards. Then, in another example of the extreme nature of his fortunes, Daniel found himself the subject of a minor bidding war in Hollywood in 1993 when Kurt Cobain, himself bipolar and perhaps therefore even more partial to Johnston's work, took to wearing a tee shirt with Johnston's "Hi, How Are You?" frog with eye-stalks design while promoting Nirvana's breakthrough *Nevermind* album. The offer, alas, came at the worst time, with Johnston in a psychiatric hospital and unable to curtail his religious mania. Johnston turned down Elektra Records because he believed their act Metallica was satanic in origin, and he wanted nothing to do with any such association. When his tireless friend and pro bono manager disagreed, Johnston soon distanced himself from him, accusing him of being the devil's messenger. Alienated and estranged, Johnston's decision to go with Atlantic Records and handle his career solo wound up with a disastrous release of his non-selling album *Fun*, with Atlantic soon dropping him from their roster.

    The Devil and Daniel Johnston details many shocking incidents in the artist's life with simple candor, and in most recalled incidents, a sweet sadness lingers. There are stretches in which Johnston loquaciously recalls an obsessive teenage crush on a local girl, a flame he still kindles all these decades later, that achieve a kind of spare, poetic beauty rarely captured in American filmmaking. But occasionally, the film also reveals a dark hint of the underlying reason why Daniel Johnston takes his religious beliefs so seriously, needing as he does a strong spiritual component to explain the larger-than-life forces that he feels have guided and shaped his destiny. For as his chastened family and friends recall to the camera, Johnston's at times barely suppressed violent impulses have occasionally resulted in his committing assault, including one horrifying time he attacked an old woman in her upstairs apartment while he was having a delusional episode. Convinced the occupant was in danger of being harmed by a demon in her living room, Johnston ran up the outside flight of stairs and banged against her front door, finally forcing his way inside, even as she screamed for him to stop. She was injured in the assault, though Johnston maintains a fervent belief that any harm was from the demon rushing by her. What is quite extraordinary is that the bipolar Peter Sellers, who was also violent at times while under manic psychosis, attacked a domestic helper in a similar fashion under a similar delusion, as previously noted, which shows such moments are not unprecedented. Another moment of raw video taken in a living room during his early college years shows a dead-eyed Daniel Johnston staring at his off-screen, videotaping host. As Johnston rocks slowly in place, narrowed eyes gleaming and his smile disturbingly stiff, his nervous friend asks Daniel what is on his mind, clearly worried by the sinister looks. Johnston's non-response and maniacal chuckle do little to reassure the host, who finally feels compelled to ask Johnston to stop his behavior, worried for his own safety. Here a glimmer of the underlying psychosis that will lead to Johnston's later problems with the old woman's assault and his attempt to crash his father's plane emerge for the viewer to see, without apology or further explanation. It is to the film's enormous credit that it can so adroitly present the darkest sides of its titular subject's life without having the viewer feel conflicted, or even judgmental, by its conclusion. There is no easy explanation for anyone involved in his life, or for Daniel himself, and so the film refuses to promote any. Instead it focuses on the acute nature of Johnston's isolation and anxiety as they relate to bipolarity, and in particular, how they influence his need to creatively express himself via unending art therapy.

There are moments of aching beauty beyond words in the film. One that is a melancholic icon for manic-depressive illness for the ages is a series of shots of the bloated Johnston, dressed head-to-toe in a plus-sized Casper gown and plastic mask, standing near an empty grove of trees and slowly swaying back and forth to his own sad music. It is as emotionally expressive as a Gothic rock video directed by Lord Byron. The corpulent phantom figure, once rail thin in earlier footage but now bloated from his daily bombardment of prescriptive meds, becomes a powerful metaphor for the constant feeling of depersonalized insignificance Daniel Johnston chronicles in his art and music. For Johnston, Casper is more than a simple comic book hero. Casper is a living symbol of mythic proportions, a representative of the lonely spirit who forever wanders among the emotionally healthy others, unrecognized and invisible, save to but a handful who see and feel his overwhelming pain and isolation. The perpetual sense of being estranged, and at the same time self-estranging, from others has rarely been so movingly rendered in bipolar cinema, even if fictional portraits such as *Breakfast at Tiffany's* and the works of Woody Allen have come very close. This ironic sense of permanent detachment is a familiar one for many bipolars. Daniel Johnston is no exception, right to the film's title, which he found objectionable,[28] owing to its linking his name with Satan's for all time (even though the film makes clear Johnston is engaged in a religious struggle with Lucifer and minions and is waging his private theological war at the behest of God). And while the name may be an issue for him, there is little doubt that *The Devil and Daniel Johnston* has not only elevated his status as one of the great outside artists of his generation, but brought much-needed attention to the manic depressive illness that underlies much of his artistic production. Johnston continues to perform at live events on occasion, and has been active in various musical, book, and filmmaking projects, including the successful funding of a short film based on his concepts and snippets of conversation recorded with him called "Hello, Hi Are You?" via Kickstarter as of this book's writing.

LARS VON TRIER'S CHRONIC STUDIES OF *MELANCHOLIA*

There is in much of Danish filmmaker Lars von Trier's body of work a perpetual fog of depression and dissolution in many of his characters and situations. While such earlier studies in lingering sadness such as *Breaking the Waves* (1996), *Dancer in the Dark* (2000), and *Antichrist* (2009) lay the stark groundwork, *Melancholia* (2011) is the triumphant masterpiece in his depressive oeuvre. It is a carefully constructed tale of rapid-cycling bipolarity, reveling in the depressions and sudden hypomanias of Justine (Kirsten Dunst), an affluent young professional, on the literal eve of her wedding. The multilayered approach von Triers uses, in which he incorporates surreal, painterly paced, digitally created imagery with embarrassingly frank handheld shots of a family in emotional crisis, works to an enormously effective degree of capturing the actual complexity of mental illness. Taking the expressionist approach to delineating the disorder allows Lars von Trier to patiently unfold his "end of the world" love story, going from the most intimate of moments wherein Justine masturbates naked beneath the stars one mystical night to a cosmic, God's eye point-of-view staged from inside our own solar system as the errant planet called Melancholia speeds toward the doomed Earth. The opening, extended sequence in which the cataclysm unfolds before we are introduced to the film's characters, set to the teary strains of Wagner's *Tristan and Isolde*, creates an immediate, lasting feel of fatalism. The tragedy is not unlike when one watches a film such as *Titanic*, the director admitted when discussing his film's construction,[29] in that one knows from the start only a handful, if any, of the characters will survive until the film's conclusion. This is also a perfect artistic expression of the foreboding, mordant sense chronic depression can create in the mind of the sufferer, a doomed sense of certainty that the worst is always yet, but soon, to come. This kind of existential despair is classic to the many films we have reviewed in this discussion, and has been equally seen in the biographies highlighted herein concerning affective actors and directors. Poe's manic-depressive works are literally haunted with this epic sense of Gothic hopelessness, so much so that they have become cultural shorthand as expressions of morbidity of thought. It is also a hallmark for a psychiatric diagnosis of bipolarity, as many manic depressives admit to thoughts of apocalypse and destruction during clinical episodes.[30]

Lars von Trier faced the enormous battle to overcome his own bout of years-long clinical depression before and during the making of *Melancholia*. The film was conceived initially as being solely to force him out of his reclusive retreat from reality and responsibilities owing to his chronic depression.[31] His previous appearance at Cannes the year he presented *Antichrist* was marked with notations in the media about his somber appearance, with murmurings about his weight gain and inability to maintain eye contact when he spoke to journalists.[32] What was little understood at this point by most, however, was that von Trier's depression was becoming so severe as to be life threatening, and that his appearance at the film festival was at great personal agony to the depressed filmmaker. His therapist convinced von Trier that he should focus his depressive state on a creative project, suggesting a paradox that has recently become evident as research accumulates in this regard. The paradox being that while depression has historically been seen as a genetic malady, it arguably confers survival advantages in some strategic situations. As von Trier's therapist posited it, neurotypicals tend to react poorly in stressful, life-and-death situations compared to melancholics, because depressive people are accustomed to seeing life as a dire series of consequences largely beyond one's control, owing to their illness.[33] Put another way, depressives are able to cope more easily because they are in a perpetual mode of coping a priori, as their affective disorder mandates they must do so in order to survive. One of the ways emotionally affected individuals cope most effectively is not by denying their depressive ruminations, as recent studies have concluded,[34] but by addressing them with self-analytic methodology, such as writing journals specifically about their negative self-focus. Which, adapted for filmmaking based on his personal screenplay, is precisely how von Trier went about addressing his condition. This very personal need to create cinema in order to manage one's own mental illness is akin to Ingmar Bergman and Woody Allen, each of whom has likewise battled severe depression and withdrawn from the world at times to focus on his screenplays and films. Faced with an inability to function daily as it dragged on, von Trier committed to making a film with the theme of depression as a means of cathartic exegesis and eventual recovery. "I used filmmaking as a tool to get out of bed,"[35] the characteristically plain-spoken director told interviewers in a short video he made about his reasons for making *Melancholia*.

Dunst said in an interview the thing she was proudest of in *Melancholia* was that she helped give back a more humane, realistic portrait of clinical depression, which she said was not very often shown as such in movies. "Depression is not really shown on screen," she said, "It's something that I think people who've gone through it, or know someone who has gone through it, will identify with."[36] Dunst would know, having battled with depression severely enough to at one point check herself into the Cirque Lodge rehab facility in Sundance, Utah, until she recovered.[37] While she has remained elusive about the personal details of her treatment save to deny her stay was drug or alcohol related, Dunst has admitted that stressors, many career related, precipitated her lingering episode. She has detailed the level of understanding she had as an actress that much of the *Melancholia* script was an evocation by von Trier of his own battle with the black dog, citing the bathroom scene in which Justine is nearly catatonic in a soothingly hot bath as caring family members help her in and out of the therapeutic waters. While grueling to shoot, Dunst believed the scene of raw, emotional intimacy would most be recognized by loved ones, as well as the depressed, as "comforting"[38] in its authenticity. While she is emphatic that she was not depressed while making *Melancholia*, Dunst did draw upon her own bout of mood disorder for Justine's character, to the point the withdrawn stare and lowered voice left the actress unable to watch her performance later, saying that "it weirds me out."[39]

Her reaction is understandable, given that *Melancholia* is such a deeply felt piece comprised of many jagged-edged slices of observed realism in regard to the horrific agonies of bipolarity. The familial connection between madness and heredity is not merely addressed, but swiftly proven as conclusive, by the introduction of Justine's estranged, but once passionately in love, parents. They are the depressive but acid-tongued mother Gaby (Charlotte Rampling) and the perpetually drunken, pressure-grinning father Dexter (John Hurt), both emotionally vacant from the proceedings as frequently and obviously as possible. Justine's own actions are indecipherable to her non-afflicted family, especially brother-in-law, John (Kiefer Sutherland), who is hosting the expensive wedding on his wealthy family's estate. Throughout the picture, John is at odds with Justine's inexplicable inability to show appreciation and loyalty to his wife and her sister, Claire (Charlotte Gainsbourg), as if Justine were choosing her condition's expression rather than the more honest reverse scenario. He is the dominant alpha male of the combined households by self-positioning, pretending to be the enlightened man of action and brooking little dissent, especially from Justine, whom he considers weak and selfish. And yet, ironically, it is John who commits suicide and leaves his own family to suffer alone because he cannot accept that the planet Melancholia will soon destroy all life, most of all his own, on Earth. Justine, however, accepts the finality of it all and acts as a spiritual guidance counselor for all left alive, herding them together to face the end of the world not apart, but huddled as one unit, inseparable until the last second of catastrophic obliteration. It is a moving testament to the power of endurance and acceptance of constant disappointment that many bipolars must face and overcome, and as *Melan-*

cholia suggests, without recognition or even much appreciation for their efforts, perhaps even by their own unaware, unappreciative loved ones, who may only see bipolars as a sum detriment and rarely a positive in their lives.

This point is not made in any way as self-aggrandizement by von Trier, quite the opposite. It rather points out the bleak trace of poetry in realizing that the neurotypical world is as much dependent upon the comforts and visions offered by their suffering artists as any mood-afflicted creators are dependent upon their caregivers without returning value in kind. This becomes even truer when the world is seemingly, or in this case literally, falling to pieces. Even as all life in the universe is coming to a decisive end (for Justine has received a psychic impression from the invading planet Melancholia that Earth is the only planet with life in the entire cosmos), Justine imagines a beatific ending that helps the assembled, helpless tribe remain united, even until the moment of their shared apocalyptic annihilation. It is a moving coda that encapsulates many of the themes of bipolar cinema. One of these is the realization that some of the most powerful imaginations in all of humanity are often accompanied by weaker states of emotional stability, but that their offered visions and creations are so moving, so perfectly expressed, that the non-afflicted hold their visions aloft as exalted representations of their own neurotypical moods. In this moment of shared recognition between mood-disordered creator and non-disordered (perhaps) participant, a momentary sense of true equality is established. For during this cathartic transference between artist and patron, the playing fields are leveled, and all is revealed as it is, without boundaries. It is this shared sense of sameness, when created by those who are perennial outsiders to their own societies, that is so important to the works of bipolarity that move audiences. In these moments wherein audience members feel the same as any depicted mentally ill patient, and/or are moved by the expressionist tendencies of a bipolar filmmaker, petty differences between what are, in the end, members of the same species of humanity drop away. What is left is a momentary, though shared, sense that what makes us unique as humans, while often valuable and to be celebrated, is not confined only to those who may classify as neurotypical, but across the full spectrum of humanity. Here the notion that the mask of mental illness is somehow different, that those who are afflicted with it are not, like their fellow non-afflicted citizens, searching for meaning in a very difficult existence in which to find it, is set aside. A more mature realization that we are all the same despite often profound differences becomes profound reality. Such revelations in popular art can, and sometimes have, led to reactionary changes in bipolar understanding and empathy. Their benefit toward nudging humanity into a sustained, successful effort to medically assist those with mental disorders is incalculable and profoundly impactful.

SILVER LININGS PLAYBOOK AND THE GROWING AWARENESS OF BIPOLARITY

The U.S. box office success ($132 million gross on an estimated $21 million budget)[40] of *Silver Linings Playbook* (2012) heralded a new era in bipolar cinema. While many successful films chronicled herein have dealt with mania and depression either directly or obliquely, and some were box office triumphs, none have ever focused so openly, and so lovingly, on the strength of family and friendships necessary for real-world bipolar patients to survive, and then thrive, despite their disorder. *Silver Linings Playbook* takes a bracing, but darkly humorous (at times) stare into the dysfunctional, but caring, Solitano family, and how the recent diagnosis of their mature son Pat (Bradley Cooper) as a manic-depressive has altered their lives. Pat has just been released after eight months in a sanitarium when the movie begins, having accepted a plea deal to avoid a jail sentence. He has previously nearly beaten a man to death after discovering the man in his shower making love to his now-estranged wife, Nikki (Brea Bee). For the balance of *Silver Linings Playbook*'s length, Pat will display obsessional thoughts about reuniting with Nikki, despite her having abandoned him and moved on with her life. He will break the terms of his court-sanctioned release and re-straining order if he visits Nikki or has any communication with her. When he moves back into his parents' Philadelphia home until he can get back on his feet, they insist he stay on his medications and avoid any entanglements with the law as condition for their help. His doting, supportive mother, Dolores (Jacki Weaver), and obsessive-compulsive father, Pat Sr. (Robert De Niro), are facing hard times financially, with Pat Sr.'s own inability to control his anger factoring into his recent loss of employment. When Pat meets Tiffany (Jennifer Lawrence), a de-

pressed widow with a hypersexual need to sleep with as many men as
she can to alleviate her grief, a romantic attraction follows. This despite
Pat's maniacal need to remain focused on his mission to reunite with
Nikki. Tiffany's own recent history of hypersexuality has cost her her
job, as well as put her on antidepressant medications, which she has
quit taking by the time she meets Pat. The complex interplay as they
first become friends, and then hover on the edge of becoming more, is
carefully delineated in a slow, awkward dance every bit as difficult to
master as the choreography they will later perform in the film's finale.
Pat's belief that he is less mentally ill than Tiffany, and therefore superi-
or, is the basis of a public scene of contention in which Tiffany is forced
to reveal the reality that everyone else views him as the mental case, not
her, at least by comparison. Pat is shaken, as he already knows the bias
against those with a history of mental illness is so severe that even their
own families sometimes presume the worst of any situation, blaming
manic depression for any bad turn of events, even when in fact it may
have had little, if any, bearing on it.

It is this level of honesty, and revelation, that director David O.
Russell and his talented cast and crew bring to *Silver Linings Playbook*
that makes it so extraordinary in the canon. His level of commitment to
the project was motivated by his own teenaged son Matthew's battle
with manic-depressive illness, and the frustrations and sadness that
arise with it, particularly in an adolescent.[41] In an interview with *The
Hollywood Reporter* with Matthew at his side, Russell revealed that
many of the scenes of emotional turbulence and manic rage in *Silver
Linings Playbook* were similar to those his own family has witnessed
and endured. He explained how isolated he has felt raising a son with a
mood disorder, with "movies over here, and here is your struggle [with
bipolarity] over here."[42] He spoke of how wonderful it was that they
could be joined in a project that he believes will not only shed light on
the illness, but make bipolar patients feel much less shame about their
illness. Matthew even cameos in the film as the pesky neighbor teen
Ricky D'Angelo, who constantly interrupts the quarreling family to see
if he can interview them with his camcorder for extra credit on a school
project about mental illness. It is this degree of familiarity with all the
nuances and variations that occur within a full range of episodic bipolar
behaviors that informs *Silver Linings Playbook* with such an aura of
having been lived, rather than imagined, by its creators. The usual Hol-

lywood clichés of straightjackets and bug-eyed killers is entirely missing, replaced with scenes of agonizing mental confusion and desperate inability to refrain from one's own worst impulses. Pat is shown violently assaulting Nikki's lover, but such an outburst is also within the expected, if extreme, range of any neurotypical spouse who stumbled into such a betrayal. Pat does not seem cruel or abusive in his assault, but rather a man who has simply momentarily lost control. Indeed, in an ironic counterpoint to this, Pat will later struggle to not join in with a tailgate party at a Philadelphia Eagles football game turned deadly, wherein neurotypical fans savage one another in a display of unmotivated racial violence. As the so-called normal people rush to pummel each other without mercy or true motivation beyond blindly releasing pent-up aggression, Russell makes his point devastatingly clear: those who would pretend only the mentally ill are subject to fits of irrational anger and lashing out are only kidding themselves. While Pat initially resists the senseless display out of a compulsion to avoid further legal problems, he is drawn into the melee out of loyalty to his beaten friends and brother. This scene, which plays to illustrate a plot point on the surface, is a deeper repudiation of the endless debates on television in which misinformed speakers promote the idea that violence and mental illness are conjoined, rather than distinct, terms of description and conditions.[43] Even the nerve-wracking sequence in which Pat and Pat Sr. come to blows over Pat's maniacal 3 AM need to retrieve his wedding video from his father's private study is not without compassion for Pat's roving, restless bout of manic depression. Pat later brags to his therapist, Dr. Patel (Anupam Kher), that his condition is improving because Pat resisted hitting his father in return, realizing in the moment of anger such an action could kill Pat Sr. This level of self-awareness is a constant struggle for psychologists in dealing with bipolar patients. Many afflicted persons succumb to believing the worst about themselves during depressive episodes, as well as having to overcome the embarrassment or recriminations from any manic episodes once they've stabilized. Dr. Patel is shown in his sessions with his patient constantly urging Pat to form a game plan for action that is more specific, and less grandiose in maniac certainty, for its probable outcome. This is a very realistic therapeutic depiction and profits from Cooper's hesitancy in accepting his diagnosis, or his need to take medication, or any other of the many changes he is required to undergo and master in order to remain free. In fact, the way in which the threat of being returned to the asylum is depicted as one of the contributing pressures Pat and his struggling family must overcome is another major stroke of realism by the filmmakers. While the court's looming threat is meant to scare Pat straight, it often acts as an unintentional source of further, unnecessary tension, only adding to his distressed family's plight, rather than assisting it, as intended. Officer Keogh (Dash Mihok), who is court assigned to oversee any problems with Pat's return integration, only appears in the film after moments of complete duress, in which Pat or his family have had a fight or screaming match and awakened the neighbors. Keogh even has the nerve to hit on Tiffany after almost arresting Pat following a street altercation.

There is another quirky anomaly in *Silver Linings Playbook* that is welcome to bipolar cinema. All the neurotypical characters we meet have their own deep-seated issues to work through and resolve, even lacking any mental illness. Besides Keogh, Pat's married friend Ronnie (John Ortiz), perfect embodiment of the everyman (at least as far as this film's quirky characters go), is oppressed with worry about his job and less-than-happy marriage. He is shown leaning on Pat's inner strength for support as much as offering any return support to Pat beyond the palest show of friendship. Ronnie corners Pat alone whenever he can when they are at parties or gatherings, whispering to Pat how terrible his life is and how the work pressures are killing him. He makes a self-strangulation gesture, eyes bugging with fear. This is a perceptive look at how many people feel much less inhibited when they are with someone such as Pat whom they know has a history of mental struggles, especially when they are one-on-one. Rightfully believing Pat will understand what it is like to suffer in silence while everyone expects you never to crack, Ronnie nevertheless uses his relationship with Pat as a form of poor man's therapy. It's well-intended, as if to tell his bipolar friend he's not alone in suffering, but likewise it's a mostly one-way street. Ronnie apologizes when he meets Pat after Pat's release, whispering with embarrassment how sorry he is that he never visited Pat in the eight months he was in the mental hospital. Ronnie ironically never seems to become aware that he is in many ways dependent upon Pat's silver linings philosophy, which Pat preaches throughout the film. At its core, the idea is attractive in its motivational simplicity. Instead of regrets and negative thoughts, one copes with positive reactions and stabilizing thoughts. While it is too easy to be effective in reality without ensuing problems, the rest of his family, and in time Tiffany, gravitate around Pat's unshakeable, if manic-derived, self-belief. They are inspired by his fight for sanity no matter their own skepticism, which is shown as coming from a lack of self-worth rather than any true disdain for Pat or his condition. Even Dr. Patel is drawn into his patient's personal life in an ethical blurring due to Pat's remaining positive despite all odds. The doctor turns out to be an Eagles football fanatic, down to painting his face in the team's colors before attending the game. While it is suggested this is within the bounds of acceptable behavior because it is restricted to game day and at the stadium (which Pat Sr. has been barred for life from ever attending due to the numerous fights he's started over the years), the director implies there is a certain lunatic element in everyone. The difference is obvious but the irony is palpable here, as in much of *Silver Linings Playbook*. If one can control one's irrational impulses and only express them when socially acceptable, one is sane. If not, one is insane. Either way, the irrational rages, fears, and obsessions expressed by bipolars undergoing an episode are not different from what neurotypicals may also experience. The feelings are the same, but the rational reasons for their expression have in fact vanished or become unhinged to any perceivable reality, and hence the manic-depressive diagnosis.

Both protagonists are depressive, but only Pat hears his wedding song, the same song his wife played while she betrayed them in their home, whenever he is stressed. This form of audio delusion is not rare in bipolars, as hallucinatory auditory experiences can occur in manic depression.[44] Another trait is his attire. Pat insists on wearing a signature garbage bag over his trademark sweat pants outfit whenever he is jogging, working out, etc., all of which he does rather compulsively. While he is in incredible shape as a result, there is a sense in his frantic jogging that Pat is as much running away from himself and his condition as he is running toward any image of physical perfection. He isolates himself with his insistent jogging to the point where the only way Tiffany can engage him in conversation is to wait for him and join him as he jogs by, tagging along despite his protests. Pat, in an earlier scene, wears a football jersey to a dinner party, where he meets Tiffany, when everyone else is conservatively attired. As in real-life accounts of bipolars, such as Heath Ledger and others, attire is often oddly mismatched and/

or even unkempt. While Pat is clean as far as we can tell, his desire to wear the same clothes in the same situations is actually as much an obsessive-compulsive disorder trait as it is one of bipolarity. Nor is this the only diagnostic anomaly in *Silver Linings Playbook*. Pat Sr. is clearly suffering OCD in the film, believing that his son is the reason the Eagles win or lose games, depending on whether or not Pat Jr. is present. He fastidiously arranges the remotes to his TV set and consoles in a specific order. Throughout the film, Pat Jr. jokes about his father's condition by clinical name, somewhat bemused that Pat Sr. will never address his own disorder, all the while insisting on being hyper-vigilant about his son's problem. But just as Pat Jr. has certain OCD-derived tendencies, so his father has manic-depressive tendencies in his own behavioral patterns. In fact, when Pat Sr. is concocting an incredibly risky bet while his horrified family objects, Dr. Patel mutters "that's very manic," though no one pays him any attention. Tiffany fares not much better, as she has a history of chronic, uncontrollable hypersexuality and exhibits many wild swings of mood within a single scene. She laments that her depressive behavior turned her off to making love to her husband. This led to his accidental automobile death after he purchased sex toys to enliven her interest. She admits she has slept with eleven men in her small office in a matter of months, effectively acknowledging at least a short duration of hypomanic, if not manic, sexuality. While it is possible these behaviors are all attributable to a severe emotional reaction to her husband's death (though that does not explain her depressive prior aversion to sex), they seem more likely lifelong, owing to their severity. Since no clear portrait is available of Tiffany before we meet her as a hypersexual widow, there is no way to be certain. However, the fact she and Pat first bond over their initial meeting by discussing which psychiatric meds they have tried, and which worked versus left them zombies, is a strong indicator that her doctors believed there was at least a possibility Tiffany was bipolar. Again, these fascinating possibilities are not indicative of deficiencies in *Silver Linings Playbook*, but further proof that comorbidity in psychiatric illnesses has become common knowledge. Many mental illnesses share similar affective responses, such as depression and social withdrawal, even as they also have distinguishing characteristics specific to each malady.

The enormous popularity of *Silver Linings Playbook* demonstrates that bipolarity has become a known disorder in American life, and that it has saturated every level of stratified class reality (as Pat and his family are distinctly middle class, or what is left of it). The enormous challenges modest households face in affording effective therapy for their suffering loved ones, as well as the lengths to which such families will go to remain united despite the forces tearing them apart, has never been more understandably or transparently rendered. It marks a paradigm shift away from the treatment and understanding of manic depression as something that needs to be pretended doesn't exist and into a realm where it is understood to be a medical condition, and not a weakness of character or a case of demonic possession. *Silver Linings Playbook* moves the ball further down the field toward an inevitable touchdown of acceptance and equality for those with mental illness. But it is not yet a touchdown, nor even a field goal, at least in terms of what is still required, both in movies and reality, to finally end all lingering taboos and understand and fully allow dignity and compassion for those who daily face such medical challenges.

NOTES

1. A BRIEF OVERVIEW OF MANIC DEPRESSION AND HOW IT AFFECTS CREATIVITY

1. Frederick Goodwin and Kay Redfield Jamison, *Manic-Depressive Illness* (New York: Oxford University Press, 1990), 14.

2. Goodwin and Jamison, *Manic-Depressive Illness*, 36–40.

3. Goodwin and Jamison, *Manic-Depressive Illness*, 40–42.

4. Richard O'Connor, *Undoing Depression: What Therapy Doesn't Teach You and Medication Can't Give You* (New York: Berkley Books, 1999), 143–46.

5. Goodwin and Jamison, *Manic-Depressive Illness*, 227–33.

6. Kay Redfield Jamison, *Touched with Fire: Manic-Depressive Illness and the Artistic Temperament* (New York: Free Press, 1993), 18–19.

7. Edgar Allan Poe, *The Works of Edgar Allan Poe* (Roslyn, NY: Walter J. Black Co., 1927), 19.

8. Goodwin and Jamison, *Manic-Depressive Illness*, 36–39.

9. O'Connor, *Undoing Depression*, 110–15.

10. Goodwin and Jamison, *Manic-Depressive Illness*, 146–51.

11. Goodwin and Jamison, *Manic-Depressive Illness*, 138–39.

12. Goodwin and Jamison, *Manic-Depressive Illness*, 146–51.

13. Goodwin and Jamison, *Manic-Depressive Illness*, 233–35.

14. Goodwin and Jamison, *Manic-Depressive Illness*, 269.

15. Gina Kuperberg, "Language in Schizophrenia Part 2: What Can Psycholinguistics Bring to the Study of Schizophrenia . . . and Vice Versa?" *Language and Linguistics Compass* 4, no. 8 (Aug. 2010): 590–604.

16. Goodwin and Jamison, *Manic-Depressive Illness*, 272–73.

17. Goodwin and Jamison, *Manic-Depressive Illness*, 231.

18. Anthony Storr, *Churchill's Black Dog, Kafka's Mice and Other Phenomena of the Human Mind* (New York: Grove Press, 1988), 258.

2. THE EARLY CINEMA AND
MENTAL ILLNESS

1. David Robinson, *From Peep Show to Palace: The Birth of American Film* (New York: Columbia University Press, 1996), 27–28.

2. Robinson, *From Peep Show to Palace*, 40.

3. Margaret Julia Hames, "I Have No Pride: William Kennedy Laurie Dickson in His Own Words—An Autobiography" (paper presented at the Proceedings of the 68th New York State Communication Association, New York, April 16, 2012), 4–5.

4. Frederick Goodwin and Kay Redfield Jamison, *Manic-Depressive Illness* (New York: Oxford University Press, 1990), 208.

5. Robinson, *From Peep Show to Palace*, 21–22.

6. Robinson, *From Peep Show to Palace*, 22.

7. Robinson, *From Peep Show to Palace*, 40.

8. Hames, "I Have No Pride," 16.

9. Steven W. Siferd, "Dickson Experimental Sound Film," *Internet Movie Database*, www.imdb.com/title/tt0177707/ (accessed December 14, 2012).

10. "Pioneers of Early Cinema 4: William Kennedy Laurie Dickson (1860–1935)," *National Media Museum*, http://www.nationalmediamuseum.org.uk/~/media/Files/NMeM/PDF/Collections/Cinematography/PioneersOfEarlyCinemaWilliamKennedyLaurieDickson.ashx (accessed May 23, 2014).

11. "Biography for William K. L. Dickson," *Internet Movie Database*, www.imdb.com/name/nm0005690/bio (accessed December 14, 2012).

12. Robinson, *From Peep Show to Palace*, 40.

13. Hames, "I Have No Pride," 11.

14. "Pioneers of Early Cinema 4."

15. Hames, "I Have No Pride," 10.

16. Hames, "I Have No Pride," 17.

17. Richard O'Connor, *Undoing Depression: What Therapy Doesn't Teach You and Medication Can't Give You* (New York: Berkley Books, 1999), 42.

18. Hames, "I Have No Pride," 15.

19. Robinson, *From Peep Show to Palace*, 70.

20. Goodwin and Jamison, *Manic-Depressive Illness*, 25.

21. Kenji Tsuchiya, Esben Agerbo, and Preben Mortensen, "Parental Death and Bipolar Disorder: A Robust Association Was Found in Early Maternal Suicide," *Journal of Affective Disorders* 86, no. 2 (June 2005): 151–59.

22. Robinson, *From Peep Show to Palace*, 19.

23. "Pioneers of Early Cinema 4."

24. Robinson, *From Peep Show to Palace*, 32.

25. Rae Beth Gordon, *Why the French Love Jerry Lewis: From Cabaret to Early Cinema* (Stanford, CA: Stanford University Press, 2001), 187.

26. Gordon, *Why the French Love Jerry Lewis*, 188.

27. Gordon, *Why the French Love Jerry Lewis*, 188.

28. Michael Leahy, *If You're Thinking of Living In: All about 115 Great Neighborhoods in and around New York City* (New York: Three Rivers Press, 1999), 10.

29. "Bloomingdale Asylum Expose-Julius Chambers-The New York Tribune," Undercover Reporting 2012, dlib.nyu.edu/undercover/bloomingdale-asylum-expose-julius-chambers-new-york-tribune (accessed May 9, 2014).

30. "The Escaped Lunatic," *Internet Movie Database*,www.imdb.com/title/tt0231547/ (accessed November 7, 2012).

31. "The Escaped Lunatic."

32. Tim Dirks, "Timeline of Greatest Film Milestones and Turning Points in Film History: The Year 1904," *AMC Filmsite*,www.filmsite.org/1904-filmhistory.html (accessed February 1, 2013).

33. David Berry, "Haggar, William (1851–1925)," *BFI Screenonline*,www.screenonline.org.uk/people/id/449862/ (accessed July 5, 2012).

34. Berry, "Haggar, William (1851–1925)."

35. "Dr. Dippy's Sanitarium," *BFI Film & TV Database* ,http://ftvdb.bfi.org.uk/sift/title/71409?view=synopsis (accessed October 12, 2012).

36. Carles Muntaner, "Socioeconomic Position and Major Mental Disorders," *Oxford Journal Epidemiologic Review* 26, no. 1 (July 2004): 53–62.

37. Kay Redfield Jamison, *Touched with Fire: Manic-Depressive Illness and the Artistic Temperament* (New York: Free Press, 1996), 18–19.

38. Richard Cavendish, "The Death of Edgar Allan Poe," *History Today* 49, no. 10 (October 1999): 38.

39. "Poe's Life," *The Poe Museum*, www.poemuseum.org/life.php (accessed August 8, 2012).

40. Edgar Allan Poe, *The Tell-Tale Heart and Other Writings* (New York: Bantam Books, 1982), 30.

41. Edgar Allan Poe, *The Works of Edgar Allan Poe* (Roslyn, NY: Walter J. Black Co., 1927), 48.

42. Poe, *The Works of Edgar Allan Poe*, 17.

43. Cavendish, "The Death of Edgar Allan Poe," 39.

44. "Poe's Life."
45. "Poe's Life."
46. Poe, *The Works of Edgar Allan Poe*, 3.
47. Cavendish, "The Death of Edgar Allan Poe," 39.
48. "The Raven," *And You Call Yourself a Rocket Scientist* ,www.aycyas. com/theraven1915.htm (accessed January 11, 2013).
49. Kevin Hayes, "Lunatics in Power (1909): A Neglected Poe Film," *Edgar Allan Poe Review* 1, no. 1 (Spring 2000): 13.
50. "Bethlem Royal Hospital," *Science Museum*, www.sciencemuseum.org. uk/broughttolife/techniques/bethlemroyalhospital.aspx (accessed August 19, 2012).
51. Jonny Metro, "Horror Explorer (Sneak Peek): 1913–1915," *Midnight Media* May 8, 2010, http://midnitemedia.blogspot.com/2010/05/horror-explorer-sneak-peek-1913-1915.html (accessed January 21, 2014).
52. Peter Byrne, "Fall and Rise of the Movie 'Psycho-Killer,'" *Psychiatric Bulletin* 22 (1998): 174–76.
53. David Brake, "Best Films Never Made: Sylvester Stallone's *Poe*," *Huffington Post*, October 17, 2013, www.huffingtonpost.com/david-brake/best-films-never-made-syl_b_4057550.html (accessed December 27, 2013).
54. Jamison, *Touched with Fire*, 80.
55. "The National Confidential Inquiry into Suicide and Homicide by People with Mental Illness" (annual report produced by the University of Manchester: England, Wales, Scotland and Northern Ireland, Manchester, England, July 2012), 6.

3. THE GOLDEN AGE OF SILENT FILMS AND MANIC DEPRESSION

1. Martin Sieff, "Chaplin Lifted Weary World's Spirits," *Washington Times*, December 21, 2008, www.washingtontimes.com/news/2008/dec/21/his-gift-of-comedy-for-a-weary-world/?page=all (accessed January 23, 2012).
2. Jan Fawcett, Bernard Golden, and Nancy Rosenfeld, *New Hope for People with Bipolar Disorder* (New York: Three Rivers Press, 2007), 40.
3. Stephen M. Weissman, "Charlie Chaplin's Film Heroines," *Welcome to the Silent Movies*, www.welcometosilentmovies.com/news/newsarchive/chaplin.htm (accessed December 23, 2012).
4. Weissman, "Charlie Chaplin's Film Heroines."
5. Fawcett et al., *New Hope for People with Bipolar Disorder*, 238.
6. Weissman, "Charlie Chaplin's Film Heroines."
7. Weissman, "Charlie Chaplin's Film Heroines."
8. Weissman, "Charlie Chaplin's Film Heroines."

9. Weissman, "Charlie Chaplin's Film Heroines."

10. Weissman, "Charlie Chaplin's Film Heroines."

11. Weissman, "Charlie Chaplin's Film Heroines."

12. Kay Redfield Jamison, *Touched with Fire: Manic-Depressive Illness and the Artistic Temperament* (New York: Free Press, 1996), 8.

13. Joyce Milton, *Tramp: The Life of Charlie Chaplin* (New York: Da Capo Press, 1998), 306.

14. Milton, *Tramp*, 421–22.

15. Milton, *Tramp*, 302–3.

16. Milton, *Tramp*, 306.

17. Milton, *Tramp*, 350–51.

18. Milton, *Tramp*, 274.

19. Milton, *Tramp*, 525.

20. Alan Vanneman, "Looking at Charlie—*City Lights*," *Bright Lights Film Journal*, February 2009, http://brightlightsfilm.com/63/63chaplin.php (accessed November 12, 2012).

21. Jamison, *Touched with Fire*, 121.

22. Milton, *Tramp*, 183.

23. D. Jablow Hershman, *Manic Depression and Creativity* (Amherst, NY: Prometheus Books, 1998), 9–10.

24. Glenys Roberts, "Revealed: The Dark Secrets about Charlie Chaplin's Mother That Fired His Genius," *Daily Mail*, December 7, 2009, www.dailymail.co.uk/femail/article-1233081/The-dark-secrets-Charlie-Chaplins-mother-fired-genius.html (accessed November 19, 2012).

25. Milton, *Tramp*, 185.

26. Milton, *Tramp*, 249.

27. Fawcett et al., *New Hope for People with Bipolar Disorder*, 310.

28. Milton, *Tramp*, 287.

29. Weissman, "Charlie Chaplin's Film Heroines."

30. Stephen Brockmann, *A Critical History of German Film* (Rochester, NY: Camden House, 2010), 61.

31. Brockmann, *A Critical History of German Film*, 64.

32. Robert Wiene, Robert Adkinson, Carl Mayer, and Hans Janowitz, *The Cabinet of Dr. Caligari: A Film* (Vancouver, Canada: Lorimer Publishing, 1984), 28.

33. Andrew Kelly, *Cinema and the Great War* (London: Routledge, 1997), 67.

34. Mark S. Micale and Paul Lerner, eds., *Traumatic Pasts: History, Psychiatry, and Trauma in the Modern Age, 1870–1930* (Cambridge: Cambridge University Press, 2001), 106–9.

35. Michael Toole, *"The Cabinet of Dr. Caligari," Turner Classic Movies*, http://www.tcm.com/this-month/article.html?isPreview=&id= 443507%7C87713&name=The-Cabinet-of-Dr-Caligari (accessed January 3, 2012).

36. Linda Badley, R. Barton Palmer, and Steven Jay Schneider, *Traditions in World Cinema* (New Brunswick, NJ: Rutgers University Press, 2006), 19.

37. Badley et al., *Traditions in World Cinema*, 19.

38. Toole, *"The Cabinet of Dr. Caligari."*

39. Kevin Brownlow, *The Parade's Gone By* (New York: Bonanza Books, 1983), 510.

40. Paula Vitaris, "The Influence of *The Cabinet of Dr. Caligari* on Upton Sinclair's *They Call Me Carpenter*," *The Conrad Veidt Society*, http://thethunderchild.com/ActorSites/ConradVeidt/page35.html (accessed November 11, 2012).

41. Phillip W. Long, "Bipolar I Disorder: Course," *Internet Mental Health*, www.mentalhealth.com/dis/p20-md02.html (accessed October 9, 2011).

42. Brockmann, *A Critical History of German Film*, 64.

43. "Depression with Catatonic Features," *Encyclopedia of Mental Disorders*, www.minddisorders.com/Br- Del/Catatonic-disorders.html (accessed September 4, 2012).

44. "Depression with Catatonic Features."

45. Fawcett et al., *New Hope for People with Bipolar Disorder*, 286–87.

46. Paul Chambers, *Bedlam: London's Hospital for the Mad* (Birmingham, UK: Ian Allan Publishing, 2009), 24.

47. "Chronic Depersonalization & Derealization," *Bipolar World*, July 2008, www.bipolarworld.net/Phelps/ph_2008/ph1752.htm (accessed January 9, 2013).

48. Jamison, *Touched with Fire*, 250.

49. Jamison, *Touched with Fire*, 262–65.

50. Clifton Fadiman and Andre Bernard, eds., *Bartlett's Book of Anecdotes* (Boston: Little, Brown and Company, 2000), 44.

51. Larry Harnisch, "Diana Barrymore Dies at 38," *Los Angeles Times*, January 26, 1960, http://latimesblogs.latimes.com/thedailymirror/2010/01/diana-barrymore-dies-at-38.html (accessed February 25, 2014).

52. Myrna Oliver, "John Drew Barrymore, 72; Troubled Heir to the Throne of the Royal Family of Acting," *Los Angeles Times*, December 1, 2004, http://articles.latimes.com/2004/dec/01/local/me-barrymore1 (accessed February 2, 2013).

53. Drew Barrymore, *Little Girl Lost* (New York: Pocket Books, 1990), 128.

54. Jamison, *Touched with Fire*, 192–94.

55. Virginie Sélavy, "Haxan (Witchcraft Through the Ages)," *Electric Sheep*, May 3, 2007, www.electricsheepmagazine.co.uk/reviews/2007/05/03/haxan-witchcraft-through-the-ages/ (accessed October 12, 2012).

56. Chris Fujiwara, "Häxan" October 15, 2001, www.criterion.com/current/posts/147-haxan (accessed October 18, 2012).

57. Fujiwara, "Häxan."

58. Sélavy, "Haxan (Witchcraft Through the Ages)."

59. S. Acharya, *Suns of Gods: Krishna, Buddha and Christ Unveiled* (Kempton, IL: Adventures Unlimited Press, 2004), 419.

60. Paul Carus, *The History of the Devil and the Idea of Evil* (New York: Gramercy Books, 1996), 314.

61. Allison M. Foerschner, "The History of Mental Illness: From 'Skull Drills' to 'Happy Pills,'" *Student Pulse* 2, no. 9 (2010): 1.

62. Carus, *The History of the Devil and the Idea of Evil*, 307.

63. Jasper Sharp, "*A Page of Madness*," *Midnight Eye*, March 7, 2002, www.midnighteye.com/features/a-page-of-madness/%20 (accessed February 14, 2013).

64. Sharp, "*A Page of Madness*."

65. Sharp, "*A Page of Madness*."

66. Amanda Doxtater, "Carl. Th. Dreyer—The Man and His Work," *Danish Film Institute*, August 17, 2011, http://english.carlthdreyer.dk/AboutDreyer/Working-method/Perilous-Performance.aspx (accessed January 18, 2013).

67. Jerry Whyte, "Soul on Ice," *CineOutsider*, February 5, 2013, www.cineoutsider.com/reviews/bluray/p/passion_of_joan_of_arc_1.html (accessed February 14, 2013).

68. Whyte, "Soul on Ice."

69. Doxtater, "Carl Th. Dreyer."

70. "Chronic Depersonalization & Derealization."

71. Whyte, "Soul on Ice."

72. Doxtater, "Carl. Th. Dreyer—The Man and His Work."

73. Whyte, "Soul on Ice."

74. Whyte, "Soul on Ice."

75. Whyte, "Soul on Ice."

76. Whyte, "Soul on Ice."

4. 1930S: BIPOLAR DISORDER SPEAKS AT THE MOVIES

1. Louis D. Giannetti, *Masters of the American Cinema* (Upper Saddle River, NJ: Prentice-Hall, 1981), 253.

2. Stephen D. Youngkin, "Peter Lorre: A Biographical Sketch," *The Lost One: A Life of Peter Lorre*, May 23, 2005, http://peterlorrebook.com/bio.html (accessed January 7, 2012).

3. Youngkin, "Peter Lorre."

4. Youngkin, "Peter Lorre."

5. Stephen D. Youngkin, *The Lost One: A Life of Peter Lorre* (Lexington: University Press of Kentucky, 2005), 55.

6. Youngkin, *The Lost One*, 55.

7. Youngkin, *The Lost One*, 134.

8. Youngkin, *The Lost One*, 238.

9. Youngkin, *The Lost One*, 313.

10. Youngkin, *The Lost One*, 284.

11. Youngkin, *The Lost One*, 314.

12. Youngkin, *The Lost One*, 392.

13. "Groucho Talks about Irving Thalberg & Greta Garbo," *Dick Cavett Show*, May 25, 1971, YouTube http://www.youtube.com/watch?v=ZzEflb-C8HU (accessed August 21, 2012).

14. Karen Swenson, *Greta Garbo: A Life Apart* (New York: Scribner, 1997), 471.

15. Diana Souhami, *Greta and Cecil* (San Francisco: HarperSanFrancisco, 1994), 65.

16. Swenson, *Greta Garbo*, 366.

17. Souhami, *Greta and Cecil*, 65.

18. Harold Bloom, *Bloom's Modern Critical Views: Eugene O'Neill—Updated Edition* (New York: Infobase Publishing, 2007), 49.

19. Frederick Goodwin and Kay Redfield Jamison, *Manic-Depressive Illness: Bipolar Disorders and Recurrent Depression*, 2nd edition (New York: Oxford University Press, 2007), 83.

20. Jan Fawcett, Bernard Golden, and Nancy Rosenfeld, *New Hope for People with Bipolar Disorder* (New York: Three Rivers Press, 2007), 261.

21. Roland Barthes, "The Face of Garbo," *Mythologies* (New York: Hill and Wang, 1972), 56.

22. Errol Trzebinski, *The Lives of Beryl Markham* (New York: W.W. Norton and Company, 1993), 253.

23. "Groucho Talks," *Dick Cavett Show*.

24. Roger Lewis, "I Want to Be Alone—with My Enormous Ego," *Daily Mail*, July 19, 2012, http://www.dailymail.co.uk/home/books/article-2176105/I-want--enormous-ego-Greta-Garbo-Divine-Star-By-David-Bret.html (accessed December 28, 2012).

25. Swenson, *Greta Garbo*, 31.

26. Jane Gunther, "There Was a Strange Melancholy in Her," *Garbo Forever*, 2005, http://www.garboforever.com/Garbo_Stories-09.htm (accessed December 29, 2012).

27. Len Sperry and Jon Carlson, eds., *Psychopathology and Psychotherapy: From DSM-IV Diagnosis to Treatment* (Philadelphia: Taylor & Francis, 1996), 79–82.

28. Jamison, *Touched with Fire*, 251–59.

29. Fawcett, et al, *New Hope for People with Bipolar Disorder*, 272–80.

30. David Kalat, *The Strange Case of Dr. Mabuse: A Study of the Twelve Films and Five Novels* (Jefferson, NC: McFarland, 2005), 76.

31. Barry Keith Grant, ed., *Fritz Lang: Interviews* (Oxford: University Press of Mississippi, 2003), 31.

32. Hubert Fernandez and Marcelo Merello, *Movement Disorders: Unforgettable Cases and Lessons from the Bedside* (New York: Demos Medical Publishing, 2013), 52.

33. Orli Van Mourik, "Hypergraphia: A River of Words," *Psychology Today*, May 1, 2007, http://www.psychologytoday.com/articles/200705/quirky-minds-hypergraphia-river-words (accessed March 14, 2013).

34. Van Mourik, "Hypergraphia."

35. Jamison, *Touched with Fire*, 16.

5. 1940S: THE EFFECTS OF WORLD WAR II ON BIPOLAR CINEMA

1. Frederick Goodwin and Kay Redfield Jamison, *Manic-Depressive Illness* (New York: Oxford University Press, 1990), 134.

2. Clinton Heylin, *Despite the System: Orson Welles versus the Hollywood Studios* (Edinburgh, UK: Canongate Books, 2005), 311.

3. Heylin, *Despite the System*, 311.

4. Simon Callow, *Orson Welles: Volume 2: Hello Americans* (New York: Viking, 2006), 413.

5. Heylin, *Despite the System*, 311.

6. Heylin, *Despite the System*, 312.

7. Heylin, *Despite the System*, 120–25.

8. Heylin, *Despite the System*, 311.

9. Heylin, *Despite the System*, 311.

10. Chris Welles Feder, *In My Father's Shadow: A Daughter Remembers Orson Welles* (Chapel Hill, NC: Algonquin Books, 2009), 180.

11. Feder, *In My Father's Shadow*, 238.

12. Feder, *In My Father's Shadow*, 238.

13. Jan Fawcett, Bernard Golden, and Nancy Rosenfeld, *New Hope for People with Bipolar Disorder* (New York: Three Rivers Press, 2007), 272–80.

14. Anthony Storr, *Churchill's Black Dog, Kafka's Mice and Other Phenomena of the Human Mind* (New York: Grove Press, 1988), 24.

15. Simon Callow, *Orson Welles: The Road to Xanadu* (New York: Viking, 1995), 26.

16. Goodwin and Jamison, *Manic-Depressive Illness*, 19.

17. Charles Higham, *Orson Welles: The Rise and Fall of an American Genius* (New York: St. Martin's Press, 1985), 53.

18. Higham, *Orson Welles*, 91–92.

19. Heylin, *Despite the System*, 312.

20. Higham, *Orson Welles*, 173.

21. Paul Huckerby, "F for Fake," *Electric Sheep*, August 23, 2012, www.electricsheepmagazine.co.uk/reviews/2012/08/23/f-for-fake/ (accessed February 26, 2014).

22. Joseph McBride, *Orson Welles* (Cambridge, MA: Da Capo Press, 1996), 117.

23. Steve Vertlieb, "Xanadu: A Castle in the Clouds: The Life of Orson Welles," *Viewzone*, http://www.viewzone.com/orson.html (accessed May 13, 2013).

24. Michael Parkinson, "Parkinson: The Orson Welles Interview," *BBC* 1974, www.youtube.com/watch?v=XlSOSuFdzfE (accessed May 13, 2013).

25. Kent Demaret, "Gene Tierney Began Her Trip Back from Madness on a Ledge 14 Floors Above the Street," *People*, May 1979, www.people.com/people/article/0,,20073581,00.html (accessed January 9, 2013).

26. Jerry Roberts, *The Hollywood Scandal Almanac* (Charleston, SC: History Press, 2012), 82.

27. Gene Tierney and Mickey Herskowitz, *Self-Portrait* (New York: Wyden Books, 1978), 44.

28. Tierney and Herskowitz, *Self-Portrait*, 32.

29. Madeline Vann, "Clang Associations in Bipolar Disorder," *Everyday Health*, July 13, 2010, www.everydayhealth.com/bipolar-disorder/clang-associations-in-bipolar-disorder.aspx (accessed January 8, 2014).

30. Goodwin and Jamison, *Manic-Depressive Illness*, 342–49.

31. Tierney and Herskowitz, *Self-Portrait*, 71–72.

32. Tierney and Herskowitz, *Self-Portrait*, 70.

33. Tierney and Herskowitz, *Self-Portrait*, 58.

34. Tierney and Herskowitz, *Self-Portrait*, 82.

35. Tierney and Herskowitz, *Self-Portrait*, 83.

36. Tierney and Herskowitz, *Self-Portrait*, 89.

37. Storr, *Churchill's Black Dog*, vii.

38. Tierney and Herskowitz, *Self-Portrait*, 84.

39. Tierney and Herskowitz, *Self-Portrait*, 148.

40. Tierney and Herskowitz, *Self-Portrait*, 160.

41. Tierney and Herskowitz, *Self-Portrait*, 37–38.

42. Tierney and Herskowitz, *Self-Portrait*, 166–67.

43. Goodwin and Jamison, *Manic-Depressive Illness*, 611.

44. Tierney and Herskowitz, *Self-Portrait*, 171.

45. Tierney and Herskowitz, *Self-Portrait*, 172.

46. Tierney and Herskowitz, *Self-Portrait*, 180.

47. Tierney and Herskowitz, *Self-Portrait*, 182–83.

48. Tierney and Herskowitz, *Self-Portrait*, 191.

49. Tierney and Herskowitz, *Self-Portrait*, 197.

50. Tierney and Herskowitz, *Self-Portrait*, 119.

51. Goodwin and Jamison, *Manic-Depressive Illness*, 660–61.

52. Kay Redfield Jamison, *Touched with Fire: Manic-Depressive Illness and the Artistic Temperament* (New York: Free Press, 1996), 191–94.

6. 1950S: PSYCHOLOGICAL REALISM IN BIPOLAR FILM DEPICTIONS

1. Karzan Kardozi, "The Cinema of Nicholas Ray," *The Moving Silent*, August 13, 2012, http://themovingsilent.wordpress.com/2012/08/13/the-cinema-of-nicholas-ray/ (accessed June 17, 2013).

2. "Nicholas Ray: Hollywood's Last Romantic," *Harvard Film Archives*, 2010, http://hcl.harvard.edu/hfa/films/2010julsep/ray.html (accessed June 17, 2013).

3. Patrick McGilligan, *Nicholas Ray: The Glorious Failure of an American Director* (New York: HarperCollins, 2011), 328.

4. Steve Ryfle, "Book Review: *Nicholas Ray* by Patrick McGilligan," *Los Angeles Times*, July 28, 2011, http://articles.latimes.com/2011/jul/28/entertainment/la-et-book-20110728 (accessed June 14, 2013).

5. McGilligan, *Nicholas Ray*, 7.

6. McGilligan, *Nicholas Ray*, 45.

7. McGilligan, *Nicholas Ray*, 87.

8. McGilligan, *Nicholas Ray*, 10.

9. Dean McKay and Eric Storch, eds., *Handbook of Assessing Variants and Complications in Anxiety Disorders* (New York: Springer Science+Business Media, 2013), 30.

10. McGilligan, *Nicholas Ray*, 330.

11. McGilligan, *Nicholas Ray*, 252–53.

12. McGilligan, *Nicholas Ray*, 279.

13. McGilligan, *Nicholas Ray*, 194.

14. McGilligan, *Nicholas Ray*, 446.

15. McGilligan, *Nicholas Ray*, 343.

16. McGilligan, *Nicholas Ray*, 276.

17. Andy Schwartz, "Not Directed by Nicholas Ray: *Wind Across the Everglades*," *New York Rocker*, July 30, 2009, www.nyrocker.com/blog/2009/07/not-directed-by-nicholas-ray-wind-across-the-everglades-film-forum-73009/ (accessed June 17, 2013).

18. Frederick Goodwin and Kay Redfield Jamison, *Manic-Depressive Illness* (New York: Oxford University Press, 1990), 360–63.

19. Hilary Smith, *Welcome to the Jungle: Everything You Ever Wanted to Know about Bipolar but Were Too Freaked Out to Ask* (San Francisco: Red Wheel/Weiser, 2010), 34.

20. McGilligan, *Nicholas Ray*, 302.

21. McGilligan, *Nicholas Ray*, 466.

22. Emanuel Levy, "*Rebel without a Cause*: Effects of Dean's Legendary Film," *Emanuel Levy Cinema*, July 24, 2005, http://emanuellevy.com/festival/rebel-without-a-causebreffects-of-deans-legendary-film-5/ (accessed March 3, 2013).

23. Joe Hyams and Jay Hyams, *James Dean: Little Boy Lost* (New York: Warner Books, 1992), 9.

24. Smith, *Welcome to the Jungle*, 126.

25. Hyams and Hyams, *James Dean*, 12.

26. Hyams and Hyams, *James Dean*, 16.

27. Hyams and Hyams, *James Dean*, 20.

28. Hyams and Hyams, *James Dean*, 104.

29. Hyams and Hyams, *James Dean*, 39–40.

30. David Dalton, *James Dean: The Mutant King: A Biography* (Chicago: A Cappella Books, 1974), 63.

31. S. Nassir Ghaemi, *Mood Disorders: A Practical Guide*, 2nd Edition (Philadelphia: Lippincott, Williams & Wilkins, 2008), 246.

32. Ghaemi, *Mood Disorders*, 244.

33. Hyams and Hyams, *James Dean*, 39–40.

34. Donald Spoto, *Rebel: The Life and Legend of James Dean* (New York: HarperCollins, 1996), 142–48.

35. Dalton, *James Dean*, 159.

36. Dalton, *James Dean*, 175.

37. Mary Ann Doane, *The Desire to Desire: The Woman's Film of the 1940s* (Bloomington: Indiana University Press, 1987), 45–46.

38. Dalton, *James Dean*, 110.

39. Hyams and Hyams, *James Dean*, 181.

40. Dalton, *James Dean*, 78.

41. Hyams and Hyams, *James Dean*, 42.

42. Hyams and Hyams, *James Dean*, 103.

43. Hyams and Hyams, *James Dean*, 182.

44. Hyams and Hyams, *James Dean*, 261.

45. McGilligan, *Nicholas Ray*, 36.

46. Smith, *Welcome to the Jungle*, 72.

47. Dalton, *James Dean*, 51–52.

48. Geoffrey O'Brien, "The Jimmy Stewart Story," *New York Review of Books* , 2006, www.nybooks.com/articles/archives/2006/nov/02/the-jimmy-stewart-story/?pagination=false (accessed June 18, 2013).

49. O'Brien, "The Jimmy Stewart Story."

50. "Hitchcock Talks about *Vertigo*," *Cine-Phile.com*, July 12, 2013,(accessed January 8, 2014).

51. Patrick McGilligan, *Alfred Hitchcock: A Life in Darkness and Light* (New York: HaperCollins, 2003), 82.

52. Ghaemi, *Mood Disorders*, 13.

53. Ghaemi, *Mood Disorders*, 13.

54. "Hitchcock Talks about *Vertigo*."

55. "Hitchcock Talks about *Vertigo*."

56. Kevin Jagernauth, "'*Vertigo*' Replaces '*Citizen Kane*' On *Sight & Sound* Greatest of All Time List," *IndieWire*, August 1, 2012, http://blogs.indiewire.com/theplaylist/vertigo-replaces-citizen-kane-on-sight-sound-greatest-of-all-time-list-20120801 (accessed January 24, 2013).

57. Rebecca Keegan, "Kim Novak Says She's Bipolar, Regrets Leaving Hollywood," *Los Angeles Times*, April 13, 2012, http://latimesblogs.latimes.com/movies/2012/04/kim-novak-says-shes-bipolar-regrets-leaving-hollywood.html (accessed November 8, 2013).

58. Keegan, "Kim Novak."

59. Keegan, "Kim Novak."

60. Keegan, "Kim Novak."

61. "Hitchcock Talks about *Vertigo*."

62. Donald Spoto, *The Dark Side of Genius: The Life of Alfred Hitchcock* (New York: Da Capo Press, 1999), 39–40.

63. Spoto, *The Dark Side of Genius*, 39–40.

64. Spoto, *The Dark Side of Genius*, 37.

65. Spoto, *The Dark Side of Genius*, 550.

66. Spoto, *The Dark Side of Genius*, 550.

67. Chelsea Lowe and Bruce Cohen, *Living with Someone Who's Living with Bipolar Disorder: A Practical Guide for Family, Friends, and Coworkers* (San Francisco: Jossey-Bass, 2010), 46.

68. Goodwin and Jamison, *Manic-Depressive Illness*, 738–41.

69. Deborah Serani, *Living with Depression: Why Biology and Biography Matter along the Path to Hope and Healing* (Lanham, MD: Rowman & Littlefield, 2011), 119.

70. Mark E. Neely, Jr. and R. Gerald McMurtry, *The Insanity File: The Case of Mary Todd Lincoln* (Carbondale: Southern Illinois University Press, 1993), 127.

71. Piers Morgan, "Interview with Larry Flynt," *Piers Morgan Tonight*, April 20, 2011, http://transcripts.cnn.com/TRANSCRIPTS/1104/20/pmt.01. html (accessed May 3, 2012).

72. Anne Edwards, *Judy Garland: A Biography* (Lanham, MD: Taylor Trade Publishing, 2013), 67.

73. Emanuel Levy, *Vincente Minnelli: Hollywood's Dark Dreamer* (New York: St. Martin's Press, 2009), 82.

74. "Biography," *Vivien-Leigh.Info*, 2013, http://vivien-leigh.info/biography/ (accessed May 19, 2013).

75. "Biography," *Vivien-Leigh.Info*.

76. "Biography," *Vivien-Leigh.Info*.

77. "Biography," *Vivien-Leigh.Info*.

78. "Biography," *Vivien-Leigh.Info*.

79. "Biography," *Vivien-Leigh.Info*.

80. "Biography," *Vivien-Leigh.Info*.

81. "Biography," *Vivien-Leigh.Info*.

82. Alexander Walker, *Vivien: The Life of Vivien Leigh* (New York: Grove Press, 1987), 214.

83. "Biography," *Vivien-Leigh.Info*.

84. Terry Coleman, *Olivier* (New York: Henry Holt, 2005), 360.

85. Scott McGee, "Behind the Camera on *A Streetcar Named Desire*," *Turner Classic Movies*, 2012, www.tcm.com/this-month/article/ 286298%7C286309/Behind-the-Camera-A-Streetcar-Named-Desire.html (accessed May 23, 2013).

86. "Tennessee Lanier Williams," *The Biography Channel*, 2014, www. biography.com/people/tennessee-williams-9532952 (accessed February 25, 2014).

87. Jack Lawler, "New Orleans: The Spiritual Home of Tennessee Williams," *Literary New Orleans*, April 2, 2013, http://urliteraryneworleans. wordpress.com/2013/04/02/new-orleans-the-spiritual-home-of-tennessee-williams/ (accessed June 10, 2013).

88. Tennessee Williams, *Memoirs* (New York: New Directions, 2006), 194.

89. "Biography," *Vivien-Leigh.Info*.

90. "Biography," *Vivien-Leigh.Info*.

91. Coleman, *Olivier*, 249.

92. "Biography," *Vivien-Leigh.Info*.

93. "Williams and the Grotesque," *Tennessee Williams Annual Review* No. 8 (2006), www.tennesseewilliamsstudies.org/archives/2006/10grotesque_panel. htm (accessed June 17, 2013).

94. "Biography," *Vivien-Leigh.Info*.

95. Anne Edwards, *Vivien Leigh: A Biography* (Lanham, MD: Taylor Trade Publishing, 2013), 287.

96. "Biography," *Vivien-Leigh.Info*.

97. Akira Kurosawa, *Something Like an Autobiography* (New York: Vintage, 1983), 72–75.

98. Kurosawa, *Something Like an Autobiography*, 45.

99. Kurosawa, *Something Like an Autobiography*, 72.

100. Kurosawa, *Something Like an Autobiography*, 13.

101. Kurosawa, *Something Like an Autobiography*, 52–53.

102. Oliver Ho, "*Akira Kurosawa: Master of Cinema* by Peter Cowie," *Pop-Matters*, March 5, 2010, www.popmatters.com/pm/review/121687-akira-kurosawa-master-of-cinema-by-peter-cowie/ (accessed June 3, 2013).

103. Ho, "*Akira Kurosawa*."

104. Kurosawa, *Something Like an Autobiography*, 151.

105. Kurosawa, *Something Like an Autobiography*, 183.

106. Ho, "*Akira Kurosawa*."

107. Ho, "*Akira Kurosawa*."

108. Kurosawa, *Something Like an Autobiography*, 191–98.

109. Kurosawa, *Something Like an Autobiography*, 191–98.

7. 1960S: THE LIBERALIZATION OF MANIC-DEPRESSIVE STEREOTYPES IN CINEMA

1. Frederick Goodwin and Kay Redfield Jamison, *Manic-Depressive Illness* (New York: Oxford University Press, 1990), 301–9.

2. James Wolcott, "Tru Grit," *Vanity Fair*, October 2005, www.vanityfair. com/culture/features/2005/10/wolcott200510 (accessed July 1, 2013).

3. Truman Capote, *Answered Prayers* (New York: Vintage, 2012), 54.

4. Deborah Davis, *Party of the Century: The Fabulous Story of Truman Capote and His Black and White Ball* (Hoboken, NJ: John Wiley & Sons, 2006), 7.

5. Donald Spoto, *Marilyn Monroe: The Biography* (New York: Cooper Square Press, 2001), 324.

6. Sarah Churchwell, "*Breakfast at Tiffany's*: When Audrey Hepburn Won Marilyn Monroe's Role," *Guardian*, September 4, 2009, www.theguardian.com/books/2009/sep/05/breakfast-at-tiffanys-audrey-hepburn (accessed February 2, 2014).

7. Barry Paris, *Audrey Hepburn* (New York: Berkley Books, 1996), 167.

8. Jere Hester, "Audrey Hepburn Bio Reveals the Pain Behind the Fame," *Chicago Tribune*, December 31, 1993, http://articles.chicagotribune.com/1993-12-31/features/9312310372_1_audrey-hepburn-roman-holiday-intimate-portrait (accessed December 19, 2013).

9. Hester, "Audrey Hepburn."

10. "Interview with Blake Edwards," *Larry King Show*, July 27, 2002, http://transcripts.cnn.com/TRANSCRIPTS/0207/27/lklw.00.html (accessed April 4, 2013).

11. "Interview with Blake Edwards."

12. Goodwin and Jamison, *Manic-Depressive Illness*, 19.

13. Dennis McLellan, "Blake Edwards Dies at 88; '*Pink Panther*' Director Was Master of Slapstick Comedy," *Los Angeles Times*, December 17, 2010, http://articles.latimes.com/2010/dec/17/local/la-me-blake-edwards-20101217 (accessed May 4, 2013).

14. Roger Lewis, *The Life and Death of Peter Sellers* (New York: Applause Books, 1997), xx.

15. Lewis, *The Life and Death of Peter Sellers*, 11.

16. Leslie Halliwell, *Halliwell's Filmgoer's Companion* (1988), 622.

17. Lewis, *The Life and Death of Peter Sellers*, 15.

18. Lewis, *The Life and Death of Peter Sellers*, 17.

19. Lewis, *The Life and Death of Peter Sellers*, 319.

20. Lewis, *The Life and Death of Peter Sellers*, 171.

21. Lewis, *The Life and Death of Peter Sellers*, 88.

22. Lewis, *The Life and Death of Peter Sellers*, 123.

23. Lewis, *The Life and Death of Peter Sellers*, 298.

24. Ed Sikov, *Mr. Strangelove: A Biography of Peter Sellers* (New York: Hyperion, 2002), 248.

25. Lewis, *The Life and Death of Peter Sellers*, 298.

26. Lewis, *The Life and Death of Peter Sellers*, 145.

27. Lewis, *The Life and Death of Peter Sellers*, 132.

28. Lewis, *The Life and Death of Peter Sellers*, 338.

29. Lewis, *The Life and Death of Peter Sellers*, 339.

30. Sikov, *Mr. Strangelove*, 272.

31. Sikov, *Mr. Strangelove*, 55.

32. Lewis, *The Life and Death of Peter Sellers*, 306.

33. "Interview with Blake Edwards."

34. Ingmar Bergman, *Images: My Life in Film* (New York: Arcade, 1995), 16.

35. Bergman, *Images*, 25.

36. Bergman, *Images*, 122.

37. Bergman, *Images*, 124.

38. "Ingmar Bergman: The Legendary *Playboy* Interview," *Playboy*, June 1964; *Euro Screenwriters* 2011, http://zakka.dk/euroscreenwriters/interviews/ingmar_bergman_02.htm (accessed May 7, 2013).

39. Bergman, *Images*, 201.

40. "Ingmar Bergman."

41. "Ingmar Bergman."

42. Bergman, *Images*, 39.

43. Bergman, *Images*, 80.

44. "Ingmar Bergman."

45. "Ingmar Bergman."

46. Bergman, *Images*, 161.

47. Bergman, *Images*, 197.

48. Costanzo Costantini, *Conversations with Fellini* (New York: Mariner Press, 1997), 73.

49. Goodwin and Jamison, *Manic-Depressive Illness*, 49.

50. Costantini, *Conversations with Fellini*, 80–81.

51. Costantini, *Conversations with Fellini*, 94.

52. Costantini, *Conversations with Fellini*, 99–100.

53. Costantini, *Conversations with Fellini*, 99–100.

54. Costantini, *Conversations with Fellini*, 141.

55. Costantini, *Conversations with Fellini*, 127.

56. Tony Maraini, "Interview with Federico Fellini," *Euro Screenwriters* 2011, http://zakka.dk/euroscreenwriters/interviews/federico_fellini_02.htm (accessed May 5, 2013).

57. Maraini, "Interview with Federico Fellini."

58. Costantini, *Conversations with Fellini*, 80–81.

59. Costantini, *Conversations with Fellini*, 192.

60. Costantini, *Conversations with Fellini*, 185.

61. Maraini, "Interview with Federico Fellini."

8. 1970S: THE MANIC-DEPRESSIVE TEMPERAMENT DEFINES NEW HOLLYWOOD

1. Kenji Tsuchiya, Esben Agerbo, and Preben Mortensen, "Parental Death and Bipolar Disorder: A Robust Association Was Found in Early Maternal Suicide," *Journal of Affective Disorders* 86, no. 2 (June 2005): 151–59.

2. Peter Biskind, *Easy Riders, Raging Bulls: How the Sex-Drugs-and-Rock 'n' Roll Generation Saved Hollywood* (New York: Simon & Schuster, 1999), 149.

3. Eleanor Coppola, *Notes: The Making of Apocalypse Now* (New York: Limelight Editions, 1979), 124.

4. Biskind, *Easy Riders, Raging Bulls*, 149.

5. Coppola, *Notes*, 266–67.

6. Coppola, *Notes*, 267.

7. Coppola, *Notes*, 267.

8. Coppola, *Notes*, 41.

9. Coppola, *Notes*, 88.

10. Coppola, *Notes*, 44.

11. Frederick Goodwin and Kay Redfield Jamison, *Manic-Depressive Illness* (New York: Oxford University Press, 1990), 39.

12. Coppola, *Notes*, 44.

13. Coppola, *Notes*, 137.

14. Biskind, *Easy Riders, Raging Bulls*, 350.

15. Biskind, *Easy Riders, Raging Bulls*, 350.

16. Goodwin and Jamison, *Manic-Depressive Illness*, 286.

17. Goodwin and Jamison, *Manic-Depressive Illness*, 336.

18. Biskind, *Easy Riders, Raging Bulls*, 367.

19. Biskind, *Easy Riders, Raging Bulls*, 372.

20. Biskind, *Easy Riders, Raging Bulls*, 372.

21. Biskind, *Easy Riders, Raging Bulls*, 276.

22. Andrew Yule, *Picture Shows: The Life and Films of Peter Bogdanovich* (New York: Limelight Editions, 2004), 5.

23. Jon Hopwood, "Biography for Peter Bogdanovich," *Internet Movie Database*, www.imdb.com/name/nm0000953/bio (accessed September 1, 2013).

24. Ryan Gilbey, "Polly Platt Obituary," *Guardian*, August 7, 2011, www.theguardian.com/film/2011/aug/07/polly-platt-obituary (accessed May 15, 2013).

25. Rachel Abramowitz, "She's Done Everything," *Premiere*, November 1993, www.maryellenmark.com/text/magazines/premiere/919V-000-004.html (accessed May 16, 2013).

26. Abramowitz, "She's Done Everything."

27. Abramowitz, "She's Done Everything."

28. Dana Harris, "Peter Bogdanovich Talks about Ben Gazzara," *Indiewire*, February 3, 2012, www.indiewire.com/article/peter-bogdanovich-talks-about-ben-gazzara-i-dont-think-they-make-actors-like-ben-anymore (accessed May 2, 2013).

29. Abramowitz, "She's Done Everything."

30. Marion Meade, *The Unruly Life of Woody Allen: A Biography* (New York: Scribner, 2000), 35.

31. Meade, *The Unruly Life of Woody Allen*, 100.

32. Meade, *The Unruly Life of Woody Allen*, 111.

33. Faith Brynie, "Depression and Anhedonia," *Psychology Today*, December 21, 2009, www.psychologytoday.com/blog/brain-sense/200912/depression-and-anhedonia (accessed May 2, 2013).

34. Brynie, "Depression and Anhedonia."

35. Goodwin and Jamison, *Manic-Depressive Illness*, 336–39.

36. Meade, *The Unruly Life of Woody Allen*, 311.

37. Robert E. Lauder, "Whatever Works: Woody Allen's World," *Commonweal*, April 15, 2010, www.commonwealmagazine.org/print/5255 (accessed May 14, 2013).

38. Meade, *The Unruly Life of Woody Allen*, 46.

39. Meade, *The Unruly Life of Woody Allen*, 70–71.

40. Meade, *The Unruly Life of Woody Allen*, 70–71.

41. Meade, *The Unruly Life of Woody Allen*, 100.

42. Meade, *The Unruly Life of Woody Allen*, 127.

43. Meade, *The Unruly Life of Woody Allen*, 104.

44. Meade, *The Unruly Life of Woody Allen*, 99.

45. Richard Schickel, *Conversations with Scorsese* (New York: Alfred A. Knopf, 2011), 9.

46. Schickel, *Conversations with Scorsese*, 25.

47. Schickel, *Conversations with Scorsese*, 33.

48. Biskind, *Easy Riders, Raging Bulls*, 151.

49. Schickel, *Conversations with Scorsese*, 341.

50. Schickel, *Conversations with Scorsese*, 12.

51. Schickel, *Conversations with Scorsese*, 6–7.

52. *Bright Wall/Dark Room*, June 19, 2013, http://brightwalldarkroom.com/post/53373216867/when-he-was-11-years-old-martin-scorsese-drew-up (accessed September 14, 2014).

53. Schickel, *Conversations with Scorsese*, 295.

54. Biskind, *Easy Riders, Raging Bulls*, 238.

55. Schickel, *Conversations with Scorsese*, 83.

56. Biskind, *Easy Riders, Raging Bulls*, 239.

57. Schickel, *Conversations with Scorsese*, 83.

58. Schickel, *Conversations with Scorsese*, 119.

59. Schickel, *Conversations with Scorsese*, 350.

60. "Navy Yard Shooter Got Clean Bill of Mental Health Just Weeks before Killing 12 People in Gun Rampage," *Daily Mail*, January 31, 2014, www.dailymail.co.uk/news/article-2549504/No-problem-VA-doctors-concluded-Aaron-Alexis-no-mental-health-issues-killing-12-people-Navy-Yard.html (accessed February 2, 2014).

61. Biskind, *Easy Riders, Raging Bulls*, 238–39.

62. Biskind, *Easy Riders, Raging Bulls*, 238.

63. Biskind, *Easy Riders, Raging Bulls*, 305.

64. Biskind, *Easy Riders, Raging Bulls*, 287.

65. Biskind, *Easy Riders, Raging Bulls*, 288.

66. Biskind, *Easy Riders, Raging Bulls*, 289.

67. Biskind, *Easy Riders, Raging Bulls*, 288.

68. Biskind, *Easy Riders, Raging Bulls*, 289.

69. Biskind, *Easy Riders, Raging Bulls*, 290.

70. Biskind, *Easy Riders, Raging Bulls*, 234.

71. Biskind, *Easy Riders, Raging Bulls*, 286.

72. Biskind, *Easy Riders, Raging Bulls*, 286.

73. Biskind, *Easy Riders, Raging Bulls*, 295.

74. Andrew Stille, "Paul Schrader: Steps to Writing a Script," *Diary of a Screenwriter*, April 18, 2012, http://diaryofascreenwriter.blogspot.com/2012/04/paul-schrader-steps-to-writing-script.html (accessed May 16, 2012).

75. Biskind, *Easy Riders, Raging Bulls*, 290.

76. Stille, "Paul Schrader."

77. Biskind, *Easy Riders, Raging Bulls*, 290.

78. Biskind, *Easy Riders, Raging Bulls*, 290.

79. Biskind, *Easy Riders, Raging Bulls*, 287.

80. Biskind, *Easy Riders, Raging Bulls*, 234.

81. Biskind, *Easy Riders, Raging Bulls*, 293.

82. Biskind, *Easy Riders, Raging Bulls*, 294.

83. Biskind, *Easy Riders, Raging Bulls*, 412.

84. Biskind, *Easy Riders, Raging Bulls*, 349.

85. John Sandford, *The New German Cinema* (Totowa, NJ: Barnes and Noble Books, 1980), 64.

86. Michael Toteberg and Leo Lensing, eds., *The Anarchy of the Imagination* (Baltimore, MD: Johns Hopkins University Press, 1992), 110.

87. Toteberg and Lensing, *The Anarchy of the Imagination*, 109–11.

88. Toteberg and Lensing, *The Anarchy of the Imagination*, 72.

89. Sandford, *The New German Cinema*, 101.

90. Toteberg and Lensing, *The Anarchy of the Imagination*, 207.

91. Klaus Kinski, *Kinski Uncut: The Autobiography of Klaus Kinski* (New York: Viking, 1996), 11.

92. Kinski, *Kinski Uncut*, 17.

93. Kinski, *Kinski Uncut*, 24.

94. "Klaus, Wrath of Werner," *Guardian*, May 21, 1999, www.theguardian. com/film/1999/may/21/comment (accessed July 2013).

95. Kinski, *Kinski Uncut*, 64.

96. Kinski, *Kinski Uncut*, 72.

97. Kinski, *Kinski Uncut*, 79.

98. Kinski, *Kinski Uncut*, 93.

99. "Asylum Records Confirm Klaus Kinski's Madness," *Local*, July 22, 2008, www.thelocal.de/society/20080722-13215.html (accessed March 27, 2012).

100. "Asylum Records Confirm Klaus Kinski's Madness."

101. "Asylum Records Confirm Klaus Kinski's Madness."

102. Goodwin and Jamison, *Manic-Depressive Illness*, 190–91.

103. Jan Fawcett, Bernard Golden, and Nancy Rosenfeld, *New Hope for People with Bipolar Disorder* (New York: Three Rivers Press, 2007), 35–36.

104. "Asylum Records Confirm Klaus Kinski's Madness."

105. Kinski, *Kinski Uncut*, 96.

106. Kinski, *Kinski Uncut*, 41.

107. Kinski, *Kinski Uncut*, 110.

108. Kinski, *Kinski Uncut*, 208.

109. Kinski, *Kinski Uncut*, 172.

110. Kinski, *Kinski Uncut*, 200–205.

111. Kinski, *Kinski Uncut*, 213–14.

112. Kinski, *Kinski Uncut*, 284.

113. Toteberg and Lensing, *The Anarchy of the Imagination*, 125, 174.

114. Kinski, *Kinski Uncut*, 240.

115. Kinski, *Kinski Uncut*, 242.

9. 1980S–1990S: THE BURGEONING DIVERSITY OF DEPRESSIVE EXPRESSIONISM

1. Frederick Goodwin and Kay Redfield Jamison, *Manic-Depressive Illness* (New York: Oxford University Press, 1990), 493.

2. Jack Mathews, "The Upstream Struggle for '*River's Edge*,'" *Los Angeles Times*, July 16, 1987, http://articles.latimes.com/1987-07-16/entertainment/ca-4226_1_script-readers (accessed October 3, 2012).

3. Goodwin and Jamison, *Manic-Depressive Illness*, 281–83.

4. Cheryl Paradis, "Mel Gibson and a Leaked Tape," *Psychology Today*, July 14, 2010, www.psychologytoday.com/blog/the-measure-madness/201007/mel-gibson-and-leaked-tape (accessed May 9, 2013).

5. Goodwin and Jamison, *Manic-Depressive Illness*, 45.

6. Elicia Murray and Garry Maddox, "Mel Opens Up, but Ever So Fleetingly," *Sydney Morning Herald*, May 15, 2008, www.smh.com.au/news/stay-in-touch/mel-gibson-talks-about-bipolar-struggle/2008/05/14/1210444527205.html (accessed May 9, 2013).

7. Joe Eszterhas, *Heaven and Mel: A Kindle Single* (San Jose, CA: Amazon Kindle, 2012), Section I: *The Passion of the Christ*.

8. Eszterhas, *Heaven and Mel*.

9. Grady Smith, "Robert Downey Jr. Asks Hollywood to Forgive Mel Gibson at American Cinematheque Awards," October 15, 2011, http://insidemovies.ew.com/2011/10/15/robert-downey-jr-forgive-mel-gibson/ (accessed May 12, 2013).

10. Peter Biskind, "The Rude Warrior," *Vanity Fair*, March 2011, www.vanityfair.com/hollywood/features/2011/03/mel-gibson-201103 (accessed March 14, 2013).

11. "Box office business for *The Beaver*," *IMDB*, www.imdb.com/title/tt1321860/business?ref_=tt_dt_bus (accessed March 17, 2013).

12. "Joe Eszterhas' Letter to Mel Gibson," *Wrap*, April 11, 2012, www.thewrap.com/movies/article/joe-eszterhas-letter-mel-gibson-36949 (accessed July 19, 2013).

13. Juan Caceres, "LatinoBuzz: The House That Joseph B. Vasquez Built," *Indiewire*, May 15, 2013, http://blogs.indiewire.com/sydneylevine/latinobuzz-the-house-that-joseph-b-vasquez-built (accessed November 26, 2013).

14. Mark Harris, "South Bronx Story: Hanging Out with Joseph B. Vasquez," *Entertainment Weekly*, June 7, 1991, www.ew.com/ew/article/0,,314529,00.html (accessed November 26, 2013).

15. Mark Harris, "Remembering Joe Vasquez," *Entertainment Weekly*, February 9, 1996, www.ew.com/ew/article/0,,291314_2,00.html (accessed November 26, 2013).

16. Harris, "Remembering Joe Vasquez."

17. Harris, "Remembering Joe Vasquez."

18. Harris, "South Bronx Story."

19. Harris, "Remembering Joe Vasquez."

20. Harris, "Remembering Joe Vasquez."

21. Harris, "Remembering Joe Vasquez."

22. Harris, "Remembering Joe Vasquez."

23. Harris, "Remembering Joe Vasquez."

24. Harris, "Remembering Joe Vasquez."

25. Harris, "Remembering Joe Vasquez."

26. Mark Salisbury, ed., *Burton on Burton* (London: Faber and Faber, 1995), x.

27. Salisbury, *Burton on Burton*, x.

28. David Breskin, "Tim Burton: The Rolling Stone Interview," *Rolling Stone*, July 1992; *The Tim Burton Collective*, www.timburtoncollective.com/articles/misc5.html (accessed March 17, 2012).

29. Breskin, "Tim Burton."

30. Breskin, "Tim Burton."

31. Ken Hanke, *Tim Burton: An Unauthorized Biography of the Filmmaker* (Los Angeles: Renaissance Books, 1999), 97.

32. Breskin, "Tim Burton."

33. Hanke, *Tim Burton*, 28.

34. Hanke, *Tim Burton*, 27.

35. Breskin, "Tim Burton."

36. Hanke, *Tim Burton*, 37–38.

37. Salisbury, *Burton on Burton*, 4.

38. Breskin, "Tim Burton."

39. Breskin, "Tim Burton."

40. Breskin, "Tim Burton."

41. Salisbury, *Burton on Burton*, 50.

42. Hanke, *Tim Burton*, 82.

43. Hanke, *Tim Burton*, 22.

44. Salisbury, *Burton on Burton*, 102.

45. Simon Garfield, "When Hell Burst Through the Pavement and Grew: Anton Furst Conjured Up *Batman*'s Gotham City," *The Independent*, July 4, 1992, www.independent.co.uk/life-style/when-hell-burst-through-the-pavement-and-grew-anton-furst-conjured-up-batmans-gotham-city-in-england-he-was-a-creator-of-dreams-but-in-hollywood-his-dreams-ended-simon-garfield-reports-1531040.html (accessed May 24, 2012).

46. Hanke, *Tim Burton*, 121.

47. Hanke, *Tim Burton*, 121.

48. Breskin, "Tim Burton."

49. Hanke, *Tim Burton*, 135.

50. Hanke, *Tim Burton*, 151.

51. Hanke, *Tim Burton*, 152.

52. Salisbury, *Burton on Burton*, 1-2.

53. Kristine McKenna, "Steeled Magnolia: It Seems as if Jessica Lange is a Supermarket Shelf of Emotions," *Los Angeles Times*, March 19, 1995, http://

articles.latimes.com/1995-03-19/entertainment/ca-44583_1_jessica-lange (accessed March 22, 2012).

54. Dana Kennedy, "A Winner Never Quits," *Entertainment Weekly*, April 14, 1995, www.ew.com/ew/article/0,,296786,00.html (accessed March 22, 2012).

55. Kennedy, "A Winner Never Quits."

56. "Jessica Lange's Dark Magic Interview," *Oh No They Didn't!* November 11, 2013, http://ohnotheydidnt.livejournal.com/83127089.html (accessed November 14, 2013).

57. Janene Mascarella, "Bipolar Disorder and Legal Issues," *Everyday Health*, November 13, 2008, www.everydayhealth.com/bipolar-disorder/bipolar-disorder-and-legal-issues.aspx (accessed June 8, 2013).

58. Mascarella, "Bipolar Disorder and Legal Issues."

59. Jeffrey Kauffman, "Frances Farmer: Shedding Light on *Shadowland*," *Jeffrey Kauffman.net* 2013, http://jeffreykauffman.net/francesfarmer/sheddinglight.html (accessed November 14, 2013).

60. Kauffman, "Frances Farmer."

61. Kennedy, "A Winner Never Quits."

62. Alan Cumming, "Jessica Lange," *Interview*, November 2013, www.interviewmagazine.com/culture/jessica-lange/ (accessed November 14, 2013).

10. 2000S: BIPOLAR CINEMA FULLY EMERGES FROM LINGERING SHADOWS

1. James Dao, "Vets' Mental Health Diagnoses Rising," *New York Times*, July 16, 2009, www.nytimes.com/2009/07/17/health/views/17vets.html?_r=0 (accessed January 8, 2014).

2. Dina Gusovsky, "Congressional Chairman Says Veterans Affairs 'Overwhelmed,'" *CNBC*, November 11, 2013, www.cnbc.com/id/101188279 (accessed January 8, 2014).

3. John Grohol, "Mental Health Care Benefits Under Affordable Care Act (Obamacare)," *Psych Central*, July 2, 2012, http://psychcentral.com/news/2012/06/30/mental-health-care-benefits-under-affordable-care-act-obamacare/41052.html (accessed January 8, 2014).

4. "State Mental Health Cuts: The Continuing Crisis," *National Alliance on Mental Health*, November 2011, www.nami.org/ContentManagement/ContentDisplay.cfm?ContentFileID=147763 (accessed January 8, 2014).

5. Matt Finkelstein, "Poll: Less Than 1 Percent Favor Repealing Coverage for Pre-Existing Conditions," *Political Correction*, January 21, 2011, http://politicalcorrection.org/blog/201101210005 (accessed January 9, 2014).

6. Janet Fife-Yeomans, *Heath: A Family's Tale* (New York: Fall River Press, 2009), 306.

7. Fife-Yeomans, *Heath: A Family's Tale*, 296.

8. Fife-Yeomans, *Heath: A Family's Tale*, 306.

9. Frederick Goodwin and Kay Redfield Jamison, *Manic-Depressive Illness* (New York: Oxford University Press, 1990), 14.

10. Fife-Yeomans, *Heath: A Family's Tale*, 265.

11. Fife-Yeomans, *Heath: A Family's Tale*, 238.

12. Jamie Alridge, "Did Heath Ledger Suffer from Bipolar Disorder? His Symptoms Suggest He Did," *Examiner*, May 14, 2012, www.examiner.com/article/did-heath-ledger-suffer-from-bipolar-disorder-his-symptoms-suggest-he-did (accessed June 19, 2013).

13. Richard Pendlebury, "Drugs, Depression and a Lost Love—the Truth about the Lonely Death of Heath Ledger," *Daily Mail*, January 24, 2008, www.dailymail.co.uk/tvshowbiz/article-510066/Drugs-depression-lost-love--truth-lonely-death-Heath-Ledger.html (accessed September 9, 2012).

14. Fife-Yeomans, *Heath: A Family's Tale*, 239.

15. Fife-Yeomans, *Heath: A Family's Tale*, 238.

16. Pendlebury, "Drugs, Depression and a Lost Love."

17. Fife-Yeomans, *Heath: A Family's Tale*, 278.

18. Pendlebury, "Drugs, Depression and a Lost Love."

19. Fife-Yeomans, *Heath: A Family's Tale*, 266.

20. Fife-Yeomans, *Heath: A Family's Tale*, 262.

21. Fife-Yeomans, *Heath: A Family's Tale*, 257.

22. Fife-Yeomans, *Heath: A Family's Tale*, 258–60.

23. Goodwin and Jamison, *Manic-Depressive Illness*, 24–25.

24. Goodwin and Jamison, *Manic-Depressive Illness*, 139.

25. Fife-Yeomans, *Heath: A Family's Tale*, 273.

26. Fife-Yeomans, *Heath: A Family's Tale*, 278.

27. "Arrested Christian Bale 'Depressed' over Heath Ledger's Death," *News.com.au*, July 23, 2008, www.news.com.au/news/arrested-bale-depressed-over-ledger/story-fna7dq6e-1111116991829 (accessed June 23, 2013).

28. Sean Desmond, "Daniel Johnston on Meds," *Medicine Agency* on Vimeo, June 9, 2010, http://vimeo.com/11938066 (accessed December 17, 2013).

29. "Interview: Lars Von Trier," *Melancholia* 2011, www.melancholiathemovie.com/#_interview (accessed December 3, 2013).

30. Goodwin and Jamison, *Manic-Depressive Illness*, 139.

31. Per Juul Carlsen, "The Only Redeeming Factor Is the World Ending," *Danish Film Institute*, May 4, 2011, www.dfi.dk/Service/English/News-and-publications/FILM-Magazine/Artikler-fra-tidsskriftet-FILM/72/The-Only-Redeeming-Factor-is-the-World-Ending.aspx (accessed June 9, 2012).

32. Carlsen, "The Only Redeeming Factor Is the World Ending."

33. Carlsen, "The Only Redeeming Factor Is the World Ending."

34. Paul Andrews and J. Anderson Thomson, Jr., "Depression's Evolutionary Roots: Two Scientists Suggest That Depression Is Not a Malfunction, but a Mental Adaptation That Brings Certain Cognitive Advantages," *Scientific American*, August 25, 2009, www.scientificamerican.com/article.cfm?id=depressions-evolutionary (accessed December 19, 2012).

35. "Lars Von Trier on His Depression," YouTube, February 22, 2011, www.youtube.com/watch?v=siegKLVZ_yQ (accessed March 28, 2012).

36. "DP/30: Melancholia, Actor Kirsten Dunst," YouTube, November 16, 2011, www.youtube.com/watch?v=PbVmBDccyak (accessed March 28, 2012).

37. "Kirsten Dunst Talks Rehab, Depression to *British Elle*," *Huffington Post*, October 2, 2011, www.huffingtonpost.com/2011/08/02/kirsten-dunst-talks-rehab_n_915931.html (accessed March 12, 2012).

38. "Kirsten Dunst Talks Rehab, Depression to *British Elle*."

39. Sandie Angulo Chen, "Kirsten Dunst: Depression Isn't an Embarrassing Topic," *iVillage*, September 26, 2011, www.ivillage.com/kirsten-dunst-depression-isnt-embarrassing-topic/1-a-386032 (accessed March 18, 2012).

40. "Silver Linings Playbook," *Box Office Mojo* 2012, www.boxofficemojo.com/movies/?id=silverliningsplaybook.htm (accessed July 19, 2013).

41. "David O. Russell and His Son Matthew on Making of *Silver Linings Playbook*," *Hollywood Reporter*, February 23, 2013, www.hollywoodreporter.com/video/david-o-russell-his-son-423721 (accessed July 19, 2013).

42. "David O. Russell and His Son Matthew on Making of *Silver Linings Playbook*."

43. *The National Confidential Inquiry into Suicide and Homicide by People with Mental Illness* (annual report produced by the University of Manchester, Manchester, England, July 2012), 6.

44. Goodwin and Jamison, *Manic-Depressive Illness*, 16.

SELECT FILMOGRAPHY OF BIPOLAR CINEMA BY YEAR

No filmography of bipolar cinema can truly be considered complete, however accurate, owing to the sheer volume of possible legitimate entries. Films that show bipolarity, or its attendant comorbid personality effects, can be argued to include every slasher film ever made, as well as nearly every film noir, war movie, superhero film, and other genre variants in which psychopathology is examined (however inaccurately). Equally, the nearly constant manic state many Hollywood musicals achieve during their exuberant dance and singing numbers could be, if isolated out of context, seen as vivid examples of mania at its most heightened states. Filmmakers and actors who were once secretive, or undiagnosed, now regularly emerge to advocate and educate about their illness without shame. This revelation alone is a cause for honest reappraisal of their works, especially in regard to bipolarity and its expressive nature. But until such connections are made by their creators, or posthumously deduced by others, it is all too easy to overlook films in their credits list that may subtly indicate manic depression but were unremarked as such during their initial release era. And so even a thorough filmography is constantly subject to sudden, but welcome, revisions, owing to such disclosures. Consider as well: if a director or actor is bipolar, should every film or performance therefore be included? Clearly, only select examples from their respective careers can be emphasized, or this select filmography would be voluminous. Finally, the vast range of motion pictures depicting states of human emotion, such as sadness, joy, despair, and passion, that are comparable in scope to bipolarity contains many that mirror some of these entries, but obviously their sheer volume precludes categorizing them as bipolar cinema here. Suffice it to say, the inclusion of any film in this comprehensive overview must be considered as merely one author's attempt to select a grouping of like-themed, or like-minded, if you will, movies that show persistent styles and themes of manic-depressive expression.

1901 TO 1920

Off to Bloomingdale Asylum (1901). US. Short.
The Maniac's Guillotine (1902). UK. Short.
The Escaped Lunatic (1904). US. Short.
Dr. Dippy's Sanitarium (1906). US. Short.
The Madman's Fate (1906). UK. Short.
The Puzzle Maniac (1906). UK. Short.
The Madman's Bride (1907).UK. Short.
The Harmless Lunatic's Escape (1908). UK. Short.
The Plumber and the Lunatics (1908). UK. Short.
Where the Breakers Roar (1908). US. Short.
The Cord of Life (1909). US. Short.
Edgar Allen Poe (1909). US. Short.
Lunatics in Power (1909). US. Short.
The Maniac Cook (1909). US. Short.
A Lunatic Expected (1910). UK. Short.
The Lunatic at Liberty (1911). UK. Short.
The House of Darkness (1913). US. Short.
The Avenging Conscience: or "Thou Shalt Not Kill" (1914). US.
The Pit and the Pendulum (1914). France.
The Raven (1915). US.
The Cabinet of Dr. Caligari (1920). Germany.

1921–1930

Häxan: Witchcraft through the Ages (1922). Denmark.
Nosferatu (1922). Germany.

The Untamable (1922). US.
Warning Shadows (1923). Germany.
A Page of Madness (1926). Japan.
The Sea Beast (1926). US.
Metropolis (1927). Germany.
The Fall of the House of Usher (1928). France.
Anna Christie (1930). US.
Moby Dick (1930). US.

1931–1940

M (1931). Germany.
The Mad Genius (1931). US.
Svengali (1931). US.
A Bill of Divorcement (1932). US.
Grand Hotel (1932). US.
Stoopnocracy (1933). US. Short.
The Testament of Dr. Mabuse (1933). Germany.
Private Worlds (1935). US.
The 39 Steps (1935). UK.
Crack-Up (1936). US.
Modern Times (1936). US.

1941–1950

Citizen Kane (1941). US.
Le Corbeau (1943). France.
Gaslight (1943). US.
Ministry of Fear (1944). US.
Leave Her to Heaven (1945). US.
Stairway to Light (1945). US. Short. Doc.
Bedlam (1946). US.
It's a Wonderful Life (1946). US.
Let There Be Light (1946). US. Short. Doc.
The Snake Pit (1946). US.
Macbeth (1948). US.

Angry Boy (1950). US. Short. Doc.
In a Lonely Place (1950). US.
Sunset Boulevard (1950). US.

1951–1960

Der Verlorene (1951). Germany.
The Idiots (1951). Japan.
People Will Talk (1951). US.
A Streetcar Named Desire (1951). US.
Ikiru (1952). Japan.
Limelight (1952). US.
El (1953). Mexico.
The Caine Mutiny (1954). US.
Johnny Guitar (1954). US.
Daughter of Horror (1955). US.
I Live in Fear (1955). Japan.
Ordet (1955). Denmark.
Rebel without a Cause (1955). US.
Bigger Than Life (1956). US.
Lust for Life (1956). US.
Moby Dick (1956). US.
The Wrong Man (1956). US.
Fear Strikes Out (1957). US.
Il Grido (1957). Italy.
Saint Joan (1957). US.
Home Before Dark (1958). US.
Vertigo (1958). US.
The Fugitive Kind (1959). US.
Head Against a Wall (1959). France.
Suddenly, Last Summer (1959). US.
Booked for Safekeeping (1960). US. Short. Doc.
Peeping Tom (1960). UK.

1961–1970

Breakfast at Tiffany's (1961). US.
The Innocents (1961). UK.
Splendor in the Grass (1961). US.
Through a Glass Darkly (1961). Sweden.
Freud (1962). US.
The Manchurian Candidate (1962). US.
Tender Is the Night (1962). US.
Whatever Happened to Baby Jane? (1962). US.
The Caretakers (1963). US.
Le Feu Follet (1963). France.
Shock Corridor (1963). US.
Dr. Strangelove (1964). US.
Hush . . . Hush, Sweet Charlotte (1964). US.
Lilith (1964). US.
The Night of the Iguana (1964). US.
The Pumpkin Eater (1964). UK.
Scorpio Rising (1964). US. Experimental.
The Collector (1965). US.
Juliet of the Spirits (1965). Italy.
Life Upside Down (1965). France.
Repulsion (1965). UK.
A Fine Madness (1966). US.
King of Hearts (1966). France/Italy.
Morgan: A Suitable Case for Treatment (1966). UK.
Persona (1966). Sweden.
Marat/Sade (1967). UK.
Titicut Follies (1967). US. Doc.
Warrendale (1967). Canada. Doc.
Hour of the Wolf (1968). Sweden.
A Quiet Place in the Country (1968). Italy.
Signs of Life (1968). Germany.
Coming Apart (1969). US.
The Cremator (1969). Czechoslovakia.
Jackal of Nahueltoro (1969). Chile.
Midnight Cowboy (1969). US.
The Alienist (1970). Brazil.

The Breach (1970). France.

The Case of Lena Christ (1970). Germany.

Reza, the Motorcyclist (1970). Iran.

Why Does Herr R. Run Amok? (1970). Germany.

1971–1980

Carnal Knowledge (1971). US.

A Clockwork Orange (1971). UK.

The Devils (1971). UK.

Harold and Maude (1971). US.

King Lear (1971). Russia.

The Last Picture Show (1971). US.

The Mad Butcher (1971). Italy/Germany.

Play Misty for Me (1971). US.

The Otherside of the Underneath (1971). UK.

Aguirre: The Wrath of God (1972). Germany.

The Bitter Tears of Petra von Kant (1972). Germany.

The Godfather (1972). US.

Ali: Fear Eats the Soul (1973). Germany.

The Finger of God (1973). Poland.

The Hour Glass Sanatorium (1973). Poland.

Sisters (1973). US.

Voices (1973). UK.

The Conversation (1974). US.

The Godfather Part II (1974). US.

Lenny (1974). US.

Steppenwolf (1974). Denmark.

A Woman under the Influence (1974). US.

Down the Ancient Stairs (1975). Italy/France.

Euridice BA 2037 (1975). Greece.

The Flesh of the Orchid (1975). Italy/Germany/France.

Footprints on the Moon (1975). Italy.

Fox and His Friends (1975). Germany.

Jeanne Dielman, 23, quai du Commerce, 1080 Bruxelles (1975). Belgium.

Lisztomania (1975). UK.

Network (1975). US.
One Flew Over the Cuckoo's Nest (1975). US.
Salò, or the 120 Days of Sodom (1975). Italy/France.
The Story of Adele H. (1975). France.
Dragonfly (1976). US.
Face to Face (1976). Sweden/Italy.
Grey Gardens (1976). US. Doc.
Taxi Driver (1976). US.
The Tenant (1976). French.
The Wishing Tree (1976). Russia.
The Closet Children (1977). France.
Eraserhead (1977). US.
Looking for Mr. Goodbar (1977). US.
Interiors (1978). US.
Magic (1978). US.
Rekolekcje (1978). Poland.
All That Jazz (1979). US.
Apocalypse Now (1979). US.
Being There (1979). US.
The Bell Jar (1979). US.
L'Enfant Secret (1979). France.
The Great Santini (1979). US.
Hardcore (1979). US.
Hospital of the Transfiguration (1979). Poland.
Woyzeck (1979). Germany.
Lightning over Water (1980). Germany. Doc.
Ordinary People (1980). US.
Raging Bull (1980). US.
The River's Edge (1980). US.
The Shining (1980). UK.
Stardust Memories (1980). US.

1981–1990

Cutter's Way (1981). US.
Possession (1981). France.
S.O.B. (1981).

Tales of Ordinary Madness (1981). France.

Domino (1982). Germany.

Pink Floyd: The Wall (1982). UK.

Veronika Voss (1982). Germany.

The King of Comedy (1983). US.

Will There Really Be a Morning? (1983). Germany.

Amadeus (1984). US.

Birdy (1984). UK.

The Illusionist (1984). Denmark.

A Man Like Eva (1984). Germany.

Paris, Texas (1984). Germany/US/UK.

Come and See (1985). Russia.

The Falcon and the Snowman (1985). US.

Ran (1985). Japan.

Betty Blue (1986). France.

Blue Velvet (1986). US.

Hannah and Her Sisters (1986). US.

Krakatau (1986). Poland. Short.

Man Facing Southeast (1986). Argentina.

Mosquito Coast (1986). US.

Night, Mother (1986). US.

River's Edge (1986). US.

Barfly (1987). US.

Fatal Attraction (1987). US.

Ironweed (1987). US.

Lethal Weapon (1987). US.

Swimming to Cambodia (1987). US. Doc.

Camille Claudel (1988). France.

Dead Ringers (1988). US/Canada.

Dogura Magura (1988). Japan.

Punchline (1988). US.

Women on the Verge of a Nervous Breakdown (1988). Spain.

Batman (1989). US.

Seuls (1989). Belgium. Doc.

Sex, Lies & Videotape (1989). US.

Talk Radio (1989). US.

Akira Kurosawa's Dreams (1990). US/Japan.

Crazy People (1990). US.

Goodfellas (1990). US.
Misery (1990). US.
Vincent and Theo (1990). UK/Netherlands/France.

1991–2000

Cape Fear (1991). US.
Hangin' with the Homeboys (1991). US.
The Prince of Tides (1991). US.
The Silence of the Lambs (1991). US.
Van Gogh (1991). France.
Beautiful Dreamers (1992). Canada.
Chaplin (1992). US.
Lunatics, A Love Story (1992). US.
Falling Down (1993). US.
Mr. Jones (1993). US.
Naked (1993). UK.
Blue Sky (1994). US.
Breaking the Dark Horse: A Family Copes with Manic Depression (1994). US. Doc.
Crumb (1994). US. Doc.
Dialogues with Madwomen (1994). US. Doc.
Ed Wood (1994). US.
L'Enfer (1994). France.
Mrs. Parker and the Vicious Circle (1994). US.
12 Monkeys (1995). US.
Brian Wilson: I Just Wasn't Made for These Times (1995). US. Doc.
Immortal Beloved (1995). UK.
Leaving Las Vegas (1995). US.
Mad Love (1995). US.
Nixon (1995). US.
Back from Madness: The Struggle for Sanity (1996). US. Doc.
The Birdcage (1996). US.
Breaking the Waves (1996). Denmark.
The People vs. Larry Flynt (1996). US.
Shine (1996). UK.
The Whole Wide World (1996). US.

In the Presence of a Clown (1997). Sweden.
Mrs. Dalloway (1997). US.
Sue (1997). Germany.
Sweethearts (1997). US.
Taste of Cherry (1997). Iran.
Buffalo '66 (1998). US.
Bulworth (1998). US.
The Butcher Boy (1998). UK.
Kurt and Courtney (1998). US. Doc.
Permanent Midnight (1998). US.
Girl, Interrupted (1999). US.
Magnolia (1999). US.
Man on the Moon (1999). US.
My Best Fiend—Klaus Kinski (1999). Germany. Doc.
My Best Friend Paul (1999). US. Doc.
The Virgin Suicides (1999). US.
Intimate Portrait: Margot Kidder (2000). US. Doc.
Pollock (2000). US.
The Sky Is Falling (2000). Italy.

2001–2014

Don't Say a Word (2001). US.
Ghost World (2001). US.
Harmful Insect (2001). Japan.
My Father and I (2001). France.
No Place to Go (2001). UK.
Prozac Nation (2001). US.
Revolution #9 (2001). US.
About a Boy (2002). UK.
Bowling for Columbine (2002). US. Doc.
Bus 174 (2002). Brazil.
The Hours (2002). US.
Love Is a Treasure (2002). Finland.
One Hour Photo (2002). US.
The Piano Teacher (2002). Germany.
A Skin Too Few: The Days of Nick Drake (2002). US. Doc.

Stoked: The Rise and Fall of Gator (2002). US. Doc.

Wilbur Wants to Kill Himself (2002). Denmark.

American Splendor (2003). US.

Off the Map (2003). Australia.

Stormy Weather (2003). Iceland.

Sylvia (2003). UK.

Tarnation (2003). US. Doc.

That Day (2003). Switzerland.

Alienations (2004). Algeria. Doc.

Alone (2004). Germany.

The Assassination of Richard Nixon (2004). US.

The Aviator (2004). US.

Bittersweet Memories (2004). Canada.

Downfall (2004). Germany.

A Hole in One (2004). US.

The Machinist (2004). Spain.

The Passion of the Christ (2004). US.

Brokeback Mountain (2005). US.

Broken Flowers (2005). US.

The Devil and Daniel Johnston (2005). US. Doc.

Grizzly Man (2005). US. Doc.

It's Only Talk (2005). Japan.

Last Days (2005). US.

Lonesome Jim (2005). France.

Lunacy (2005). Czechoslovakia.

Neverwas (2005). US/Canada.

Wayfarers (2005). Ukraine.

The Art of Crying (2006). Denmark.

Breaking and Entering (2006). US.

The Bridge (2006). US. Doc.

The Last King of Scotland (2006). US.

The Namesake (2006). US.

Revolutionary Road (2006). US.

Romulus, My Father (2006). Australia.

Running with Scissors (2006). US.

The Saddest Boy in the World (2006). Canada.

Stephen Fry: The Secret Life of the Manic Depressive (2006). UK.
Doc.

Wristcutters: A Love Story (2006). US.

Charlie Bartlett (2007). US.

Control (2007). UK.

Does Your Soul Have a Cold? (2007). Japan. Doc.

Michael Clayton (2007). US.

Nick Drake: Under Review (2007). US. Doc.

Numb (2007). US.

Opium: Diary of a Madwoman (2007). Germany.

A Summer in the Cage (2007). US. Doc.

Goodbye Solo (2008). US.

Phoebe in Wonderland (2008). US.

P.S. Kroyer: What a Life! (2008). Denmark.

Rachel Getting Married (2008). US.

Synecdoche, New York (2008). US.

Two Lovers (2008). US.

Valvert (2008). France. Doc.

The Wrestler (2008). US.

Boy Interrupted (2009). US. Doc.

Bright Star (2009). Australia.

The Daily Moods of the Final Certainty (2009). US. Doc. Experimental. Short.

The Father of My Children (2009). Germany.

Helen (2009). US.

Henri-Georges Clouzot's Inferno (2009). France. Doc.

The Informant! (2009). US.

My Suicide (2009). US.

Observe and Report (2009). US.

A Single Man (2009). US.

Tetro (2009). US/Spain.

Afflictions: Culture and Mental Illness in Indonesia (2010). Indonesia. Doc.

Bedlam: The History of Bethlem Hospital (2010). UK. Doc.

It's Kind of a Funny Story (2010). US.

Look It in the Eye (2010). US. Doc.

OC87: The Obsessive Compulsive, Major Depression, Bipolar, Asperger's Movie (2010). US. Doc.

Shutter Island (2010). US.

Barrymore (2011). Canada.

The Beaver (2011). US.

Black Butterflies (2011). Netherlands.

Insanely Dangerous (2011). Denmark. Doc.

It's Such a Beautiful Day (2011). US.

Melancholia (2011). Denmark.

This Must Be the Place (2011). US.

Waking Madison (2011). US.

We Need to Talk About Kevin (2011). UK.

3 (2012). India.

Bipolar: A Narration of Manic Depression (2012). US. Experimental. Short.

Mother (2012). South Korea. Doc.

Of Two Minds (2012). US. Doc.

Silver Linings Playbook (2012). US.

The House That Jack Built (2013). US.

Magic, Magic (2013). Chile.

Running from Crazy (2013). US. Doc.

Side Effects (2013). US.

INDEX

ABOUT THE AUTHOR

David Coleman has written screenplays for Michael Douglas, Phillip Noyce, Dino De Laurentiis, Sony, Universal, and many others. He distributed movies and created the award-winning *Bijou Cafe* website. His previous book is *The Bigfoot Filmography*. Coleman is a graduate of the University of Southern California School of Cinema Arts. He lives in Lago Vista, Texas, with his wife and children.

CPSIA information can be obtained at www.ICGtesting.com
Printed in the USA
BVOW07*1044020714

358009BV00001B/1/P